THE PSYCHEDELIC DIGEST

By David W Handyside

ISBN: 978-0-578-25864-5

Any references to historical events, real people or real places are written from the author's own perspective and based entirely on research and conversations held with the people directly involved.

First paperback edition December 2021.

David W Handyside

PO Box 342

Everett, WA 98206

FORWARD

When it comes to learning about Psychedelic Music, the underground bands and musicians coming out of what is arguably the most experimental time in musical history, this is a book unlike any other you'll find. This is a culmination of information coming from the artists themselves, obtained over the past several decades by the author, my father Dave.

Telling a bit about my Dad, music is his heart and soul, especially when it comes to the rare and eclectic. He's been an avid collector for his entire life, since his first purchase in 1966 *KRLA Solid Rocks Vol. 1*. In 1967 he obtained his first band LP, *Easter Everywhere* by ***The 13th Floor Elevators***. To date, it is said among the collector's community that his is possibly the most extensive collection of LPs in the US.

Growing up immersed in the artistry and history of so much underground and mainstream music spanning multiple decades was quite an experience. As a recording artist myself, my own experimentation is a direct product of that environment and my Dad's passion for it. That same passion makes this book a special piece.

The artists whose stories are contained here were dedicated to their craft and it took somebody equally as dedicated to put this book together. As the reader, you'll learn the ups and downs of these nearly forgotten musicians, passed through candid conversations with many of the artists themselves. In my eyes, few if any are more qualified authors on this subject. So, sit back, hold on and get ready for a far out journey into an era of music of the like we may never experience again.

Cam Handyside

Recording Artist | Apologue www.apologuemusic.com

PREFACE

About 40 years ago I realized that I had a huge inventory of records. I had been buying out of catalogs that were sent out by personal collectors and thought (well) I could do that, maybe make some money and buy a few more elusive records with the money I made. So, I started an in home business called Ina-Gadda-Da-Records, put a catalog together myself on my new personal computer, developed a list of buyers and sent them out. Sometimes I would list the records for sale in Goldmine Magazine, but the twist was I would give a brief description of the band, where they were from, who they became and who they sounded like. Over time, I compiled a small synopsis with bits and pieces about several bands. I had written little paragraphs of verbiage about some of the bands I enjoyed and began calling it *My Psychedelic Digest*.

Every collector has their favorite band or artist. My resources initially came from record magazines with interviews of band members. Then the computer came along where other collectors who were passionate about a band knew every detail. There are a lot of collectors that have many more psych albums than I do and I don't claim to have it all or know everything. I'm still learning about bands and discovering albums that were completely off my radar.

I was able to obtain some details about a specific obscure one album wonder band with an LP that was in my collection through the internet which I thought highlighted some of the key points. But I discovered that some of the source information wasn't quite accurate or was lacking details. This prompted me to go right to the source which was near impossible considering some of the bands I was trying to find the story about. Many LPs only pictured the band members on the cover with no formal names of the players mentioned. Many of these albums only listed the players by first name and the songs didn't mention the last name of the composer of the music or verse. The label or back album cover simply stated "All songs were written by the band."

In the Psychedelic era, it was all about the art and most of the cover art was bright and colorful with little or no information about the players themselves. However, through extensive research I was able to locate some of the actual members of these bands and get their story on record (if you'll pardon the pun). Some couldn't remember all the details from those "daze" and others still did not want to talk about the past. But more than a few were surprised that anyone remembered or even cared about the record they recorded and released and were happy to give me information about their band.

It is truly a reference guide and details the highs and lows of bands that may have only been together for a year. Their one artifact and legacy left to the "cut-out" bins. Great albums and the record collectors were hot and heavy about the music spewing from the grooves. But few knew the real story about the players behind the music. I found their stories remarkably interesting and the aftermath of some of the members who became quite famous elsewhere later was surprising.

The LPs I chose were strictly at random. Many are highly collectible in the record collecting marketplace and the source for most of the album covers shown, with a few exceptions, are from my personal collection. Many of the stories happened because I was lucky enough to converse with somebody who was involved with a band and remembered what happened back then. As we talked, more information would come forth as memories came to light. Any rumors about the band were either verified or denied and put to paper. Most of these bands experienced and were influenced in some way by the psychedelic times. Most are or were unknown on the national scene. But many of these bands were heard in the early days of underground radio where the restricted 3-minute song was expanded to anywhere from 5 to 20 minutes in length.

There were very few commercials on underground FM radio and most of the advertisements relayed information about the weekend's protest gathering, "love festival", head shop sale or what rock band was playing and where. There were no dance party hit singles found and played as on AM radio. Most of these bands made one or two LPs, lasted a year if that, made no money and were gone but the music they made swayed many and influenced an entire generation. Not all the bands detailed here in the book are considered psychedelic musically according to those in the know but they were from that era and had some influence of the times.

Of the bands I've been able to correspond with, I have tried to keep the details short and sweet. I don't talk about each song on the LP or give an album rating. Rather it's all about the details of the players in the band from beginning to end and beyond. The digest gives you just enough information to make you curious about the album or music. I've tried to make comparisons to other bands where I could. Many of these are comparable to other psych bands that may be unknown to most people. But those who follow the bands from those hazy days will probably agree. I think these comparisons are accurate, but there will always be folks who disagree. However, somebody who doesn't listen to a lot of this type of music may not be familiar with the comparison. I've tried not to be opinionated, but sometimes my enthusiasm about a band gets in the way and I might say (for instance) "These guys were awesome".

The best resource for knowledge about these bands is the internet. Some of the more familiar psych bands have a dedicated website. Discogs.com is a website where you can buy the album if available and hear some of these bands via a YouTube link on their website. Other psych bands have websites run by hardcore fans that never let their "hero's" die. But, with some of the more obscure psych bands there was little to no information.

Three of the best books on the subject are Fuzz, Acid and Flowers (US Bands), Tapestry of Delights (UK Bands) and Dreams, Fantasies and Nightmares (Canadian Bands, Australia and Bands from other lands). These books have evolved over the years. They were released in limited quantity and are thick and expensive if you can find a copy. They are also out of print, but these three books would probably be the best reference guide for information on Psychedelic bands from the 60's and early 70's. If nothing else, they state that there was an album recorded by a band and maybe who the players were. These books were printed in the UK. Another informative reference book includes The Acid Archives that was edited by Patrick Lundborg, a world renown psych enthusiast who had some details about many psychedelic bands. Magazines like Ptolemaic Terrascope, Flashback and Ugly Things were/are other useful sources that interviewed bands in depth with PT long out of publication.

The digest here has a lot of colorful album covers included. The artists vary from the marginally famous to the local artist in town. Sometimes the cover artist was one of the band members or a mutual friend of the band. Sometimes the wife or girlfriend was asked to draw or silkscreen a picture. At any rate, the covers are diversified, from the very amateurish to the very intricate in detail. I think all the album covers from this time were vibrant with color and had a very strange drawing or picture that was used to grab your attention. It certainly worked for me. I bought a lot of records back then based on the cover picture alone.

For about 6 years from 1965 to 1971 the bands were trying to be as outrageous sounding as possible. The record companies were signing bands as fast as they could and artists were going beyond the kaleidoscope, developing a wild and colorful picture to grace the album cover. The Psychedelic Digest does not include every band that made a record in the 60's. Far from it, but I've been working on it for more than 26 years and truthfully, I'm running out of time. We only live so long, so please don't be offended if your favorite obscure band is missing.

This was a long and arduous project. To find any information on some of the bands was daunting. The books that were out of print, the newspaper articles that were hiding in the depths and the articles from magazines that no longer exist were proof that history never dies.

I should note that many singles, 7"er's or 45's are listed throughout the book with ***b/w*** between the song names. Lots of questions about this. Curiously even I didn't know what that meant, but it's pretty simple. Typically, a single release is two songs on a single 7" record. With an A side song ***backed/with*** a B side song.

My hope is that this digest will be informative and pleasingly colorful. I've enjoyed communicating with all the folks who were gracious enough to talk with me, a stranger, who invaded their privacy and dared to ask the questions. I have left acknowledgments to the mystery bands that moved me in my lifetime and left a piece of history for all to listen to long after we are gone.

*****PSYCHEDELIC MUSIC*****

Psychedelic music is just like anything else, there is good to go with the bad. Music in the 60's came out of an era of experimentation. It varied in style and most of the music recorded resulted from some type of drug experience or envisioned drug experience. Not all musicians took drugs. Ted Nugent and Frank Zappa were living proof of this. To me, psychedelic music is full of special effects, backwards guitars, chants, unusual noises, poetry, phase shifting, echoes, mega stereo or true stereo effects. Generally, these were alterations that took place within the studio by some very turned-on producers and engineers. All these strange things and altered sounds were added to what would otherwise be a simple melody. Whereas the drugs supposedly expanded the human mind, the special effects were added to the music and expanded the song.

The various styles fell into the following categories with examples of the bands who played them listed here. Country psych (The Byrds, Goosecreek Symphony, Hearts And Flowers, West, Plain Jane), Flower psych (The Stone Poneys, We Five, The Sunshine Company), Flowered underground (Sweetwater, Flat Earth Society, Complex), Folk psych or Acid folk, (The Incredible String Band, Fairport Convention, Steeleye Span, Trees), Pop psych (The Monkees, The Five Americans, The Pleasure Fair), Baroque psych (Ars Nova, The New York Rock 'n Roll Ensemble, Amazing Blondel), Blues rock (Taste, John Mayall and the Bluesbreakers, Johnny Winter), Garage sounds (The Standells, The Chocolate Watchband, The Leaves), Raga (The Orient Express, Magic Carpet), Christian psych (The Concrete Rubber Band, Indelible Inc., Azitis, Rainbow Promise), Jazz psych (Herbie Mann, The Soft Machine), Electronic or instrumental (Silver Apples, Syrinx, Mother Mallards Portable Masterpiece Company, Tonto's Expanding Head Band), Strange and Weird (The Godz, The Mothers of Invention, The Fugs, Captain Beefheart & the Magic Band, The Deep), Horn psych (Blood, Sweat & Tears, Linn County, Ambergris) and even Big Band sounds with (The Don Ellis Orchestra). You could also add the many three or four-member Blazing guitar bands (Cream, Chariot, Fat, Grand Funk Railroad, Black Sabbath and Sacred Mushroom) to the mix as well. The list goes on and the names of some of the bands were as strange as the music put forth.

In many cases the cover artwork on the album is what sold the band. Much of the music was heard during the very infant stages of FM radio. If you heard the music at all, the DJ who was playing it would rarely state who the band was. I had been buying records for a long time, but when I got serious about collecting, I didn't know what I really liked musically and spent a lot of money on rare albums. And that's just what they were. Rare and hard to find. Musically they weren't always up to my standards. Of course, what I like is not always what someone else might prefer. Musical tastes are always a matter of opinion and many times only a matter of one's mood. I can listen to Tony Bennett and turn to Captain Beefheart in a San Francisco heartbeat.

I guess the direction I'm going here and the advice I would give is if you are going to buy a vinyl record for musical content, don't spend a bundle of bucks on it unless you are familiar with the record you are buying. The true psychedelic enthusiast enjoys what comes from the grooves, regardless of value. Remember that expensive doesn't always mean good, expensive means rare and difficult to find. A copy of *The Collectors* first album is one of the select few early LPs I purchased and still own to this day. This band was from Vancouver, B.C. in Canada. The album was quite common in the record bins, it was on a common record label and even in today's market is comparatively inexpensive. Their records were distributed here in the states by the truckload. To me their music is some of the most incredible psych to ever be etched into the vinyl grooves. My preference for psychedelic music involves melody, harmony, plenty of weirdness and special effects. Most of my personal collection reflects this.

Finally, I would like to add, most of my Psych Rock collection is now over 50 years old. Except for some of the more popular and known bands, they don't make albums anymore like they used to. That's why they call them collectible. Many of the bands and records shown here have been re-released on CD, but as stated earlier the beauty of a vinyl LP record is the packaging. It has very colorful artwork and it is BIGGER.

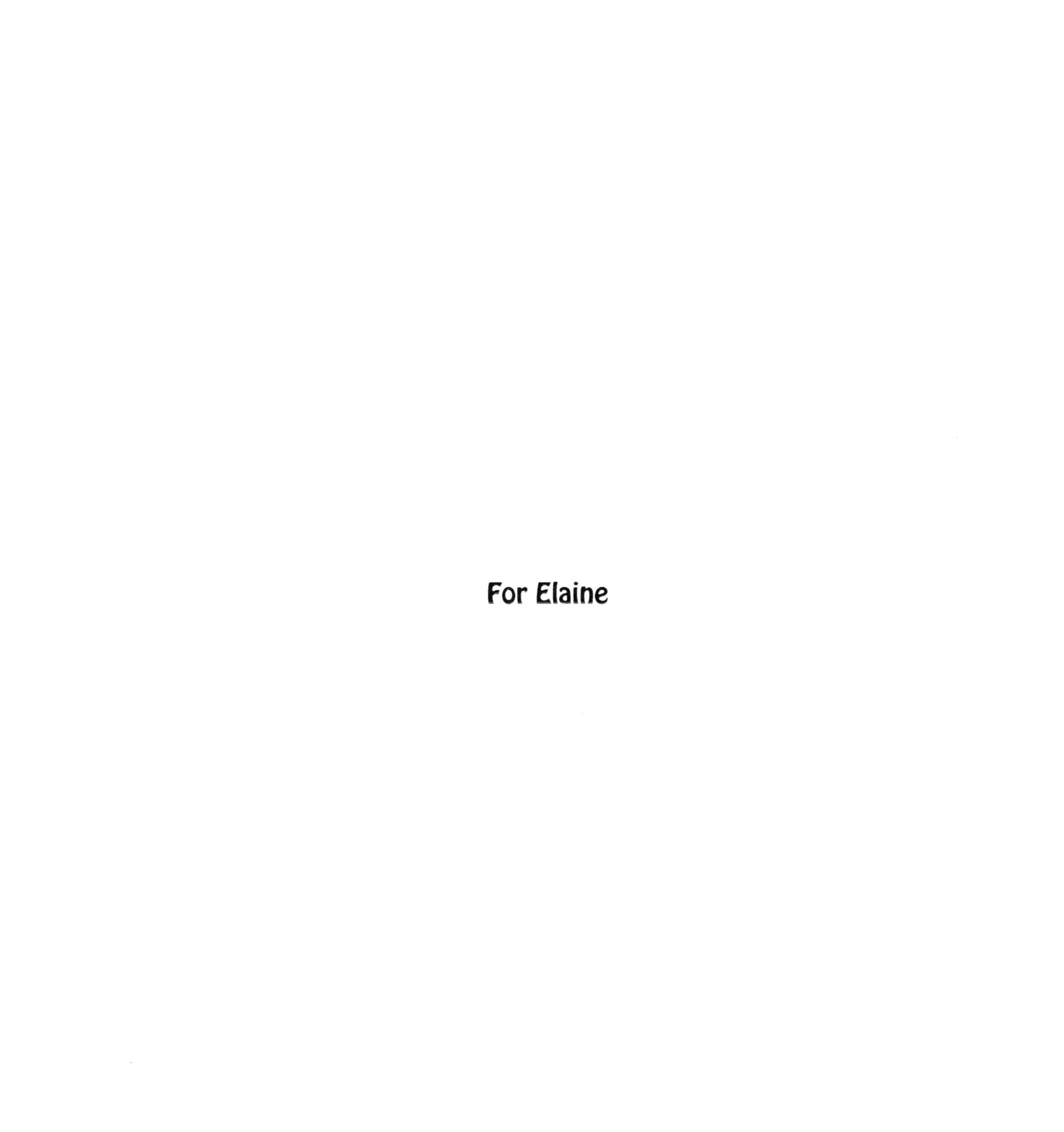

For Elaine

"Stories last forever. But only if you tell them."

THE ABSTRACTS
STEREO
SD 6002
POMPEII

THE ABSTRACTS 1968

Tony Peluso, Henry Dandini and Pierre Vigeant were lifelong friends from an early age. All played instruments. Henry was versed on saxophone and Tony was a piano player. Tony's family had been high rollers in Hollywood with his Dad, Thomas Peluso, a composer, conductor and musical director for NBC TV and Mom, Emily Hardy, who was a leading soprano singer for the Metropolitan Opera in New York and the San Francisco Opera Company. Their circle of friends included Hal David, Les Paul and Burt Bacharach. As high school sophomores they formed a band called The Delighters with Hank who now played (organ), Tony who graduated to (guitar), Pierre (bass,) David DeNinno (guitar) and Tommy Jacobson (drums). Tommy was Tony's cousin and Tony was already writing songs.

They were all attending Blessed Sacrament School on Sunset Blvd and knew Danny Hutton Sr. who was a janitor there. He was the father of Danny Hutton Jr., a member of a band that became Three Dog Night. Practice and rehearsals were here in the auditorium when it wasn't in use. Gigs and shows occurred at various high schools in Central Hollywood. It was agreed to update the band name to The Abstracts to reflect the psychedelic times and one demo recording was made. Then David left the band and Tommy joined Dave Callens to form The Children and The Third Eye. Mike Thatcher had just won the LA County Drum Contest and he became Tommy's replacement.

They were all underage but would sneak into Gazzarri's located at 9039 West Sunset Blvd on the Sunset Strip to see the latest bands. They got to know Pat and Lolly Vegas who would play there often before the official formation of the band Redbone. As underage kids they lied about their age and managed to convince Bill Gazzarri to hire them to perform. Their first big club gig was at Gazzarri's where they would alternate one hour shows with Eddie James and the Pacific Ocean, October Country, The Doors, The Human Expression, The Third Eye and others. The Abstracts were a terrific band. Mike Thatcher's parents had to move to Texas so the band picked up, packed their equipment and travelled to Dallas with his folks. They lived with Mike at his parents' house.

Tony usually booked the band but they found Marc MacCord in Texas, who had been with the oddly named band Licorice Tadpole, to become their manager. The rock venue they played the most in Texas was The Cellar in Fort

Worth and they were paired with Bugs Henderson as well as The Barons with John Nitzinger. This was a non-alcoholic venue with scantily clad girls serving non-alcoholic beverages. But there was a back room for the players that had a punch bowl full of Everclear mixed with Green Chartreuse to guarantee a “buzz” and remove any jitters on stage. It was here that The Abstracts got notice from Darrell Glenn who took a real interest. He produced Ike and Tina Turner. Darrell was also a song writer credited with singing the first version of *Crying in the Chapel*. This song was written by his dad Artie Glenn that became a big hit for Elvis Presley.

Through Darrell they signed to an obscure Atlantic Records label subsidiary called Pompeii Records owned by Joe Perry and club owner Pat Morgan. The record label was known for early singles recorded and released by Ike and Tina Turner. Sessions occurred at Sound City which was a small recording studio located in the basement of the KXOL Radio station located at 1705 W 7th St. in Fort Worth. The studio was formerly The Clifford Herring Sound Studios. The name was changed to Sound City studios when the radio station took over the building. Their station jingle was “KXOL The Sound of the City”.

As a producer of Rock-a-Billy and Soul type music, Darrell was not able to capture the energy of the band’s rock music sound. This was the early days of T Bone Burnett, listed as J Burnett on the LP, who was the engineer for the sessions. The self-titled LP *The Abstracts* does have some nice echo chamber harmonies, fuzz guitar and minor effects with Hank’s Hammond M-3 organ featured for a softer blued-eyed soul sound. But the production was much less than it could have been. Those who knew the band and were witness to their shows knew better. The band really cooked as a live act and the LP never did them justice.

The album cover was very colorful with a bright orange background and rainbow-colored faces. Hank’s name was listed on the back but was misspelled as Henry Dondini. Featured clockwise on the front cover from the top is Tony Peluso, Mike Thatcher, Pierre Vigeant and Henry Dandini. One single was distributed locally, *A Smell of Incense b/w See The Birdies* with the song *Incense* being a rehash of the original West Coast Pop Art Experimental Band song. There was no promotion of the LP and it sank like a brick. This resulted in Mike Thatcher leaving the band.

The Abstracts were no more but Tony, Hank and Pierre hired Gary Stovall (guitar) with Fred Alwag (drums) and continued to perform as a band called Pestovadandiwag as a reference to their last names **Pe** luso, **Stova** ll, **Dandi** ni, Al **wag**. After a few months they renamed as Instant Joy and backed Bobby Sherman for about a year. Then Gary and Fred left the band. Former Third Eye band members Dave Callens joined on (guitar) and Tommy Jacobson came back on (drums). They remained as Instant Joy backing Mark Lindsay of Paul Revere and the Raiders. Jim Hilton, producer for Iron Butterfly, took interest in the band and Instant Joy recorded an album for the Warner Brothers record label but it was never released and still sits on the shelves. At one point Instant Joy opened for The Carpenters who eventually hired Tony Peluso permanently. The nucleus of the band then fell apart after he left.

You can see Instant Joy playing in the shadows backing *Bobby Sherman-Julie Do You Love Me* live on YouTube.

Pierre Vigeant lost his battle with drugs and depression in 1992. He was only 42 years of age.

Mike Thatcher became a notable studio drummer finishing the Blues Image hit song *Ride Captain Ride* after Manuel Bertematti up and left the recording session. He played with several Christian rock bands throughout his life that sadly ended in July 2006 due to complications from Sleep Apnea.

Henry Dandini became a Respiratory Therapist for more than 30 years but has been able to play keyboards and participate with Cannibal and the Headhunters, Bobby Sherman, Otis Day and many others including Richard Nader's 30 Years of Rock and Roll Tours that led directly to "oldies radio" and proved the commercial value of Rock 'n' Roll nostalgia. Hank still lives in California.

Tony Peluso played in the studio and toured with The Carpenters for twelve years until Karen's death in 1983. Their fourth LP *A Song For You* included the hit song *Goodbye To Love.* He is credited with the wild fuzz guitar solo at the end of the song. His solo here not only freaked out fans of The Carpenters but goes down as one of the great historic guitar riffs of all time. *Goodbye To Love* has been credited as the first real "power ballad" that spawned many others. After The Carpenters, Tony worked for Motown records co-producing several bands, The Fixx, Animotion, Kenny Loggins, Boyz To Men and many others. He won four Grammy Awards and was part of several gold and platinum records throughout his career. Sadly, he departed us in June of 2010 due to heart failure.

The Affection Collection
Evolution
a stereo dimension recording
STEREO
2007

THE AFFECTION COLLECTION 1969

Seeing The Beatles on The Ed Sullivan Show in 1964 inspired Mike Doggett to form this band with friends at Idaho Falls High School in Idaho. All sophomores, the band included Mike Doggett (guitar), Hal Rowberry (vocals), Keith Kennedy (bass) and Tim Comeau (drums) and they started as a surf band jamming together in the basements of their parent's houses trying to get a sound. Their first gig was at the Ward Building at The Church of Jesus Christ of Latter-Day Saints where they made a whopping $20 for the night. More gigs came along by playing parties and high school dances. They were known as the Mystics because Tim was originally from Mystic, Connecticut.

Mystic was located near Groton, Connecticut, where the 1st nuclear submarine was built (The Nautilus SSN-571). Tim's dad had a part in building that first of its kind underwater boat back east. But he was transferred out to Idaho and was working at the Nuclear Reactor Testing Station(NRTS) and the S1W/S5W prototype reactor core 4 near the town of Arco and Atomic City 30 minutes west of Idaho Falls. After a year in the band Tim had to leave due to his folks transferring back east.

They hired Alan Strong to take Tim's place as drummer and Ray Hassell to replace Keith Kennedy on (bass) who had also left. Ray said he had toured with Johnny Rivers and Bobby Vee, so that's why he was hired. There were stable playing gigs and dances every weekend. The Lovin' Spoonful was a heavy influence and they decided to rename themselves as The Affection Collection which seemed to be a similar band name. By the end of high school Tim moved back to Idaho and took his old spot banging on the drums. So, the members were Mike Doggett (guitar), Don Christensen (keyboards), Ray Hassell (bass), Hal Rowberry (lead vocals) and Tim Comeau (drums). Both Ray and Mike had composed some tunes.

Ray apparently had done some recording with Norman Petty in Clovis, New Mexico. Finding their way there, Norman took a real liking to the band and became their manager. They recorded some demos and he shopped the band around and gained some interest from the United Artists label. A single was recorded, *In Apple Blossom Time b/w Time Rest on My Hands*, but UA was in turmoil and instead bet the farm on Bobby Goldsboro's single *Honey b/w Danny*. The Affection Collection single was not promoted and the band was dropped.

Norman went ballistic and eventually sued UA settling for lost profits. Unrelenting, the band continued and put together a couple more locally released singles. By this time, the Evolution Record label picked them up and they traveled back to The Petty Studios in Clovis, to record a full album. The sessions took place and the self-titled album called *The Affection Collection* was released. With pitch perfect three-part harmonies, they veer towards many of the flower pop bands. The Association, JAIM, Blades of Grass and Orange Colored Sky come to mind. Admittedly, the album was a little more lightweight than what they showed on stage.

Evolution was a sub label for the Longines Symphonette Society in New York, a classical music label that had yet to roll out a rock 'n' roll record. Promotion for a teen band was new territory and frustration set in when sales didn't materialize. The band figured the rain of money just wouldn't happen and Ray began giving them problems, so he was fired. Hal Rowberry took over on (bass, vocals).

They all packed up and attended Brigham Young University in Provo, Utah. Another single was recorded and released *Plastic Flowers b/w Feeling So Good* that found little radio interest. They continued to play concerts and gigs throughout their stay in Utah changing the band name to Moose which was Don Christensen's nickname. All the profits were used to pay for the costs of college education.

They opened for the likes of The Moody Blues, The Byrds, Herman's Hermits, Gary Lewis and the Playboys, Gary Puckett and the Union Gap and a few others in local towns like Pocatello, Ashton, Blackfoot, Boise in Idaho, Butte in Montana, Jackson Hole, Yellowstone in Wyoming and Salt Lake City in Utah. There were no rock clubs to speak of in the area but because of the military training and troops, there were some National Guard Armories with Recreation Halls and College Auditoriums where they did play to a modest fan following. Several songs were recorded during this time that shows a band with full hit potential, more than enough songs for an entire second LP. However, few of these songs were released until later. After college, the band all went their separate ways.

After he departed, Ray Hassell took off for Pampa, Texas and worked for Norm Petty at the Clovis, New Mexico Studio.

Tim Comeau married and stayed in Utah where he currently lives.

Hal Rowberry and Don Christensen stayed close playing with known country artists all over the country. Then Don spent time in Branson, Missouri as music director for one of the showplaces there.

Mike Doggett formed a new group called Goodwill that played together into the 80's. He then opened and still operates Mike's Music, an instrument sale and leasing business that caters to young up and coming artists.

Don and Hal eventually moved back to the stability of Idaho Falls. A recent resurgence for the Affection Collection brought Mike, Hal and Don back together along with former members of Goodwill, Larry Thatcher and Jon Holst. A full retrospective of songs including the full remastered original album and 13 unreleased singles were put out on CD by the Super Oldies label in 2007. They still play occasional local shows in and around Idaho Falls.

MTS 5010
MTA
RECORDS
STEREO
Afterglow

AFTERGLOW 1966-68

Afterglow began in the very remote rural area of Fort Jones about 12 miles SW of Yreka in Northern California. Tony Tecumseh from Klamath Falls, Oregon (guitar), Mike Moreno (bass), Mike's wife (vocals) and Larry Alexander from Fort Jones High School, California (drums) began as GT and the Go Go's. Mike was working full time at another job at the Dorris Lumber Mill and he and his wife decided to leave the band. Mike realized they would need a lead singer and he knew a guy from church who could sing and play guitar. So, Gene Resler from Butte Valley High School (guitar, vocals) came aboard. They practiced at Gene's house in the town of Dorris to get the sound they wanted. The first gigs were at the local Pizza Parlor. There were no teen dance venues in the area, but they expanded to playing weddings, high school proms and any other events that came their way. Tony was the driving force behind the band.

They sought out a bass player and found Ron George (bass) along with Roger Swanson (drums). Both were from Mt Shasta High School and had been playing in another band but agreed to join Tony, Gene and Larry. Ron filled their need for (bass) and Roger as a drummer could also play (keyboards). So, the band was set with Tony Tecumseh (guitar, lead vocals), Gene Resler (guitar, lead vocals), Ron George (bass, vocals), Roger Swanson (keyboards, vocals) and Larry Alexander (drums).

After high school graduation they all moved on to the College of the Siskiyous in Weed, California. They practiced in Mt Shasta and Fort Jones and retitled themselves as The Medallions. Their music covered many of the popular bands like The Strawberry Alarm Clock, The Byrd's, The Beatles and Tony wrote many new songs. He was the inspiration and spiritual leader for the band. He especially wanted the band to have a certain uniqueness and quality. They continued to play at colleges, Battle of the Bands, pizza parlors and county fairs. After two years they transferred to Chico State College, this galvanized their popularity, and they played venues all over Northern California and Southern Oregon. Opening for The Turtles and The Beau Brummel's at the Armory, located in Yreka, got them some real attention. When they played the auditorium at the College of the Siskiyous, they found Bill Glenn who knew some folks in San Francisco and he signed them to a recording deal.

The thing was, they had to come up with 20 of their own songs within a three-month period. It was summer and college was on break. Larry's parents were supportive and offered up their house back in Fort James for practice and rehearsal. All the furniture was moved out of the living room, they were fed and they housed the boys for the full term. The band was able to compose new songs, arrange and polish the songs they had rehearsed and play occasional local gigs. After three months they were all set to travel to the big city. The boys had never been outside of their comfortable rural surroundings.

Once in San Francisco they were overwhelmed with the vastness and immensity of such a metropolis. They went to Golden State Recorders located at 665 Harrison St. to lay down songs and record an album. Glenn introduced them to the studio owner and engineer Leo De Gar Kulka. They were ready and started recording their songs, but something wasn't quite right. Each song had only one take and they were told to move on. The band knew their stuff but there were minor mistakes. At first, they thought once through a song meant it was a trial recording and would be rerecorded. When Tony questioned what was going on, they were told not to worry, that the songs would be tweaked afterwards through studio engineering.

One song was written by B. Byron Boots, a California Highway Patrolman (CHP) who was an avid fan of the band. He wrote the song *Susie's Gone* which was weird and strange and it stopped the studio session guys in their tracks. The engineers and producers got all excited. It was completely unlike any of the other songs and didn't fit their style. They loved it and it was the song that put them into the psychedelic realm. The sessions were completed in about three days including pictures of the band for the album cover. Hank Levin was one of the producers and mentioned that there was another band called The Swinging Medallions and the name might cause concern and confusion. He suggested that they rename themselves as Afterglow and there were no objections.

Musically their album falls somewhere between Country Joe and the Fish and a British Invasion sound. Nice three and four-part harmonies ala The Association, fuzz guitar, farfisa organ, echoes and special effects. Directly after the sessions Afterglow was offered the chance to play both The Fillmore and The Avalon Ballroom, but Tony had heard that The Beach Boys, a band he loved, was booed off the stage at both places. They were already frustrated about the recording session, a little bit intimidated and didn't want to chance a possible disheartening embarrassment in front of a boisterous crowd so they turned the gigs down. Back at home in friendly territory, they played the same familiar haunts.

There was some front money put forth to have the original tapes remastered before distribution and sales would occur. MTA was a small-time record label located in New York and the studio felt that the original recordings required no additional mastering and were good as is.

Six months later they got a call from Golden State who said a box of records was there awaiting pickup. Larry was extremely excited and made the 8-hour trip to San Francisco to pick up the package. When he opened the box, he saw *The Afterglow* album cover where there was this wild cartoon pictorial of the band in phosphorescent colors. To make matters worse, the music as promised was certainly tweaked but included lots of studio effects. This was not at all how the band envisioned their sound and the albums psychedelic cover was not the image they had hoped for. Worse yet MTA was told by the studio that the band had broken apart so there was no promotional tour set up. No single was released from the LP and it was as if MTA treated the whole thing as a tax write off. Located 3000 miles away, it also appears that the record label was in a fog about the band, relying strictly on what the studio guys had said.

Afterglow did a two-week self-promotion, traveling in person to interview and talk about the LP to many pop radio music stations in the Northwest. There was interest and some of the stations played a song from the album but there were no live performances. The local radio stations in Yreka, KSYC 1490, and Redding, KRDG 1230, did play a song from the album *Riding Home Again* which had a local #1 rating for several weeks. But the band didn't see a penny in royalties and they became discouraged. Empty promises and disappointments abound.

They kept playing gigs and then graduated from Chico State. There was some discussion about going on a west coast tour, but there were no backup dollars to pay for the costs. Tony didn't want to tour everywhere and left the band, followed shortly afterwards by Roger Swanson.

Gene, Ron and Larry decided to continue and hired two new vocalists and another keyboard player where they spent the next four years playing night clubs in the Northwest, in Las Vegas and Hawaii.

Afterward Ron George got into Mechanical Engineering and Building Construction for the greater San Francisco area.

Roger Swanson became a Certified Public Accountant.

Gene Resler got into politics and wound up the Mayor of Isleton, California.

Larry Alexander owns and operates a Natural Resource Consulting Firm doing hazardous fuel reduction, watershed analysis and restoration work.

Tony was a jack of all trades and always focused on music, but he never stayed at a job for more than 3 years before moving on. As a Native American he received a Lifetime Achievement Award for his contribution to music. Sadly, he died in 2012.

But the story does not end here. The players thought the endeavor was a complete failure but as it turned out years later, the music of the band and the album cover graphics got resurrected. In 1995 the Sundazed Record label reissued the album, a rerecording from an original disc. Afterglow was rediscovered and the original members found. The world heard their music and took notice. Overwhelmed with emotional resurgence, the band reunited in 2007. A studio was put together in Fort Jones where the original members reassembled and recorded a second LP (CD) with new songs called *Afterglow Unearthed*. They played a full concert for fans 40 years later at The Ford Theater on the campus of The Siskiyous College in Weed. Afterglow was tagged with the phase “Forty years ago they thought they failed ~ the world says they didn’t”. Justification for all the efforts are well deserved.

CAN YOU DIG IT?

The Aggregation
MIND ODYSSEY
STEREO
lhi
RECORDS
S-12008

THE AGGREGATION 1968

These guys were all graduate students at California State University at Long Beach (CSULB). Initially a five-piece band that included Leo Potts (flute, clarinet, saxophone, recorder, kazoo, vocals), Lemoyne Taylor (flute, clarinet, saxophone, recorder, slide whistle, vocals), Dale Burt (organ, bass, piano, vocals), LeWayne Braun (guitar, vocals) and Bayard Gregory (drums, timpani, bongos, tambourine, vocals). The band name came from the diversity of styles and instruments played all molded into one unit. They were known to have played gigs at the college and at The Lido Ballroom in the Pike area of Long Beach.

It was New Year's Eve 1968 when they were invited to join some other bands like The Mustangs, Sir Douglas Quintet, The Turtles, The Bobby Fuller Four and others to play several shows during that summer at Disneyland. Listed as a Guest Rock Band in the brochure they were hired to play full time (6 shows a day) in the park located at Tomorrowland on the Coke Terrace Stage. Aggregation basically played for the teenage crowd popping out the latest radio hits, but they also played a few originals as well. Leo was the band leader and was looking for that "big break". He took advantage of the situation by contacting folks in the music industry in Hollywood to come out for a listen. The rest of the band wasn't keen on the idea, but nonetheless Leo provided free passes to enter the park and encouraged them to catch one of their shows. It was a great way to audition.

Lee Hazelwood was one of those who had a small record label, LHI, and was looking for new talent so he took advantage and came to see their show. He liked what he saw and brought them aboard. First a single was recorded. A Dale Burt instrumental called *Maharishi* with the flip side an instrumental version of Donovan's *Sunshine Superman*. The single was distributed to all the major cities and had decent interest on the east coast, especially Boston. Based on this, Lee encouraged the band to record a full-albums worth of material.

He put up all the money for studio time at United Western Recorders located at 6000 Sunset Boulevard in Hollywood and told the band to record whatever they wanted. They could produce themselves with Eddie Brackett as sound engineer and decided to record a concept album based upon an LSD trip in the amusement park. But the band had certain limitations for what they needed to address the sessions. Dale Burt played keyboard bass and they wanted to free him up on keyboards, so they hired another CSULB buddy Bill Sissoev to play (bass guitar). The band was also weak vocally, so they found Richard Jones who played (rhythm guitar) and became the (lead vocalist). Linda O'Hara, Bayard's fiancé at the time, was hired to help as lyricist for the project.

The band was incredibly talented and multi-instrumental. It is shown on the album called *Mind Odyssey* which was truly diverse. Musically some say it's a psychedelic masterpiece, with dreamy choir-like sounds, eastern influenced instrumentals, flute with spoken word, echoes, special studio effects, psych guitar passages and horns in spots. It approaches The Freak Scene or The David (the US band) with horns like those of Linn County. One song has a Swing Pop feel about it with a toilet flush at the end. An album that draws you in with each listen. The unusual cover artwork was an illustration drawn by Phil Rich who worked with the Nasus Art Studio in LA.

They didn't play anywhere after the LP was finished. Lee Hazelwood liked the final product and tried to promote it as best he could, but the label distribution folks thought otherwise. Very few albums were pressed, the public didn't get a chance to hear the album or songs on the radio and the band fell apart.

Lemoyne Taylor developed his own swing band billed as Lemoyne Taylor & Valley Jazz. He was also director of The Phoenix Jazz and Swing Band for a while.

Bayard Gregory became a Sociology Professor at a Northwest University. He got his PhD, moved to Idaho and does lectures at Boise State University.

LeWayne Braun stayed in Long Beach playing for several bands. He has been with The Topics Band for many years, long time local idols out of San Pedro, California that are still active today.

Leo Potts traveled to France and studied at the National Conservatory of Music in Paris. The list of contemporary artists he and his sax have backed is a mile long. He is world renowned for his teachings, improvisations and creative concepts. Accolades are warranted.

AIR
Promotional
Copy
NOT FOR SALE
STEREO/SD 733
EMBRYO

AIR 1971

Carolyn Brooks Gottlieb aka "Googie" and Tom Coppola had both been in bands in high school and College in New York. Both played piano and organ. When a junior at Manhattan College, Tom attended a concert at Smith Auditorium on campus where he heard an extraordinary 16-year-old girl with a voice from heaven singing in the band. About two years later they crossed paths again playing in bands opposite each other at New York's Maritime Academy. They remembered each other, traded phone numbers and within a year they were married.

Moogy Klingman had made some demo recordings and was looking for a singer for his songs. He put an ad in The Village Voice. Googie and Tom responded and showed up. Moogy introduced them to John Siegler (bass) and Mark Rosengarden (drums) who were also there to help. The Moogy recordings got finished and they decided to form their own band together. The official members included Googie (piano, harpsichord, organ, lead vocals), Tom Coppola (Allen organ, electric and acoustic piano), John Siegler (bass guitar) and Mark Rosengarden (drums). They called themselves AIR. The band name came up out of the blue, out of thin (AIR).

Mark's dad was Bobby Rosengarden who was a well-known studio musician (drummer) playing with such acts as Miles Davis, Quincy Jones, Duke Ellington and worked for NBC and ABC TV as bandleader for Johnny Carson, Dick Cavett and others. He lived in Great Neck on Long Island and had built a guest house that was converted to a rehearsal studio. Mark invited Googie, Tom and John to come up and practice. By this time Tom and Googie had a little girl and brought her along to the sessions. Called the "Little House" this is where they rehearsed every day for a year.

They would venture out to Greenwich Village and play places like Gerde's, The Village Gate and others and made some demo recordings of their own songs at Atlantic Studios at 1841 Broadway. Herbie Mann was given a copy and was extremely impressed and decided to hire them as backing band for his shows.

Herbie had a history of playing all over the world as a jazz flutist. He was recognized as one of only a few jazz musicians that made the billboard charts (25 chart ratings within a 30-year period). By the mid to late 60's he had been playing clubs in Greenwich Village where a few live albums had been recorded and released to some success. Once AIR was on board, the Little House rehearsals ceased and they were off on a world tour with Herbie to far reaching places like Mexico, South America, Scandinavia and the Middle East.

1967-70 was the psychedelic era in America. During this period all the focus was on the experimentation and innovation of all the rock bands. Jazz music was losing record industry attention. Herbie was aware of this and in 1969 recorded and released an album called *Memphis Underground* with studio musicians that fused rhythm & blues, jazz, rock and funk. Jazz was declining, but this influential album had the naysayers of jazz stand up and listen. The album merged rock and jazz and kept Herbie afloat during all the psychedelia happening.

Because of the success of this LP, he formed his own record label, Embryo, under the backing of the mothership label Atlantic Records. The psychedelic scene was in full bloom and he took notice of his talented backup band especially Googie, whose songs seemed special. He saw the opportunity to feature AIR on his new record label as one of the first jazz rock bands. A contract was signed and they went to Media Sound Studios, a converted church located on 57th St. in Manhattan, to record their own album of music.

It was a great and infectious LP with help from The Brecker Brothers. Randy (trumpet), Mike (sax) and Barry Rogers (trombone) who were established with Columbia records and the band Dreams. Herbie produced the album with the help of sound engineers Fred Christie and Tony Bongiovi, a cousin of the later superstar Jon Bon Jovi. The album has some brilliant laid-back folk sounds with a jazzy feel and lots of piano and organ. The horns are only there as spice on the cake. Overall, there is a sound like the band Seawind. The focal point of the band was 19-year old Googie, who looks and sounds a lot like Laura Nyro. Her voice was a dream and she had all the vision and drive for the band. Pictured on the album cover going clockwise is Googie, Mark, Tom and John.

There was little to no promotion for the record album release simply called *AIR*, but they were featured at New York clubs as well as The Western Front in Cambridge, Ma and at Stonehenge located at 4 South Main Street in Ipswich, Ma. Most of the time was spent backing Herbie Mann and they were not able to concentrate on their own music projects. One single was released *Baby, I Don't Know Where Love b/w Mr. Man* that did nothing.

Unfortunately, the album didn't sell well here in states, but it did gather a cult following in the UK. The record showed no financial promise and the contract ran out. Soon after the album release the band fell apart. Googie became a born-again Christian, a move that influenced her later song writing.

Mark Rosengarden and John Siegler both reconnected with Moogy Klingman on the 2 albums that he released. Then Moogy and John Siegler moved on to several albums and touring with Todd Rundgren's Utopia. John was also a session bass man for several bands including Hall & Oates, Baby Grand, Roger Daltry and others throughout his career. Mark Rosengarden guested on a few LPs and went into sound techniques for a short while but disappeared musically by 1980.

Googie and Tom continued to play cameo parts on other albums by jazz artists Herbie Mann, Hermeto Pascoal, Flora Purim, John Blair, Bette Midler, Ray Barretto, Lenny White, Jeremy Steig, Airto and others. As Googie and Tom Coppola they released an album in 1980 called *Shine the Light of Love* and had a huge hit in Detroit with the single *Joyous Flame b/w Family of Man*. As a result, they were invited to play their hit single on *The Scene*, a TV program hosted by Nat Morris and based in Detroit highlighting the current hit-making funk and soul groups. The album has all the influences of the early days as AIR with soul heard here for a highly polished disc of music. Tom and Googie stopped performing. He went to work for NBC as a music producer for NBC's *Saturday Night Live* from 1984-1990 and played in the Broadway Show, Dreamgirls. He attended USC for film scoring and got a graduate degree in jazz studies.

In the 80's the band reformed for a short while, minus John Siegler and recorded two albums *In Need of You* and *Can't Let Go.* With a sudden sadness Googie left us in 2008. Tom formed a jazz trio and set up a website at www.tomcoppolajazz.com featuring the works of both him and Googie. The CDs of the two previous recordings were released from the website and distributed through CD Baby in 2009.

Tom and Googie's daughter had been heavily influenced by all the musicians her parents were involved with and is now a world-renowned artist known as EvaEva.

←STEREO→
ALEXANDER'S TIMELESS
BLOOZBAND

STEREO
73021
ALEXANDER'S TIMELESS BLOOZBAND
UNI
PRINTED IN U.S.A.
©UNIVERSAL CITY RECORDS • A Division of MCA Inc.

ALEXANDERS TIMELESS BLOOZBAND 1967-68

Reed Lockart was a blues historian at University of California Santa Barbara (UCSB) and was well versed in blues history. He formed a band called Alexanders Timeless Bloozband (ATB) whose members initially were Reed Lockart (bass, keyboards, sax, vocals), Larry Marks (harmonica, trombone, vocals), Dennis Geaney (guitar) and Spencer Conway (drums). Reed Lockart was the lead singer and his voice sounded a lot like Howlin' Wolf or Don Van Vliet (aka Captain Beefheart).

Charles Lamont was a keyboard player and Ralph Parrett was a guitar player who both attended college at UCLA. The two of them formed The Glass Family who had some success in the area around Hermosa and Redondo Beach. But that band was in love with The Doors and wanted to emulate their sound. This was contrary to Charles thoughts about more of a pop music sound, so he left The Glass Family and joined Reed Lockart who was a childhood friend growing up together in Santa Ana, CA. to play keyboards and sing for ATB.

The band played the college circuit in and around the LA area with a heavy following at UCSB in Santa Barbara and played a gig or two at The Whiskey-Au-Go-Go on The Strip. They were the exclusive house band at The Golden Bear in Huntington Beach and had quite a local following. An album was recorded at the small Sound Recorder Studios, owned and operated by Fritz Ashauer behind the Record Rack store that he also owned in Santa Barbara. He engineered this first album called *Alexanders Timeless Bloozband*. It was pressed and released in limited quantity on the very private label Smack Records.

They hooked up with Tony Cary (born Tony Luton) who owned Miramar Records in Hollywood. He produced The Roadrunners, James Burton and The Dover's and was known to cruise down Hwy 101 at 100 MPH in his Cadillac while talking on his Motorola car phone to DJs trying to get his records played on the radio. ATB was picked up in the signing frenzy of psych bands with the UNI Record label and recorded a second album at Sunset Sound Studios in Hollywood.

There was national distribution of their second album entitled *For Sale*. With completely different songs, the band members were pictured on the back cover without names mentioned. Those who were unfamiliar with the band and their first album release were wondering who these guys were. The front cover of the LP had a great Bob Masse picture that really helped sell the unknown group. Musically the band has a lot of blues numbers due to Reed Lockart's passion for that style. There are some horns and sax with some psych guitar and minor studio effects. Charles Lamont's addition added some songs worthy of AM radio airplay. A single *Love So Strong b/w Horn Song* was the only single that had any airplay on the radio. There is some resemblance in sound to another band called Linn County.

One story was about ATB opening for Country Joe and the Fish and Janis Joplin for a show at the Robertson Gym at the University of California Santa Barbara. After the show, a groupie came backstage and hooked up with Charles Lamont. They retired to a nearby hotel room and spent a couple of days and nights there, until she realized that Charles Lamont from the other band was not the famous Country Joe MacDonald leader of The Fish. She was outta there in a hurry.

The UNI LP did have some minor underground FM radio airplay, but by then the band had split apart and gone onto other things. Charles Lamont recorded one more album for the UNI label called *A Legend in His Own Mind*. The players were Charles (keyboards, vocals) along with Dennis Geaney, Jon Hill and Chris Pritchard (guitars), Chuck Domanico (bass), Tom Scott and Jimmy Horn (saxophone), Bobby Bryant (trumpet), George Bohannon (trombone) and John Guerin (drums). They all were very highly praised session and jazz musicians playing for a virtual who's who in the musical industry (Frank Sinatra, Joni Mitchell, Taj Mahal, The Beatles, Linda Ronstadt, Earth Wind & Fire, the list goes on forever). Produced by Tony Cary, the album sounds a lot like the first Blood, Sweat and Tears LP with horns and some wah-wah guitar.

Unfortunately, in 1974 Tony Cary died of a drug overdose at the early age of 27. Alexanders Timeless Bloozband did try and reform with Jonathan Hill (guitar, sax) and added Chuck Marchese on (drums). They gigged around for a while, but no recordings were ever made. The band was done.

Spencer Conway and Larry Marks moved on to the relative security of steady daytime work.

Reed Lockart became a history teacher at UCLA.

Dennis Geaney played the tours with Ike and Tina Turner & the Kings of Rhythm band for a while and then moved to San Francisco where he pursued his passion for Photography. He continues to play freelance with other bay area bands as the featured guitarist.

Charles Lamont continued playing and traveled to Europe. He was able to make a good living throughout the years and currently is back with Ralph Parrett (now Jim Callon) and the Glass Family members gigging occasionally in Redondo Beach during the year. The ATB band members are all still living in California and there is some talk of reforming again.

Stereo / A10101
THE AMERICAN DREAM
AMPEX RECORDS
1.
GOOD NEWS
BIG BROTHER
THE OTHER SIDE
CREDEMPHELS
STORM
CADILLAC
2.
MY BABE
I AIN'T SEARCHIN'
FUTURE'S FOLLY
I AM YOU
FRANKFORD EL
RASPBERRIES
NICK JAMESON
First Guitar, Piano, Vocals
DON LEE VAN WINKLE
Second Guitar, Vocals
NICKY INDELICATO
Rhythm Guitar, Lead Vocals
DON FERRIS
Bass, Vocals
Engineer/TODD RUNDGREN
RECORD PRODUCTION
and Designer/BOB CATO
to Albert, Mike, Lloyd and everyone else.
/PAUL FISHKIN
Madison Avenue/New York City 10022

THE AMERICAN DREAM 1970

Don Lee Van Winkle, Don Ferris and Mickey Brook were all high school buddies growing up in the Holmesburg area of Philadelphia on the south edge of Pennypack Park. The usual afterschool shenanigans occurred, drinking, smoking and kissing girls at the golf course, the graveyard or down on the railroad tracks. History was made when The Beatles played on The Ed Sullivan Show and that was that. Mickey had a set of drums and both Don Ferris and Van Winkle were dabbling with guitars. They started jamming together after hours in the basement of a luncheonette. Realizing they needed somebody to sing, they went to Rittenhouse Square located in downtown Philadelphia where everybody hung out to tell stories and play music and found Pat Cush.

So, the band had their start with Don Van Winkle (acoustic guitar), Don Ferris (bass, guitar) Mickey Brook (drums) and Pat Cush (vocals). Pat had been reading a book The Great Gatsby and came up with a band name of The Great American Dream. Then word got out that Skip Drinkwater, a record producer with Brooke Productions Inc. from California, was coming to Philadelphia looking for bands to sign up. They practiced for 12 hours a day to make an impression and score a record deal, but Skip never showed up.

Undeterred they continued hoping to make it on their own. Pat Cush left to sing for Slim Pickens, this was another local band not the California actor. They hooked up with Paul Fishkin who was managing Todd Rundgren's previous band Woody's Truck Stop. Paul saw promise with the new guys and left Woody's to manage The Great American Dream. He introduced them to Nick Jameson (guitar) and vocalist Richard Johnson. The band dropped the Great from their name. Richard left and was replaced by rock and roll singer Nicky Indelicato. He brought some light-hearted comedy to the mix but had serious vocal pipes that could bring chills to the ears. So, The American Dream was solidified starring Nick Jameson (guitar, vocals), Don Lee Van Winkle (guitar, vocals), Nick Indelicato (lead vocals, rhythm guitar), Don Ferris (bass, vocals) and Mickey Brook (drums).

They found a rehearsal place underneath a parking garage, would practice all day long for 6 days a week, started writing songs and began to get their sound. Just starting out Don Van Winkle didn't own an electric guitar. The

Guitar Workshop located in Rittenhouse Square would lend him a guitar to play on stage, but he couldn't take the price tag off. They moved to a house in the old city area at 136 N 3rd St just minutes from downtown. The American Dream played places like The Trauma, The Magic Theatre, The Second Fret, The Artists Hut and other small clubs geared for local bands. When visiting Philadelphia, Bonnie Raitt and Jerry Miller (lead guitar with Moby Grape) would come to the house on occasion to jam with the boys.

One night, Larry Magid, co-owner of The Electric Factory where all the national acts played, got a hold of Paul and said he "needed a band now". The new venue was only in their second week of operation. The band Elizabeth had canceled their show and Larry needed somebody to fill in. The band only lived about 6 blocks away and had to hoof all the equipment over on carts. The American Dream appeared on the big stage opening for H.P. Lovecraft.

Todd Rundgren had formed the band Nazz and scored a national hit single on the airwaves with *Open My Eyes b/w Hello Its Me*. He moved on as a solo artist and was beginning to show signs as the new "wonderkid" in the studio, still writing songs but engineering as well. He worked at the newly built Bearsville Sound Studio in Woodstock, New York. Paul Fishkin asked Todd if he could help with production for the new band. He agreed and they went to The Record Plant located in New York to record their first album. The American Dream was Todd's maiden voyage as a producer. He and Lloyd Zane Remick, who represented the band, were instrumental in getting them signed by Alex Grossman and Ampex Records.

The recording was completed and the self-titled album *The American Dream* with three-guitar assault and four-part harmony sounds much like Moby Grape. It's a strong album from start to finish and should have gotten the band more attention. The single *I Ain't Searchin' b/w Good News* was released and played on local radio stations and was popular but never hit the national charts. The LP sold well locally at about 50,000 initial copies but truly little promotion occurred by the Ampex Record label so, they remained local hero's and that is as far as they went.

Out on tour they got as far east as The Ludlow Garage in Cincinnati opening for The Allman Brothers Band, played places like The Electric Circus in New York opening for Santana on a three-night stretch. St. Marks Place and Café Wha? in New York opening for Steppenwolf, Jefferson Airplane, The Doors and others along with places in New

Jersey and back home at The Electric Factory in Philadelphia where, on their new album debut, Seals and Crofts and Elton John were the opening act for them. They were huge in their hometown.

The band eventually broke apart.

Nick Jameson left and wound up with Foghat. He played bass and produced & engineered Foghat's multi-platinum album *Fool for The City* in 1975. He also put out a solo album in 1977. He currently does voice-overs, TV work and starred as the President in the TV series 24.

Mickey Brook opened a bar in Philly called the Sand Trap Tavern. It lasted a short while, but sadly Mickey passed away due to a drug overdose.

Unfortunately, Don Ferris also passed due to cancer in April 2011.

Nick Indelicato and Don Lee Van Winkle remained active recording and producing in the Philly music scene. Nick Jameson came home on occasion and with Nicky Indelicato and Don Lee Van Winkle reunited American Dream for various events over the years. They were part of an Electric Factory tribute and several Earth Day events.

Nicky Idelicato sadly passed in 2019 which leaves Nick Jameson and Don Lee Van Winkle as the last standing pillars of "The Great American Dream".

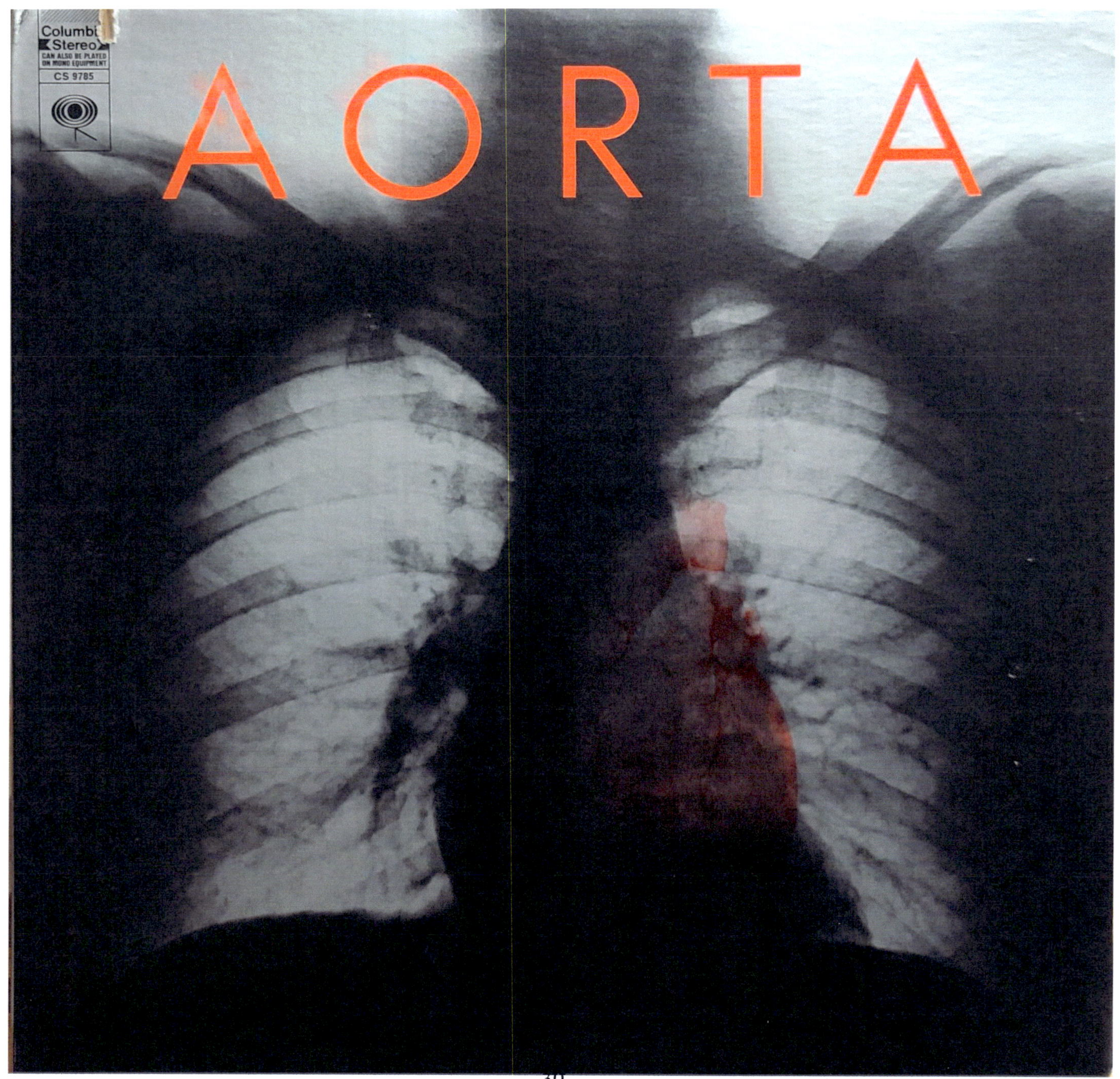
Columbia
Stereo
CAN ALSO BE PLAYED ON MONO EQUIPMENT
CS 9785
AORTA

STEREO | HAPPY TIGER RECORDS
AORTA 2

AORTA 1969-70

James Vincent Dondelinger hailed from Chicago. His first formal guitar band was The Quintones. They were an instrumental combo covering most of the hit songs, *Apache* by Jorden Ingmann, *Honky Tonk* by Bill Doggett, *Walk Don't Run* by The Ventures, etc. Jim befriended Doug Sahm (Sir Douglas Quintet) when they came through town and he learned a few guitar chords, riffs and tricks from this talented man. After a while he got a call to audition for The Five MCs, a band of brothers located in Fayetteville, Arkansas. They were an established band and were much older than Jim (then 17 years old), but they hired him anyway and made travel plans.

Canada was hot on bands from the American south and the Five MCs were booked to The Grange Club in Hamilton, Ontario. Then they found themselves in the heat of it all in the Yorkville area where they played the Le Coq d'Or club along with The Conway Twitty Band and Ronnie Hawkins and the Hawks. This version of the Hawks eventually became The Band.

The Peppermint Lounge in New York was another club they played along with Joey Dee and the Starlighters. This band rode the sails with their top hit *Peppermint Twist* and later evolved into The Young Rascals. The two bands were asked to open a new discothèque in Hollywood, California called The Peppermint West. The Five MCs were popular for private house parties of the stars as well.

After 8 weeks, they were done. Returning to New York, they all said their goodbyes and took a long hiatus. Jim left for home and after a few years playing with various bands joined Kal David and the Exceptions, a band that included former members of his old combo The Quintones. Kal David left and joined The Rovin' Kind who later became The Illinois Speed Press. He was replaced by Jim on (guitar). So, the band included former Quintones alumnus Marty Greeb (organ) and Denny Ebert (drums) along with a yet unknown (bass) player Peter Cetera. The band name was shortened to The Exceptions and they were the premiere band playing clubs in and around the local Chicago area. They were well established and opened for most of the bigger named bands that came to town.

Over time Denny Ebert got drafted and was replaced on (drums) by Bill Herman. Marty Greeb left to join The Buckingham's and was replaced on (keyboards) by Jimmy Neyholt. They played clubs in Illinois like The Palmer House. Jim D was growing musically and wanted to write and record original songs. Peter Cetera preferred the steady income of the nightly gigs. Differences ensued and after a meeting of the minds, Pete was fired. He was devastated and was replaced on (bass guitar) by Bobby Jones.

A new direction and a new band name was needed. Thus, began Aorta. Bill Traut ran the local Dunwich Production company and signed the band. Bill was a proven producer who gained some national recognition with the bands The American Breed and The Shadows of Night. He was sure Aorta would become the next big thing. By now, Jim, had simplified the spelling of his last name to Dolinger.

Several original songs had been written, so they went to the Great Lakes Recording Studios in Sparta, Michigan and recorded their first album. Enhanced with special effects, echoes, church pipe organ and psych guitar, the self-titled *Aorta* album is touted by many to be a psychedelic masterpiece. Vibes of Hamilton Streetcar with heavy guitar come closest to their sound. *Strange b/w Ode to Missy Mztsfpklk* was the featured album single that was highly regarded on the radio.

Backing the likes of Led Zeppelin and The Who, Aorta toured the Midwest States, played to big crowds and received high accolades for their shows. Clubs like The Jaguar in St Charles, The Green Gorilla in Des Plaines and Barnaby's and The Kinetic Playground in Chicago were places that were full of flashing lights and general psychedelia. Ready for the big time, they were scheduled to be the showcase band at the Fillmore East. Columbia executives would be there to hand this up and coming band the golden key to fame and fortune. Opening for them was Chuck Berry, Savoy Brown, Johnny Winter and Procol Harum. A chance of a lifetime and easy, they were hyped and ready for the world.

But during the Savoy Brown performance, Bobby Jones was in the sound booth talking to a member of Procol Harum and was offered a couple hits of LSD. Bob told Jim what he had attained and his thought was that they would take the "dot" after their show was over. But Jim persuaded Bob to pop 'em in now to give the band an extra lift for their performance. Understand that up until this point none of the band members had done much more than the occasional marijuana joint.

They didn't think about the unsuspected effects of an LSD hit before they went on stage and they weren't sure how to handle it, everything was enhanced and paranoia set in. The show was a disaster. During the performance, Jim was so detached from the music he chose instead to observe the perceived phosphorescence of his audience. His guitar playing was so intense that he got way out of tune. Bob was a madman on bass guitar. Anger and confusion overshadowed the other band members and it became obvious that they blew their big chance. The labels turned their back and any support for the band went out the door.

Billy Herman quit immediately and joined The New Colony Six. Aorta seemed to be done. Bob Jones left for California. Jim's brother Tom was playing drums with The Rotary Connection starring Minnie Ripperton and they needed a guitar player. So, Jim Dolinger and Jimmy Neyholt joined the band and recorded the album *Peace*, a psychedelic Christmas album. The band toured everywhere playing all the festivals. They were asked to play Woodstock at the last minute but turned it down because they saw how big the audience was and felt they had done enough festivals. A reluctant decline in retrospect.

The Rotary Connection alliance didn't last long and Aorta was reformed with brother Tom Donlinger on (drums). They toured that summer and played before a crowd of 100,000 at the Denver Pop Festival. But Bobby Jones was disheartened and split to California for good. He was replaced by Michael Been (bass). One more album *Aorta 2* was recorded at Universal Recording Corp. located at 32 W Randolph Street in Chicago with some nice songs, but it didn't quite live up to the previous imaginative bliss of the first. The single *Sandcastles b/w Willie Jean* went unnoticed. The band as Aorta fell apart quickly. Jim Dolinger and Micheal Been then joined Michael Tzega with Marty Greeb to revive HP Lovecraft who had fallen apart and recorded their third LP *Valley of the Moon*.

Bobby Jones moved on and played bass with Joe Cocker recording and touring for over 30 years.

Michael Been formed The Call in San Francisco to great success and played with Pendragon and others. He retired as a player and ran the soundboard for his son Robert Levon Been who plays bass guitar for his popular band Black Rebel Motorcycle Club.

Jim Nyeholt got out of music and worked for a medical research organization near Chicago.

Jim Dolinger dropped his last name and became James Vincent. Guesting with other bands in the studio and on the road like Azteca, Rufus, Greg Allman and others. He found Christianity and had a long career as a songwriter and released several solo LPs eventually finding peace in his life after the realization that existence as a musician can really take its toll.

FTS-3042
STEREO
THE APPLETREE THEATRE
PLAYBACK
PLAYBACK
PLAYBACK
PLAYBACK
Verve
FORECAST

THE APPLETREE THEATRE 1968

Terence Boylan was brought up in Buffalo, New York. His initial claim to fame came when he was 9 years old. He wrote a letter to The National Institute of Health (NIH) requesting money to build a rocket ship. At The Center for Scientific Review at the NIH, the people who review grant requests were certainly amused at Boylan's bold ambition. But Ernest Allen, the director of the Center, saw something in the request and awarded the $10 grant to Terence and his friend Bruce Cook to complete their project. Unbeknownst to his dad the check was hand delivered to his home along with reporters from both local newspapers, The Courier Express and The Buffalo News, who wrote an article about the two rocket ship builders. They ultimately did launch a small rocket with quite an impressive flight height.

Terence also enjoyed music and played guitar. He formed a band called the Pre-Teens at age 12 and performed a song he wrote on WBNY's Buffalo Bob's Radio Show. Later, as a sophomore in high school, 1962, he had a chance meeting with Bob Dylan in Greenwich Village and the two traded off singing songs at The Folklore Center on MacDougal Street. Inspired by Dylan's encouragement, Terence returned to Buffalo and began playing at local folk coffee houses, such as The Limelight and The Lower Level as well as The Bell, Book and Candle in Ontario, Canada.

He attended Bard College, located at Annandale-on-Hudson about 90 miles north of New York City, where such alumnus included Christopher Guest, Mia Fallow, Chevy Chase and other famous celebrities. Bard had a lively and progressive music scene. Forming another band called The Ginger Men with his older brother, John, the band included Terence Boylan (guitar, bass, vocals), John Boylan (rhythm guitar, piano, vocals), Peter Meekel (lead guitar), Rick Smith (harmonica) and Michael Equine (drums, harmony vocals).

They started playing at The Night Owl Café in Greenwich Village, sharing the stage with other notable acts such as The Lovin' Spoonful, Richie Havens, Stephen Stills and James Taylor's fledgling band The Flying Machine. This was a time when rock and folk were beginning to fuse. Terence also played solo at Folk Clubs like The Gaslight Café, Gerde's Folk City, and was introduced by Pete Seeger at the Village Gate for a young songwriter's festival held there. This garnered a brief but favorable write-up in The New York Times by Robert Shelton, one of the leading music and film critics, and then record companies came calling.

Terence wound up signing a contract with the MGM/Verve Forecast label as a staff songwriter and solo act. But before recording solo he decided to recruit his brother and a few studio musicians for an experimental album, combining rock songs and satirical comedy sketches. The result was The Appletree Theatre, a "concept" album with parodies of different musical genres that became a masterpiece of psychedelia.

At Regent Studios in New York, they mixed studio musicians with musician friends from other Greenwich Village bands, including Larry Coryell, Eric Gale and Zal Yanovsky on guitars, Chuck Israels and Chuck Rainey on bass, Paul Griffin on keyboards and Buddy Saltzman, Joe Butler and former patron with The Ginger Men, Michael Equine, who later formed Cat Mother and the All Night Newboys, on drums. Terence and John performed all the vocals and "skits" and the brilliant engineer, Bill Szymczyk, contributed lots of special studio effects, backwards passages, stereo panning, echoes, all combined with wild guitar solos and an eclectic range of vocal styles. Appletree Theatre was one of the first concept albums to tie a storyline, comedy and rock music into a single album. The band's name was inspired by a mythical theatre touring group called the Appletree Players from the 1500s in Britannia.

Entitled *Playback,* the album cover was drawn and designed by Nick Gaetano. A very unusual, colorful and wild illustration. Even if you never heard the tunes, the album cover was a marketing showpiece. The LP was released and had an immediate impact on those in the psychedelic genre. With much airplay on underground FM radio John Lennon was being quoted in an interview that Appletree Theatre was one of his favorite new albums. The Boylan brothers received a brief but rave write-up in Time Magazine. They never toured as a band, but two singles were released to popular fanfare: *Hightower Square b/w Who Do I Think I Am* and *What A Way To Go b/w Lotus Flower.*

Terence then recorded the solo album he had originally prepared, called *Alias Boona,* at the Hit Factory in New York, with fellow Bard College friends, Walter Becker and Donald Fagen who later went on to form Steely Dan, plus three session drummers, one of whom was Darius Davenport who later formed the well-regarded Autosalvage.

His brother John had relocated to Los Angeles and established himself as a premiere producer. He was producing former Stone Poneys lead singer Linda Ronstadt, at the time, and was responsible for putting together a new band to back her emerging solo career for an upcoming national tour. This back-up band included Don Henley (drums, vocals) (from Shilo), Glenn Frey, (electric, slide & steel guitar, vocals) (from Longbranch Pennywhistle), and later, Randy Meisner (from Rick Nelson and The Stone Canyon Band) and Bernie Leadon (from Hearts and Flowers and The Flying Burrito Brothers). All of these players, some between bands, met often at Doug Weston's The Troubadour, located on Santa Monica Blvd. in West Hollywood. John Boylan sealed the deal with a handshake for Glenn Frey and Don Henley to tour with Linda Ronstadt on the road, and later coordinated the addition of Meisner and Leadon. Of course, this backup band would later become famous as The Eagles.

John Boylan worked with and produced Pure Prairie League, Rick Nelson, Commander Cody and The Little River Band, and had his largest selling album in the mid-70's producing the first LP by Boston, headed by guitarist Tom Scholz. He became vice president of EPIC Records on the west coast. Then he produced albums for children by The Muppets, The Chipmunks and won a Grammy Award for the soundtrack album *Elmopalooza.* John has been involved with several movie soundtracks including *Urban Cowboy* and *Born on The Fourth of July* and is currently a professor at Citrus College in Glendora, California teaching critical listening skills for their recording arts program.

Terence Boylan continued to write songs and released a self-titled album called *Terence Boylan,* again backed by his Bard College buddies Walter Becker and Donald Fagen, plus members of the Eagles and a bevy of notable LA session musicians. This album was a national breakout in 1977 on Billboard for 5 weeks, reaching their top 200 album charts, and garnered high marks from the critics. He played and promoted this album in 50 cities nationwide after the release and then released a third LP *Suzy*. Back in New York he began writing songs for movies and other artists and has released three other LPs and CDs. He currently owns a record label, Spinnaker Records, and a book publishing company, The River Press. Everything has come full circle as he became the Executive Director of the Boylan Foundation for Medical Research, and Chairman of the Board of The MDI Biological Laboratory located in the state of Maine.

EKS-74020 STEREO, also playable on mono phonographs
ARS NOVA

STEREO
ARS NOVA
SUNSHINE
&
SHADOWS
ATLANTIC
SD 8221

ARS NOVA 1967-69

Wyatt Day met Jon Pierson in New York at the Mannes College of Music. Wyatt was a classical guitarist and piano player while Jon played (bass trombone) and could sing. They were musicians, playing with small symphonies and had formed The New York Baroque Brass Ensemble. After graduation both left for Spain where Wyatt learned his diverse skills on Spanish guitar. After a year and a half both Jon and Wyatt had returned to New York. The psychedelic music scene was in full bloom and Wyatt contacted Jon to form a rock band.

They gathered two friends and players from Mannes College and formed a band that included Wyatt Day (rhythm guitar, keyboards, vocals), Jon Pierson (bass trombone, bass guitar, vocals), Jonathon Raskin (bass, lead guitar) and Maury Baker (drums, percussion) and chose the name Ars Nova, a Latin term meaning New Art.

They hadn't written any original songs yet, but they did get a gig at The Electric Circus on St. Marks Place in New York City. The club was pretty-wild with sheets hanging from the ceiling, black lights, clowns, mimes, fire eaters, trapeze artists swinging on either side of the stage and the featured liquid light show from "Lights By Pablo." Folks would dress in costumes and paint their faces with bright fluorescent colors. Playing basically cover songs, the Ars Nova performance was completed with psychedelic props and strobe lights that were unnerving. The band was only weeks old and felt that their first performance was not up to their standards. Nevertheless, the club was known for altered substances that made for a good impression and the audience seemed delighted with their stage show. The years-long phase for this club was "If you remembered much of what happened at the Electric Circus, you weren't really there." But Ars Nova did feel magic from the experience.

Their early influences of Medieval and Renaissance music along with the burgeoning rock sounds was something unexplored and completely different. So, they decided to move to Vermont and stayed at Jonathon Raskin's cabin to write music and develop an original sound. Wyatt and Jon wrote a handful of songs together and they played a local ski lodge to get their show set. Tiring of the seclusion and a daily diet of rice, they went back to the big city in

New York. Jonathon Raskin decided to leave the band. In his place Wyatt knew Giovanni (Johnny) Papalia who came in on (lead guitar, sitar) and he brought in his friend Bill Folwell who played (trumpet & bass).

A handful of songs had been written and their sound was quite unusual combining the baroque styles that the players were familiar with along with rock music. Wyatt had a friend in the business that knew Arthur Gorson. He represented several folk acts including (Phil Ochs, Judy Collins, Tom Rush & others) that were at the cusp of going electric. They were able to audition for Arthur who was involved with Jac Holzman at Elektra Records and he was impressed by their unique sound.

At that time, there was a huge media frenzy over the psychedelic bands and a buzz was happening locally about Ars Nova. They put a demo recording together and Jac Holzman signed them up immediately for an album. The band had not played any of their new songs at a rock club in front of a live audience and knowing all the intricacies of the music they were playing the band was nervous about being thrown to the wolves. But they were booked to open for Egg and The Moody Blues at The Electric Factory on 22nd and Arch Street in Philadelphia. The show went better than expected and the band was flown to Los Angeles to start the 3-month process of recording their first album at Sunset Sound Studios in West Hollywood.

Paul Rothchild who discovered The Doors oversaw the production. But the band didn't have quite enough material for a full album. So, Elektra brought in Gregory Copeland, a proven song composer who collaborated with Steve Noonan and the Nitty Gritty Dirt Band and the national top 50 Billboard hit single *Buy For Me The Rain b/w Candy Man*, to work with Wyatt to write enough songs to fill the void. After a month they began to record but were not used to recording in a big studio, the band was out of sorts, never getting a real feel for each other during practice and rehearsal. All tracks, voice, instruments and special effects were recorded separately. Bill Folwell was a trumpet player who had problems in the studio with the bass parts. The first album was finally finished, but it was rough sounding.

They went back to New York and recalled Jonathon Raskin to rejoin the band and overdub the bass lines for the recording. LIFE magazine had a huge write up on Ars Nova as part of the new rock flourishing all over the country.

But Elektra wanted to keep the band under wraps waiting to debut them as the next big thing. The showcase was initially supposed to happen at Carnegie Hall with mimes, dancers, jugglers and jesters and the event was to be called "Automatic Love" named after one of their songs. When the show was done, the audience was supposed to meet down the street at a banquet hall and dine to Renaissance Food with candles, handmaidens and tumblers. But due to the exuberant costs, the whole thing was cancelled.

Instead, they were booked to open for Elektra labelmates The Doors at The Fillmore East. A disaster in the making, they hadn't played together on stage for months. Crome Syrcus opened the show and overplayed their time slot. Ars Nova was the second act and they only had about 15-20 minutes to make an impression. The promoter wanted to have the stage darkened to enhance the mysterious effect for the band. During the stage show they forgot some of the words to the songs and couldn't get coordinated with each other while playing. The crowd was screaming for The Doors wanting to hear Jim Morrison instead. Ars Nova were so humiliated afterwards that the band fell apart.

Giovanni and Bill Folwell went back to studio work. Jonathon Raskin and Maury Baker headed back to Los Angeles followed by Jon and Wyatt in hopes of giving the band a fresh start, but it didn't work out.

Meanwhile the album was officially released. The self-titled album *Ars Nova* is unique and infectious, full of brass horns, lute, harpsichord, fuzz guitar and medieval harmonies. Unique in the fact that they merged baroque sounds with a touch of psychedelics much like The New York Rock & Roll Ensemble and UK bands Gryphon and Amazing Blondel. The album cover pictures clockwise from the top right Giovanni Papalia, Jonathon Raskin, Bill Folwell, Wyatt Day and Maury Baker with Jon Pierson centered. Two singles were released for radio airplay *Fields Of People b/w March of the Mad Dukes Circus* and *Pavan For My Lady b/w Zoroaster.* The album was distributed all over the US but only heard outside of New York on underground FM radio. There were no plans for a scheduled national tour.

While still in California Jon Pierson called his mother and explained that Ars Nova was done and that he was coming home. But she revealed some great news. The Village Voice praised the album with stellar reviews. So, after hearing this revelation Jon called a friend of his in New York (Sam Brown) who played (lead guitar) and plans were made to reform the band back there. However, Jonathon Raskin and Maury Baker stayed behind in LA due to a side deal with Paul Rothchild and Elektra Records. Wyatt and Jon weren't happy with this and forced the label to compensate them for travel expenses back home. Once back in New York they were able to gather different players. The new band consisted of Wyatt Day (guitar, vocals), Jon Pierson (bass trombone, lead vocals), Sam Brown (lead guitar), Stu Wasserman (bass), Ronnie Puddu (trumpet), Warren Bernhardt (keyboards) and Joe Hunt on (drums).

Jon Pierson's father was a Lutheran Preacher and because of his connections in the religious circles, they were able to practice at an unused Episcopal church rectory in the Bronx. Their first gig with the new band was at The Bitter End. But, after that show, Elektra head, Jac Holtzman, bid them farewell. They no longer had a record label, but they continued to play clubs in and around New York including The Boston Tea Party with Ford Theatre. Stu Wasserman was replaced by Art Koenig on (bass) and Ronnie Puddu was replaced by Jimmy Owens (trumpet).

Finally, ATCO Records came calling. They went to Century Sound Studios with Brooks Arthur and recorded a second album called *Sunshine and Shadows*. But it wasn't officially released until a year later. This album had the same feel as the first but was more electric in sound. Pictured counterclockwise from left to right is Sam Brown, Jimmy Owens, Wyatt Day, Jonathon Pierson, Warren Bernhardt, and Joe Hunt. Art Koenig is not pictured.

There was a small tour established that took them to Thee Image in Miami, The Love Auditorium in South Carolina, The Black Dome in Cincinnati, The Kinetic Playground in Chicago, and other places in New York with a final seven day schedule at Ungano's in Manhattan. Fans in Europe adhered to their unique sound but with unfilled promises from the record labels, little promotion of the second LP and no interest for the corresponding single release *Sunshine & Shadows b/w Walk On The Sand,* Ars Nova broke up for good.

Ars Nova was a very melodic band that was truly innovative for the times and woefully overlooked.

An instrumental album by The Terminal Barbershop called *Hair Styles* was released by ATCO that included Wyatt Day, Jon Pierson, Jonathon Raskin, Sam Brown, Joe Hunt and others with songs from the popular stage musical Hair.

Sam Brown was a jazz guitarist who continued with artists like Jeremy Stieg, Paul Desmond, Paul Winter and others.

Jimmy Owens played with Miles Davis and was tutored by Donald Byrd. He was side trumpet with Charles Mingus, Maynard Ferguson, Lionel Hampton and many others over the years.

Warren Bernhardt is a seasoned musician as a classical jazz pianist. He began his career with Paul Winters Sextet and played with George Benson and Bill Evans who became his mentor. Warren has toured and recorded with Paul Simon, Steely Dan and several other known bands and musicians and has released about 20 solo LPs.

Art Koenig toured and recorded with Danny Kalb, Joe Beck, Morgana King and others.

It appears Giovanni Papalia's whereabouts is unknown.

Jonathon Raskin was tabbed to play bass with the new super band *Rhinoceros* being put together by Paul Rothchild. It's not known what happened and he may have been in the initial sessions but he was never credited as a player with the band. He returned to New York and played in recording sessions with Tom Paxton and Tom Rush.

Bill Folwell was a bassist and trumpet player with Albert Ayler both before and after Ars Nova in studio recordings in New York. He also played with Buddy Guy and was in session with The Insect Trust as a bass player. Sadly, he left us in October 2019.

Maury Baker was at Woodstock with Janis Joplin and toured with her until she passed away in 1970. He also toured with Tim Buckley & Frank Zappa and has remained a session drummer playing with many known artists and bands throughout his illustrious career. He is currently fronting his experimental jazz band Baker's Brew.

Jon Pierson performed songs with Lou Reed and Brother Jack McDuff. He wrote songs and performed with Nick Holmes and Mike Mainieri on *Soulful Crooner* and the *White Elephant* album that included fellow bandmate Warren Bernhardt, The Brecker Brothers, Steve Gadd, Hugh MacCracken, Tony Levin and several others.

Wyatt Day settled down in New York and developed an established business that is still active appraising, buying and selling old and rare books.

ARZACHEL
ROULETTE
bellaphon

ARZACHEL 1969

Steve Hillage (guitar, vocals) and Montgomery (Mont) Campbell (bass, guitar, vocals) met at The City of London Boys Day School in the shadow of St Paul's Cathedral. Steve was a budding guitarist and Mont also played guitar. They met Dave Stewart who played (piano and organ) and aspired to form a band, so Mont agreed to play bass guitar. Honing their skills, they put an ad in Melody Maker hoping to find a suitable drummer. Clive Brooks answered and the band was complete. Inspired by John Milton's Paradise Lost, they called themselves Uriel (pronounced OO-Re-EL), the name is Hebrew for Angel of Light, Flame of God.

Their first show was at a youth club in Sheen, a suburb of London, playing cover versions of Cream, Hendrix, The Nice and others. Steve Hillage was known for long, drawn-out guitar jams for the sparse few who showed up. They began writing their own songs right away. During the summer of 1968 they played the clubs around town but were mostly featured at The Ryde Castle Hotel located on The Isle of Wight.

A demo recording, *Saturn, The Bringer of Old Age,* was recorded in a small area of Lansdowne Studios in Holland Park, London, where Mr. Aker Bilk recorded the worldwide hit song *Stranger On The Shore*. Mont was classically trained and began to influence the band towards a different keyboard based direction. This prompted Steve to leave the band and finish his schooling. He eventually went on to the University of Kent.

Uriel continued to play as a trio and they were managed by Dave Howson and Paul Walden. After meeting Bill Jewett, Uriel highlighted at The Middle Earth located on King Street in the Covent Garden district in London, famous for bands like Pink Floyd, The Soft Machine, Tomorrow, Ghost, Captain Beefheart and the Magic Band and o many others. Bill owned the club that was influential for bringing these psych bands to the masses in Canterbury.

Uriel was no different and they gained notice from Decca Records. The band name sounded a lot like Urinal, so at the suggestion of Dave and Paul they agreed to a name change. The new moniker, Egg, would be more acceptable to the record industry. They signed the record deal and were under contract to record their first album.

When they weren't on stage, the band would show up at a café where Bill Jewett's wife worked as a waitress.

There they met Peter Wicker who owned a small recording studio called Studio 19. He suggested that the band should record a psychedelic album and take advantage of all the focus on the underground bands like Pink Floyd and The Soft Machine. The only stipulation was that they could only use minimum time and max out the costs at 250 UK lbs. Three songs *Egoman, Swooping Bill* and *The Salesman Song* were recorded here. The problem was that the band Egg was under contract to Decca and couldn't use their proper names or the band name to release any additional recordings as Peter suggested.

Dave, Mont and Clive asked Steve Hillage to come back for this one recording. Dave Stewart came up with the name Arzachel, taken from one of the craters on the moon. The album session was recorded at Denmark Studios in London and only took about 6 hours. In and out and undetected. The choices for band member pseudonyms were as follows: Sam Lee Uff was Dave Stewarts Latin teacher, Basil Downing was Clive Brooks Math teacher, Simon Sasparella was the best name Steve Hillage could come up with for testing microphones and Njerogi Gatetaka was an African name chosen by Mont Campbell because he was born in Africa. Fictitious biographies for each were written up. Dave Stewart drew up the album cover design with a felt pen. The original self-titled album *Arzache*l came out on the Evolution label. The cover was in black and gray with no Arzachel name written out. Other versions came out on the Roulette label with pink and black with the name on the cover or blue and black without the name on the Vogue label.

The music best depicted the sound of Uriel on stage, they recorded and mixed the album all in one day. 6 songs in all, what they came up with is killer starting out in a slightly mellow mood and building with each song into a psychedelic frenzy. The Egg influences are present with heavy organ. The album is a must for every psych enthusiast.

Afterwards Egg with Dave, Mont and Clive recorded three albums *Egg, The Polite Force* and *The Civil Service,* and then broke apart in 1974.

After the Arzachel recording, Steve Hillage formed the band Kahn with Dave Stewart for one album called *Space Shanty* and then joined the band Gong, on and off with Daevid Allen before recording his own solo albums.

Clive Brooks joined The Groundhogs for two albums *Hogwash* and *Solid* and became a drum tech for Pink Floyd and others over the years. He passed on in May of 2017.

Dave Stewart formed Hatfield and the North for a couple albums, then on to the band National Health. He toured on and off with several bands gaining two number one hits with Colin Blunstone and Barbara Gaskin.

Mont Campbell tired of the rock scene and gravitated towards more traditional World Music and odd instruments. As an environmentalist and alternative energy specialist he is the founding director of the Ouse Valley Energy Services Company (Ovesco), a solar energy installations company, located in Lewes, East Sussex, UK.

Because of the interest in Arzachel over the years, all 4 members gathered to remix the original recordings adding the earlier Uriel studio recordings plus demos and released everything out there including outtakes from the Arzachel session on CD by Uriel called *Arzachel (Collector's Edition)* and stuff from Egg on CD called *The Metronomical Society* including Egg archives, remixes and live stuff back in 2007.

bead game
WELCOME.
AVCO EMBASSY
STEREO AVE 33009

BEAD GAME

BEAD GAME 1970

Robert Gass grew up in Newton, Massachusetts. He took accordion lessons and was influenced by orchestra music. His interest stayed in classical music throughout high school and he studied piano and music composition in Boston at both the New England Conservatory of Music and Tanglewood Institute of Fine Arts. When he moved on to Harvard University, his interest changed and he focused on rock n' roll. It was here in Cambridge that he formed the band Bead Game. The band name was inspired by the popular Herman Hesse book called The Glass Bead Game. The players, all Harvard students, were Robert Gass (Hammond CV organ), John Leone (lead vocals, harp), Will Dick (guitar), Joe D'Amico (drums) and a gal named Tina (vocals). Their first gig was in the offices of Vogue Magazine where they auditioned for Vanguard Records. But they were not signed. A few other small shows were played before Tina left and was replaced by Joel "Lassie" Sachs a (bass) player. John Leone had some disillusionment about the band and left. Will Dick followed shortly thereafter. Joey D'Amico left as well but afterwards spent a lifetime on drums with the band Crack the Sky.

Robert revamped the band keeping the same moniker. The players included himself on (keyboards, vocals), Lassie Sachs (bass, vocals) and Jim Hodder on (drums, vocals). He found Kenny Westland Haas (guitar, vocals) studying at The Berklee School of Music and met John Sheldon (guitar) at a B&M Pizza joint in Cambridge, who got the audition and became lead guitar for the band. He was a bit of a prodigy and had previously been on tour with Van Morrison. The new recruits had wonderful song writing abilities.

They met Ray Paret who said he could rent them rehearsal space at Amphion Productions located at 331 Newbury St. in Boston where he worked. There was a small practice area behind his office location. They had been writing their own songs. Once he heard the band, he felt the urge to represent them as manager and found the Bead Game some live shows opening for Jethro Tull, Blues Image, The Allman Brothers, Fat Mattress and others. They played many of the big clubs, The Fillmore East, The Cheetah Club located at Broadway and 53rd, in New York, The Boston Tea Party and the Wax Museum in Washington DC. The critiques who saw the band said they were musically way ahead of their time.

Some members of the band relocated to a communal house, the gigs they played were solid and the fans showed up in droves. Jim Hodder had a very distinctive voice and Robert was known for jumping up and down pounding the keys to his organ until his hands bled, one time it short-circuited on him. He would unintentionally break the legs of the stools, so much so that the road crew set up a full shrine of broken stools in their practice room with a sticker noting the date and location of the occurrence.

Record labels were beginning to take notice and Gary Kannon aka (Gary Katz) found them. He was a junior A&R man with the newly formed Avco Embassy Record label. They were a movie production company that was still lavishing the benefits of two years and one hundred million dollars later with the blockbuster movie *The Graduate*. Gary got the band signed and part of the deal was to be part of a major movie that was in the works.

But first they traveled to New York and the Record Plant located in Manhattan to record an LP. They stayed at a Travelodge but were upgraded to the Park Plaza because The Richmond Organization (TRO) as their music publisher, was pouring out a lot of money for promotion into the band. The sessions were long and grueling and had the notable occurrence of Jimi Hendrix present with Buddy Miles awaiting their studio time to record the *Band of Gypsies* LP. They were on the sidelines watching the sessions and were quoted as saying "they were blown away by what they heard".

The recording was finished and Kenny came up with an embroidered tapestry cloth which became the album cover. The word *Welcome* was woven into the cloth thus the name of the first album. There was no promotion from the label and the album wound up in the cutout bins from the start. The record is psychedelic and jazzy with some phasing, echoes, psych guitar and special effects. Jim Hodder's voice is unmistakable. No single was released, so there was no radio airplay other than through the FM underground stations.

Avco then concentrated their thoughts on a movie, *The People Next Door*, which starred Eli Wallach and Julie Harris about a teenager caught up in the counterculture, experimenting with drugs, sex, rock and roll and all the angst from her parents. The Bead Game is featured at the start of the movie during opening credits playing a dive joint. Called The Shake It Club, this place and the film location was located in Scarsdale, New York. There were a few patrons sitting in chairs and at the bar and the band was auditioning for a gig trying to impress the owner who was sitting by himself. When the opening credits and the song ends the owner states "Ya can't dance to it!" twice. But here is rare footage of the actual band playing live. Pretty cool. The film was a bust but seeing the band in action was a bonus. A soundtrack LP was put out featuring the Bead Game and other Avco label mates The Glass Bottle. The label did release a single of the opening song *Sweet Medusa mono b/w Sweet Medusa stereo*. A great song but it was not written by the band and very few found their way to the radio airwaves. Nothing happened with the sales, so Avco let the Bead Game go.

The next project happened with Ray Paret who knew people at Mercury records. They were looking for a group to back the Buddy Miles horn section for an LP. Buddy was on the road with Hendrix and his Band of Gypsies at the time. They went to Natural Sound Studios in Maynard, Ma. and recorded a full album with horn players James Taum, Bobby Pittman and Tom Hall. The album came out as the band Freedom Express entitled *Easy Ridin'* and musically is completely different than the *Welcome* LP showing signs of Chicago and other popular horn bands.

After this, Bead Game used Natural Sound Studios, offering a 50/50 split of revenue in exchange for studio time and engineering costs to record a second LP. Kenny Haag wrote all the music. Many songs simulate Steeley Dan with minor vocal effects and fuzz guitar. John Sheldon's uncle, Bradley Phillips, was a successful artist and painted the cover picture for the album jacket. A full album of songs, that was to be entitled simply *Bead Game,* was recorded but there were no takers and the tapes wound up sitting on the shelves for over 26 years. A limited press of the LP called *Baptism* was released on American Sound Records in 1996.

The new LP had potential because of all the radio friendly tunes but it wasn't meant to be. They played shows to self-promote the album, but it was frustrating. Then Joel Sachs was mugged outside his home and nearly died. Shortly afterwards the band fell apart.

John Westland and Kenny Hass moved to San Francisco and formed a band called Sneakers. They had some success, but no recordings were made.

John Sheldon hooked up with Linda Ronstadt and then James Taylor traveling all over the world in performance. Throughout his 50-year career, he has released over 13 CDs as a solo artist and with his band Blue Streak.

Joel "Lassie" Sachs became a studio engineer for a while and had a loving family. He was in poor health towards the end of his life and sadly died due to pancreatic cancer in August of 2016 at the age of 65.

Kenny Westland Haas was a bit of a recluse and lived in New York but unfortunately passed away in April of 2019.

Jim Hodder went on to play for Steely Dan and was their voice for the first three LPs that the band released. He did session work and played with Linda Ronstadt, Sammy Hagar and The Rowan Brothers. Sadly, in 1990 he accidentally drowned in his swimming pool. A talented loss.

Robert Gass and his wife moved to Colorado and set up a motivational school, teaching leadership skills along with two non-profit organizations, *The Rockwell Institute* and *The Social Transformation Project*. Robert remained a musician and has recorded and released about 20 spiritual CDs including one that has sold over ½ million copies.

FTS-3059 STEREO
Greetings, Children Of Paradise
BEAR
Verve
FORECAST

BEAR 1967

The story of Bear begins initially in New York, 1965, with Happy & Artie Traum. Happy Traum had been playing the folk clubs in Greenwich Village and starred with The Broadsides in 1963 recording with Bob Dylan, Phil Ochs, Pete Seegar, Peter LaFarge and The Freedom Singers. He was also a member of The New World Singers. Both he, Artie and Eric Kaz were part of the Washington Square Park Riot where folk singing was banned at the fountain. All who were there protested by singing songs like *Glory Hallelujah, Home of the Brave, The Star-Spangled Banner* and other Hail America songs. Meanwhile, the police beat a few folks up and arrested many simply for the lack of a permit to sing in public.

Artie was five years younger than his brother and both had been heavily influenced by the Greenwich Village scene with sounds of folk from early James Taylor and jazz with Miles Davis and John Coltrane. Artie began his career playing with the True Endeavor Jug Band and then The Danny Kalb Quartet which later became The Blues Project. With the advent of Bob Dylan at the Newport Folk Festival, the songs took a twist for a more electric sound. So, Artie and Happy formed Children of Paradise with fellow folksters Marc Silber (bass), Eric Kaz (keyboards, harmonica) and Bobby Colomby (drums).

The band was together for about two years playing in Greenwich Village at clubs like The Café Au Go Go, The Village Gate and Café Bizarre, where Andy Warhol first saw The Velvet Underground and came up with some ideas for his "Expanded Cinema". They were also featured at The Electric Circus in New York and opened for The Beacon Street Union at The Boston Tea Party in Boston, Mass. They traveled to Canada and toured Montreal, Ottawa and played the clubs in Yorkville near Toronto as well.

During this time (drummer) Bobby Colomby left and joined Al Cooper to form Blood, Sweat and Tears. Jerry Angus replaced him. The Children of Paradise signed a contract with Colombia records and recorded one single *What Am I Doing Here b/w Hey You Got Something*. The A side was written by Eric Kaz and fits right in with many of the psych pop sounds of the times with infectious three-part harmonies, guitar, echoes and special effects. Shortly after the recording, Happy left the band and moved upstate to Woodstock. Artie evolved The Children of Paradise and replaced his brother with J. Steven Soles who was a great vocalist and could write a tune. There wasn't a huge following for the band and there were others like Children of Paradise with a similar type of name, so Steven suggested a new moniker as Bear.

The new lineup was Artie Traum (guitar, vocals), Eric Kaz (keyboards), J. Steven Soles (guitar, vocals), Skip Boone (formerly of The Sellouts) (bass) and Darius Davenport (drums). There was some connection between Artie and Brian de Palma who was directing a new film called *Greetings*. This was the film debut for Brian de Palma and the first major role for a new actor named Robert De Niro. Artie was asked to write the theme song for the movie and Bear got the go ahead to record it.

After the movie recording, they went to The Hit Factory Studio located at 353 West 48th St in Manhattan, New York and made a formal album with lots of special effects and wondrous harmonies. Entitled *Greetings, Children of Paradise*, an obvious tribute to the former band, the album released on the Verve label, was produced by John Boylan. He was brother to Terence Boylan who was responsible for the psych masterpiece album by Appletree Theatre. John's talent as a music producer was just blossoming and Bear's sound approaches that of Chamaeleon Church and a lighter Ultimate Spinach. The only single released was the theme song to the movie backed with another album cut *Greetings! b/w Don't Say A Word.*

The album has a diversity of songs noted for the writing talents of each individual band member. They played a few gigs locally, but the band began to drift. Shortly after the album release, they fell apart and began solo careers. Skip Boone was already a seasoned musician and had recommended his brother Steve Boone to John Sebastian and Zal Yanovski to be a drummer for the newly forming Lovin' Spoonful.

Skip Boone and Darius Davenport formed the highly rated Autosalvage, a band that many considered way ahead of its time.

After the break-up of that band Skip became a high-end paint contractor, but never lost the passion for music and guitar. Sadly, he died peacefully in April of 2015.

Darius Davenport joined Terence Boylan along with Donald Fagen and Walter Becker (the Steely Dan guys) for the album called *Alias Boona* before moving to California where he dedicated his life as a Social Worker & Clinical Psychologist.

J Steven Soles was asked to join Bob Dylan and his Rolling Thunder Review and then joined Tidbits for one LP in 1973 called *Greetings From Jamaica.* He formed The Alpha Band with T Bone Burnett and David Mansfield for three fledging LPs released 1976, '77 and '78. Then, in the 80's released two highly regarded Christian LPs *The Promise* and *Walk By Love.* He went on to produce several records by Elvis Costello, The Monkees, Olivia Newton John and many others.

Eric Kaz joined Peppi Castro as the only remaining member of The Blues MaGoos when that band signed with ABC records. Eric then formed American Flyer with Craig Fuller (from Poco), Doug Yule (from The Velvet Underground) and Eric Katz (from Blood, Sweat and Tears) for two albums, the self-titled *American Flyer* and *Spirit of a Woman* and had a long studio career. But his claim to fame was his song writing skills, where he's garnered several ASCAP and Country Music Awards for almost every well-known artist known at the time. George Strait, Bonnie Raitt, Kenny Rogers, Linda Ronstadt, Alison Krauss, Art Garfunkel, The Sawyer Brown Band all are just the tip of the iceberg of artists that Eric has collaborated with. He is truly a living legend in the music industry.

Artie Traum joined his brother Happy Traum and formed a popular folk/pop duo. They got their big break at the Newport Folk Festival and recorded a couple albums in Nashville. The highly influential Albert Grossman was their manager and they continued for quite a few years as opening act for The Paul Butterfield Blues Band, Seatrain and Bob Dylan among many others. Artie was guest musician and or producer for artists too many to mention that included Maria Muldaur, John Sebastian, Richie Havens, James Taylor and The Band. He toured all over the world as an award-winning guitarist, song writer and producer. Unfortunately, he departed us in July of 2008.

SPACED OUT

STEREO
BEAST
SD 9012
Cotillion

STEREO
2017
BEAST
Evolution
a stereo dimension recording

BEAST 1969-70

Robert Yeasel started playing guitar at a Pentecostal Church in or near Denver, Colorado. He was raised in the church because his Dad was the preacher. He loved his guitar and spent 8 hours a day practicing. He began writing songs and ventured out from the church to play parties and school sock hops. He was in a band with Roger Bryant who played (bass).

Then he met Ron Morgan who was a guitar player and part of the tour group for The West Coast Pop Art Experimental Band (WCPAEB). Ron was back visiting in Colorado and asked both Rob and Roger if they wanted to fly out to LA and join the touring band. After landing in Los Angeles, they traveled up to Trousdale Estates above Hollywood and met Bob Markley, leader of WCPAEB, at his house. Robert remembers setting the couch on fire almost spreading to the house itself, but things got under control. Markley wasn't too upset and both Rob and Roger were brought aboard for the tour.

It was 1967 in the summer of love. They played the clubs on the LA strip and had a grueling 10-day stint at the Teen-age Fair at the Hollywood Palladium. Methamphetamine was the drug of choice just to keep things going. The band toured all over the country opening for Moby Grape, Iron Butterfly, The Byrds and others. Their album *Volume 3 – A Child's Guide to Good and Evil* featured the song *Watch Yourself* written by Bob Yeasel. By the Fall of 67, Bob and Roger had had enough of LA and wanted to go back home to Denver. Jimmy Greenspoon was also part of the touring band and was talked into leaving as well along with Ron Morgan.

Once back in Denver, Bob Yeasel (guitar), Roger Bryant (bass), Ron Morgan (guitar) and Jimmy Greenspoon (keyboards, vocals) formed Superband with Myron Pollock on (drums). This band minus Ron Morgan recorded one single *Acid Indigestion b/w I Ain't Got Nobody*. Ron got sick and couldn't participate forcing Bob into uncomfortable lead guitar duties. Soon after this single was put out Ron Morgan and Jimmy Greenspoon left and went back to LA.

Bob then formed another band with himself Robert Yeasel (guitar), David Raines (vocals), Kenny Passarelli (bass), Gerry Fike (organ), Larry Ferris (drums), Mike Kearnes (sax, flute) and Dominick Todero (trumpet). Before they played anywhere publicly, they moved to a big ranch up near Colorado Springs and took a year there to get their sound perfected. It was a communal setting with wives, girlfriends, cats and dogs and lots of high-quality drugs. When they went back to Denver, there was a big buzz and anticipation about their sound. They hired a manager, John Philbin, and their first gig was on Aug 18th, 1968, at Kelker Junction in Colorado Springs opening for The Who.

It wasn't long before they found themselves at Norman Petty's studio in Clovis, New Mexico recording their first record album. The album released on the Cotillion record label was entitled *Beast.* The cover art to this album looks much like a Jackson Pollock painting, however it was done by a local Denver artist Carson Weaver. They were featured at The Junction mentioned above for most of their shows with bands like Ivory, Warm, Pacific Ocean and others. Jimmy Gilmore ex of The Fireballs became Beast's manager. After a few months Kenny Passarelli left to join Joe Walsh and he was replaced by former bassist Roger Bryant.

A second album on the Evolution label followed shortly thereafter. This LP appropriately called *Beast* was recorded at the revamped and new state of the art Norman Petty Studios. Both albums are full of great guitar and organ passages, flute and sax with 3-part harmonies slightly like The Collectors and maybe BS&T because of the horns, but this was a rocking band. One single hit the airwaves *Move Mountain (You Got It) b/w Communication* from the second album output. They had a short tour in Canada and came back to play at a new place called The Establishment.

Robert Yeasel grew disappointed with all the unfulfilled promises from the record company's and decided to leave the band. Micheal Kearnes obtained the rights to the Beast name and kept the band going for about a year, but it was not the same after Bob left. Beast eventually parted ways.

Ron Morgan was an extraordinary guitarist. He and Jimmy Greenspoon left Supergroup for LA to form Three Dog Night. He left the band before their first breakout album and joined The Electric Prunes for their last two LPs. He passed away in 1989.

Jimmy Greenspoon stayed with Three Dog Night until his death in 2015.

Mike Kearnes and Larry Ferris have also since passed.

Kenny Passarelli stayed with Joe Walsh for 2 albums, then played with several of the biggest stars in the world, Elton John, Stephen Stills, Hall & Oates, Dan Fogelberg and others.

Dominick Todero moved to LA and hooked up with the band Cordova Rock and played at the clubs on the strip for a short while. Then he did a lot of studio work backing the recordings of famous musicians. He got into the early stages of the video business where he remained. Sadly, cancer got the best of him in 2011.

Little is known of Roger Bryant, David Raines or Gerry Fike.

Robert Yeasel played with Sugarloaf on their second album *Spaceship Earth* and traveled with the band for about two years before he got burned out from touring. He then formed The Freddi-Henchi Band back in Colorado and started a glass art and cutting business to supplement his income. Some of his works are displayed at the Broncos Mile High Stadium in Denver. He hung up his guitar for a while but came back again to form 2D Max and then The Nightcrawlers. He was a well-loved and an unknown genius on guitar and lived life to the fullest, but sadly died in June of 2016.

BIG LOST RAINBOW

BIG LOST RAINBOW

BIG LOST RAINBOW 1973

Ridley Pearson began playing guitar at five years old and was voice trained singing in church every Sunday. His family and relatives were very musical with weekend gatherings where the family met for food and musical jams. He took voice lessons from Met professionals in New York and when he was 13 years old played the son of Noah on stage in a version of Benjamin Britton's Noye's Fludde. This was a big production play/opera which recounted the story of Noah's Ark. By the time he attended Pomfret School he was playing guitar and piano and met Otis Read who was also a guitar player. The natural influences were Bob Dylan, The Everly Brothers, Donovan and other folk artists of the time. The two hit it off and began playing together as a duo and performed for friends and family.

Tony Morse and Robin Pfoutz were fellow students who had previously played with jazz and rock ensembles. Both were classically trained and played flute, guitar and cello, respectively. They joined Ridley and Otis and began practicing at The Clark Memorial Chapel. Located on the school grounds, this was a Norman inspired Stone Church that had fabulous built-in reverb perfect for acoustic instruments and voice. They began honing their sound and originating new songs when J.P. Bailhe (aka Zip) joined in on bass guitar.

Ridley's older brother Brad, a former graduate of Pomfret, was also a musician and songwriter. He lived in the Big Lost River Valley near Pocatello, Idaho. Ridley always saw this place as magical whenever he visited and was inspired to name the band as Big Lost Rainbow. Officially the members included Ridley Pearson (lead vocals, guitar, piano, sax), Otis Read (guitar, vocals, piano, harmonica), Tony Morse (flute, guitar, vibraphone), J.P. Bailhe (Zip) (bass) and Robin Pfoutz. (cello). They were young and began promoting themselves as a band.

Their first gig was in front of 5000 people performing at the Connecticut Ecology Festival in Hartford celebrating the first year of Earth Day. Opening for Pete Seegar was somewhat intimidating. They all sang and played the occasional party event here and there venturing to small clubs and coffee houses in Newport, Rhode Island and Cape Cod, Massachusetts. After graduation from Pomfret in 1971 the band all separated. Tony and Robin had moved on to other colleges. Otis traveled to the far east and Australia. Zip had been living in Thailand previously and he with Ridley headed back there to do some recording.

It had been a year since Ridley and Zip had written quite a few songs and returned to the US with thoughts of recording. Establishing themselves in Woodside, California they convinced Tony and Robin to join them out west. Otis was in Australia, but when he got word, he flew to San Francisco and met up for the reunion. They did find a small studio in Los Angeles and recorded some demo songs but there was no record company support and nothing panned out, so they piled in Zips station wagon and migrated back east.

Back on the east coast they stationed themselves in Cape Cod, Massachusetts in the town of West Dennis and then relocated to Mashpee 20 miles southwest where they rehearsed the songs they had written. By now Adam Berensen, a former Pomfret School friend had also joined the band on (keyboards). Zip and Ridley took over scheduling and booking. A friend they knew, Todd Holland, backed the band with dollars for high-end stage equipment and had a minor management role.

They became the house band in the town of Chatham at a small club called The Lightship opening for Dave Van Ronk, John Herald and NRBQ. It was here that a big fan following started to sprout. Other places they played were The First Encounter Coffee House, a converted church in Eastham, they opened for Livingston Taylor at the Cape Cod Community College in Hyannis and shared the stage with The James Montgomery Blues Band at Tufts University in Boston. Regular gigs occurred at the Killington and Stratton ski resorts in Vermont.

There was an abundance of new songs and it was decided that they should record a full record album. Otis had a brother, Charlie Read, who knew Tom Igelheart. Tom offered to invest in studio time for the band and back the costs to make the vinyl LP. They went to Sheffield Recording Studios in Timonium, an outlying suburb of Baltimore, Maryland and started to record a limited pressing of their LP, finalizing the sessions at Dynamic Sound Studios in New Haven, Connecticut. Charlie was also a graphic artist and knew how to put things together for the LP cover artwork. They set up in their practice space at the house where Tony designed an illustration for the album cover. All homemade, the record front jacket was silk screened on a plain white generic album cover and the backside had a paste-on print with details of the recording. Only about 150 self-titled *Big Lost Rainbow* LPs were pressed with a blue record label and white lettering, taken to the shows and surprisingly sold out immediately.

The music is very pleasant surrealistic folk/rock with flute, cello, occasional sax and acoustic guitar, with vocals and one long jazzy show off cut with slight hints of special effects. There were no drums as it overwhelmed the acoustics and just didn't fit the music they were writing. Nearest comparisons go Simon and Garfunkel or Appaloosa. There was no record store distribution of the LP Tom Igelheart had part in booking gigs for some promotion of the LP. There was another second silk screened limited pressing of homemade LPs, this time with a black cover and white record label. A third edition was pressed with a white cover and label that was numbered to take with them on a self-promoted tour.

Big Lost Rainbow traveled across the country to promote the LP in a refurbished school bus they called The Wizard where the seats were removed in favor of mock bunk beds and an illegal wood stove in the back for heat. This was only fired up once in a foolish and dangerous sense of desperation in below zero-degree weather during their travels through Wyoming. When the tour was over and they got back east, they continued playing venues throughout New England and although the fans were crazy about this band, they never got the interest from a major record label. By 1975, they called it quits and moved on. Ridley and Otis did stay together, acquired an agent named Bob Greene and formed a rock ensemble called The Otis Ridley Band with other players. They played the New York clubs but only lasted together for about 6 months opening for Pure Prairie League and other bands. This band never did any recording.

Robin Pfoutz is a noted celloist who toured with Livingston Taylor, Paul Horn, Pete Seegar and others. Singled out in The Oracle of Orleans for his unique style of rock, jazz and folk, he currently plays with the Celtic folk/rock band Border Lord.

J.P. (Jacques) Bailhe left music, headed for California and graduated Magnum Cum Laude from the Art Center College of Design in movie and TV films. He involved himself in documentaries and commercials but found himself mostly producing and writing music. Selling his film production business, he bought a synthesizer and began composing music. Playing shows now and again he had some success with modern classical pieces. You can hear his music on Sound Cloud.

Adam Berensen completed his master's degree in jazz at the New England Conservatory of Music in Boston. He was a correspondent for Pulse! Magazine and has written articles for the Philadelphia Weekly Newspaper. He has released at least twenty equivalent CDs as MP3s with a plethora of inventive and experimental songs for jazz, all available on Amazon.

Tony Morse went to art school and dedicated himself to painting.

Otis Read has had a long history in music production and released several CDs as a solo artist and with others over the years. He formed The Cambridge Harmonica Orchestra for 40 harps in the 80's and was part of many stage productions. As producer he oversaw the music for the 5 CD pack called *The New England Music Collection.*

Ridley Pearson went on to Kansas and Brown Universities. He continued to write songs which eventually led to script writing and then on to full novels. His first published work was called *Never Look Back* in 1985. He has since become a well-known suspense and crime writer, winning many awards and publishing over 22 bestsellers as well as several adventure-story books for children. As a musician who also writes novels, he was a charter member of The Rock Bottom Remainders, a band that was founded in 1992. A 20-year run playing concerts and shows they were not the greatest of rock and roll bands but the inclusion of such well knowns as Ridley Pearson, Steven King, Roy Blount, Dave Barry, Scott Turow, James McBride, Amy Tan and a host of other author/wannabe rock stars got them 150,000 hits on YouTube every year. Dave Barry said it best "We played music as well as Metallica wrote novels".

A Message From
BIRMINGHAM
SUNDAY
STEREO AA-5718
ALL-AMERICAN
RECORDS

BIRMINGHAM SUNDAY 1967

Birmingham Sunday was initially formed in 1966 at Carson High School in Carson City, Nevada by Monty and Ward Johns. They were in the high school band along with John Kvam and Phil Gustafson and all belonged to separate rock bands. Monty and Ward played drums and guitar respectively for The Contrasts. John played bass guitar for The Scroachers and Phil was with The Keningtons on keyboards and sax. Joe LaChew was also at Carson High and played guitar and sang for The Velours. They joined together and became a band called The Freedom Five playing many of the popular hits and cover songs written by the British invasion bands like The Rolling Stones, The Animals and The Kinks. Joe wrote a campaign song for Nevada Governor Grant Sawyer's re-election in 1962. The song *It's Gotta Be Grant* was a one sided single that was recorded by The Freedom Five and handed out at election rally turnouts and gatherings.

English bands were all the rage at the time so they renamed themselves as Birmingham Sunday after the Sunday concerts they read about occurring in Birmingham, England. The name was very English sounding. They found a loft above the garage in Carson City where they practiced and began playing teen dances at places in northern Nevada.

Joe, Phil and Monty began college and attended the University of Nevada, Reno (UNR) where the band got a bigger fan base. In 1967 they became the house band at the American Legion Hall in Lake Tahoe. Playing five nights during the week and opening for the frequent weekend headliners that came east from San Francisco like Santana, The Grateful Dead, Sly and the Family Stone, The Family Tree and others.

Jim Burgett, who leased the American Legion Hall promoted a rock festival there featuring The Grateful Dead and other bands from San Francisco along with local acts. They were witness to one band, The Justus V, which included the appearance of 15-year old Debbie Parke who had a strong voice. The boys took notice and she joined the band with her vocals blending perfectly.

Officially the band was established, playing bigger shows and gaining notice from record labels. Members were Joe

LaChew (guitars, vocals), Debbie Parke (vocals), Ward Johns (guitar), John Kvam (bass), Phil Gustafson (keyboards, sax, vocals) and Monty Johns (drums, vocals). That summer Phil joined the National Guard and left temporarily for boot camp. His brother, Dave Gustafson, came aboard and quickly learned to play all the songs. Monty also left the band to pursue a heavy medical career at the University of Nevada. They auditioned other drummers who couldn't really sing. But Joe could also play drums, so he dropped playing guitar and became Monty's replacement. They hired Jean Heim on (rhythm guitar and vocals) and Phil came back after his summer hiatus.

They entered a Battle of the Bands called Teen Scene sponsored by Bruce Blaylock. Pat Boone was a Spokesperson for the event. It was judged by members of The Sunshine Company who were a band noted for some recent success themselves. The prize was playing for the state finals in Las Vegas. Birmingham Sunday and two other bands were chosen to compete. The Vegas event was judged by members of The Strawberry Alarm Clock and their manager Bill Holmes who owned All-American Records. Unfortunately, they lost the contest to a band called the London Fogg, but impressed Bill Holmes enough that he asked them to make a demo and gave them the possibility of becoming their band manager.

There was much interest so Bill Holmes and Bruce Blaylock brought them to Los Angeles to record demos at Sunset Sound Recorders and Gold Star Recording Studios in Hollywood. Jim McKuen, a talent scout with Liberty Records, also set them up for an audition and a possible record deal through that label. Then they had a choice decision to either sign with Liberty Records or Bill Holmes and All-American Records. They chose the deal with Bill. There was a movie in the making at Paramount Studios called *Romeo and Juliet* and the title song *A Time For Us.* There were thoughts of Birmingham Sunday recording this but it didn't work out. It should be noted that *A Time For Us* went to number #1 on the charts performed as an instrumental by Henry Mancini.

Bill Holmes knew Paul Buff, an engineer at Original Sound Recording Studios at 7120 Sunset Boulevard in Hollywood. 10 songs were chosen from the demo tapes. Paul was a former partner with Frank Zappa at Pal Studios which he sold to Frank Zappa. There was a Chamberlin Keyboard in the studio, an early mellotron, that was used for the string arrangements. Musically they make all the right psych moves with five part harmonies including

Debbie's dreamy vocals, psychedelic guitars and a sound that fits into the mold of such Mainstream label acts like Art of Lovin, Growing Concern and The Sunshine Company who were with the Imperial record label.

Per Joe LaChew there were 1000 copies of the album that were pressed. But it's an album that is extremely hard to come by. Entitled *A Message From Birmingham Sunday* they were distributed to most of the stores in Southern California and Nevada, in Seattle and Portland on the west coast and as far east as St. Louis and Chicago. The single *Prevalent Visionaries b/w Egocentric Solitude* was also released. It did very well locally and in Santa Barbara where it went to #1. Over time the albums have all since disappeared and are difficult to find.

Bill Holmes was concentrating on The Strawberry Alarmclock and Giant Crab so promotion for this band and the LP was dismal. They played shows after the release of the LP at The Civic Auditorium in Carson City, the Genoa Town Hall, the University of Nevada Reno, Sacramento and other California places, but were disappointed for lack of promotion and money and decided to split apart.

Frankie Fanelli was a casino lounge singer that had some clout in the industry. He appeared on *The Tonight Show* with Johnny Carson and was a featured performer on Ed Sullivan. John Kvam, Debbie Parke, Dave and Phil Gustafson and Jean Heim decided to back him on the Nevada and California casino and lounge circuit. They also recorded an LP in 1970 *Saturdays Only* that was given away at the shows. There was no mention of the players on the LP. Disappointed and frustrated they broke apart for good.

Joe, Monty and Ward along with three members of the UNR jazz group formed a horn band as Brother Rock. This nine piece band had a style based on Tower of Power, Chicago, Sons of Champlain and others.

Montgomery (Monty) Johns eventually became a Doctor but still dabbles in music and still has a part time band.

Phil Gustafson became an Army National Guard Colonel and retired after 30 plus years.

Ward Johns became a talent scout and Vice President of Missile Records out of Mississippi but passed on in 2009.

John Kvam became a journeyman cabinet maker and played in some local bands. Sadly, he passed away in 2013.

Jean Heim got into country music and played gigs in Nevada. Unfortunately, he also left us in 2014.

Dave Gustafson played for 20 years in the casino circuit with his partner Chip Human as a duo called the Two of Clubs. They recorded one LP simply titled *'76* that was sold or given away at their shows. He always said, "He got into the music business but could never figure how to get out." Well, he did and later became very successful in Real Estate. Unfortunately, he also left us in 2010.

Debbie Parke was a teacher and school counselor in the Lewiston Idaho school district for 35 years before retiring. She sang occasionally at community school districts and church events.

Joe LaChew pursued a music career as a session musician at Larrabee Studios in Hollywood and did movie soundtracks including *Dirty Mary, Crazy Larry*. He played guitar for successful artists Billy Preston, Bobby Hatfield, The Drifters, The Coasters, Little Jimmy Dickens, he was on TV with *Rich Little's Comedy Show* and others. Retiring from life on the road he began teaching music at UNR and the Carson City School district while still playing shows in the Reno Carson City area.

All the members of the band stayed in contact and recorded more original music which resulted in a second album release on a double CD *Prevalent Visionaries: The History of the Birmingham Sunday* available on the internet. It includes the full original LP plus outtakes and demos recorded previously along with newer songs recorded prior to 2012.

Joe and Debbie are happily married and are still doing session work.

STEREO SRF 67591
PLAYABLE ON MODERN MONAURAL EQUIPMENT
fontana
Libby's
PEAS
HOUSE LEATHER
The Blackwood Apology
OVERCOME
NEWPORT

THE BLACKWOOD APOLOGY 1969

The Castaways were a band from Minneapolis, Minnesota that had a Billboard hit single reaching #12 with *Liar, Liar b/w Sam* on the Soma record label. This put them on the map and over a 3 year period they released other singles but none of them did as well as their first. By 1968 The Castaways were still an active band that included Denny Libby (lead vocals), Tom Husting (guitar), Greg Maland (keyboards), Roy Hensley (bass guitar) and Dennis Craswell (drums). Mercury Records came calling and asked them to record a full LP with all recording expenses paid.

Dale Menten was a local noteworthy songwriter who had formerly been with Soma labelmates The Gestures and their Billboard top 50 single *Run, Run, Run b/w It Seems To Me.* The Castaways approached Dale, told him about the album deal and asked if he had any songs that he could help with. He was also asked to produce the album project. He played them some songs including a rather long one he entitled *The House Of Leather.* It was agreed that this could be the song featured on the A side with five other songs on the B side of the album. Rehearsals took place at Universal Audio Recording located at 2541 Nicollet Ave in Minneapolis. The players were Dale Menten (guitar, vocals) Denny Libby (vocals), Tom Husting (guitar, vocals), Greg Maland (keyboards), Dennis Craswell (drums) and Ron Beckman (bass) who replaced Roy Hensley. Once the sessions started, the 15 minute *House of Leather* extended well beyond 30 minutes. This precluded any need for additional songs for the B side of the LP.

The album entitled *House of Leather* was theme based on a brothel during the Civil War. It was not a rock opera per se, but did have some special effects, backwards guitar & psychedelic moments. Mercury wanted to release the album but the players' representative group, Dunwich Productions, felt it was too experimental and underground for a Castaways record. Dale was asked if he would be willing to form a band to promote the album live. So, Dennis Libby left The Castaways and joined Dale who hired the best players he knew in the area including himself (guitar, vocals), Dik Hedland (bass), Bruce Pedalty (Hammond B3 organ), and Joe Piazza (drums, vocals). Joe was visiting in Minneapolis at the time and had formerly been with a host of bands including The Strangeloves with their #1 national hit *I Want Candy* and was the drummer in studio for The McCoys national #1 hit song *Hang On Sloopy*. Dale named the band The Blackwood Apology. The LP cover was designed by the Mercury Art department.

Released on the Fontana Record label, they promoted the LP and performed at places like The New City Opera House and the West Bank Hippie capitol Dania Hall in the Twin Cities where bands like The Paisleys, Zarathustra, The Litter and others played. They were one of the first underground bands in the area and opened for The Grateful Dead at the Minneapolis Labor Temple where most of the big name acts like Jethro Tull, Jeff Beck, Procol Harum and others performed.

The owners of the Cricket Theatre in Minneapolis asked Dale Menten if he would be willing to work with rising playwright, Frederick Gaines. The result of this collaboration became a stage play based on *The House Of Leather* album. It was an interactive play transforming the album into a full theatre production with actors in dialogue on stage. The band was stationed to the right on a side stage above the audience and performed all the songs from the album during the performance. The theatre production took place at The Cricket Theatre (formerly The Ritz) on March 26th, 1969. There were fifty continuous sold out shows each night including four shows on the weekends. After this, Dale had an interim period where he wanted to spend time writing and the band briefly parted ways.

They were then asked to play the Crawford Livingston Theatre in St Paul which was an Arts and Science Center. Bruce and Joe had moved on so Dale hired Dick Reese on (keyboards) and Scott Sansby (drums) as replacement players for this event. *The House of Leather* was showcased there from July 18th through August 24th, 1969.

Based upon this, a show was scheduled in New York at The Ellen Stewart Theatre just off Broadway. Scott Sansby had other commitments so Dick Borotolussi replaced him on (drums). *The House of Leather* previewed for eight nights leading up to the big Grand Opening debut on March 18th, 1970. Starring Peter De Anda and Barry Bostwick, who later became notable on TV and in film, the show only lasted one night and was cancelled. Clive Barnes was the most powerful theatre critic in New York and worked for The New York Times. He could make or break a theatrical production with the swipe of a pen. After the show everyone sat at the famous Sardi's Restaurant and read all the reviews as they came pouring in. Enough favorable praises came in from The Village Voice, Wall Street Journal and others to keep things going but Clive Barnes dropped the axe and gave them an awful review. As simple as that, the show was cancelled. After this the members of The Blackwood Apology split off to do other things.

As far as the studio session players, Greg Maland played as a solo artist in and around the Twin Cities and then settled into work outside of music. He passed away in 2012.

Ron Beckman is a retired accountant living in Pewaukee, WI. He still plays bass with two local Pewaukee bands.

Tom Husting started Husting Brothers Electrical Instruments and they built tube amps and guitars out of Sheboygan Falls, Wisconsin.

Denny Craswell went on to bang away on (drums) with the band Crow. This band had a hit single with *Evil Woman b/w Don't Play Your Games with Me*, they recorded four albums and toured all over the US. He has since come full circle and currently plays with a group called The Original Castaways.

Bruce Pedalty went back to stable session work and plays with bands in the general Minneapolis area.

Dennis Libby married and became successful in Minneapolis with Real Estate Properties.

Dik Hedland continued playing in bands throughout his bass playing career. He developed Dik Hedland Music and built a sound studio, recording local bands and artists through his business Loud Neighbors Sound.

Joe Piazza stayed in Minneapolis for ten years playing with such jazz artists as Bobby Lyle, Roberta Davis and Monfredo Fest. He booked and represented well-known jazz acts like Sonny Rollins, The Bill Evans Trio and The McCoy Tyner Quintet. When he moved back to New York he was responsible for setting up events as the Art Director for the Snug Harbor Cultural Center and has become an integral part of New York's uptown jazz scene.

Dale Menten started a theatrical production company with Frederick Gaines and Wesley Balk. He developed another Menton/Gaine's creation called *The 7th Indiana Calvary* that was moderately successful and showcased for three months back at the Crawford Livingston Theatre in St. Paul but it did not have the same response as The House of Leather. Dale moved on and became well respected for recording other bands through his Cookhouse Recording Studios, Weekend Records Label and ran a full-service production company composing and arranging music for advertising agencies at Menten Music, Inc. located in Excelsior, Minnesota.

STEREO ST-435
BLOODROCK
BLOODROCK
Capitol

STEREO ST-491
Bloodrock
2
Capitol

BLOODROCK
3

BLOODROCK 1969-75

Jim Rutledge (drums, vocals), Nick Taylor (guitar), Ed Grundy (bass) and Dean Parks (guitar, organ) started out in Fort Worth, Texas as The Naturals. They were a basic covers band that played the various small clubs around town. They changed their name to Crowd + 1 and recorded one single called *Mary Ann Regrets b/w What'cha Trying to Do to Me.* After this, larger venues came their way with Corporate events, big ballroom dances and more money for paying gigs.

John Nitzinger was a fabulous song writer with his band The Barons, which had broken up, and was playing with his new band, The Dream, at The Cellar in Fort Worth. This club had no dance floor and you would lay around on big pillows and couches to relax and watch the shows. Scantily clad waitresses would serve sodas (no alcohol) to all the patrons. Jim Rutledge happened to be in attendance and he and John became lifelong friends after that.

Capitol Records staff producer, Terry Knight, was in town for the Texas International Pop Festival with Grand Funk Railroad and happened across Crowd + 1 playing at an SMU Frat party in a small club called Lou Ann's. They were still just a cover band then, but Terry saw huge potential and signed them to Capitol records immediately. Dean Parks was the genius behind the band as a multi-instrumentalist and was writing some original songs. They went to Sound City Studios in Fort Worth and recorded two more singles *Don't Hold Back b/w Try* and *Circles b/w Most Peculiar Things*. They'd been together for over three years and had a reputation, then Dean Parks up and left for a more lucrative career working for the *Sonny and Cher* TV show along with backing bands Steeley Dan, Stevie Wonder and many others. In his place, Lee Pickens (guitar) and Stevie Hill (organ) were hired. John Nitzinger was always hanging around and became the featured songwriter for the band.

Terry Knight really believed in them and the full band now included Jim Rutledge (drums, lead vocals), Lee Pickens (lead guitar, vocals), Nick Taylor (guitar, vocals), Stevie Hill (organ, vocals) and Ed Grundy (bass, vocals). They traveled up to The Cleveland Recording Company, a studio located at the Loews Theatre building at 1515 Euclid Ave and recorded their first LP. The band name change is credited to Terry who had a conceptual idea for the first album cover (blood and broken glass with a rock). Blood and Rock seemed to fit nicely, so Bloodrock became their band name. The self-titled *Bloodrock* LP has a heavy band sound with guitar and organ interplay in the vein of Deep Purple and Uriah Heep, but with so many more hooks courtesy of John Nitzinger. These guys rocked and Lee Pickens was a surprising guitarist that delivered with wild flow and oddball chords in unexpected moments.

Opening shows and festivals all over the country for the likes of Jimi Hendrix, The Almond Brothers and especially Grand Funk Railroad, they gained notice and adulation of many fans. Terry wanted Jim to leave the drums and front the band as lead vocalist. This was expected, as so many other drummer vocalists have wound up leaving the drum set and fronting their respective bands. Karen Carpenter (The Carpenters), Don Henley (The Eagles) and Phil Collins (Genesis) are three of the more famous drummers who stepped out front to sing. So, they hired Rick Cobb on (drums) to replace Jim Rutledge who now fronted Bloodrock on (lead vocals).

Their second album *Bloodrock 2* got them real attention with the song *DOA*. It had a lot of FM airplay and the short version single *DOA b/w Children's Heritage* reached number #36 on the billboard charts. Lee Pickens wrote the song about his friend who died in a plane crash that he was witness to when he was younger. The song put the band on the map, but it wasn't without repercussions. The song on the LP was over eight minutes long, slow and drawn out, and it was about death and dying which wasn't new. But changing the major chords in the song to minor and seventh chords in a certain sequence suddenly brought on a demonic feel according to church and religious groups. Some radio stations wouldn't play the song. There were also loud siren sounds dispersed throughout the song which, at the time, were illegal to play on the radio airwaves. But *DOA* became very popular and was the highlight of every concert.

Terry had Bloodrock and Grand Funk Railroad together for a nationwide tour and sellout crowds everywhere they appeared. The band toured extensively and recorded three albums in two years *Bloodrock, Bloodrock 2* and *Bloodrock 3*. Capitol was reaping benefits from the band and put out a *Bloodrock Live* LP. But the pace was taking its toll, they were being tabbed as the "Little Brother of Grand Funk" everywhere they went and wanted to move on. In the early days Jim Rutledge had been producing the singles he did with Crowd+1 at the Sound City Studio so it was decided to part ways with Terry Knight. They recorded and self-produced their 4th studio LP called *Bloodrock USA* with help from John Palladino at Capitol Records Studio A in the famous round building in Hollywood. By now Bloodrock had released several singles and were a regular hit making machine. But Jim Rutledge had been contemplating a solo career and left the band along with songwriter John Nitzinger. Lee Pickens left shortly thereafter because he felt the band wouldn't be the same without Jim's voice.

With Jim gone, Warren Ham came to Bloodrock as his replacement on (vocals, flute, sax & harmonica). Warren had a history with Stevie Hill in a band called The Rocks during their high school years. Two more Bloodrock albums were recorded *Passage, Whirlwind Tongues* and were released to the public. But one other LP *Unspoken Words* sat on the shelves only to be released later in a packaged CD compilation of the albums after Jim Rutledge and Lee Pickens had left called *Triptych*. Lots of organ and flute with less guitar and progressive sounds of (some say) Jethro Tull and King Crimson, but unmistakably like a band called AD, formed by Kerry Livgren after he departed Kansas. This was Stevie Hill and Ed Grundy's band and they showcased a totally different sound. The music here is wonderful, but fans of the old hard rock sound were surprised with Bloodrock's new direction. The albums didn't sell well and although the band was proud and satisfied with the recordings, they separated for good.

Jim Rutledge was still under contract and had to stay with Capitol records. But he chose to produce albums for John Nitzinger. He still owed Capitol one more album to satisfy his contract. So, he put together an LP with tunes, all written by John, and submitted it to the label who turned it down. The powers to be said "It was too out of the mainstream and wasn't something that would appeal to the Bloodrock/Rutledge fan base". It wasn't until 1976 that he was finally able to put out an album for release with help from Michael Rabon of The Five Americans called *Hooray for The Good Times*. It was a contractual album that went directly to the cutout bins and Jim was finally released from his Capitol Records contract. It should be noted that a self-published CD called *Bloodrock 2013* was released and included several songs all written by Jim Rutledge and/or John Nitzinger.

Lee Pickens released his own LP called *Lee Pickens Group* that had highly favorable reviews and he continued session work thereafter.

Rick Cobb became a logistics specialist for Raytheon Technical Services.

Nick Taylor lost his life in a car wreck in March of 2010.

Ed Grundy retired from music but still lives in Texas.

Stevie Hill continued to play on and off with other bands and released at least one solo effort. He was diagnosed with Leukemia sometime in the early 2000's. It had been a while since anyone had heard about the band members, then out of nowhere they decided to come together to the delight of all their rabid fans for one reunion show. A tribute and benefit concert for Stevie Hill happened at The Ridglea Theatre in Fort Worth, Tx. in March of 2005. The show was recorded, filmed and released on DVD. All proceeds were to benefit Stevie and his fight to beat Cancer. In 2011 the band reunited once more at the Texas Music awards to rousing fans. Sadly, Stevie Hill passed September 2013.

John Nitzinger was a player, songwriter and producer all his life. He released three albums, the self-titled *Nitzinger, One Foot In History* and *Live Better Electrically* between 1972 and 1976. Then played with several other bands including Alice Cooper for a while. He formed *Thunder* for one rare LP on the Capitol label that included Bugs Henderson and former Crowd + 1 member Dean Parks. Collaborating with Carl Palmer, of ELP, he helped form the band PM. They rehearsed for a year in Los Angeles and London then flew to Germany to record the album *1:PM* which is a 1980's AOR novelty.

A real legend in Texas, he has released several solo CDs and developed Nitzinger's Music Factory that teaches music writing skills and technical instruction on how to play an instrument to kids and adults alike. A Rock Camp is held periodically in his name for intercity kids in need of direction.

TURN ON, TUNE IN, DROP OUT

STEREO
BLUES IMAGE
BLUES IMAGE
ATCO
SD 33-300

SD 33-317
BLUES IMAGE/OPEN
STEREO
ATCO

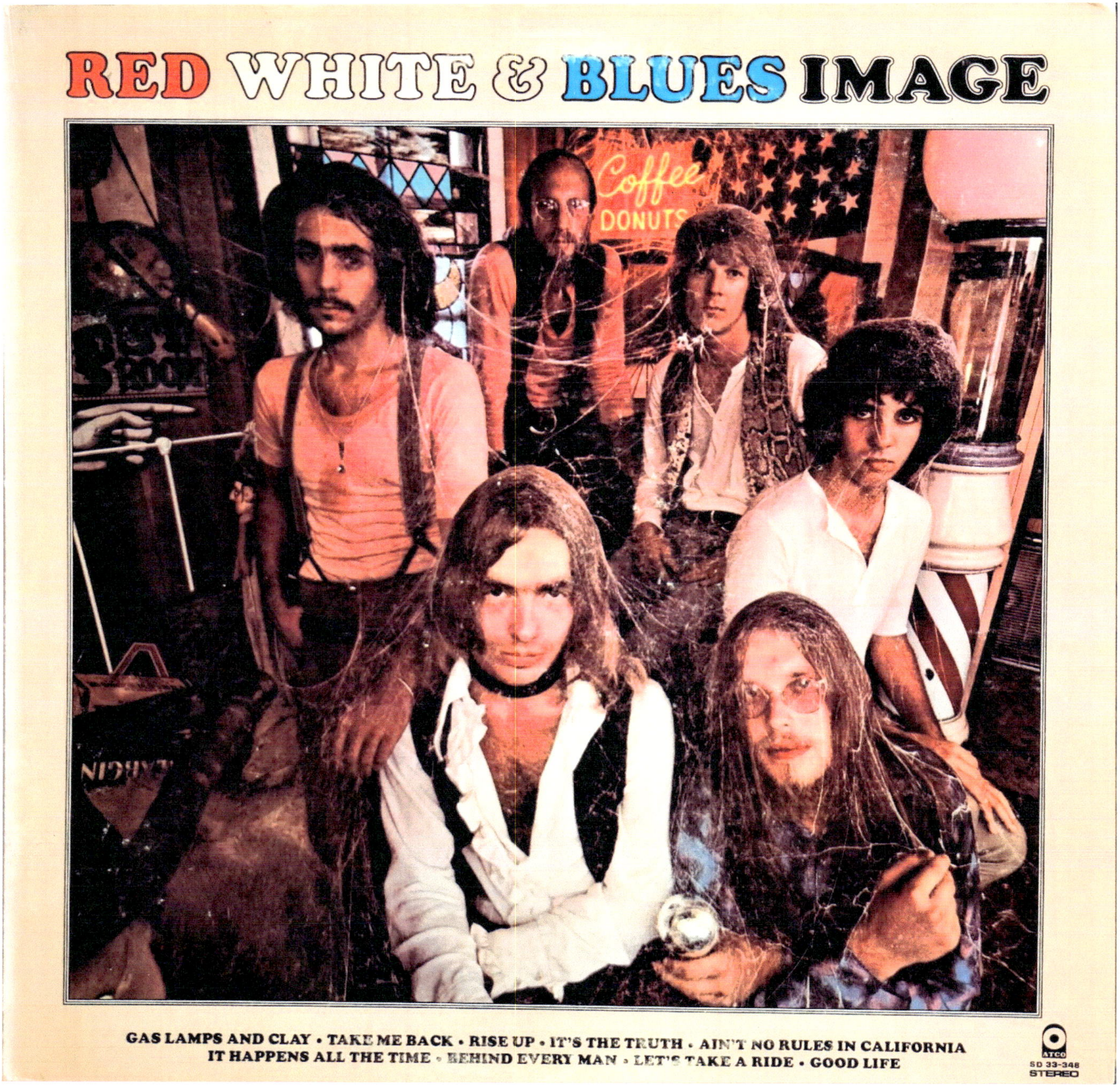
RED WHITE & BLUES IMAGE
Coffee
DONUTS
GAS LAMPS AND CLAY • TAKE ME BACK • RISE UP • IT'S THE TRUTH • AIN'T NO RULES IN CALIFORNIA
IT HAPPENS ALL THE TIME • BEHIND EVERY MAN • LET'S TAKE A RIDE • GOOD LIFE
ATCO
SD 33-348
STEREO

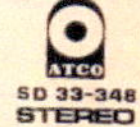

BLUES IMAGE 1969-71

Mike Pinera grew up in Tampa, Florida. He started playing guitar at 15 because of tunes he heard on the radio by Chuck Berry and James Burton, the guitarist for Elvis Presley, Ricky Nelson and many others. He formed a band in high school with Manuel (Manny) Bertimatti called The Impalas and they played all the cover hit tunes of the day. The band included Mike Pinera (guitar), Manny on (drums) with Joe Lala (conga, percussion) and Emilio Garcia (keyboards, bass). Joe and Emilio were both older seasoned musicians having played in other bands. When they added Malcolm Jones to play (bass guitar) they became The Motions. Most of the pop band competition played typical AM radio dance songs whereas Mike leaned towards more R'n'B and blues and the band was gaining a reputation as the one to see.

The best place to see bands at the time was at The Clearwater Star Spectacular. This venue was a big auditorium owned by Paul Cochran and featured acts from New York and elsewhere. Popstars like Bobby Vinton, Chubby Checker, Dion and others would come to play a short set of songs including their radio hit single. Paul had set up bands like Terry and the Pirates, The Roemans and The Mystics to back the stars when they came to play. Emilio Garcia formed a band called E. G. and the Hi-Fi's who became The Mystics. They were the house band at the big venue for months and included Rodney Justo who later fronted The Candymen, a band that evolved into The Atlantic Rhythm Section. But the Mystics eventually fell apart.

Mike would frequent this place and offered his band, The Motions, as back-up to the stars. Paul Cochran agreed to hire The Motions if they were worthy enough to pull it off. He already knew Emilio Garcia very well and set them up with Gene Pitney who was coming in two weeks. Gene was a huge star with several hits and would normally hire musicians to travel and back him on tour. But Paul gave The Motions their chance and they went to work learning Gene's complicated tunes. A tape of the songs they learned was dispatched to Gene. He was impressed enough and agreed to come to the venue without his backing players. Two weeks later it all went well with Gene Pitney stating that The Motions were a great band.

After a year of backing the stars, Emilio decided to leave the band as he wanted to be an airline pilot. Mike then hired Bob Hoffman on guitar and decided that the band should go out on the road. Mike handled all the bookings, the money and general duties normally assigned to a manager. Calling themselves Mike West and the Motions they traveled to venues on the east coast and wound up playing at clubs in Virginia Beach like Rogues, Peabody's and The Peppermint Beach Club.

Skip Konte was from Anchorage, Alaska and was a keyboard player with his band called Blue Chip Stock. They were on summer break from college and were also playing in the clubs in Virginia Beach. Between gigs Skip happened across Mike Pinera and his band playing one of the clubs and was impressed with Mikes guitar work. At the end of summer, the members of Blue Chip Stock decided to go back to Alaska and continue their college studies but Skip stayed behind and joined The Motions. He fit right in and with the new member it was Mike who came up with a new name for the band as Blues Image. Traveling to Greenwich Village they figured they would take the New York club scene by storm. Presenting themselves at the Café Wha? they were unable to even get an audition. Other clubs in Greenwich Village also passed on the band.

Devastated, they were stuck in New York and out of money. But Manny knew a small club owner in Tampa who owned Deano's. He wired money to the guys and they left New York with their tail between their legs. The gigs there as the house band at Deano's repaid their traveling expenses to get back home. Over the next few months Blues Image had gained a reputable fan following selling out night after night. They had written songs and decided to record a single. Bob Hoffman decided to leave the band and they journeyed to Criteria Studios in Miami to record a demo single *Can't You Believe in Forever b/w Parchmant Farm*. It was decided they would stay in Miami to write songs, promote themselves at bigger clubs and hopefully get noticed.

In May of 1968, Michael Lang and his friend Richard O'Barry decided to promote a rock festival in Miami called the Pop & Underground Festival. They put things together with Hector Morales in New York. The 2-day gathering was held at Gulfstream Park which was a horse racetrack north of Miami and it turned out to be the "dry run" for the famous Woodstock Festival a year later. Invited were bands like John Lee Hooker, The Mothers of Invention, Chuck

Berry, Blue Cheer, The Crazy World of Arthur Brown, Blues Image, local bands These Vizitors and Sun Country with featured artist The Jimi Hendrix Experience.

Hendrix was well known at the time and the audience was anxious to see him live based upon his first two album releases and his now famous showing at the Monterey Pop festival. The bands in attendance were scheduled for two shows per day and The Jimi Hendrix Experience did not disappoint. But the following day a torrential rainfall occurred and no electrically amplified bands were allowed to play. Hendrix left but was inspired to write the song *Rainy Day, Dream Away* found on his third double LP *Electric Ladyland*. The two day festival only lasted a day due to the rain but Hendrix had witnessed Blues Image live and was extremely impressed.

Meanwhile Marshall Brevetz was an important part of the early rock scene in Miami and had owned a small club called Thee Experience. He needed a larger club and found that the Sunny Isle Bowling Center was no longer active and up for lease. Workers were brought in to rip out the lanes and convert it to a psychedelic ballroom. Once finished the club was labeled as Thee Image which became a major stop for the underground rock scene. Blues Image was one of the better bands around and were featured here shortly after the May festival. They helped Marshall woo some of the unknown bands from the UK but they were never owners of the club as was rumored. It was August 1968 when they decided to travel to California and try to make their mark.

They rented a house in Santa Monica with a huge maze in the backyard to amuse themselves. Skip and Manny stayed in separate apartments in town. They practiced constantly and with demo in hand the guys walked the streets trying to find any record label interest but all the record companies turned them down. About this time an issue of Rolling Stone Magazine came out where Jimi Hendrix gave an interview praising Blues Image as a great up and coming band. His admiration for Blues Image, who was without a recording contract, in a nationally syndicated "rock" magazine brought on much interest.

They still had no manager to oversee the business side of things but were playing clubs locally and on the LA Strip. Eric Burdon happened to see them and offered to have his manager, Kevin Deverich, take them under his wing. But things soon fell apart and they found Todd Shiffman and Larry Larson to take on management duties. Busy playing many music venues over the next few weeks they found themselves at a small club in Torrance, Ca. called The Bank. This was a small venue featuring bands on the cusp of record label interest to showcase themselves and audition. A compact audience included friends, family and label emissaries looking for new talent and bands to sign. The Atlantic label representative loved Blues Image and a few months later, they signed with Ahmet Ertegun and ATCO records.

Blues Image had songs in hand and ready to record. Bill Halverson engineered the sessions at Wally Heider's Studio. He was fresh from Crosby, Stills and Nash and their first album. The self-titled LP *Blues Image* showed the talents of Mike Pinera on guitar. We're talking blues with a punch and a little Santana affect. The single picked for release to the airwaves *Lay Your Sweet Love On Me b/w Outside Was Night* got slight radio play but the LP died on the racks. They were back at the LA Strip clubs promoting the album and gigged up and down the west coast opening for other established superstar psych bands. The energetic stage presence and Mikes jaw dropping guitar licks proved that this band would be a difficult act to follow.

A second LP was in the works and recorded at American Recording Company in Studio City. By now Atlantic Records had brought in Richard Podolor to engineer and produce the sessions. The second album entitled *Open* was complete as they had more than enough songs written and under their belt. Richard, being a known hitmaker for Three Dog Night and Steppenwolf knew the songs were good but he didn't hear a "hit" and asked if there was anything else. Skip had written something months before that didn't sit well with the band. It just seemed to be too sappy for the hard rock and blues for which they were known. But Skip played the song with unfinished lyrics for Richard and he liked it.

The rest of the band wanted nothing to do with this atrocity but Richard was determined to include it on the album for the final add-on. Mike and Skip put the lyrics together but when they went to record it Manny refused to play the song and left the studio. Mike Thatcher, formerly of The Abstracts, was a session drummer sent in to play drums on the official recording and when Mike Pinera completed his studio portion of the song, he also quit the band. The song was unfinished and Kent Henry formerly with Pacific Ocean, Genesis (the California band) and

Charity came aboard to add the final details. The single *Ride Captain Ride b/w Pay My Dues* shot up to #4 on Billboard, #1 in Record World and #1 on *American Bandstand* 1970. It climbed the charts and became a worldwide hit. Those in the band who were completely against selling out to hit radio suddenly saw the dollar signs and Skip, who had full credit for writing the song, reciprocated by giving them all a percentage of the royalties.

Mike Pinera's departure from the band was unexpected. He had been advanced big bucks to play with Iron Butterfly helping to fill the void left by Eric Braunn who was now gone from that band. It left a bit of a conundrum for Blues Image who now had a huge hit on the radio. They chose Kent Henry (guitar) and Denny Correll (vocals) as Mikes replacement. Promoting the second album on tour, the first show was in front of a huge audience in Peoria, Illinois. When they started to play *Ride Captain Ride*, the crowd was wild with excitement but band members pelted Skip with chewed bubblegum jokingly showing their disapproval of the song. Being featured on Dick Clark's *American Bandstand* was a lifelong dream come true for Skip and the shows went very well with Kent mimicking Mike on guitar and Denny singing vocals without a hitch.

A third LP was recorded at American Recording Studios. The band had to write new music on the spot and experiment in the studio. The songs weren't quite the same, the dynamics were off and the synergy was gone. The third LP *Red, White and Blues Image* was released to little fanfare. Mike was flamboyant and outgoing on stage and Kent Henry was a great guitar player but he was reserved as a showman. Promoting the album, they traveled all over the country and Canada and found themselves on a radio DJ interview in Austin, Texas. Arguments occurred on air and a fist fight happened. This was the last stand and after a short two year stint in the limelight Blues Image split apart due to irreconcilable differences.

The members moved on to other ventures.

Denny Correll had a lengthy career as a Christian artist but passed away 2002.

Kent Henry replaced Larry Byrum in a later incarnation of Steppenwolf and did session work. Unfortunately, he died due to heart failure March of 2009.

Manuel Bertematti also passed 2001.

Malcolm Jones developed Gold Hill Music which was a publishing company for the likes of REO Speedwagon, Firefall, Joe Walsh, Bob Segar and nearly all the record releases by Steven Stills and Crosby, Stills, Nash & Young. He was the oldest member of the band and seemed to be the ageless one but moved on about 2012.

Joe Lala stayed in LA as a session musician for several album appearances guesting with Joe Walsh, Steven Stills, Manassas, Barbara Streisand, Whitney Houston, The BeeGees and others. He was part of many movie and TV soundtracks and guest starred as an actor on TVs *Miami Vice, Seinfeld* and others. Carpal Tunnel ended his career as a percussionist, but then he did voice overs for several movie and TV animation series. Sadly, he succumbed in 2014.

Skip Konte moved on to Three Dog Night and dressed like a mad Wizard while playing keyboards. Known as The Wizard of Northern Realms, he toured with them for over five years. Afterwards he presided over Skip Konte Enterprises for Television editing and transfer services and started Morningstar Entertainment Inc. for Motion Picture production. He then wrote, directed and provided the full music score for a sci-fi film complete with full cast and crew called Meridian.

After Iron Butterfly, Mike Pinera formed Ramatam with Mitch Mitchell on (drums) and then formed a reincarnation of the band Cactus that included former Blues Image partner on drums, Manuel Bertematti. After this he formed Thee Image for a couple of albums and released solo LPs. Opening his own Illusion Record label, Mike produced and recorded several local Florida bands (Hopney, Sage, Fanz, Charmer) along with other Blues Image LPs. These albums had outtakes, re-recording's and other songs not previously released. He is now involved with The Classic Rock All-stars. They are a premiere hit singles band relative to Ringo's All-Star Band of original players each presenting their original hit song live on stage.

STEREO
bo grumpus
before the war
SD 33-246
ATCO

BELL 6031
"HOME"
JOLLIVER ARKANSAW
STEREO
BELL
RECORDS

BO GRUMPUS / JOLLIVER ARKANSAW 1968

In the early 60's guitarists Eddie Mottau and Joe Hutchinson were both playing in small venues separately as duos. Joe was with Eric Anderson and Ed was working with Jerry Corbett who later went on to play with The Youngbloods. Eddie and Joe met and formed a duo called Two Guys from Boston. They played clubs and coffee houses in the area and found favor with Paul Stookey of (Peter, Paul and Mary) who became their producer. They managed one single on Scepter Records *Come On Betty Home b/w I Wish I Could Shimmy Like My Sister Kate*. Meanwhile back in Dayton, Ohio, (drummer) N.D. Smart II had been playing in a band called Thee Rubber Band that included Jim Colegrove. Eddie and Joe had previously met N.D. at The Lemon Tree, a small club in Dayton and discussed the club scene in New York. N.D. was intrigued so he left Thee Rubber Band to explore his opportunities back east.

A short while after he arrived, he met up with Felix Pappalardi who had previously played (bass) with Eddie and Joe during their recording session for the single. Felix happened to be looking for a drummer for a band called The Remains who were on the verge of making the big time nationally. Their drummer Chip Damiani had just up and quit. The band was in the middle of backing The Ronettes and Bobby Hebb and they were chosen as the opening act for The Beatles during their final east coast excursion. So, N.D. took the gig. But it wasn't long before The Remains flame burned out and they fell apart.

The Rubber Band had by now signed a contract to record back in New York. N.D. heard about the deal, headed back to New York and awaited their arrival to rejoin the band. Long story short, Thee Rubber Band backed out of their original agreement and signed with John Kurland who managed many bigtime bands including Paul Revere and the Raiders and The Mamas and Papas. They were booked at The Scene and made the "A" list, partying with all the influential people. Lou Adler came to a band audition and he was impressed. There was talk about The Rubber Band going to Los Angeles to do some recording there.

They were riding high. John Kurland set them up to fill in some scheduled dates back in Ohio left vacant by The Remains. That was okay while they waited for the west coast trip to develop. The main club they were set to play at in California was The Whiskey A Go Go. But the Riots on Sunset Strip were making nationwide news. The area was beset in turmoil and spurned by weeks of police harassment of the hippies over curfew laws. It got so bad that The Whiskey was temporarily closed. The tour west was cancelled and Thee Rubber Band was back to square one, playing the Dayton clubs. Meanwhile, Frank Weber, former manager of their old haunt The Lemon Tree, was now bartending out in New York and called N.D. to say that Ed and Joe were looking for a drummer and a bass player for a band they were forming. Thee Rubber Band was at a dead end and although Jim Colegrove was a guitar player, he agreed to head back to New York with N.D. and play bass in the unnamed band. The two picked up and left for Boston, they met up with Eddie and Joe and together they became The Bait Shop.

Eddie Anderson provided his house in Avon, Massachusetts for practice and musically getting a feel for each other. They played various Love-ins and Be-ins happening in the area honing their sound and may have gigged at clubs like The Ark, The Unicorn and Crosstown Bus. After a few months, Eddie called Felix to come up for a listen back at a club called The Loft located in Boston. He liked what he heard and offered to record the band back in New York.

Initially rehearsing and writing songs in a small back room at Atlantic Studios located at 1841 Broadway in New York, they moved to Talentmaster Studios on 42nd Street to complete the demo sessions. Everyone was pleased and they were set up to play their first gig at The Gas Light Café, but Felix wanted to change their moniker. His wife, Gail Collins, was an artist and had a weird drawing with creatures crawling out of a stomach she called Bo Grumpus. Felix thought the name was weird enough and perfect for the psychedelic times and Bo Grumpus was born.

They were mostly featured at The Café Wha? Other noted bands who played there included The Hello People, Cat Mother and the All-Night News Boys, Peepl, who later became Banchee, The Cherry People, Kangaroo and others. The LP was being recorded back at Atlantic Studios at 157 W 57th St. under the guidance and production of Adrian Barber, but things were going slow and the sessions were drawn out. Felix was a fabulous producer and bass player who was in high demand. He had just finished production and oversaw the sound for Creams *Disraeli Gears* and was starting duty with their *Wheels of Fire* album which was the first LP to go platinum. His focus was no longer keyed on Bo Grumpus. N.D. was spending time going to clubs watching and filling in spots for other bands. He grew frustrated over the lack of studio time for the Bo Grumpus LP and decided to quit again opting to play for the afore mentioned band Kangaroo. Joe and Ed wanted to continue so they hired Ron Blake to (drum) in place of N.D. He had just quit The Hello People because he was tired of acting in silence and mime for the public and painting his face for every gig.

After some slight resistance to finish the album project, Felix came back aboard, played guitar, bass, sang and absorbed himself in the Bo Grumpus sessions. Newly recruited, Ron Blake was not quite up to speed with the songs so Herb Lavelle, a session player was brought in on drums. The album entitled *Before the War* was finally finished and released. Some folks say it's comparable to The Byrds *Notorious Byrd Brothers* album with three-part harmonies, echoes and some cool psychedelic moves which made it worthy of underground radio. It seems to be closer in sound to Bear or Ars Nova without the baroque sounds. The recording was a bit of a fabrication because as a live band, they had more of a Jim Kweskin Jug Band sound. There were no singles specifically but an EP featuring four songs from the LP was distributed to the radio stations. The song *Brooklyn* was featured on the air by Scott Muni several times at WNEW 102.7 FM. This song and the album never made the charts.

They appeared at the Metropole Café and played at the Boston Tea Party three times sharing the stage with The Velvet Underground, The Staple Singers and Eden's Children. The Bell Record label asked Felix to record an album and he thought of the guys with Bo Grumpus. The Richmond Organization (TRO) had ownership rights to Bo Grumpus and they couldn't use that band name for recording purposes. So, Eddie came up with a new name and they became Jolliver Arkansaw.

Another album was recorded at Gotham Sound Studios at 2 West 46th St. with Felix on bass guitar and several other instruments and the session also included Leslie West for one song on lead guitar. The album called *Home* has none of the weirdness of Bo Grumpus, but because of this recording and the impressive guitar licks, Felix Pappalardi and

Leslie West formed Mountain. The album cover shows left to right Ronnie Blake, Jim Colegrove, Joe Hutchison (holding the baby) and Eddie Mottau. One single was released from the LP called *Lisa My Love b/w Mr. Brennan*.

Jolliver Arkansaw played in a few local clubs and traveled to Cleveland to play on *Upbeat*, the TV dance show broadcast on WEWS featuring several up and coming new bands. They spent a week playing at Cleveland's top dance club, Otto's Grotto, located in the basement at the old Statler Hotel. A place where most of the bands performed when they stayed in town. But things didn't last and Jolliver Arkansaw, aka Bo Grumpus, split up a few months later.

Eddie Mottau wound up producing Paul Stookey's first album and then got involved with John Lennon for several LPs. He opened a cabinetry and wood finishing business but still recorded and released albums and CDs into the new century.

Joe Hutchinson met up with Jim Colegrove who had since moved to Woodstock and they formed another band with David Wilcox and Billy Mundi called Jook. A full album of songs was recorded but none were ever released. Afterwards Joe took a hiatus to Alaska, played clubs as a solo act and raised a family. He moved back to mainland US in the mid-90's and settled in Florida where he formed The Smackwater Retrievers with his son John and son-in-law Jereme Neill. They have released two albums of traditional blues and still play the club circuit in the Tallahassee area.

N.D. Smart joined Leslie West and Felix on the first Mountain LP. His long career featured him as drummer for Great Speckled Bird with Ian and Silvia, Moogy Klingman, Gram Parsons, James Cotton Blues Band and he played with The Hello People on their last three albums.

Jim Colegrove joined N.D. with Great Speckled Bird and had four good years with them before Ian and Sylvia moved on. Hungry Chuck was formed with noted members of the backing band that released one self-titled LP on the Bearsville record label. Jim is well respected and has been busy musically throughout his career with Borderline, John Hall, The Juke Jumpers, Lost Country and is currently working with Roscoe West composing songs and recording as Men of Extinction.

STEREO/ABCS-705
BOLD
abc
RECORDS

BOLD 1970

Steve Walker grew up in Wakefield, Massachusetts. There was always music in the house, but it was only when he saw Elvis Presley on TV that he became serious. His first guitar was a Stella acoustic loaned to him by a teacher in school. His parents took notice and provided him with guitar lessons. Dad surprised him with a brand new Gretch Firebird guitar. At Wakefield High School, he put a band together with himself on (guitar), Bunky on (bass) and Rick Lodico (drums) and called themselves The Shepherd Kings. Practice was set up in his mom and dad's living room. They were young and only played the occasional party, teen dances and sock hops.

After graduation both Steve and Rick attended The University of Massachusetts. There was no thought about a band. Steve was studying for his Bachelor of Arts Degree in Physics. But he befriended fellow classmate Taj Mahal. Yes, that Taj Mahal. Both were really into music and Taj talked Steve into forming another band. He found the players for a new band he called The Esquires. Included were Steve Walker (guitar, vocals), Rick Lodico (drums), his dorm roommate Brew Harding (bass) and Bob LaPalm as a 16-year old (guitar) wizard from Easthampton, Ma. Taj secured empty classrooms at the College for practice sessions and would set them up to play frat parties and college dances. Taj was acting like their manager and got gigs for them to play through radio sponsored dances. They started getting a fan base and were featured at some of the local bars and taverns. Taj eventually left to find his stardom in California with The Rising Sons, then he began a solo career rising to fame and fortune.

Meanwhile, The Esquires traveled to Continental Recordings Inc. in Framingham, Ma. to record a single *Down the Track b/w Shake A Tail Feather*. They were invited to an audition for the New York Playboy Club. Admittedly they were not the best sounding band there, but Steve did a back flip off the stage during their performance and impressed someone enough to get them hired. It was supposed to be an eight-week gig but was extended for a 6-month period due to the excitement they created on stage.

After the steady gig at the Playboy Club ended, Rick Lodico and Brew Harding left and the band evolved with new players added. With Brew gone Steve took over on bass. They named themselves as Bold and the players were

Steve Walker (bass, guitar, lead vocals) and Bob LaPalm (lead guitar) with new guys Dick LeFreniere (lead guitar, vocals), Mike Chmura (keyboards, vocals) and Tim Griffin (drums). The name Bold was chosen in response to the other one name bands, Them, Love, The Who, Nazz, Free, etc. There were some live-in cabins located in Granby, Ma. where they rehearsed and wrote songs. They went to New York to record a couple of garage sound singles *Gotta Get Some b/w Robin Hood* and *Train Kept a-Rollin b/w Found What I Was Looking For*.

After a year they settled in a house in Huntington, MA and honed their skills there. Psychedelia was settling in and their sound changed. Showcasing in clubs around Massachusetts, they opened for the likes of Big Brother and the Holding Company, Hendrix and others including their former friend Taj Mahal sharing the stage with him at The Ark. Venturing outside the state, they played in Cleveland at D'Poo's Tool and Die Club and Otto's Grotto. It was nearly three years before ABC Records took notice and signed them to a contract. They went back to New York and The Hit Factory located at W 48th St and Broadway to finally record their self-titled album. Bill Szymczyk, who oversaw The James Gang, Silk, J. Giles Band and eventually The Eagles was brought in for production duties.

He brought out all the bands best qualities for the album, but the group was uncomfortable in the studio. They felt subdued, they were frustrated and thought the studio couldn't capture the raw sounds and excitement they stirred up during their live shows. Some of the songs were cut short and some of the studio finagling didn't set well with the band.

Regardless of how they felt, the self-titled *Bold* album does not disappoint. With dreamy vocals, driving organ, echoes, dual lead guitars and mild special effects, they are sometimes described as clones to Cleveland's Damnation. The Songs *Changing Seasons*, *Child of Love* and *Words Don't Make It* come close to Space Opera and Big Star territory. The band members are shown left to right, Mike Chmura, Bob LaPalm, Steve Walker, Dick LaFreniere and Tim Griffin in that order. When the album was released, it wound up directly in the cut-out bins, but it is an album that holds up even today. There were no singles released from the LP, there was no promotion and little public interest certainly didn't help.

Bold fell apart, knowing that they had their one shot.

Bob LaPalm and Tim Griffin formed Clean Living for a couple of countrified psych albums. Sadly, Bob committed suicide in November of 1977.

Tim Griffin started a successful home security business.

Brew Harding opened and operated a nautical gift shop in Portland, Maine.

Dick LaFreniere exports merchandise and has a DJ Company.

Mike Chmura became head of the computer department at the University of Massachusetts.

Steve Walker moved to California and played with several bands before settling in Lake Tahoe. He put together the Steve Walker Band and played the club and casino scene before landing a 35-year steady gig playing on the lake cruise boats Tahoe Queen and M.S. Dixie. These are paddle boats that cater to around 500 patrons per cruise.

The band members minus Bob are still in contact with each other but there are no plans for a reunion.

STEREO
BTPS 1026
bow street runners
B.T. Puppy Records

BOW STREET RUNNERS 1970

It all started in the small city of Fayetteville, North Carolina, 1967, when George Graham, a drummer, got together with his classmates at Terry Sanford High School. They decided to form a band and would practice at each other's house with a collection of 45's learning the radio hit songs of the times. The band included George Graham on (drums), Steve Darling (guitar), Mike Dees (vocals), Bill Joyner (keyboards) and Frank Hardwick (bass). They all collaborated and developed the songs and decided to call themselves Bow Street Runners. One of the guys had been reading the "taboo" novel by John Cleland called Fanny Hill and noted the connection of the Bow Street Runners, an early version of Scotland Yard, mentioned in the book and the Fayetteville Police station that was located on Bow Street in the center of town. (Coincidently, there was an English band that also had a similar name as The Bo Street Runners which was used to describe London's first police force circa the 16th century.)

They spent their high school years playing at the YMCA, teen clubs, high school parties and sock hops. The band separated temporarily after high school graduation. Bill Joyner was a year behind and had one more year of high school to complete. The others went on to college except for Frank who played bass with other bands. He eventually joined with Randy Smith (keyboards) and Steve Struthers (guitar) who attended E. E. Smith High School. Steve S. was into The Jefferson Airplane and Frank was also drawn into the San Francisco sound as a big fan of The Grateful Dead so they began writing songs and together with Randy did some recording at a small studio owned by Bill Cain.

Bill was well known in the area at the time. He also managed the Fort Bragg Teen Club where he set up gigs for bands and was the one to go to in town for a chance at better things musically. The location of his studio was in the Haymount suburb of Fayetteville just west of Hwy 87. Two songs were recorded there which were basic demos by Steve S, Frank and Randy. Frank stayed in contact with his former band mates from high school and the following summer after a full year of college they all met Bill Cain and signed a contract. Bill Joyner had moved on and was no longer involved with the band.

The band included Steve Struthers (lead guitar, vocals), Steve Darling (guitar, vocals), Frank Hardwick (bass, vocals), Mike Dees (vocals) and George Graham (drums). They used two different agents to book the shows, Don Silva and Don Perry. Bill Cain got them back into his Haymount studio with producer Bob Laroy who was a bit of a sound magician. Bob's real name was Robert Folschow and he was the distinctive high-pitched voice on the big national hit *Liar, Liar* by The Castaways in 1965. Bill also knew somebody at B.T. Puppy Records. This label was an offshoot of Bright Tunes Productions started by The Tokens who made a chunk of change with their #1 hit *The Lion Sleeps Tonight*.

The deal was for free time in the studio to record during the summer of 1970. The band never saw any of the B. T. Puppy label representatives. All the songs were recorded live with some vocals and other effects overdubbed in. There was no keyboard player. Bill Joyner was long gone and Randy Smith (remember he played keyboards) was not part of the band or the album sessions. But the two songs he did play on, *Watch* and *Another Face,* were the demos that were initially recorded previously before the band was back together. These two songs were elaborated on in the studio and became part of the album.

The completed self-titled *Bow Street Runners* LP has some psychedelic guitar with added backwards shenanigans and special effects. There's great guitar work with wah-wah jams and wonderful harmonies, echoes, flute and acid guitar replicating bands like The David, Fifty Foot Hose and H.P. Lovecraft. The stunning female vocalist who was also uncredited on the LP was Franks wife Rusty Hardwick. She added that mysterious folk sound with jangling guitars. Some guest players also appeared with Ed Tomolonius (horns) and Mike Mazarick (sax and flute). Although they never played live with horns or woodwinds, George states that they had one shot to show their versatility and decided to expand on the sound.

No singles were released but they had some local radio airplay of the song *Electric Star* and by now, rock clubs were sprouting up in Fayetteville like Roland's and The Electric Coffeehouse, two clubs where the band played often. The two booking agents were busy. Sunday events occurred at the Rowan Street Park, a place named for

Robert Rowan, a leader of the Patriot cause during the Revolutionary War. The Bow Street Runners teamed up with another local band called Valley and both were featured there.

Once the promotional gigs started, they played big clubs, hotel ballrooms and theatres all over the east coast from Maryland to Florida and paired up with bands like The Box Tops, Wet Willie, The Strawberry Alarm Clock and others. There was one night at a drive-in in Virginia opening for Big Brother and the Holding Company (after Janis died) and their final show was opening for Bloodrock at the Cumberland County Memorial Auditorium in Fayetteville. They spent two years basically on the road and by this time the band had run its course. There were no fights, feuds or disappointments, but there was also no money from the record sales. Only about 100 copies of the LP were pressed and there was no distribution, but they were happy to have made the album. An LP that record collectors are fond of and something the band should certainly be proud of.

In the aftermath the members played on and off with other local bands.

Bill Joyner still plays keyboards locally for other bands.

Mike Dees left music altogether and moved to Virginia.

Steve Struthers set up near Little Rock, Arkansas and currently plays with Carl Mouton's Jazz Jam in various clubs nearby.

George Graham still lives in North Carolina. He still plays drums for bands and has had a passion for challenged children over the years helping to provide inspiration, hope, comfort and healing through stories and music on a website he founded called "Dare to Do Your Best".

Frank Hardwick played with Ted Ray and David Guy in a jazz ensemble for over 10 years. Then he on (bass, vocals) with David Guy (keyboards, vocals), Steve Darling (guitar, vocals) and George Graham (drums) reformed Bow Street Runners and released a CD of music in 2000 called *New Classic Rock*. All new tunes from three of the original members. They booked gigs around the greater Fayetteville area playing all the new and old songs live. Sadly, only 2 years later both Steve Darling and Frank Hardwick were laid to rest.

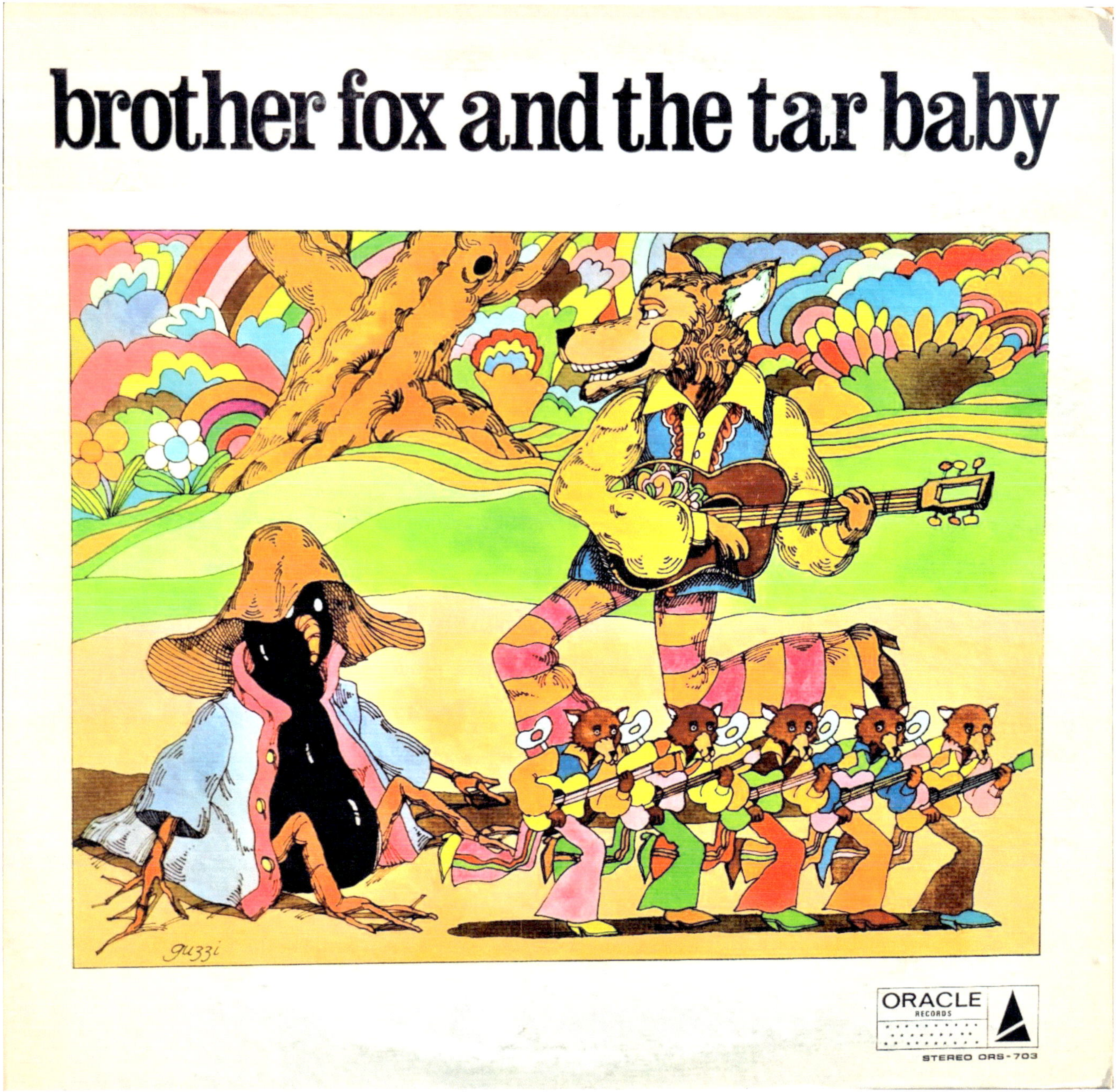
brother fox and the tar baby
guzzi
ORACLE
RECORDS
STEREO ORS-703

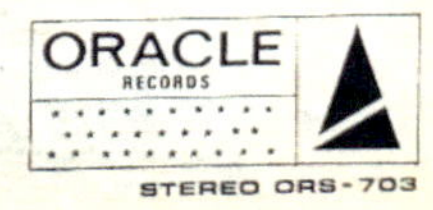

BROTHER FOX AND THE TAR BABY 1969

It's possible (but officially unconfirmed) that this band started out in the early 60's as The Profits. Calling the Boston area their home, they played some of the teen clubs around town. At some point the band changed their name to The Front Page Review and included Richard Bartlett (guitar), Dave Christiansen (guitar) Tom Belliveau (bass), Joseph Santangelo (keyboards) and Dave Weber (drums). They played a lot of the "Surf" clubs (owned by Bill Spence). These were teen clubs located in the New England Beach communities in and around Cape Cod catering to college and non-college kids. Two clubs they frequently played were the Surf Hyannis and the Surf Nantasket.

Steve Cataldo (singer, songwriter) had also been playing these clubs with his band. When he and Rich Bartlett met, Steve became (vocalist) for the Front Page Review. The songs he wrote were deep and unusual and given the times were inventive and psychedelic. Playing clubs like The Crosstown Bus and The Psychedelic Supermarket, they had developed into quite a band. This was also a time when Alan Lorber was putting together his plan to market some of the local talent.

A quarter of a million college students in the area and bands like The Ramrods, The Beacon Street Union, The Lost and others inspired Alan with a good money-making idea. Big time producers, recording studios and record labels were located less than an hour away in New York. He chose MGM records as the label of convenience and had already signed the Beacon Street Union, Orpheus and Ultimate Spinach to record deals. Other bands were being looked at and The Front Page Review fell into the mold of Lorber's Boston Sound concept.

The band had charisma and Steve brought in deep thought lyrics. An album was recorded at Mayfair Studios in New York and was produced by Alan Lorber himself. Lots of special effects, heavy psych guitar, spooky Farfisa organ and dreamy vocals permeate the disc. But all the negative media surrounding the Bosstown Sound and the bands Lorber had signed, spelt doom for any release of this album and so it sat on the shelves for 30 years.

When the media dust had settled, The Front Page Review had ceased to exist. Steve Cataldo went back home to Cape Cod and (drummer) Dave Weber found session work, but Rich, Tom, Joe and Dave Christiansen continued, hiring Bill Garr (drums) and Steve High to provide (vocals) for their new band Brother Fox and the Tar Baby. Dave Christiansen had written several songs and they wound up at Natural Sound Studios in Maynard, Ma. to record an LP. The small Oracle Record Label released *Brother Fox and the Tar Baby* which is a far cry from their former psychedelic sound. A much more rock-oriented sound with heavy fuzz guitar, the record was only released locally and in small quantity. The cover illustration was an early work by George Guzzi who did album cover artwork and was later an aviation artist for the military and traveled abroad painting for the USAF and NASA Arts programs.

The music has some diversity about it with some heavy guitar and phase shifting. The nasal screams of vocalist Steve High reminds me of Axl Rose at times and of the lead singer in Power of Zeus. The album was worthy enough because Capitol Records picked it up and re-released it again nationally. One confirmed club they played at was The Warehouse for two nights in Providence, Rhode Island. A single was put out by Capitol trying to reap the benefits, *Electric Chair b/w Steel Dog Man,* but by this time the band had broken apart.

Tom Belliveau then formed Pugsley Munion and they recorded an album on the small J & S record label.

Richie Bartlett found stability with a band called The Fools throughout the 80's and into the 90's.

The Front Page Review LP was finally released on CD 30 years later entitled *Mystic Soldiers* in 1997 and as an LP on the Akarma Record label circa 2000. Psych heads will want this one.

After leaving the Front Page Review, Steve Cataldo peddled his music around New York and found the liking of the ABC Probe label to put his songs down. His music was recorded with session musicians and the strange album *Saint Steven* was released. Steve confesses that these songs were a continuation of the Front Page Review, which is evident had that band caught on. Afterward, he formed and had a long and lucrative career with the punkish/new wave outfit The Nervous Eaters.

STEREO S-21002
SENATE records
DISTRIBUTED BY

THE BUBBLE GUM MACHINE 1968

Vicki Spencer was a young and talented girl whose parents were in show business. They lived in New York but they were on the road quite a bit so Vicki lived with her Grandparents in an area near Covington, Kentucky. She went to the Conservatory of Music in Cincinnati, Ohio for vocal lessons via Fraternity Records located there and recorded some songs as demos. As luck would have it, she traveled back to New York with her Dad who was meeting a producer with United Artists. They were making a movie called *Teenage Millionaire* and Vicki got a bit part and sang a couple songs. This movie included Dion, Jackie Wilson, Chubby Checker and fighting sensation Rocky Graziano. She was a true teenage sensation with a great voice and the looks of every boy's dream.

Then the call came and she was offered a chance to be in another movie *Twist Around the Clock* where she sang two new songs and the movie finale. As a result, she went to Los Angeles to further her career, but nothing panned out. She did however meet up with Clay Cole who had a TV show back in New York much along the lines of Dick Clark and he was able to book talented acts that were less known and take them on the road. Vicki was a teenage star on the rise and toured with Clay Cole and many others all over. She was on Clay's TV show for WPIX in N.Y. many times and was a regular at Palisades Park for Clay's live shows there.

After the movies and the "twist" craze had ended, she was in other bands like The Nomads and helped in sessions with The Bad Seeds in Kentucky (not the band from Texas) and recorded a single for the Columbia label *King of the Soapbox b/w He's Lying* with jangling bell-like guitars and wonderful harmonies. Her brothers were putting a band together with Bill Spencer (guitars, vocals), Dan Spencer (drums), Dan Evans (organ, piano, keyboards, vocals) and George Peel (bass, vocals). Vicki joined them as (lead vocalist) and they became The Rottin' Kids. They were showcased on *The Tonight Show* with Johnny Carson and, during this time, they also got sponsored by Hazel Bishop who was promoting fake nails for women. This is when they became The Fabulous Fakes. The product ended up being defective and pulled off the market which is when they shortened their name to simply The Fakes.

Soon after, the band thought of a new name as The Bubble Gum Machine which was based on five different flavors (five band members) and had nothing to do with bubblegum music. However, when Wes Ferrell and Tony Romeo got a hold of the band and signed them up, they wanted to expose the band as just that. They jumped at the chance to put out a full album's worth of tunes. The sessions occurred at A&R Studios located at 322 West 48th Street in New York. For the album, the band played all their own instruments and did all the singing just as they had been doing for live performances. There were some studio horns and other instruments that were added and some vocal overdubs. Unusual for the times as most studio sessions had session players substituting for band members.

When *The Bubble Gum Machine* album was released, there was a lot of thought that this band was a studio fabrication. Wes Ferrell and Tony Romeo were known for producing recording sessions with studio players that were never bands as such. LPs were released that had no information with pictures of supposed band members that were really actors dressed like hippies for a photo op. This was a popular practice for record labels used as a tax write off. The album packaging along with members listed on a first name only basis and the fact that the band had previously called themselves The Fakes took hold and rumors abound, the public never thought they were a real band. This was something that haunted them for years.

On the LP there are several cover songs and some teenybopper sounds, but they show signs of pure magic mushroom brilliance with spacey guitar and mysterious vocals with the song *No Love to Be Found* which was written by Billy. Two singles were released with songs from the LP and another non-album promotional single *Do You Really Love Me b/w One More Mountain To Climb* all on the Senate label. Several east coast appearances occurred at festivals, venues and other TV variety shows like *The Merv Griffin Show* and *The Mike Douglas Show*. They got back on *The Tonight Show* and then played Army and Navy bases along the east coast. Their contract expired with Wes Farrell and then they renamed themselves as Horatio.

They were busy playing venues in Canada and Argentina and there was a one month stay at Caesar's Palace in Las Vegas where they opened for Frank Sinatra. While playing at a club in New York, Jim Henson was a witness to their show and asked if they would like to be part of a PBS Broadcast and they became one of the very first rock bands to be seen live in Stereo on Public Television. Different players came and went. About 6 years were spent touring and doing live TV, radio and interviews. During this time, they released about 10 singles. Vicki married their current guitarist Harry Perlow in 1972. But all good things come to an end and eventually the band broke up.

Brothers Bill and Danny then reformed, calling themselves Spencer and an album was recorded. But, before the finalization and release of the LP, Billy was in a freak falling accident that unfortunately caused his death. He was a brilliant guitarist and song writer. Vicki and Danny were devastated, but eventually moved on. The Spencer album still sits on the shelves awaiting release.

Danny Spencer was trained by family friend Buddy Rich who at the time was a world-renowned drummer. B.B. King tried to steal him away when the band played Caesars Palace but Dan stuck it out. After Horatio broke up, he moved on to a career away from drums and currently lives in Kentucky.

George Peel writes and publishes songs and still lives in Kentucky.

Dan Evans did all the arrangements for the band and afterward married, moved to Carlsbad, California and became a jazz pianist going by the name of Danny B. He is a one-man show playing clubs and events and does film scores.

Vicki Spencer is still married to Harry Perlow. To set the record straight, The Bubble Gum Machine outlived all the rumors of being a studio band fabrication. Currently, Vicki has reconnected with most of the original band members, set up a dedicated website to The Bubble Gum Machine and is working on an official release of the dormant album recorded by Billy and Dan called *Spencer-The Legacy.*

Footnote: There were rumors that The Bubble Gum Machine members were killed during a USO tour of Vietnam. This is not true. Many areas in Vietnam were cleared out and shows were put on for entertainment of the troops. Most of the bands were local Vietnamese or flown in from the Philippines, Asia or Korea and they could mimic English and American rock groups and their hits with uncanny accuracy even though they couldn't speak a word of English. Both USA and Australia also had a connection for music entertainment during the war.

Bob Hope had his own extravagant show with lots of heavily armed artillery and security sitting watch, but there were many other unknown entertainers and bands that would play for troops in very isolated and remote areas with little or no security. There were many bands from Australia such as The Beaumarks and The Vamps along with Joan Harvey and The Four Ways who had several popular singles and were already playing US military bases all over Europe and in Thailand.

To play in Vietnam, bands had to audition for a panel of judges in Saigon and if chosen would be assigned an agent to set up gigs and negotiate deals for the entertainment. Joan and The Four Ways played in one remote area about 7 miles from the DMZ for about 500 troops. Unbeknownst to anyone the Viet Cong had surrounded the camp with snipers set up in the trees. Apparently, they (the snipers) sat and enjoyed the music. After The Four Ways completed their show and left the site, the military audience took a heavy toll, most perishing under gunfire. As a result of this their agent made sure the army made extra efforts to secure areas before they played.

One of their shows was cancelled due to reports of snipers being seen along the ground route leading to that show location. So, to appease the troops, Brandi Perry and the Bubble Machine (a USA band) was chosen and scheduled to replace them. One single was recorded by the band as promotion only in Southern California *Just Passing Through b/w Round Trip* on Dore records. They were to play in a remote area near Vong Tau and took off at about 10 in the morning, but the beat-up van they were driving was a smoke bomb. It was so bad that they were pulled over by the "White Mice", a term used for the Saigon Security Police, before they could get out of the city. They were told that the route they were taking was dangerous and that they must return to their Hotel. When their agent, Jack Salvason, found out they were still in town, he threatened to ruin their music career if they didn't show up as intended. It was about 5 PM and being young and scared they snuck out of Saigon unseen and unescorted for the gig.

One military guy Dave (a Sergent) was riding with them but he was off duty and was Brandi's boyfriend. About halfway there on the roadway they heard gunfire. Dave said that the gunfire was just "home guard" protection for the village that was just off the road. But they pulled over when five guys with machine guns approached. The boys got out and explained that they were all entertainers, that they were unarmed and were just traveling to Vong Tau to play music. The gunmen opened fire killing Curt Willis (the drummer) and Phil Pill (the piano player) instantly. Brandi (real name Paula Levine) was in the car and was not hit but had several deep cuts from the shattered glass. Jack Bone (bass) was only hit in the hand. The gun party took off. Gathering his wits Jack tried to restart the van and get it out of the side ditch. But, with nowhere to hide and all the noise he was making the gunmen came back and fired bullets again. The three survivors on a hope and a prayer played dead as the gunmen left the scene. This time Sargent Dave was severely wounded. It was 2 hours before they were found by Thai Soldiers patrolling the roadway and they were airlifted to the nearest Hospital.

So sad but this rumor amongst record collectors can now be laid to rest. There was no connection between "Brandi and the Bubble Machine" and "The Bubble Gum Machine" other than similar in name. Thanks in part to Jack Bone and the Independent Star News article out of Pasadena July 7th, 1968, describing the incident.

DL 74927
STEREO
THE CAKE
DECCA

STEREO
DL 75039
A Slice of THE CAKE
DECCA

THE CAKE 1967-68

Barbara Morillo and Jeanette Jacobs were two teenage girls from New York. They both hung out at clubs and house parties wherever there was a happening. As they were usually both out late and into the early mornings, they would crash at somebody's house. One such morning they found themselves sharing a mirror together throwing makeup on in the bathroom of one of those places getting ready for the day. They didn't know each other but hit it off immediately with a chemistry they both felt.

Barb moved in with Jeanette who lived in her Dads apartment in Queens, NY. They started singing and began to write songs. Jean's dad had a sound-on-sound tape recorder where they would record the songs they wrote adding vocal harmonies. Deciding that they should have a third voice they started going to the nightclubs trying to find that one other voice to complement their proposed trio. Ending up at Steve Paul's The Scene, which at the time was the hottest after-hours club around, they saw Eleanor Barooshian up on stage singing with Tiny Tim doing a spoof of Sonny and Cher's hit song *I Got You Babe*. Eleanor was a young blonde bombshell who could not only sing but brought the house down with her presence on stage. This was a scene that occurred every night with Tiny Tim and Eleanor being immortalized in the 1967 documentary *You Are What You Eat.*

After this performance, Barb and Jeanette approached Eleanor and asked if she wanted to join their group. She agreed and moved in with Barb and Jeanette. They decided on The Cake as their name, it just had a female sound about it. They dropped LSD together and this brought them remarkably close. Because Eleanor knew Steve Paul so well, the three girls began singing at the club in a slot between Tiny Tim and The Chambers Brothers. Their reputation grew and they were singing for everyone and sang at clubs all over New York.

Jimi Hendrix was an unknown and playing with Curtis Knight at the time, but he liked the three girls and said their vocalization soothed him. He would hang-out with the girls and eventually got intimate with Jeanette. The girls showed up one night at the Ondine Discotheque located in Mid-Manhattan under the 59th Street Bridge. They were underage but were allowed inside because they were so beautiful, they could draw a full house of patrons on looks alone. This night The Daily Flash were playing. They were one of the hot bands managed by Charlie Greene and Brian Stone who recently had major success with Sonny and Cher and just signed The Buffalo Springfield and Iron Butterfly.

They saw the girls dancing and singing to the band on stage and Charlie took a liking to Eleanor. He asked her to come over and sit at his table where she told him that her, Jenette and Barbara were a band. They all went outside to sing for him and he flipped. He wanted to sign them up right away. The next day they were recording a demo at a studio vocalizing to familiar songs *Walking the Dog* and *Big Boy Pete*. Greene and Stone took this demo back to Los Angeles and indeed after a couple of months had arranged a deal for the girls with the Decca Records label.

Meanwhile during the two-month wait, the girls had been tabbed to back-up The Band who were just starting to get huge notice. But Jean, Barb and Eleanor decided instead to travel west to all the sunshine in LA. Once in Hollywood they were set up in Vince Edward's old house (he of the huge TV series *Ben Casey*). It was a beautiful round mansion overlooking LA and the Strip. Bags of LSD were flowing. Jimi Hendrix and Eric Burdon were frequent visitors. Rodney Bingenheimer was a big-time LA DJ who raved about them and Ed Caraeff was his sidekick who did all the photoshoots of the girls. Caraeff was only 15 years old at the time but became an iconic figure that was later noted for his photographs of all the famous rock stars.

They recorded at Gold Star Studios in Hollywood. The plan was to record known standards by the girls, but Barbara was very rebellious about singing their own compositions and any cover songs would have to be done their way. Harold Battiste arranged the songs with a pool of high-end studio musicians including Mac Rebennac (Dr. John) (piano), Don Peake (guitar), Carole Kaye (bass), Plas Johnson (saxophone), Michael Rubini (keyboards), Darrel Terwilliger (viola) and John Boudreaux (drums).

The self-titled first album entitled *The Cake* was done and the three songs written by the girls are certainly worth it as they have a weird high on substances feel about them, somewhat baroque in sound with lots of harpsichord, sitar and recorder added. Most of the cover tunes are R'n'B sounds like a Phil Spector production. Decca released the singles *I Know b/w You Can Have Him* and *Baby That's Me b/w Mocking Bird* from the LP. Immediate national attention happened as they were booked for *The Smothers Brothers* show on national TV.

Unique for the times, Cake was strange to watch. Eleanor and Barbara would sing and dance around like crazy to the beat of the song while Jeanette stood completely motionless. Everyone stared at Jeanette waiting for her to break-out but she never did. But it was unintentional. Apparently, Charlie Greene and Brain Stone turned off her microphone because they told her she couldn't sing R'n'B. So, when she did raise the mic to sing (and that wasn't often) she was only lip-syncing. She felt rebuked, embarrassed and showed it. She never said anything to the others. Everyone thought it was part of her "gimmick" and it all added to the mystique about this new girl band.

They were asked to play the *Miss Teenage Beauty Pageant* in Dallas, Texas (a TV broadcast of about 30 million viewers) but when they showed up for rehearsal their attire was wet from all the rain outside and they were bra-less. There was a stink from the TV executives that thought their look was not proper for the show and they were squelched from the live broadcast for so called time constraints. Scheduled to play The *Woody Woodbury* Show on TV, Eleanor was wearing a tee-shirt with a picture of the flag that she was given by Skip Spence of Moby Grape. Ultimately, the broadcast showed the girls but only focused on Barbara and Jeanette. They would not show the "flagship" Eleanor.

Five songs were already recorded for their 2nd LP release but Barbara and Eleanor were sensing that their management and the record label wanted to depict an image for them of something that they weren't, so they split for New York. Jeanette stayed behind. A few weeks later a breach of contract lawsuit was threatened so the two girls headed back to LA. Greene and Stone were not expecting to see them. Upon arrival the, the girls found that Jeanette had completed three other songs with other girls. One song *Sadie* was of particular concern to Barbara as this was a song that she wrote. It was personal as she remembered the time and inspiration for when she wrote it right after she attended The Monterey Pop Festival. A riff occurred between her and Jeanette, she blew up at Charlie Greene and wound up walking out. The Cake was done.

The album was not complete and things were bad. Jeanette and Eleanor just picked up and moved back to New York. They hooked up with Dr. John and his Night Tripper tour. The label still wanted to put out the second album but needed more songs. They had 5 completed songs from the first sessions sung by the girls proper and three sung by Jeanette singing lead with backing harmonies by Diana DeRose (former lead singer with the recently dismantled Rose Garden). The rest of the album was filled with outtakes and polished demos. The album called *A Slice Of Cake* was better than the first as it had seven songs written and recorded by the original three girls themselves. One single *Have You Heard About Miss Molly? b/w P.T. 280* was put out.

They were rebellious and trendsetters as the first girl group that refused to be manipulated in a man's world. As rebels in an industry that disrespected woman, they showed so much promise, but they imploded from within. Jeanette and Eleanor moved to London and became part of Ginger Baker's Air Force. Jeanette wound up marrying Chris Wood of Traffic. He was gone on the road quite a bit and she was not known to be faithful in his absence. They separated and he began to self-medicate even more. Shorty, after the split up, she developed seizures and unfortunately died in 1981 at the early age of 32. Chris was truly in love with her and was severely depressed over her passing. He developed liver problems and stopped indulging but the medication he was taking for his liver caused other problems. His good friend Paul Kossof (guitarist with the band Free) had just passed away from heroin and Chris was gone shortly thereafter due to pneumonia, only a year after Jeanette died.

Eleanor Barooshian moved to Japan and recorded with Tetso Yamauchi, bass guitarist for Free and The Faces. She left the music business for years doing Civil Service work in the UK, then she married and became Chelsea Lee before she returned to the US.

Barbara Morillo changed her name to Ilana Iguana for a while and sang with several bands before scoring another album as *Barbara Morillo and Shrine* on CD in 1984. She and Chelsea Lee were asked to commemorate Jimi Hendrix at a show in New York 2006. They dedicated the one-off concert to Jeanette Jacobs garnering the wows of the crowd. Sadly, Chelsea Lee (Eleanor Barooshian) passed away in 2016. Although there may be similarities in sound, these gals are *not* "The Supremes" and both albums belong in every psych collection.

STEREO
CS 9471
CL 2671
COLUMBIA
STEREO
360 SOUND
Of Cabbages And Kings/Chad Stuart And Jeremy Clyde

Stereo
CS 9699
COLUMBIA
The Ark
Chad Stuart
&
Jeremy Clyde

CHAD AND JEREMY 1964-69

Directly out of the English Pop invasion David Stuart Chadwick, aka Chad Stuart, and Jeremy Clyde first met at the Central School of Speech and Drama in London. Both had previously been choir vocalists at Durham Cathedral and Eton College, respectively. Rock and Roll was in the air and they formed a quintet with Ray Stiles (bass), Liam Hill (drums) and Stephen Holder on (vocals) called The Jerks. Stephen Holder wanted to be a Ricky Nelson clone. After a few months of not so notable shows Chad and Jeremy branched off on their own acoustically and played the local coffee houses.

They both left school with Jeremy opting to act in theatre and Chad working for a music publisher. The two worked nearby and would join at Tina's Coffeehouse for a short set during the lunch hour. John Barry overheard them playing and asked if they would like to make a record. They signed a record deal with the obscure Ember Records and released *Yesterdays Gone b/w Lemon Tree* as their first single. Chad wrote the song and it got some airplay reaching number 37 on the UK charts, but the two were found out as upper-class kids.

Jeremy Clyde was of royal blood and was the triple great grandson of Arthur Wellesley, the 1st Duke of Wellington. Once the tabloids got wind of who he was, the duo was labeled as misfits, lacking the work ethic of ground roots musicians and deemed as ones who were handed a golden platter. The press published an older picture of Jeremy Clyde during the coronation of Queen Elizabeth circa 1953. The papers displayed them as upper-class twits who had no right to play in the working-class rock n roll playground. They never had a chance in their homeland.

But the song was picked up in the US by the World Artists label in Philadelphia and it climbed nationally to #21 on the charts. They followed it with *A Summer Song b/w No Tears for Johnny* which climbed to #7. Seeing success across the Atlantic they decided to move to California and after being snubbed in the UK, had serious thoughts about becoming US citizens. However, doing so would make them eligible for the draft and the war in Vietnam. Instead, they retained their UK citizenship and kept up their working VISAs. Within their first year here Columbia Records picked them up as hitmakers in the industry.

Starring on several television shows like Batman, The Patty Duke Show and Dick Van Dyke along with numerous teen shows, they became teen idols. In two years-time, they wrote seven top 40 hits and within a five-year period released eight studio albums all recorded here in the US and toured several cities all over the country promoting their hit songs. Most of the album songs were 3-minute AM radio ditties, but after The Beach Boys released the album *Pet Sounds* and The Beatles put forth the *Sgt. Pepper's Lonely Hearts Club Band* album, music changed considerably. This prompted an outburst of Beatlesque music extraordinaire.

Chad and Jeremy's answer to all of this came in the form of two albums called *Of Cabbages and Kings* followed by *The Ark*. Both albums were recorded at Columbia Studios at 6121 Sunset Blvd Studio D and are highly experimental with genius production by Gary Usher and Curt Boettcher. Gary Usher pulled out all the production stops for both magical recordings that make them the absolute best of the Beatle-psych albums out there. Lots of special effects, orchestration, sitar, phase-shifting, harpsichord, unusual instruments and dreamy vocals. Everything good about melody and psychedelia is here on these wonderful albums by the duo.

The Ark cost a very extravagant $75,000 to produce. Gary wanted to push production limits and ignored the Columbia executive demands to cut costs. The albums were complete and two singles were released, a promo only *Sister Marie b/w Rest In Peace* and public distribution of the single *Paxton Quigley's Had The Course b/w You Need Feet (You Need Hands).* But Columbia refused to spend any promotional costs and both albums went unnoticed. Gary Usher was fired for insubordination. They never toured in support of either LP and by this time both Chad and Jeremy had tension anxiety and needed to find their own space. They took a hiatus. Mike Curb approached Chad Stuart to do a soundtrack album, something he had been wanting to do for quite some time. The movie and LP called *Three's A Crowd* was released on the Sidewalk label. This record continued the magic of the previous two albums, but it too went nowhere.

Chad stayed in California as music director for *The Smothers Brothers Comedy Hour* and eventually did production work for A&M records. He stayed in the US writing and recording songs in a studio on his own. Jeremy went back to London for several acting jobs in theatre, film and TV. But he too did some recording on his own. They were communicating and by 1982 they both heard each other's studio tapes and decided "Hey!" that sounds like the old Chad and Jeremy. Rocky Davis signed the duo to Rocshire Records and they made plans to record another album together. Some songs had already demoed separately and were to be included. But the official sessions had to stop before it started because Chad was in a terrible auto accident that nearly took his eye. But he did recover.

During the 12 years they were separated, the music world had changed. Initial recordings for another LP occurred at Audio International Studios in London. In the studio a band was hired to bring the songs up to date with more of a rock sound. Jeremy was acting in a stage play during the sessions, so the focus wasn't there. The album has a typical 80's pulsing rock beat with horns which although updated for the times, didn't fit Chad and Jeremy's original musical magic. All the promises from Rocky Davis never happened as he got into some money trouble. Rocshire Records went bankrupt and Rocky went to jail. The reborn Chad and Jeremy with the new album *Chad Stuart and Jeremy Clyde* was only released in the USA, had no promotion and the record wound up in the cut-out bins.

Undeterred, the two got involved with a play in England which filled the time until they were offered a spot with The British Invasion II. They wound up touring the States with Gerry and the Pacemakers, Freddie and the Dreamers, Herman's Hermits, The Searchers and others. The tour lasted six weeks and was rewarding. The summer of 1987 seemed to be the end. They played Harrah's in Lake Tahoe and had a week at the Reno Hilton before calling it quits.

20 years later they reunited and played concerts all over the world. Disillusioned with the record industry any recordings were produced and recorded by themselves and distributed at concerts or through their website.

Jeremy Clyde followed his dream, went back to England and starred in movies, theatre and on TV.

Chad Stuart moved out of LA to Ketcham, Idaho where he married and had kids. He wrote a book and began teaching music. He built an in-home studio he called the Electric Paintbox and never stopped writing and recording. Sadly, he passed away after he fell and developed pneumonia just before Christmas December 12th, 2020.

SR 42037
STEREO
ROULETTE
CHARISMA

CHARISMA: BEASTS AND FIENDS

CHARISMA 1969-70

Charisma began in New Britain, Connecticut with Rich Tortorigi (drums), who was highly influenced by jazz and funk, and George Tyrell (bass) both members of The Mantiques. They were a hot and heavy horn band who along with The Detroit Soul and The Paramounts were emulating Chicago and Blood, Sweat and Tears. Both The Paramounts and The Mantiques were falling apart. Rich and George wanted to continue and Tom Majesky (guitar) was asked to join. He suggested Bernie Kornowicz who had been with The Last Five to join in on (organ and guitar). Finally, Mike DeLisa, a known folk singer in the area, was added on (vocals). Tom and Bernie brought a real rock background to their sound and they dismissed the horns. They practiced and honed their sound at Richards house.

Playing in various clubs in Hartford, New York, Boston and Philly, Roulette Records took a liking to their sound and offered them a record deal. They were established as The Mantiques and had a big following, but the label wanted to rename them. This didn't set well with the band. On top of that, the label had their resident song writer Bruce McGaw write most of the songs for the promised album release. Turmoil occurred during the recording process and the band was given the ultimatum of recording the songs given them and changing their name to Charisma or the deal was off. They weren't happy but accepted the management deal.

The initial recording sessions began at Vanguard Studios located at 71 W 23rd Street in New York. Arguing ensued right from the start and after the first song was completed George Tyrell quit. The sessions were moved to Incredible Sound Studios. Bernie took over on (bass) and they hired Bob Mocarsky on (keyboards) to finish the album. Horns were added after the fact and the self-titled *Charisma* album was finished. It has a sound comparable with The Buckinghams and Central Nervous System. Pictured on the cover from left to right is Bernie Kornowicz, Bob Mocarsky, Tom Majesky, Richard Tortorigi and Mike DeLisa. They did the college tour for promotion in several northeastern states. A promo single with a *MONO b/w Stereo* version of the song *What's It Like?* was distributed to the radio stations that did nothing.

Songwriting was already in the works for a second album. Bob, Tom, Bernie and Richard were in collaboration writing all the songs. Mike DeLisa decided to part ways, leaving the vocal duties for Tom Majesky. Suzi Langlois was an artist and friend of the group, who designed the front cover for the new album and is credited for writing most of the lyrics on the second LP.

Jack Hunt was a sound master for engineering and one of the tops in the business. He was behind the sound of the first *Woodstock* movie album and was involved with Frank Zappa, The Eire Apparent, Silver Apples, Tiny Tim and others. With assistance by Dave Rango and Tom Flye, former drummer of Lothar and the Hand People, the second album was recorded at The Record Plant studio A and studio C on the tenth floor in New York. Credit was given to Bruce McGaw for production in name only as all the songs were written and produced by the band and Jack Hunt. This album blossoms with great songs and has an edge not found on the first LP. It has jazz, rock and blues vibes with influences of Miles Davis and The Mahavishnu Orchestra on keyboards from Bob and vocals as a cross between Joe Cocker and Dr. John. The showcase song was the same as the album title *Beasts and Fiends.*

The band was aware of Roulette Records, the corruption of Morris Levy and his connection to the mob. No real promotion for either album happened in the US but both LPs did do well in Europe. They toured both Charisma albums playing the college circuit in most of the northeast states and traveled to Ohio. Instead of staring at their instruments Suzi Langlois was also responsible for the stage scenery and gave them a more animated stage presence during their live shows for better public appeal. They were featured on a Saturday night in Philadelphia on WKBS TV Channel 48 for *The Hy Lit Show*. Performing at the Fillmore East was special and they gigged at other clubs locally, but never saw a dime from the Roulette record label. They were offered studio time for a third album but turned it down. Original members Rich Tortorigi and Bob Mocarsky were frustrated and left, but Tom and Bernie were determined to keep things going.

Hiring Jim Roselle (drums) and Mike Reynolds (keyboards) they continued. It turns out Mike was Bob Mocarsky's second cousin. They didn't know each other until that moment. Going back to horns and woodwinds they hired Paul Midney (sax, Flute) and Ray Mase (trumpet) as well. For a while they renamed themselves as Midney but opted back to Charisma. To relegate costs to keep themselves going and contrary to their sound, they compromised their principles and did commercial work for radio and TV. The band made enough money to build their own studio. Enlisting Brian Salke on (vocals), they began recording new songs.

There was enough recorded music to put out another album on their own. The songs are/were available on the internet for a while and show an amazing band that developed into a progressive jazz/rock anomaly much like that of Todd's Rundgren's early days in Utopia. But an album was never released. By 1976 Charisma was done.

Brian Salke is the director of a company that builds large steel structures.

Paul Midney got heavy into meditation and is believed to be living in Florida.

Ray Mase went on to play with the American Brass Quintet.

Bernie Kornowicz left music and is a retired financial and computer information specialist.

Bob Mocarsky is based in Hong Kong and tours the world playing jazz with The Bob Mocarsky Trio.

Suzi Langlois is still an accomplished artist who sells paintings and tapestries in New York.

Tom Majesky teaches at The Hartford Conservatory of Music and has been seen on the Today Show several times. He is also involved with The Cartells, a band of famous and infamous musicians that play large gatherings in New York whenever needed.

Ritchie Tortorigi stayed involved with music playing with several big names in the business, Clarence Clemmons, Jimmy McGriff, Roland Kirk and others. He had his own bands The Zingers, RIFF, and was involved with the Claymation sounds that were so familiar a few years ago. He taught drums at The Madison Academy of Music in Connecticut until they closed and continues to teach drums privately.

Both original LPs were rereleased as CDs on Wounded Bird Records in 2008 and are highly recommended. To hear the unreleased list of songs, go here: www.leisureland.us/audio/Charisma/Charisma.htm

CB 701
CHIRCO
VISITATION
OLDER THAN ANCIENT - YOUNGER THAN NEW

CHIRCO 1972

Tony Chirco was a great drummer from Fairfield County in Connecticut. He was taught how to play the drums by Henry Adler, had studied at the Conservatory of Music in Milan, Italy and had post graduate work at Juilliard in New York. As a percussionist and vibraphone player he had a musical vision and wanted to record a piece that he had written. Enlisting producer Michael Cuscuna, they began recording sessions at Syncron Sound Studios in Wallingford, Connecticut along with studio musicians for a project that entailed strange instruments and rock music.

Sassafrass was a local band that hailed from Worchester County near New York. Tony approached them to help complete his project. The band sessions took place at Media Sound Studios located at 311 W 57th Street in Manhattan. He named the band project Chirco, after himself, and the completed project was met with high hopes for all members involved. The band included Tony Chirco (vibes, percussion), Anvil Roth (lead vocals), John Naylor (guitar, vocals), Bruce Taylor (bass, vocals), S.H. Foote (keyboards) and Ted MacKenzie (drums). The LP was somewhat diverse with Bill Wich (Ram's Horn, Piston Bugle) and additional (guitars) from Lou Sulkazi and Billy Chanaka.

When Tony shopped the taped sessions around there was little interest, but they somehow got a hold of Carlos Schidlowski who was just starting the Crested Butte label in Denver, Colorado. He wooed them in. The post mix of the master tapes were completed at Good Vibration Sound Studios (formerly RKO Studios) located at 1440 Broadway in NYC. The LP called *Visitation- Older Than Ancient, Younger Than New* and a single *Golden Image b/w Mr. Sunshine* was pressed up in Denver, Colorado. The band was flown out to Denver and introduced to some of the Crested Butte label executives and influential music patrons at a party near Boulder, Colorado. Most of LPs were given away here by the Crested Butte label for promotion. You got a free belt buckle with the Crested Butte logo pressed in polished aluminum. The LPs that weren't given away were tossed into the trash.

A few singles found their way to local radio stations. The band never saw any money. Chirco only played a couple of live shows in Boulder at a club called Tulagi's. This was the top night club in town where The Moonraker's hung out and The Eagles and ZZ Top were featured. Anybody who was at either of these shows were lucky ones indeed, as they were the only known live occurrences for this band.

Unfortunately, marketing failed miserably as Carlos, the promoter, spent every dime generated on this project for his own amusement and put nothing towards the band or record label itself. Of course, the label was short-lived, he split for his homeland, Chile, for apparently having several other mis-dealings and unpaid debts. The federal authorities finally caught up with him two years later and brought him back to face 20 plus charges of fraud, etc. He spent two years in a US prison and then was deported.

As for the band, they broke up in failure, but left behind one magnificent and breathtaking album. Progressive in nature with all kinds of unusual instruments including Electronic Vibes, Ram's Horn, Piston Bugle and Timpani along with guitar, vibes, drums, keyboards and bass by the band. They do assimilate the band Bold at times.

Most of the band members have disappeared without a trace. Although John Kaye played percussion with other bands like Nick St. Nicholas, Mark Murphy, The Bob Kindred Jazz Quartet and Morgana King.

Anvil Roth was really Bobby Lindsay who was a well-known vocalist for white doo-wop bands The Orchids and The Run-Aways in the early 60's. He was a big guy that had a high piercing yet delicate voice. He became the vocalist for Sassafrass but had changed his name to reflect the times. This was the last recorded effort for Bobby Lindsay (aka Anvil Roth). He died in 1989.

Tony Chirco wound up playing with several bands, including The Volunteers in the 80's before any recordings were made. They were a Grateful Dead covers band that evolved into The Zen Tricksters. But Tony's claim to fame was in music education. When he wasn't in a band, he was teaching drums in seminars and giving drum lessons one on one. He taught Master Classes including a jazz series with Dave Brubeck and was featured in The International Musicians publication. Well-loved by all who knew him, he passed away peacefully in the year 2013 at his home in Fort Mill, South Carolina.

STEREO
A&M RECORDS
SP 4169
THE CHURLS

STEREO
A&M
RECORDS
SP 4233
The Churls | Send Me No Flowers
PRINTED IN CANADA

THE CHURLS 1967-69

Formed in Willowdale, a neighborhood of Toronto, Ontario, Canada The Churls were a group of young musicians dedicated to the Blues legends who influenced the British band onslaught in America. Initially the band had formed and included Nick McCombie (guitar, vocals), Harry Southworth (known as "Hal") Ames (guitar), John Barr (bass) and Brad Fowles (drums). Nick came up with The Churls for a band name as it was English sounding and was akin to The Stones. Original meaning of the word "churl" was simply "manservant", but the term evolved into meaning an uncouth English Peasant.

They worked hard rehearsing in the basement of Brad Fowles' house. Nick was trying to emulate Jimi Hendrix and Eric Clapton and he just wasn't up to the task, so he left. Sam Hurrie was a great guitarist, so he came in as Nick's replacement. They also needed a lead vocalist and John met Bob O'Neill (lead vocals) at a "slop shop" who agreed to audition for the band and was hired. They practiced songs redone by the British bands covering tunes by Muddy Waters, Otis Redding, Howling Wolf, The Rolling Stones and others and composed some original tunes as well.

In the beginning they were playing high school dances and small basement clubs in Etobicoke, North York, Mimico and other suburbs of Toronto. But the hot spot was Yorkville with over 60 clubs and coffee houses. Places like The Mynah Bird, The Purple Onion, The Mousehole, The Riverboat and others were all in the hub of this area, Canada's hippie counterpart to Greenwich Village in New York, The West Bank in The Twin Cities and Haight Ashbury in San Francisco. They were playing at one of the clubs, Charlie Brown's Place and were discovered, groomed and nurtured by Bill Riley, an Englishman who knew all the right people and had some influence. He asked the band if he could take over management duties. They agreed and as an enthusiast he got them many gigs, including The Churls being featured as the house band at The Penny Farthing. They became the hottest band in town. As their manager Bill Riley took them from $25 a night to a real stage presence demanding $1000 a show.

Leonard Seeds was a jazz drummer from New York who had just finished a leg of shows on Broadway as drummer in the band for the original Broadway play "Hair-The American Tribal Love Rock Musical". He was in Canada playing with friends at The Colonial Tavern on Yonge St in Toronto and had wandered up to Yorkville. He asked some folks where he could listen to a good band and was told that The Penny Farthing was the best place to hear great bands. The Churls just happened to be playing when he walked in. Lenny was impressed and he told Paul Sloman and Andy Muson at PAIJ Music in New York about them. Andy kept traveling north to see the band and by now Bill Riley had fulfilled his purpose and had given up the reigns. It took seven months to get a US VISA approved and once they got to New York, they were set up at The Hotel Earle in Washington Square right next to Greenwich Village.

PAIJ set them up with Bennett Glotzer and Dennis Katz who represented the number one band in North America at the time, Blood Sweat and Tears. They auditioned at Steve Paul's Scene and were immediately set up to play there for six weeks. Here, the likes of Buddy Miles, Van Morrison, Paul McCartney, John Lennon and Yoko Ono witnessed their shows. Jimi Hendrix had befriended Hal who was awe inspired. One night, Jimi, Hal, Sam (who played bass) and Randy Zehringer, the drummer for The McCoys, got up on stage and jammed. They all just basically took cues from Hendrix as they played. Few familiar songs were played as Hendrix was trying out some new things he was working on.

Recording demos in New York, they had hoped to find a label that would take them on. As the house band at Steve Paul's Scene, they were busy but also played other places, opening for The MC5 at Unganos and The James Cotton Blues Band at The Electric Circus. Then it finally happened. A&M Records signed them to a two-record album deal. A tour was scheduled on the way out to Hollywood where they played at The Newport Jazz Festival in Rhode Island, The Electric Factory in Philadelphia, The Grande Ballroom in Detroit, Barnaby's in Chicago and a Debutant's Ball at the De Vousier Estate near St Louis. The bands they shared the stage with included Taj Mahal, Raven, Creedence Clearwater Revival and others. In California they played The Whiskey A Go Go on Sunset Blvd.

They were only the second rock band signed to A&M Records. Herb Alpert was the head honcho and imposed his own vision of sound on the band, this included some horns which were only minor in detail. The sessions for the first album were recorded at A&M Recording Studios located at 1416 N. La Brea Ave. in Central Hollywood. The photo shoot for the album cover depicts the band in rented Hollywood movie costumes for a downtrodden peasant look. Really? The players on the record are pictured but not identified. Left to right is Bob, Hal, Brad, Sam and John in that order. Bob O'Neill and Hal Ames wrote most of the songs. The first album *The Churls* has twin heavy guitars with minor special effects. The Kinks and The Rolling Stones with an edge come to mind.

In retrospect, the first self-titled album was quite good but lacked the sound and excitement that the band had displayed during their live shows. It was apparent that Herb Alpert wanted a more AM radio friendly sound and the energy of stage shows seen by the audience was toned down for the LP. The band toured back across the US and Canada promoting their release and playing all the big clubs. But there was a small place in El Paso, Texas called The Kingsmen Lounge located a mile from the border near Juarez, Mexico at 3626 Doniphan Drive. This was the only venue in town that dared to book rock and psych bands. Most of the known rock bands played at the college or the County Coliseum but it's known that Vanilla Fudge also played here. The Churls set up on stage and saw rattlesnake skins everywhere. This freaked the guys out just a bit.

Steven Hill of Bloodrock caught their act when they played at The Cellar in Fort Worth, Texas and could not get a song out of his head. The original version of the song and a highlight from the LP *Time Piece* was later covered by Bloodrock on their first album. This song should have been The Churls single release representing the band. Instead, the single *City Lights b/w Where Will You Be Tomorrow* was released to the radio airwaves and charted only in Canada albeit only briefly.

The shows got them a grand fan following but garnered little interest from the record buyers. Sam Hurrie was older, he was married, had a child and he was tired of the road so he left the band. They knew a fellow Canadian, Newton Garwood (keyboards), who had previously played with the band Leigh Ashford. This band had just broken apart, so he was hired to replace Sam.

They went back to Hollywood. A second album *Send Me No Flowers* was recorded and put on the market. Hal's guitar shines as never heard in the previous studio mix. Another single *I Can See Your Picture b/w Long, Long Time* was released with little or no public reaction. The band still put on great shows and filled the clubs, but they were frustrated by the lack of records sales. Musically, both albums show a quality band with all the right moves, heavy guitar, three-part harmonies and inventive songs that should have had a major impact. But the A&M label failed to promote the band and then lost interest. Hal was also married and was tired of the constant touring, so he departed. There were some auditions for Hal's replacement on guitar, but nobody was found that could fill his shoes. Discouraged, the Churls decided to call it quits.

Newton Garwood moved on to the fourth version of the band Motherload for a while then retired from music and became the manager at Long and McQuade, a music instrument retailer in Toronto. He died suddenly in 2005 at 57 years of age.

Brad Fowles got into Real Estate and left music behind.

John Barr became an auto mechanic and disappeared from the music industry.

Hal Ames became a carpenter and cabinet maker but continued to play music with bands on the weekends. He's still around and lives in Canada.

Sam Hurrie moved back to Toronto and released several guitar-instruction videos and CDs. Moving to British Columbia he worked at the Catalyst Paper Mill in Powell River for 35 years. He retired but still plays small clubs in the Lake Kootney area of British Columbia where he lives.

Bob O'Neill married and sold automobiles for a 30-year career. Retired, he now lives in Ontario.

STEREO SRS 67101
DB
the Collage
SMASH
RECORDS

THE COLLAGE 1968

Jerry Careaga grew up in California. He had joined the Air Force for his tour of duty and was stationed at Luke AFB near Phoenix. After completing his active duty, he ventured back to LA and found a job at the Hollywood Ramblerland selling cars. One day Ron Joelson walked in to buy a new Rambler. He had moved to LA with his wife from Fargo, North Dakota. They talked about music and agreed to meet at Ron's new house to discuss the possibility of a collaboration. Ron wrote poems that were unstructured and freeform. Jerry was a guitarist who was quite structured and wrote songs that qualified for commercial radio ads. They were complete opposites, but some-how they found a common bond in music. Ron was the wordsmith and would write poems and lyrics in a journal. Jerry would comb through the words and when something hit his fancy, he put it to music.

After a few weeks, they had enough songs and decided to make some demos to shop around. Ron knew some musicians and booked some time at Paramount Studios in Santa Monica where they made some acetates to shop around. Initially they had a deal through Equinox Records, but it didn't work out. They shopped around some more and found Abe Hoch who worked with a Capitol Records subsidiary. He loved the songs and had a vision of Ron and Jerry with two girl singers. He became their manager. Abe's ex-girlfriend Donna Byrd was a terrific singer and Jerry had a friend back in Arizona, Jodie Cline, who showed up the next day. So, with Ron Joelson, Jerry Careaga, Donna Byrd and Jodie Cline they became an acoustic vocal quartet. The Collage was born.

The music industry had freed up quite a bit from the tight suit times and Abe was determined to find the best record deal. The demos were left behind and he would have The Collage promote themselves live for each A&R personality. The thought was that Beat Poetry and Hippie Beads would sell the band, but it was really all about the two hot chicks up front and center. Record labels were falling over themselves to sign them up, but Abe was holding out. Even Capitol Records had a keen interest and were ready to set them up with production guru Nick

Venet, but Abe said that the Capitol deal wasn't quite good enough. A bad move because Abe was promptly fired leaving him and the band completely broke.

The only income at the time came from a part time job, packaging mail order dildos for a Melrose Ave sex-toy shop. It worked out as they set up at Ron's house and could practice when the packages were done and ready for pick-up. Abe was welcomed back into their graces when he found an interested record label with the right deal. Mercury Records subsidiary Smash Records invited them up to perform their three songs and they were signed on the spot. Ron and Jerry began writing new material and refining older songs for the upcoming recording session. The label wanted them to augment some other familiar songs to mold with their own material.

Several sessions occurred at Amigo Studios, Gold Star Recording and Wally Heider Studios all in Hollywood and had the Wrecking Crew to back their voices and bring life to the tunes they wrote. Jerry was especially overwhelmed at the professional sound these musicians came up with. J.J. Cale engineered the recordings and it was musically wonderful. With tandem boys and girl's beautiful harmonies, the self-titled album *The Collage* emulates a very flower pop style. Orchestral maneuvers, harps, acoustic guitars and emphasis on the vocals, they sound like many others, The Sunshine Company, The Free Design and The Pleasure Faire to name a few. Ron Joelson and Jerry Careaga showcased their music, they also did justice to cover tunes from The Collectors *Looking at A Baby*, The Stone Poneys *Driftin'* and Sagittarius *Would You Like to Go* as well. The music was high quality and magical sounding but it was viewed as lightweight. There weren't any rock songs with bite.

Radio airplay was virtually non-existent. One single *Driftin' b/w Any Day's A Sunday Afternoon* was released but it stalled, so the band requested another session of songs that were more rock oriented. Somehow, they convinced Mercury to provide more recording time. They put down some quality pop/rock songs, but Mercury Records was unconvinced and put these in the can. The Collage ventured out to promote the album as best they could. Several TV spots came along, *The Mike Douglas Show, American Bandstand, Its Happening, Steve Allen, Playboy After Dark* and others. They played most of their gigs in Nevada at The Sands in Las Vegas and Hurrah's in Lake Tahoe. But they didn't want to be a Vegas act.

They happened across Harry Nilsson playing a song *Story of Rock and Roll*. It had yet to be claimed (or so they thought). Harry gave his blessing to The Collage and they went to the studio to make a recording. Smash records released *Story of Rock And Roll b/w Virginia Day's Ragtime Memories,* but unbeknownst to everyone The Turtles also recorded and released Nilsson's song. The Turtles were hot off the song *Happy Together* and the stations chose The Turtles version for airplay. Another song *Someday Man* written by Paul Williams was initially going to be released by The Collage, but Paul instead gave his approval to The Monkees for this one. That was pretty much it for The Collage. So many near misses, they couldn't get a break.

Donna Byrd wound up with The Gringo's for a few years.

Jodie Cline retired from the music business.

Ron Joelson went onto a successful business with his wife Marjorie, but unfortunately crossed to the other side in 1997.

Jerry Careaga finally put together a full CD of the album including outtakes and six unreleased songs by the band. He was still musically active as of this writing and publishing songs for several artists including many for The Bellamy Brothers.

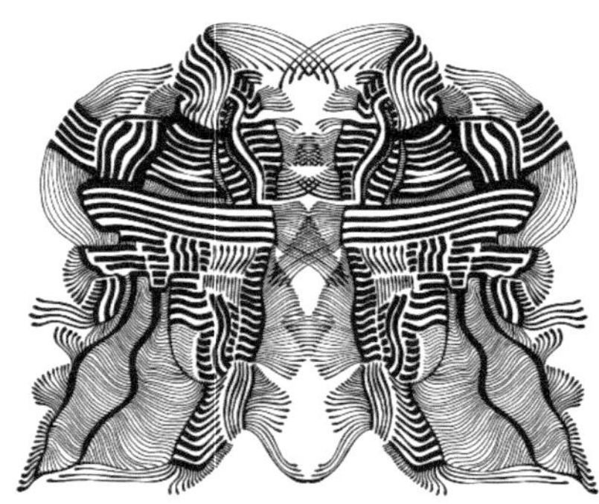

DOT
RECORDS
STEREO
DLP 25854
COLOURS

DOT RECORDS
STEREO
DLP 25935
Colours
atmosphere

COLOURS 1968-69

Colours infancy started with The Dalton Boys (Dan, Jack and Wally) who grew up in Dearborn, Michigan. They were folk singers playing at clubs and coffee houses in New York, Philadelphia, San Francisco, Los Angeles, New Orleans and finally settled in Cleveland for a while where they owned and operated a folk club. During this time there were TV appearances as well on *Hootenanny* and *The Mike Douglas Show* which was broadcast from Cleveland when that show first started. When the Beatles were shown to the world on *The Ed Sullivan Show* the folk music scene began its decline.

The band broke apart. Dan Dalton left and traveled to California. He joined the folk singing group called The Back Porch Majority. Jack and Wally closed shop and moved to Windsor, Ontario, Canada where they played as a folk duo in clubs there and across the river in the general Detroit area. But the folk scene burned out completely. They were at a Windsor bar and poolhall and were discussing their next move when somebody came up to them and asked if they were singers. His name was Gary Montgomery and he explained that he played piano, could sing and could write songs. Jack took him up on his offer to collaborate musically.

They started writing songs together and when they thought their songs were good enough, they decided to try and get work with Motown Records located just across the river in Detroit. They schmoozed their way in by getting notice from Henry "Hank" Cosby, a former Funk Brother who worked as a song writer and producer for the label. Jack with Gary were the first "white" dudes to be signed by Motown. Still calling themselves The Dalton Boys they wrote and recorded a few songs with The Funk Brothers who in Detroit and at the Motown label where the equivalent to The Wrecking Crew in Los Angeles. Top of the heap session musicians that were dependable and really knew their stuff.

Their single *I've Been Cheated b/w Somethings Bothering You* was released the same week as The Supremes *I Hear a Symphony b/w Who Could Ever Doubt My Love*, so it wasn't really promoted and although there was some airplay of the song the band was back shelved by the label. Gary and Jack felt that Motown wasn't giving them any respect and they were a little down and out. Try as they might, they eventually asked to be released from their Motown Records contract.

Brother Dan was a producer now in California. He heard the news and told Jack that he should come out to LA. So, he did. Gary followed and the two continued writing songs out there. Because of Dans influence and the fact that they were former song writers for the big Motown label, they were hired to write for the White Whale Record label. Officially calling themselves Dalton & Montgomery, they had written numerous songs already and started recording demos right away. Two singles that were composed by them were released by The Turtles, *Outside Chance b/w Making My Mind Up* and *Can I Get to Know You Better b/w Like The Seasons.*

Neither single did very well at the time but they continued to write songs for the likes of The Spiral Staircase, The Outsiders, Nino and April and White Whale released one single *All At Once b/w Tomorrow's Women* as Dalton & Montgomery. But no hits were happening. They decided to put together a formal band with members Jack Dalton (guitar, vocals), Gary Montgomery (keyboards, vocals), Rob Edwards (lead guitar), Carl Radle (bass) and Chuck Blackwell (drums). Rob, Carl and Chuck had all been with bands in the past and were seasoned studio session musicians. Their fashionable look and the music simulated a Beatles sound.

Since they were so heavy into The Beatles, they termed themselves as Colours (the English spelling). DOT Records signed them up and they went to Columbia Studio D on Sunset Blvd in Hollywood. The result was the self-titled *Colours* album full of over the top psych and pop music. The record is full of orchestration, magical harmonies, special effects and real dream-like songs that take strange turns. There are several unusual instruments including sitar, harpsichord, flute and bagpipes along with three-part harmonies. Their sound closely resembles The Moon and Michael Lloyds Smoke. But you can also hear what must have been a huge influence on Mark Mikel and his band Marikesh in the 1980's and later, his fantastic band The Pillbugs. Big plans were in mind for Colours and for their album. Pictured on the cover left to right is Chuck, Jack, Carl, Gary and Rob.

There was massive distribution of the LP, but there was only one live show ever played at a small unnamed bar in the San Fernando Valley. Gary did not like the stage and was uncomfortable playing live. The single *Love Heals b/w*

Bad Day at Black Rock, Baby climbed the charts to #9 locally. But, during an interview with one of the Boss Jocks at KHJ radio 93, he cold cocked the DJ for referencing Colours to The Moody Blues who Gary thought was an inferior band. This sealed Colours fate and the radio stations banned them from airplay.

Gary and Jack stayed together and continued to write songs for the likes of Aorta, The Moon, Harper & Rowe and others but the other band members moved on. Still owing an album to DOT records Gary and Jack reformed the band with David Marks (lead guitar, vocals) and David Jackson (bass) (both members of The Moon) and Richard Crooks on (drums). The decision was to change direction musically and not to sound so much like the Beatles. Their second and final album was mostly recorded at Sound Recorders Studio in Studio City. This album had no big production, studio effects or orchestration and brings out the raw musicians. Blues with some horns permeate the album called *Atmosphere*. Expectations of another Beatles style album were not present, although a couple songs would fit well on The White Album. A disappointment to most of their fans, the album tanked and the band split apart.

Wally Dalton moved to the Seattle area where he still lives.

Dan Dalton became a big-time producer in LA. He formed Dan Dalton Productions and continued as CEO for the company until his passing in June of 2018.

Richard Crooks moved east and drummed for Dr. John touring and recording for over 25 years. He was a highly regarded session drummer and has a list of credits that reads like War & Peace. He died in Key West, Florida January 2015.

David Marks moved to Boston and went on to Berkley College of Music to study jazz guitar. He remained a credible session guitarist and rejoined The Beach Boys on and off touring all over the world.

David Jackson was another solid bass player who continued session work throughout his career.

Rob Edwards vanished back to studio work.

Carl Radle became a well-respected session bass player and toured with Derek & the Dominoes. He was with Joe Cocker, George Harrison and too many other superstars to list. However, drink and drugs caught up with him and he died of kidney failure in 1980.

Chuck Blackwell moved back to Tulsa, Oklahoma and continued drumming with Leon Russell, Joe Cocker, Eric Clapton, et al.

Gary Montgomery, disillusioned with the record industry, moved to Tulsa, OK and did not pursue music as a profession. He did do some vocal work for T. Bone Burnett but ultimately became a stone mason and then painted for a living. Sadly, he passed away in 2005.

Jack Dalton moved back to Detroit and started a "jingle" company called The Road Company. This became a successful business where Jack wrote, sang and arranged most of the commercials seen on TV or heard on the radio in Detroit. By the 1980's he got back into playing music in clubs either solo or with a band and played over 250 nights a year. He currently resides in Columbus, Georgia.

STEREO
SPS 542
CONDELLO :
SCEPTER RECORDS
PHASE 1

CONDELLO 1966

Mike Condello was born in New York, but his folks moved to Phoenix, Arizona. He took a real interest in music and guitar and by 14 he was writing music and had a band called The King's Four. He looked older than he really was and hung out at Jack Curtis' teenage nightclub Stage 7 where he eventually became part of the house band there. Mike and his band became The Stage 7 Combo and they ventured out to other clubs in the valley and wound up on a local kid's show called Wallace and Ladmo.

This was a zany comedy hour that has been compared to Monty Python for kids. Mike starred as Commodore Condello and was in several parody bands (Hubb Kapp and the Wheels, Commodore Condello's Salt River Navy Band, The Ladmo Trio). As Hubb Kapp and the Wheels they put out a single called *Let's Really Hear It b/w Work, Work* that got a lot of local radio airplay and went to number one on the Phoenix charts. The success of this song garnered interest from some big wigs in Los Angeles.

The band wore fake wigs, long eyelashes and eyebrows. The same costumes and make up they used for Wallace and Ladmo gave them a bit of an alien presence. This is noteworthy, as Vincent Furnier credits them as inspiration for him and his Cortez High School buddies to form The Earwigs, The Spiders, The Nazz and eventual superstardom as Alice Cooper. Hubb Kapp and the Wheels traveled to LA and were showcased on the *Steve Allen* and *Joey Bishop* TV shows. They also played The Whiskey-Au-Go-Go on the strip. They dressed for a comedy show, but LA didn't get the joke. They chose to wear the ridiculous garments, but had to be serious musicians, so they told LA to stuff it.

The band broke up, but Mike stayed on with Wallace and Ladmo as a musician and musical director. He was a well-respected session artist in the Phoenix area and put together Condello. Sessions for an album occurred at Audio Recorders located on 7th Street in Phoenix, Arizona. The session band was Mike Condello (guitar, vocals, keyboards, celeste), Bill Spooner (guitar, vocals), Ray Trainer (bass, flute, keyboards) and Dennis Kenmore (drums). Some consider the album entitled *Phase-1* a psych masterpiece and it certainly deserves the title. There are obvious flower-pop influences, with great harmonies, some slight special effects, great psychedelic and chiming guitar. The band Wildweeds with an edge comes to mind with some songs rivaling The Chad and Jeremy LP *Of Cabbages and Kings*.

It was a one-off production as Mike kept with his steady job and continued playing the club circuit as well. He released a couple more EPs as Commodore Condello's Salt River Navy Band, then formed Last Fridays Fire and released three singles for Lee Hazelwood's LHI Record Label *The Lady Barber b/w Rose Colored Corner, I Can't Help The Way I Feel b/w What Is She Thinking Of* and *Something's Happening b/w Stand Up* and *Shout.*

Later in the mid to late 70's he formed Elton Duck with Michael Steele (bass, vocals), Michael McFaden (lead guitar, vocals) and Andy Robinson (drums, vocals). They recorded a full LP at Rumbo Studios in Canoga Park near the Simi Valley in California. A deal with Arista records was in the works for release, but Clive Davis, owner of the label, baled on them for unknown reasons. Elton Duck played clubs in the greater LA area like The Troubadour, Madame Wong's West and Club 88 but eventually fell apart. The self-titled Elton Duck LP was released on CD in very limited quantity circa 2012 and sounded like the band Be Bop Deluxe.

Michael Steele the (bass) player with Elton Duck, was formerly with the Runaways, she wound up as Micki Steele and played with The Bangles.

Bill Spooner helped to form The Tubes with Fee Waybill and had a long career with them for over 20 years.

Ray Trainer played with Jackie DeShannon and joined The Tubes for quite a while.

Dennis Kenmore went on to the band Pollution for two LPs, was with The Goose Creek Symphony for a while and then had a long stay with John Stewart. He got into Real Estate and worked for Century City Mortgage. During the off hours he was a drug and alcohol counselor.

Mike Condello's influences in the Phoenix area are legendary. In California between playing in bands, he produced several other bands over a few years, but nobody saw the severe depression that hovered over him. Sadly, he took his own life in 1995.

ABCS - 729
STEREO
COTTONWOOD
camaraderie

COTTONWOOD 1971

The five members of Cottonwood were Gary Rowles (lead guitar, vocals), Doug Phillips (lead vocals, rhythm guitar), Rick Allan (drums, vocals), Dave Farrell (bass) and Dave Weyer (keyboards, vocals, equipment special effects). Doug was the principal song writer. The band began to coalesce in Los Angeles in the spring of 1970 with the chance meeting of Doug and Gary.

Gary happened to be the son of Jimmie Rowles, an influential jazz pianist, who recorded with all the big names of the day (Stan Getz, Herbie Mann, John Coltrane, Ella Fitzgerald, Billie Holiday and others), recording numerous albums from the 50's into the late 80's. Carrying on his father's legacy, Gary had been busy himself, touring with Dewey Martin and the New Buffalo Springfield before joining Arthur Lee in the reformed Love lineup and recording the LP *Out There*. Touring took them to Europe where they met up with and played backing tracks for Jimi Hendrix at the Olympic Studio sessions. A snippet of these sessions was released by Love & Jimi Hendrix as *The Blue Thumb Acetate,* on 8-track tape only, occurring on St Patrick's Day of 1970.

Gary, Arthur Lee and the band returned to Los Angeles three days later and began recording the album, *False Start* which was released in December of that year. One of the songs from the aforementioned Hendrix sessions, *The Everlasting First* was included on the LP. The album did not sell well however and Gary had long since grown weary of Arthur and his drug problems. After the tours with John Mayall and the Bluesbreakers and Love, Gary was longing for a musical venture where he was more than just a guitar-slinger for hire. After returning from England, Gary met Doug Phillips and brought him over to Dave Weyer's Hollywood house for an afternoon jam session. A few days later, Doug introduced him to Eddie Tuduri, a popular session drummer from the Valley and the nucleus of an original group was formed.

Doug Phillips had been the lead singer in a band called The Dartells and had enjoyed a rather remarkable hit single in 1963 with *Hot Pastrami b/w Dartell Stomp*. Doug was also anxious to get involved with an all original country rock band and seeing Gary's talents at producing and arranging, began to picture the nascent group in his own mind. Doug, Gary and Eddie were soon together at Eddie's Matilija Street house working out arrangements and looking for a bass player. Matilija Street was also known as Musician's Street, after the many recording artists who were living there.

Rick Allan had formerly been the drummer for The Dartells and had recently been playing for the Illinois Speed Press. Boston native Dave Ferrell had been in a popular East Coast band called Roger Pace and the Pacemakers but had moved out to California looking for opportunities and a new start in life. He landed a gig in Lead Bottom, later joining Illinois Speed Press with Rick Allan, over which time the two became best friends. When Doug called Rick to inquire about a bass player for his yet-unnamed new band, Rick recommended Dave Farrell. The Speed Press was disintegrating into individual elements, one of which (Paul Cotton) became a member of Poco. Rick Allan introduced Dave Farrell to Doug, Gary and Eddie, filling out the band roster.

Dave Weyer was an amp builder and an electronics expert at West Coast Organ and Amp Service who had formerly been the keyboard player in a band called The Beauregard Mansion. He was the amp and effects doctor for Jimi Hendrix, Neil Young and many other guitar Gods of the day, working partly from a rented old Hollywood mansion located on Hemet Place in Laurel Canyon, next door to another rented Tudor style house used by The Turtles and later The Flying Burrito Bothers. The police were often seen at Dave's Hollywood digs checking up on extremely loud guitar sounds emanating from the shop area. Many notable musicians would stop by to try out an amp or gadget he had made and would often participate in highly experimental jam sessions, sometimes into the late hours. Dave had built some special effects for Gary's vintage Strat guitar, so they knew each other quite well, so well in fact that Dave was eventually persuaded to join the yet-to-be-named band, on keyboards.

Three of the guys were married or spoken for; Dave and Eddie were hanging loose at the time, but trouble was brewing just ahead and it had nothing to do with girls. Eddie was kicked out of the band by Doug Phillips in favor of Rick Allan and a long deep wound inflicted which would have lasting consequences for the group. A troubled no-name band would re-form with Doug, Gary, Dave Farrell, Rick Allan and future member Dave Weyer waiting in the wings.

Relationships improved with the addition of Dave Weyer to the group. In the meantime, a break took Doug to Oregon to retrieve his wife Darla and her children. While traveling across northern California on the way down to Los Angeles, Darla had gotten to thinking about the camaraderie of the new members of the group. Staring out the window she saw one of those green town signs on which she read, Cottonwood; she put Cottonwood and Camaraderie together, accidentally naming the band and their first ABC Dunhill record.

Dave Mancini owned Devonshire Studios in North Hollywood and through the efforts of young engineer and mutual acquaintance Duane Scott, did front studio time for the original band to record some songs. Although that project would go nowhere, Dave remained open to the boys, knowing that Doug Phillips was thick with Harvey Bruce, A&R man for Dunhill/ABC records.

The backstory of the formation of the group through the tragic dismissal of Eddie Tuduri is its own novella. Rick Allan, then current drummer for Illinois Speed Press, was looking at the end times for his band. Doug had known and loved Rick for many years, secretly hoping he would become his drummer again one day, but strangely, after all the excitement and energy over his newly formed band, had never felt any loyalty or musical gravity to Eddie, the very drummer he had introduced to Gary only weeks before. Gary, it should be said, was extremely fond of Eddie and his straight-ahead rock style, even going so far as to write tunes around Eddie's grooves.

Upon hearing The Speed Press had dissolved Doug asked Rick to join Cottonwood. Troubling times for Rick, because he knew Eddie was well established and had already recorded four songs with the group. Doug told Rick he would handle it and promptly fired Eddie. Devastated, Eddie called Gary, who told Eddie he had not been informed in any way about the change. Gary, as might be expected, blew a cork and left for Oregon. Cottonwood ended momentarily and Dave Mancini was left with worthless material and some serious doubts about the band. Doug would later erase the material and record it over with Rick as drummer. The unreleased song *Concentrated, Liberated Being* has survived.

A couple of months later Jim Guercio called Rick out of the blue to see what had been happening since the breakup of Illinois Speed Press. Rick told him about Cottonwood and sparked his interest. Jim sponsored the group to an all-expenses-paid trip to Mammoth Hot Springs for writing, rehearsal and potential album tracks. Doug scrambled to get Gary back who was still very reluctant and Rick was even more apprehensive because of the circumstances surrounding Eddie's dismissal. Even though back in the flesh, Gary was distant in spirit and the band wasted nearly six weeks at Mammoth getting stoned and goofing off, barely finishing three songs. Highly dissatisfied (especially Gary) with their progress, they called Jim Guercio out from New York for a listen anyway. He wasn't pleased. Expecting music more along the lines of top chart band Chicago, or at least something solid and well-rehearsed, he flew back to New York slightly miffed over his colossal waste of money. He and Rick have never spoken since.

So, Cottonwood looked up Dave Mancini one more time, hoping he would forgive them for their misadventures. As reluctant as he was, he still enjoyed Doug's writing and thought he heard something in those tunes that might sell. He fronted studio time that would give the band a chance to produce five new tunes and a call to ABC Records would help bring the bosses out for a listen, the second time around with Jay Lasker himself, CEO of ABC Dunhill Records. It was the third tune, *Holdin' On*, that clinched the deal and that song did indeed become the preferred single for the radio stations, well played and giving the band a definite shot at superstardom.

The band knew that Dave Weyer had been a builder and lover of pipe organs, so when Gary Rowles came to recording his closing hymn *Mother Earth* for the album, he arranged with Doug to have a session booked at Lorin Whitney Recording Studios in Glendale California so Dave could add an organ part. The studio housed a beautiful Robert Morton theater pipe organ which had once lived at the Fox Theater in Redwood City. The organ had since been used for accompaniment on Lorin Whitney's Haven of Rest Christian radio programs and had also made dozens of records with famous theater organists of the day such as Don Baker, one of Dave's favorites.

The sixteen track tapes were brought over from Devonshire Studios and spooled onto Whitney's machine and the session began. As Dave played, the band tripped around inside the pipe organ chambers looking and listening to the incredible instrument, a pipe organ experience neither of them had ever seen or felt so intimately. Several tries were made at inventing a suitable organ part for Gary's song, but before a good take had been officially recorded, the session was over and the band had to pack up. When the tapes were played back at Devonshire

Studios, the Organ was not in tune with the rest of the instruments, so the most in-tune sounding part had to be used. It surely wasn't the best take and Dave didn't want it to go on the record, but time had run out. A re-recorded organ part did not make it onto the album.

Whitney Studios was an extremely popular destination for Christian groups; bands like The Xanadu's, The Acid Test and Stone Garden recorded there, but most notorious of these was the religious psych band Fraction. Of the secular rock bands who used the organ, Lee Michaels was probably the most famous, with his 1971 hit *Do You Know What I Mean* and the song *Spare Change* from his *Recital* LP. The studio building was curiously constructed to resemble a boat, complete with a moat around the periphery and the bands who recorded there had to walk over a ramp to get across the water and inside.

With the first album completed and several songs already partly recorded for the second album, the band began to drift apart and rehearsals slowed down to a crawl. The Cottonwood *Camaraderie* album had been released in late spring of '71 and the long grind toward bookings and touring began. To introduce their new bands for 1971, ABC Dunhill threw a big party at the Grand Ballroom of Century City Plaza, inviting record people and disk jockeys from all over the country, expecting Cottonwood and their other new bands to appear with their wives or girlfriends on stage for promotion. The new bands posed for pictures on stage while their music was played over the speaker system. Out in the audience, drunken partygoers gorged on their filet mignon with cream sauce, hardly noticing the music but having a seemingly good time.

Another showcase was set up in Manhattan Beach at a place called Cisco's, but this event was deadly serious, putting the band to the live test for several shows and challenging their skills at communicating with real disk jockeys. The record company's idea was to have the band impress the disk jockeys with their musical skills, encourage them to become personal fans and of course, to play their record. The fiasco at Cisco's would be the final straw for the record company, but for now the dream was still alive and the band was preparing.

With Cottonwood's *Camaraderie* out in the marketplace and the single *Holding On b/w Mother Earth* promoted heavily on KRLA radio, holding up well against established names and other new artists, the band became more confident. The album is a real grower musically, with obvious signs of later Love influences, Glory Road similarities and a countrified Joe Walsh feel. With wonderful three and four-part harmonies, wavering vocals, echoes with high-strung psychedelic guitar, some special effects and Dave's piano and organ parts. The album cover depicts the band tripping around the hills at Big Sur with a decidedly party-going atmosphere, long hair blowing in the breeze and apparent rediscovery of the earth's wonders at their feet.

The boys are seen on the album cover jumping over a chained-off gate on a country lane, supposedly "coming down from the sky" as the lyrics from the song *Cottonwood* detail, with Doug on the left, then Dave Weyer, Rick, Dave Farrell and Gary in the hat on the far right. Some magic mushrooms powered the trek through the hills and tangled brush. As a result, there were some serious cases of poison oak blistering the next day. The band played about 50 gigs, if that, mostly in the San Fernando Valley clubs like The Brass Ring and The Sundance Saloon. It's said that The Eagles absorbed some influence for their four-part vocal harmonies because of attending a couple of the Cottonwood shows.

So, the shows were happening and the drugs were happening. Apart from Gary, the band members were all ingesting various quantities of LSD, PCP, Nepalese hashish, Colombian weed, mushrooms, plenty of Quaaludes and of course, the big 'H', smack. Doug and Dave Farrell had all the signs of an addiction problem, particularly regarding smack and would manifest it painfully for the rest of the band by disappearing into darkened rooms for an entire day or more. For the moment though, despite the obvious trouble brewing, the band was riding high on the drugs and the advance money from the record company and had graduated to rock festivals, peppering them with long, blues-oriented jamming. During a Jane Fonda rally in Granada Hills, Gary Rowles, hearing the dark drug blues influence begin to take over the soul of the band, unplugged and walked off the stage, telling the rest of the band he was through with musical bummers and that he had suffered enough of the same old drug laden paranoid dark BS he had seen with Arthur Lee and Love. Playing gigs without the true musical arranger of the group was a wake-up call for the rest of the Cottonwood band members and worries grew over the upcoming showcase at Cisco's.

It wasn't long after this affair that Darla kicked Doug out of her house on Burnett St, furious over his waste of the entire record company advance on drugs and his inappropriate sexual behavior with her two oldest daughters. Knowing of no other place where they could easily move in with available girls, Doug and Dave Weyer moved to Venice, Ca. where Doug hooked up with a hippie girl named Patty and Dave moved in with an ex-nun named Tori. The second album was slowly filling in and the buzz about the band was good. Dave Mancini had fronted enough time for three songs, Dave Weyer's *If I Die*, Dave Ferrell's *You Know How It Is* and Doug and Gary's *The Blue and The Grey*. Gary did not rejoin the band until *The Blue and The Grey* was recorded and did not appear on the other two tunes. But the showcase at Cisco's was coming up and the band wanted to be ready.

Dave and Doug grabbed a couple of Quaaludes at Psychedelic Mary's apartment the morning of the show, but Doug took off for Patty's around noon and told Dave he'd be back at 4:00 pm. During the ensuing hours, Dave packed up his piano system and Doug's gear and waited. With plenty of time to get to Cisco's there seemed to be little worry, but by 4 PM and no sign of Doug, the nervousness set in. After numbers of frantic phone calls to anyone who might know where Patty lived, Dave finally gave up and drove to Cisco's, knowing he would face both the band and Harvey Bruce from the record company, with the worst possible news.

Doug had OD'd at Patty's place on a cocktail of downers and was completely oblivious of the showcase. He didn't die, but nobody saw him for a day or so. After all the promotion of Cottonwood, ABC representative Harvey Bruce went ballistic, skewering the dumbstruck band members with numerous expletives. He showcased his backup band, Hamilton, Joe Frank & Reynolds, instead and that was the end of the Dunhill relationship for Cottonwood. Doug blew it and secretly the other members knew why; it wasn't an accident. Gary, Rick and Dave Ferrell decided to leave, breaking the band up for good.

Gary Rowles continued his career by joining Richard Torrence and Eureka, making three albums and touring the world. His talents have also graced Flo and Eddie albums and numerous individual sessions. After a spiritual awakening he moved to Corvallis, Oregon and set up Wake Robin Recording. He is now owner operator of Audio

Media Services in Lebanon, Oregon. Playing on and off for the past 30 years with Chuck Holst, the duo frequents two places in Corvallis, Bombs Away Café and Imagine Coffee House.

Dave Weyer went on with his own musical creations, hooking up with Eddie Tuduri and David Vaccaro for a project called *Land Of Goshen*, an animated special about growing up spiritually, complete with LSD characters remembered from the psychedelic experience and another project with Eddie, Gerry McGee and Larry Taylor, a Cajun rock blues album featuring Delaney and Bonnie as guest artists. He continues to build amps and effects in his electronics building, plays and edits music and is actively involved with The Jimi Hendrix Foundation of America as a historical consultant on Jimi's gear and as a designer of new equipment for the Jimi 69 Corporation. He lives with his loving and beautiful partner Olivia west of Billings, Montana.

Rick Allan lives in Santa Cruz California with his wife Juanette and communicates regularly with the remaining band members. He loves playing tennis and winters in Arizona to enjoy his game. Although as of this writing, both Darla and Nancy are gone, Rick stays in close touch with Lori and the rest of Darla's family and keeps up with Nancy's children.

Surprisingly, Eddie Tuduri did well after the Cottonwood fiasco. He recorded many albums as featured drummer on at least one album by bands like Boxer, Wah-Koo, Jim Messina, Pink Lady and many others, eventually forming a foundation dedicated to using drumming and rhythm to heal trauma and various forms of brain disconnection. He is doing well and living in Southern California.

Dave Farrell never overcame his addiction and died of alcohol poisoning in his car. Dave was the first to go.

Doug Phillips fared little better, catching the HIV virus from a contaminated needle in Reno, Nevada.

Rick Allan, Dave Weyer and Darla, found an 80 lb. Doug Phillips withering away in a hospital bed in Reno, Nevada sometime in 1995 and gave him both their blessings and forgiveness. He was completely overjoyed to see them and burst into tears. Enthusiastic as ever to start a new musical group, he begged to come to Montana with Dave.

Unfortunately, even though he did manage to leave the hospital in Reno, he only made it as far as a nursing home in the Ventura County area, never recovering from AIDS and dying in 1996 from its complications.

The Cottonwood Camaraderie experience is a testament to Doug Phillips' profound dual nature, his amazing musical levitation and his category five self-destructive storm. No one in the group, however, was deprived of their own self-realization through Doug's tortured betrayals, even though at the time it seemed a monumental waste of career opportunities and heartfelt loyalties. What can one possibly conclude from the retrospective other than that Doug Phillips was an inadvertently sagacious personal teacher, whose classes were hard and lessons were deep. The sum and substance of Cottonwood should be and is much more than an aching review of Doug's troubling character traits and personal suffering, but even despite the wonderful musical developments, lifelong loving and supportive relationships and individual post-Cottonwood achievements of every band member, the Cottonwood *Camaraderie* story always seemed to start and end with Doug.

BAD MANORS · CROWBAR

CROWBAR
CROWBAR
lbs
100
HEAVY
DUTY
CROWBAR
CROWBAR

Crowbar
Epic
KE32746

CROWBAR 1970-74

The start of Crowbar begins with Ronnie Hawkins who was a huge draw in Canada. He is now known as the Granddaddy of Canadian Rock as he launched many Canadian artists on to international stardom. Domenic Troiano, Roy Buchanan, David Foster and Skylark, Larry Gowan now of Styx, actress Beverly D'Angelo and David Clayton Thomas with Blood, Sweat and Tears all got their starts with this man. Ronnie's former backup band included Robbie Robertson, Richard Manuel, Rick Danko, Levon Helm and Garth Hudson. As The Hawks they had just left to pursue greener pastures and eventual stardom as The Band.

Richard Newell (aka King Biscuit Boy), a vocalist and harp player, had been playing on and off with Ronnie Hawkins and was asked to put together another band to replace those who had just departed. So, he and Rick Bell (keyboards) were responsible for the formation of a new backup band. The players included Rhéal Lanthier on (guitar), Roly Greenway (bass), Blake Fordham (aka Kelly Jay) (vocals, piano), Richard Newell (vocals, blues harp), Richard Bell (keyboards), John "The Getto" Gibbard (guitar) and Larry Atamaniuk (drums). They all had a history with previous bands playing clubs around Ontario, Canada. Hawkins' new band began rehearsing at a building located at Ronnie's residence in the Streetsville suburb of Mississauga, Ontario near Toronto. They formally called themselves "And Many Others" a term Ronnie came up with (as in) Ronnie Hawkins and Many Others.

They played several venues around Toronto and with Ronnie Hawkins they opened for the likes of Mountain, Lee Michaels and Joe Cocker's Mad Dogs and Englishmen at the Fillmore East in the States. On the road their stage shows were wild and it must have gotten to Ronnie. He was a bit of a drunk, he was controlling and very unpredictable. During a gig in Hamilton, Ontario, Ronnie fired the band over an argument that developed regarding the band's pay. In a later interview, he was quoted as saying: "They were so crazy that they could fuck up a crowbar in about *ten* seconds!" They left Ronnie Hawkins, adopted their befitting new name as Crowbar and settled into a big mansion on 25 acres of land in Ancaster, Ontario. The house and acreage was appropriately nicknamed Bad Manors where they rehearsed and had some hellacious parties.

As Crowbar, they backed "King Biscuit Boy" for a successful album called *Official Music*. But Richard Newell was a blues guy who felt the band was too rock 'n roll for him so he went solo. Richard Bell left the band to join Janis Joplin and Full Tilt Boogie, Larry Atamaniuk joined Sea Train with Peter Rowan and Andy Kulberg. He was replaced with Sonnie Bernardi on (drums, percussion) and they replaced Rick Bell with Jozef Chirowski (piano, organ, keyboards). Kelly Jay took over lead vocals and all the other players could sing as well.

The album *Bad Manors* was recorded at Toronto Sound Studios located at 14 Overlea Blvd in Toronto and generated the hit single *Oh! What a Feeling b/w Murder In The First Degree.* The A side song over the years has become a national rock anthem in Canada. They were featured at The Whiskey A Go-Go in Los Angeles, but the song was banned from radio airplay in the USA because of perceived drug connotations. This spelled death for the band in the US marketplace. A real shame because the actual inspiration for the song was about all the good things happening in the year 1969. John Lennon and Yoko Ono had their "Bed-In for Peace" at The Hilton in NY, the world witnessed Buzz Aldrin and Neil Armstrong landing on the Moon, and over half a million people joined together in peace and love without incident at Woodstock, a concert for the ages. It was just another summer of love.

The *Bad Manors* album was an adaptation of Boogie hits redone or written that just flat cooked. With the heavy dual guitars and howling vocals by Kelly Jay, if you didn't tap your foot, you were either Deaf or Dead. The album got high ratings in Canada and in Europe. Margaret Trudeau was the wife of Pierre Trudeau, who was then Prime Minister, and she adopted the band as personal favorites of Canada. They played a few dates as part of his 1972 re-election campaign.

Pierre loved the Canadian rock artists and wanted them to get some recognition. A Maple Music Junket was set up to market and promote Canadian music artists. They flew in nearly 100 critics and promoters to Montreal and Toronto from the UK, USA and Europe for a four-day excursion to recording studios, lunches, press conferences and a topper each night of a concert featuring several Canadian bands on stage. The artists involved were unknown to the rest of the world at that time. Bands like The Stampeders, Mashmakhan, The Guess Who, Lighthouse, April Wine and Fludd all played a part with Crowbar headlining the final concert evening at Massey Hall in Toronto.

It was grueling for the audience and the fans, but Crowbar put on one heck of a show pulling all the stops. Kelly was a big strong guy. During one of the songs, he appeared to be a giant, walking around the stage with both The Getto on his shoulders and Roly in his arms blazing on their guitars. It was incredible and this one show made their career.

Crowbar is notable in history as the inspiration for legislation that was initiated requiring one third of radio airplay in Canada to consist of a Canadian artist. There was a lot of reluctance by the national radio stations to do this, but Trudeau wanted to be sure that Canadian musicians got a distinct advantage for recognition. In the long run it paid off. Bands like Alanis Morrisette, Rush, April Wine, Blue Rodeo, Sarah McLachlan, Loverboy, Men Without Hats, Nickelback and The Tragically Hip all owe some debt to becoming world famous through this law which is still on the books today.

Crowbar had released 4 albums with *Official Music, Bad Manors, Heavy Duty* and *Larger Than Life*. But musically as a rock and early blues band, the last studio LP *KE32746* on Epic records was their magnum opus. They had met many top artists of the day including John Lennon who was recording at the same studio where the sessions occurred. Recorded at The Record Plant in NY, the Epic label had brought in a high production team and the band was proud of their work. Kelly's powerful vocals shined with several well thought out ballads. This is an album full of wonderful songs approaching the planets of the band Klaatu. The last song on the record is entitled *Nothing Lasts Forever*, a significant final goodbye. Alas, they needed a high-profile manager and backing to put them up and over the top. Ultimately it was mismanagement that did them in.

Richard Newell sadly moved on in 2003 due to long abuse of alcohol.

Keyboardist Josef Chirowski joined Alice Cooper and Peter Gabriel and toured the world.

Roly Greenway played with several bands before and after Crowbar. He found stability playing for TV commercials and movie soundtracks.

Rhéal Lanthier was born in Quebec and had played in too many bands to mention. He moved back to Quebec in the 90's but passed away in March 2020.

John "The Getto" Gibbard did well enough to retire early and write his own music. He guested with bands periodically over the years.

Kelly Jay continued the legacy of Crowbar playing gigs at small clubs near and around Hamilton where he lived. Towards the end hard times and health problems set in and he sadly crossed over July of 2019.

Sonnie Bernardi became a session drummer and has played with such well known bands as The Guess Who, Shooter and David Wilcox. He is president of a successful firm Bernardi Consulting and Show Services Ltd. that sets up and coordinates major shows, concerts, events and music festivals in and around Toronto. He currently heads the www.CrowbarCanada.com website.

Three of the original members Roly Greenway, John Gibbard and Sonnie Bernardi are keeping the band alive playing shows now and again with other players.

PAS — 5016
Paramount Records
CROWFOOT
IN GOD WE TRUST
1970

CROWFOOT
ABCS 745
FIND THE SUN

CROWFOOT 1970-71

Russell DaShiell grew up in Hawaii. His dad, Daniel Harrison DaShiell, was a radio electronics engineer and had several patents in the early stages of tape recording. Russ picked up the guitar at an early age and took to it right away. He and his folks moved to Melbourne, Florida and he joined a rock band. They played at the Melbourne Beach Casino and other venues. As a band they were two guitars, drums and a lead singer.

Russ eventually took over on vocals and as a three-piece band they were playing a new club called The Sugar Shack. One night a bass player from another band (Doug Killmer) overheard Russ singing and playing and asked if he would like to join their band (The Sonics). Russ agreed and he and Doug meshed very well. So, well in fact, that they both decided to depart The Sonics and found the best drummer in the area, Rick Jaeger, to help them form a new band. Rick was with a band called The Rogues who were popular in the Satellite Beach area. He and Mike Melby both decided to leave and join Russ and Doug.

Rick suggested the band name should be The Beau Gentry. So, the initial band included Russell DaShiell (guitar, vocals), Mike Melby (guitar, vocals), Doug Killmer (bass, vocals) and Rick Jaeger (drums). They spent a year playing the beach clubs around Melbourne and college fraternity gigs in central Florida from Orlando to Clearwater. Beatles cover tunes were the theme of each night. Problems occurred within the band and Mike left because of irreconcilable differences. Lance Massey then joined in on (guitar, keyboards, vocals) as his replacement.

Rick suddenly left the band and moved to Wisconsin. They wanted to hire Bobby Caldwell from the band Noah's Arc in his place, but he was underage for the clubs they were playing at, so they hired John Cox instead to fill the void left by Rick's departure. (note: Bobby Caldwell played with Johnny Winter and Rick Derringer, joined Keith Relf with Armageddon, played with Iron Butterfly for the Metamorphosis LP and went on to form Captain Beyond). The Beau Gentry continued to play local gigs.

Meanwhile Rick Jaeger had found representation with Ken Adamany up in Wisconsin and asked Russell if he and the guys would like to come up north. Ken was involved with several bands and later became the man behind

Cheap Trick. They agreed and traveled north to Wisconsin to play the clubs up there for the summer. The Beau Gentry found a big fan base in Wisconsin. Ken promoted them at clubs around the Midwest states. By the end of summer Rick Jaeger rejoined Russell and Doug with Lance and the band decided to set up permanent residence there.

After a year went by, they grew tired of playing cover tunes and broke apart. Doug Killmer headed west to the new evolving scene in San Francisco. Meanwhile back in Wisconsin, Russell (guitar) and Rick (drums) merged with The Wylde Heard members Bill Sutton (bass) and Jim Croegart (keyboards) to form The Masque. But the band didn't last long as Doug asked Russ and Rick to come out and join him out near San Francisco. Lance stayed behind to form the band Fat Water. With the three original band members together again, they were writing their own music and at Doug's suggestion they became Crowfoot.

Rehearsals for the new band, a trio, occurred in the basement of the house they shared with A. B. Skhy, another Wisconsin band that had relocated to the west coast. Doug landed a spot with Erik Jacobsen, Lovin Spoonful's producer, and a project he was working on. Erik was looking for a lead guitarist and Doug suggested Russell. They wound up backing Norman Greenbaum, formerly of Dr. Wests Medicine Show and Junk Band, on his latest album and his soon to be #1 hit single *Spirit in the Sky b/w Milk Cow*. Norman had a fuzz box used for the droning buzz chords throughout the song, but its Russell's guitar licks that you hear in the solo and the song's fade out.

Several months before *Spirit in the Sky* was released Doug moved back to Wisconsin. Rick had joined A. B. Skhy in the studio and helped to record their second album release. Russell was then offered a solo record deal to record at Wally Heider's Studio located on Hyde St. in San Francisco. Other notable recordings for such LPs as *Volunteers* by The Jefferson Airplane, *Déjà Vu* by Crosby Stills Nash and Young, *American Beauty* by The Grateful Dead, *Electric Warrior* by T. Rex and many others were recorded here. Basically, it was Russell who wrote, arranged, produced, sang and played guitar, keyboards and bass. Rick Jaeger joined in on drums. The only other session guy was Jack Cassidy from The Jefferson Airplane who only played on the song *California Rock 'n' Roll* that was later released as the A side to a single from the sessions.

During this time Norman Greenbaum's *Spirit in the Sky b/w Milk Cow* single started gaining momentum on the charts. So, Russ called Doug back and they joined Norman's band on tour all over the country backing The Doors, Chicago, Iron Butterfly, Spirit, Grand Funk Railroad and others and played Dick Clark's *American Bandstand* on TV. The song hit the big time nationally. It was then that Russell was offered a record deal with Paramount records. The previous sessions were complete and processed. The self-titled *Crowfoot* album was released and distributed to the marketplace and has a great Crosby, Stills, Nash & Young feel about it. Nice harmonies and heavy guitar riffs.

The album cover picture of the Indian was the first noted record album cover to be painted by Ruby Mazur who went on to become in high demand in the 70's and 80's for his LP cover artwork. He was the actual designer of the Tongue and Mouth logo that became world famous for the Rolling Stones. The New York Times had initially credited John Pasche with the design but it was later corrected and Ruby became the noted creator of the insignia.

The first album was complete and Russell needed a band to support the record release. The tour band was Russell DaShiell (guitar, vocals, keyboards), Sam McCue (formerly with the Everly Brothers) (guitar, vocals), Bill Sutton who was a former member of The Masque on (bass) and Rick Jaeger on (drums). They played clubs on the LA strip, most notably The Whiskey Au Go-Go, and traveled back to Milwaukee, Wisconsin to open for The Allman Brothers Band on September 4th and 5th 1970 at The Scene. Located in the old Antlers Hotel at 624 North 2nd St, this was an acoustically perfect ballroom which featured some of the hottest acts of the era like Jimi Hendrix, Miles Davis, Love, The Mothers of Invention, SRC, Steppenwolf and others.

A year later and with the help of Sam (guitar), Bill (bass) and Don Francisco who had been with Atlee Yeager on (drums) one more album *Find the Sun* was recorded back at Wally Heider Studios and released on the ABC Dunhill label. But the band as it was split up shortly afterwards.

Don Francisco teamed up with his buddy Michael Stevens from Atlee Yeager and formed the hard rock 3-piece band Highway Robbery. He was with Linda Ronstadt and Andrew Gold then wound up with Danny Douma and the wonderful band Wha-Koo for three albums. Most of the songs from this band just bring tears of joy. Don Francisco left us in 1998.

Doug Killmer remained as a session bassist in San Francisco until his passing in 2005. He was bassist on recordings with Mike Bloomfield, David LaFlamme of Its a Beautiful Day and Commander Cody.

Rick Jaeger was permanent drummer for Dave Mason in the studio and on the road. He spent the next 30 years with him and played as a mainstay session drummer. He also starred with Tim Weisberg for several LPs and later was with The BoDeans. He died in 2000 from liver cancer.

Russell DaShiell migrated to the Hollywood Hills of Los Angeles and was featured on and off with Creedence Clearwater Revival and solo projects over the years. He toured with Tom Fogerty and members of Creedence Clearwater. This band evolved into The Don Harrison band for 2 albums. He built a 24-track studio in Malibu, Ca. then went solo and released his own album with the help of Doug Clifford and Stu Cook (of Creedence) called *Elevator*. He had many studio projects during the 80's and reformed Crowfoot with Doug Killmer and Rick Jaeger for an EP called *Messenger* in 1994. Extremely rare, this was only available from Russell DaShiell himself. It was never formerly released to the marketplace for distribution. Moving back to his roots in Hawaii he stayed there for a while before finally settling down in California.

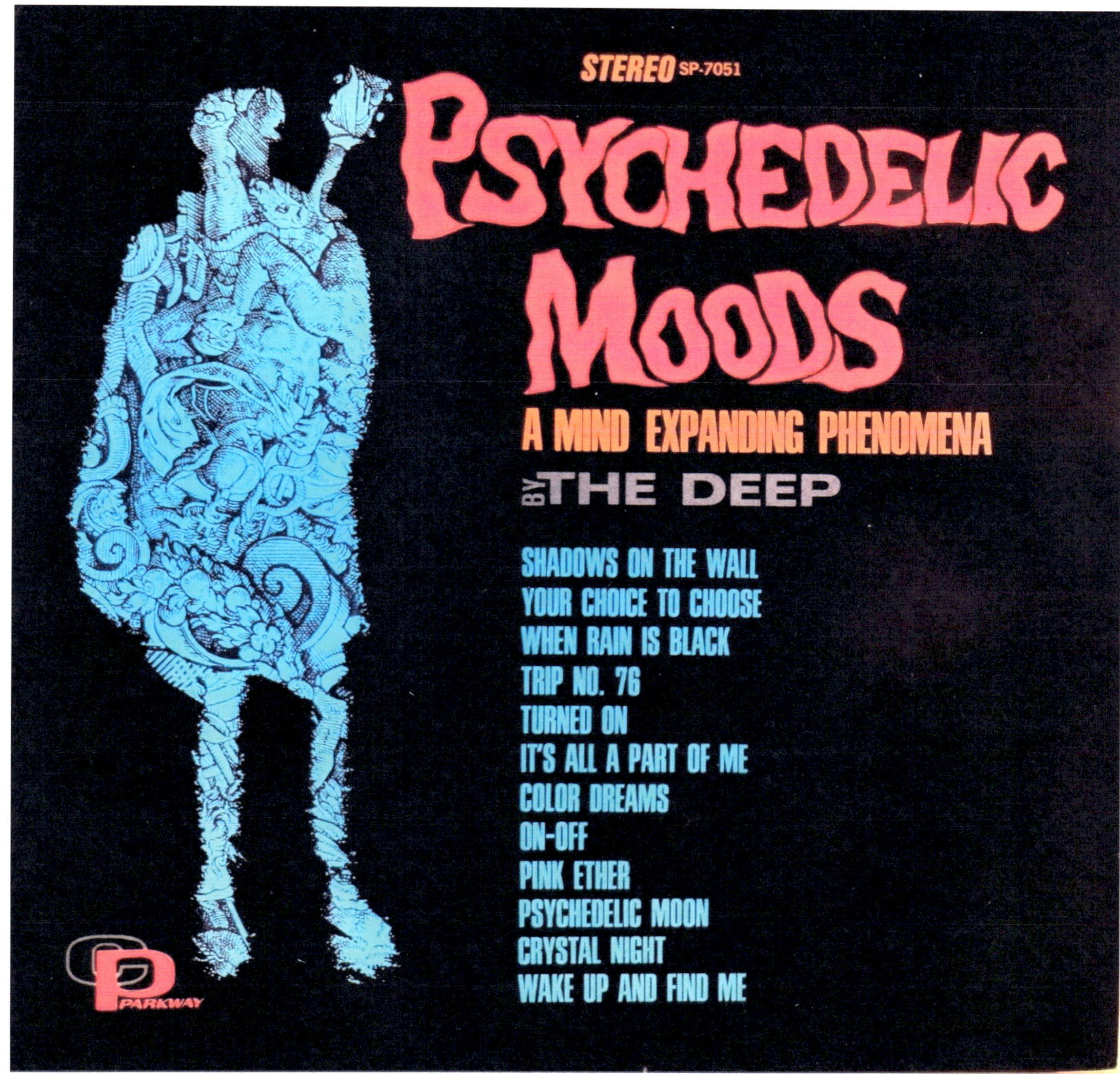
STEREO SP-7051
PSYCHEDELIC
MOODS
A MIND EXPANDING PHENOMENA
BY THE DEEP
SHADOWS ON THE WALL
YOUR CHOICE TO CHOOSE
WHEN RAIN IS BLACK
TRIP NO. 76
TURNED ON
IT'S ALL A PART OF ME
COLOR DREAMS
ON-OFF
PINK ETHER
PSYCHEDELIC MOON
CRYSTAL NIGHT
WAKE UP AND FIND ME
PARKWAY

STEREO
CS 9456
STEREO
"360 SOUND"
CL 2656
COLUMBIA
PSYCHEDELIC
PSOUL
THE
FREAK
SCENE

THE DEEP/THE FREAK SCENE 1966-67

Rusty Evans (Marcus Uzilvesky) was born and raised in New York City. His early influences are unknown, but after graduating from the School of Art and Design he picked up a Martin guitar and penned some country tunes. He formed a band as Rusty Evans and his Rock-A-Billys and then peddled some songs to the Brill Building and got signed to the Brunswick Record label. A single was made *When I'm Alone With You b/w I Lived, I Loved and Lost*. Playing several dance clubs and sock hops, his Rock-A-Billy sound found a way to Greenwich Village where he jammed with Fred Neil and a yet unknown Bob Dylan. By 1965 he had released four singles and three LPs, *Songs Of Our Land, Let 'Er Roll* and *Showdown!* on the Mount Vernon Music label as a folk and Rock-A-Billy artist.

He traveled to LA for a short while and there he experimented with LSD and the psychedelic scene. He then joined The New Christy Minstrels. But he grew tired of Los Angeles, packed up and moved back to New York.

He hired Mark Barkan, a producer most notable for writing the #1 song *Pretty Flamingo,* later covered by several artists, and had a vision to record an album that would highlight a psychedelic sight and sound experience. Gathering known players and session musicians, he and Mark each hired a player they knew who dropped acid with hopes that these folks could generate their personal insight of the experience into music. Rusty knew David Richard Blackhurst who had taken many acid trips and Mark had an army friend named Lenny Pogan.

They traveled to Cameo Parkway Studios located at 309 Broad Street in Philadelphia, which 2 years later became Sigma Sound Studios, and laid down the tracks for Parkway Records as any normal band would. Echoes, chimes, bells, vibraphone, Theremin, and an RCA Etherphone were all added with primitive special studio effects. There were recordings of actual sex between one of the session players and his girlfriend with voiceovers and a general weirdness that was overdubbed to liken a sound similar to The Fugs or The Godz. It got so weird for the unnamed session drummer he left the studio upon completion and didn't return. An album called *Psychedelic Moods: A Mind-Expanding Phenomena* was recorded crediting the music to a band that Rusty called The Deep.

Other than Rusty Evans the actual musicians were shrouded in mystery. It was only years later that the players were identified as Rusty Evans (guitar, lead vocals), David Bromberg (bass, guitar, vocals), Caroline Blue (vocals), Lenny Pogan (guitars, flute), Richie Rome (keyboards), David Richard Blackhurst (recorder, vibraphone), Arthur Geller (guitar, percussion) and several other unnamed studio session players.

The LP cover illustration was designed by Rusty and is credited as the first use of the word "Psychedelic" as a descriptive meaning for music. It was on the market a month before the 13th Floor Elevators and their *Psychedelic Sounds* album or the Blues Magoos LP *Psychedelic Lollipop*. They did not play live and there were apparently several versions of songs and effects recorded at the sessions, enough to fill more than one LP. No singles were released and there were no promotional gigs. They all went back to their respective session work.

During the following year, Rusty got involved with the one and only recording session by a band called The Third Bardo penning or helping to write six songs for the band. They released one single officially, *I'm Five Years Ahead of My Time b/w Rainbow Life* which some say is a psychedelic masterpiece.

Rusty continued his freaky sounds again with former members of the The Deep, David Bromberg, Lenny Pogan, Arthur Geller and David Blackhurst with David Rubinson in production. He added Victoria Pike, who was with him in The Third Bardo sessions on harmony vocals. This time he named the band The Freak Scene and recorded an album called *Psychedelic Psoul*. Another in studio band release, this time recorded at Columbia Recording Studios (Studio E) located at 49 East 52nd St in New York, it was a continuation of the strange and odd sounds found on The Deep album with Rusty writing all the material. Pictured on the LP cover left to right is Rusty Evans, David Bromberg, Victoria Pike, Lenny Pogan and Arthur Geller.

This album is much more cohesive with a much more sophisticated sound. The beefy bass comes out with added sitar effect (although no real sitars were used) and echoes for more consistent psychedelia than the earlier effort. Many more studio effects were involved. No club dates were set up for this album either, but it did get quite a bit of FM underground radio airplay. After completion, the players all departed and went their separate ways.

David Blackhurst and Arthur Geller have disappeared, with their whereabouts unknown.

Victoria Pike was a session vocalist for several bands both before and after The Freak Scene well into the 80's.

Caroline Blue continued as a vocalist, but there are no other records crediting her as such.

Lenny Pogan was a session guitarist and had a 40-year career mostly playing theatre shows and played both on and off Broadway in New York.

Mark Barkan was a New York producer and an avid songwriter. He was the musical director for *The Banana Splits Adventure Hour* that aired on TV for two years. Along with Richie Adams, Mark helped write the tunes for that show. He departed us in May 2020.

David Rubinson was most notable for representing Herbie Hancock, The Pointer Sisters, Taj Mahal and Santana. He also won a best documentary film award for *Suguhara: Conspiracy Of Kindness* circa the year 2000.

David Bromberg went on as a session musician and has released at least 20 albums. He toured all over the world with his David Bromberg Big Band but has officially retired. He also has the largest known collection of American fiddles in North America and owned a violin and fiddle repair business in the state of Delaware.

Rusty recorded a third album in 1970. He reverted to his given name of Marcus Uzilvesky and released another album simply called *Marcus* on the Kinetic record label. The LP was more of a mellow folk effort with minor psych overtones, flute, orchestration with Rusty's quivering voice. Again, a studio band was used but with no apparent involvement from any of the previous musicians. However, he did play some live gigs of note for promotion and admittedly opened for the Grateful Dead at one place where Jerry Garcia complimented him on his songs.

He then quit the music business for about 10 years concentrating on painting and design and became quite successful nationally developing paintings of what he called *Linear Landscapes*. In 1979 he returned to music and refocused back to his country, folk and Rock-a-Billy sounds of the past. He formed a band called Ring of Fire reviving Elvis' songs. Sadly, he found his maker in December 2015 due to heart failure.

STEREO/E 30224
design
EPIC
STEREO

64653
EPIC
Stereo
design
Free Inside Lyrics & Colouring Card
tomorrow is so far away

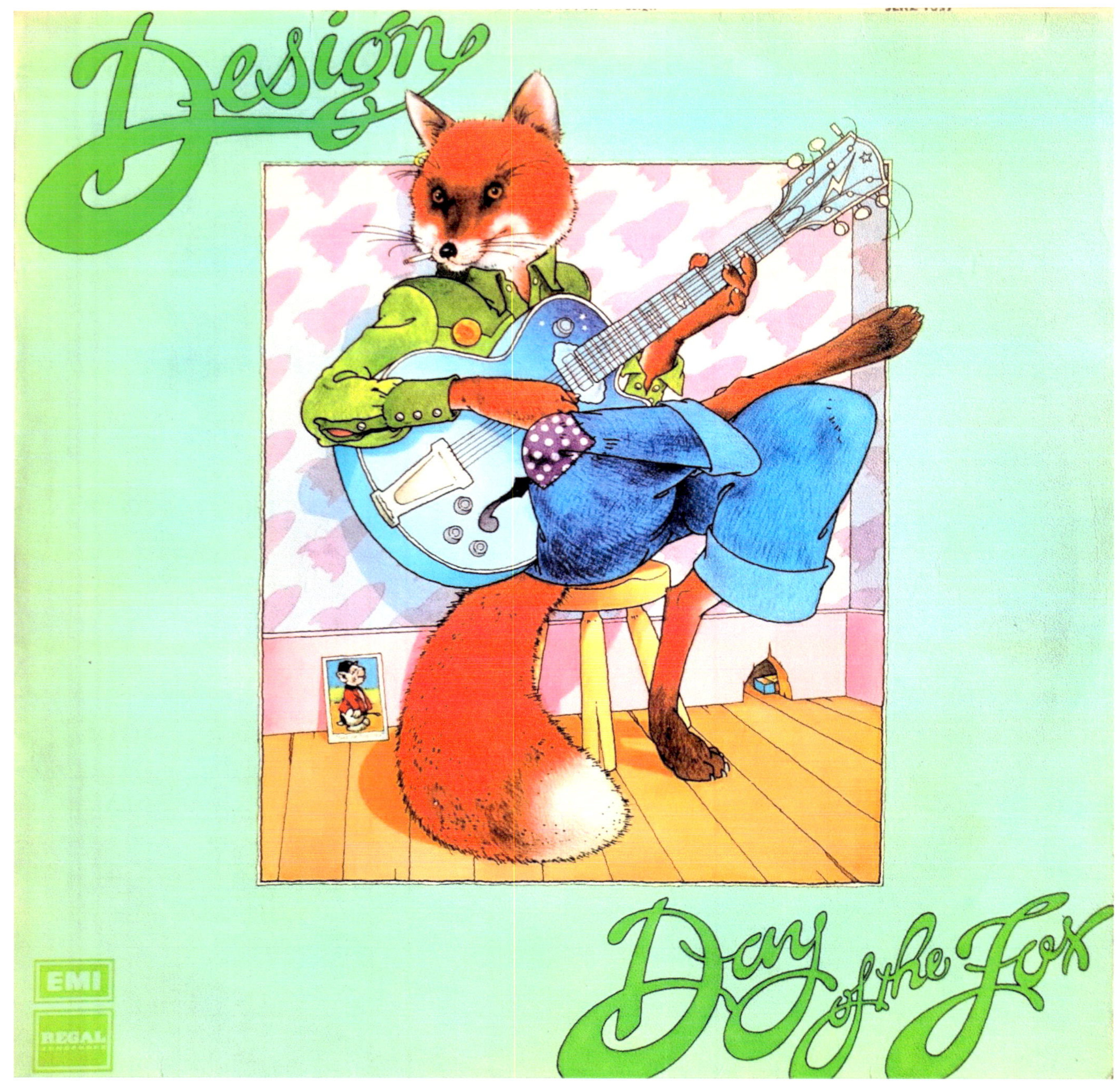
Design
Day of the Fox
EMI
REGAL

DESIGN 1969-76

Tony Smith was born in Cambridge, England about 50 miles north of London. He spent a good portion of his early life traveling abroad with his family as his Dad was in the military. He became a song writer and started a vocal group with Gabrielle Field and Kathy Manuelle who were childhood friends. They had gone through school together and had been with another vocal group called The Stevettes. He had a friend Barry Johnston who was also a singer songwriter and was involved with Apple Records. A recording session was set up involving Tony (vocals, guitar), Barry Johnston (vocals), the girls (vocals) and two guys from The Free Expression, John Mulcahy-Morgan (vocals) and Geoff Ramseyer (vocals). The sessions went well and they decided to form as a band.

The first rehearsals were at Tony's flat, but as they all had day jobs and lived far apart, the decision was made to find a place and live together. Located at Earl's Court near Chelsea, they found a basement flat where they could rehearse more often. Tony knew Peter Gallen who engineered for Lansdowne Studios in Holland Park where many famous bands recorded including Colosseum, Uriah Heep. Marianne Faithful, The Strawbs and Queen. Peter convinced Adrian Kerridge, who was head of the studio, to have a listen to Tony's band and he was delighted to sign them to a recording contract.

But problems arose right away as they only vocalized in six-part harmony with Tony's twelve-string guitar as the only instrument. The vocal style filled the gaps where instruments were used. So, for recording, they had to lay down all the vocal harmonies first and then instruments were added afterward. This was completely opposite to how it was normally done. They began singing for BBC radio and put the finishing touches to their first album.

It was unusual to break an English band in the USA, but it was decided to do just that. The album tapes got to Larry Cohn at EPIC Records and after hearing the first three songs, he gave them a $25,000 advance and a two-album record deal. The album deal and radio shows became lucrative, so they all quit their day jobs. Lead guitarist from the band Free Expression, Jeff Matthews, was hired to fill out their sound. They did a few TV shows, but still had not played before a live audience. The single *Willowed Stream b/w Coloured Mile* had been released in the states to positive reviews, but the album was still sitting in limbo.

The US rep (Alan Frey) told them that they had to perform live before the album could be released in the states. He set them up on a US tour of army bases and a NATO tour of gigs in Germany and Italy. Meanwhile Tony had suffered an ulcer and ruptured hernia and really could not perform. But he did play in Germany while sitting in bandages. The audience was not receptive to the band or their music. The US tour didn't happen and the album would not be released until the band could promote it on the road. The UK album release wouldn't happen until the US album release occurred.

Tony wound up quitting for health problems and the band was on the verge of collapse. But Geoff Ramseyer pulled them together and they found a manager. The first self-titled album *Design* was finally released in the US albeit a year later and with Tony gone. They showcased on more radio and television shows in the UK, but never got that one hit they were seeking. Overall, the critics liked them, but they were up against Led Zeppelin and ACDC as competition for climbing any charts. Vocal groups like The Mamas and Papas, The Seekers and The Fifth Dimension were diminishing as chart toppers.

They continued to promote themselves on radio and TV, becoming the most televised band in Britain. Then Gabrielle gave them a month and said she was leaving to get married. The band was in shock. They didn't even know the guy. When she left Geoff Ramseyer also said goodbye.

In all Design were part of over 150 radio shows and more than 50 TV shows. They released 5 wonderful albums with *Design, Tomorrow Is So Far Away, Day Of The Fox, In Flight* and *By Design* with several singles over their 8-year career. Those involved on tour and with the recording sessions included Chris Speeding (guitars), Clem Cattini (drums), Herbie Flowers (bass) and Alan Hawkshaw (organ), but they weren't credited as official band members. On the later albums, they show signs of ABBA and Steeleye Span. Every song is wonderful through and through. Eventually they fell apart.

Tony Smith wound up living in France and has recorded a few songs.

Jeff Matthews married and became a quantity surveyor and worked on several big building projects in the UK.

Gabrielle's marriage didn't work out, but she became Gabrielle Shootingstar and along with her new husband had five children and performed as a family band for over twenty years.

Kathy Manuelle partnered up with Dave Goodman former producer of The Sex Pistols. They moved to Malta and recorded ambient music as the Internet Café Orchestra. Successful as producer's, they established their own record label and owned a studio until Dave's sudden death in 2005. Kathy now works with a band called Mandala Malta.

After Geoff Ramseyer left the band, he only survived 6 months and died suddenly at the early age of 25 years.

John Mulcahy-Morgan moved to India on a spiritual quest. He worked for the Siddha Yoga Global Community for 6 years and this is where he met his wife. They moved to the United States in 1990 where they got into lighting and design.

Barry Johnston became the manager of The New Seekers when they reformed. He DJ'd the morning radio show on KLOA in Los Angeles for a while, but then moved back to England where he worked for the BBC. He has since authored several books and developed Barn Productions where more than 100 audio books have been released.

CL 2664
COLUMBIA
The Devil's Anvil
Hard Rock From the Middle East

THE DEVIL'S ANVIL 1967

Elierzar Adoram was already a well-known and established folk musician playing the folk circuit in Greenwich Village. He was from Israel and grew up living with his Mother and brother in The Kibbutz which was basically a Utopian Community. His father was in the British Army and was rarely around. Elierzar's interest was initially in theatre as an actor. He studied acting at the Habima Theatre in Tel Aviv, Israel where directors from the US would come to direct shows. After his dad got out of the military, he wanted to move the family elsewhere.

Elierzar was granted a scholarship to and graduated from The Neighborhood Playhouse School of Theatre in New York and studied at The Mannes School of Music. Already a multi-instrumentalist with accordion being his primary instrument his interest had changed from acting to music and he began playing traditional dance songs, Israeli shepherd songs and performed with a band called The Halutzim that released two LPs in the late 50's or early 60's *Canti E Danze Di Israele* and *Hava Nagila*. Then he worked with The Players of the Arie Theatre, a dance troupe, that played all over the US and Canada and ventured down into South America as well. He was always involved with traditional and Hasidic folk songs and artists.

By the mid to late 60's he and his band found themselves in New York playing the club scene in Greenwich Village. One place they played called Café Feejon on MacDougall Street was a coffee house that featured folk personalities like Ritchie Havens, John Sebastian and others. Felix Pappalardi frequented the place and fell in love with the eastern influences and strange rhythms of this band that was playing. They sang in the Arabic, Greek, Turkish and Hebrew languages and were a band far different than those who were experimenting with Eastern music at the time. The band used original instruments like oud, bouzouki, tamboura and durbeki (darbuka – drum instrument).

The band members on stage were Elierzar Adoram (accordion, vocals), Steve Knight (bass, bouzouki, vocals), Jerry Sappir (lead guitar, vocals) and Kareem Issaq (oud, vocals). Felix saw a vision and was inspired to incorporate this sound into a rock format. He wound up as a participant of the band trading guitar and bass licks with Steve Knight and as Devil's Anvil, they became the house band for the club.

Felix had the reputation as a studio wizard. He used his influence to sign the band to Columbia records and got them studio time at CBS Studio B located at 49 E 52nd St. in New York to record an album. The addition of Bobby Gregg on (drums), farfisa organ and echoed guitar added a real psychedelic effect to their sound. Musically, they are an intoxicating band, tabbed as Middle East Rock with a hard-core dance beat predating the acid-techno-dance bands like Joi and Spiritualized by 30 years. The best comparison goes to maybe The Monks and Kaleidoscope (US). The cover of the LP pictures from left to right Elierzar Adoram, Jerry Sappir, Kareem Issaq and Steve Knight.

After the album called *Hard Rock From The Middle East* was completed, Felix and the band members shopped it around the New York radio stations, hoping for some interest and airplay. But, on the day of the albums official release, the Six-Day War broke out between Saudi Arabia and Israel. It didn't help that Kareem Issaq was pictured on the cover in full Arabic dress and hijab at the time. Politics and prejudice really dampened the album's chances of any significant distribution and the radio stations wouldn't touch it. The album found its way directly to the cutout bins. One rare single was put out *Karkadon b/w Hala Laya* from the LP but it went nowhere.

Kareem Issaq moved to Las Vegas and performed with various showcases provided for entertainment at different casinos in the area. He backed the well-known Loretta St. John and the long running feature at several casinos called Nymphs of the Nile in Las Vegas and Laughlin. He passed away in June 2014.

Jerry Sappir joined a folk band called The Trade Winds that released one traditional worldly folk song LP called *Around The World with…* on the BT Puppy label in 1970. This band played clubs in Greenwich Village.

Steve Knight played keyboards with the band Wings and joined Felix Pappalardi, Corky Lang and Leslie West to form the band Mountain to enormous success. He succumbed to Parkinson's disease in 2013.

Felix Pappalardi was a wizard on bass guitar but was more known for his production skills in the studio. He was accidentally shot by his wife, Gail Collins, in 1983.

Elierzar Adoram had a long musical career and was a revered musician in Israel before he retired. He died of natural causes in Tucson, Arizona in 2000. He was only 69 years old.

EKS-74016
STEREO
EARTH OPERA
ALSO PLAYABLE ON MONO PHONOGRAPHS

EKS-74038
STEREO, also playable on mono phonographs
THE GREAT AMERICAN EAGLE TRAGEDY
EARTH OPERA

EARTH OPERA 1968-69

Peter Rowan started out in Massachusetts as a Rock-a-Billy singer in the late 50's with his band The Cupids. They played dances for the Christian Youth Organization (CYO) in the basements of Catholic Church's in Boston. By the early 60's he was influenced by Eric Von Schmidt and Joan Baez and put his electric guitar away, trading it in for an acoustic blues guitar. Huddie Ledbetter, otherwise known as Leadbelly, became his model along with Josh White and Lightning Hopkins. The Leadbelly song *In the Pines* became the touchstone for Peter. When he heard Bill Monroe's rendition of the song, he saw a connection between bluegrass music and the blues. He began learning Bill Monroe's music by listening to records and hearing The Lilly Brothers at the Hillbilly Ranch in Boston.

He started playing mandolin and singing tenor with Bill Keith and Jim Rooney, playing as The Keith and Rooney Band at Club 47 on Mt. Auburn St. Joe Val mentored Peter in traditional bluegrass harmony singing. They formed a duo as Joe and Pete and played clubs in Boston. When Bill Monroe came to town as a solo artist, Bill Keith put a backing band together that included Peter on guitar. After this, he was hired by Bill Monroe as a lead vocalist and guitar player. He and Bill co-wrote songs together including *The Walls of Time* that became a bluegrass standard. He was part of The Bluegrass Boys for almost four years and toured all over the country.

Peter left Bill Monroe in 1968. He returned to Cambridge, Massachusetts and teamed up with David Grisman. They had originally met in Union Grove, North Carolina. David had been a (mandolin) player with The Even Dozen Jug Band, a Jim Kweskin type band that included John Sebastian, Maria D'Amoto (Muldaur) and Steve Katz, all of whom became famous. Peter and Dave were both stalwart bluegrass musicians known amongst many and at the top of their game. When they decided to form the new band, the intention was to promote a bluegrass theme. It was just the two of them initially and they were playing simple tunes in the folk clubs. They shopped some original songs around to the record companies, but the executives were all caught up in the psychedelic trend and were uninterested. With all the experimentation in music during the times it behooved them to put together a real band and explore this new territory.

They rented a place in Allston-Brighton, Massachusetts and began auditioning players they felt would fit their vision of a band. Strictly word of mouth but several players came and went until they had the right mix. John Nagy came in on (bass) and Bill Stevenson on (keyboards) from Toronto. He was a tremendous help because he was able to arrange the music into a rock type format. Peter and David were getting into Indian music, Avant Guarde and Free Jazz. They began playing saxophones because of some influences from John Coltrane, practiced and got the songs down. Several drummers auditioned but none of them were the right fit. The name Earth Opera was something going around in Peter's head at the time. Voices heard all over the world were protesting the war. Earth Opera was a depiction ere the thoughts of all those people protesting in unison during the time of Vietnam. The music was quite different but was perfect for underground FM radio.

David Grisman knew Peter Siegel who was a producer for Nonesuch Records, an affiliate of Elektra Records and he hooked them up with Jack Holzman who signed them to the label. The full band included Peter Rowan (guitar, vocals), David Grisman (mandolin, mandocello), Bill Stevenson (piano, organ, harpsichord, vibraphone) and John Nagy (bass). They didn't have an official drummer so both Warren Smith and Billy Mundi, fresh from The Mothers of Invention, were brought in to play (drums) for the sessions that occurred at A&R Studios on the fourth floor of Mogall's Film and TV building located at 112 West 48th and at CBS Studio B at 49 East 52nd, both located in New York.

Musically the self-titled album *Earth Opera* approaches another Boston band The Freeborne at times. There was no bluegrass sound, but all the guys were experienced professionals. The recording had a lot of piano, harpsichord, special effects, mysterious sounds, fuzz and electric mandolin. It all had an infectious weirdness. Peter wrote all the songs and he must have had some odd dreams as the lyrics are very "Pearls Before Swine" like. When you listen to the music, you're not quite sure at first but then you hear a real enlightening sound and understand. One single was released from this album that was only available in Europe, *Close Your Eyes and Shut The Door b/w Dreamless*. The album sold well in Europe and there was some local airplay. Earth Opera was played frequently on the FM stations cropping up around the country.

Paul Dillon came aboard as permanent (drummer) for the band. Their album release showcase was at Steve Paul's Scene in New York and they opened for the Jeff Beck Group with Rod Stewart on vocals. They didn't have great management but got a particularly complimentary review from Jon Landau who later produced or managed famous groups including Bruce Springsteen. He worked for Crawdaddy Magazine stating that Earth Opera was like "New England Gothic" and likened Peter's lyrics to that of romantic novelist Nathaniel Hawthorne. Earth Opera was teamed up opening for The Doors. Peter Rowan and Jim Morrison were both avid poets and both bands were sponsored by Elektra Records, so it made sense that they were paired together. The Doors were just starting out, so Jim Morrison at this point was focused and serious. They played the local venues while The Doors were in town and branched out to other larger venues like The Westbury Music Fair in New York, The Boston Tea Party in Boston, The Merriweather Pavilion in Columbia, MD, The New Penelope in Montreal, The C.N.E. Coliseum in Toronto, The Cincinnati Music Hall, The Electric Theatre in Chicago and others.

Although the first LP didn't sell that well, the label believed in them enough and a second album was put together. Bill Stevenson left the band. Back at A&R Studios the basic band was Peter (guitar, vocals), David (mandolin, vocals), John Nagy (bass) and Paul Dillon (drums). Included was John Cale (viola, fiddle), Dave Horowitz (piano, organ) with Jack Bonus (horns) and Richard Grando (sax, flute, recorder). Also included was Peter's old friend Bill Keith on (pedal steel guitar). Somewhat different from the first album. Peter and David showed their heavy bluegrass roots and rock with a more rural sound, absent on the first album. There were lots of anti-Vietnam war connotations. The title song from the second LP called *The Great American Eagle Tragedy* became an anthem at anti-war rallies in the Boston Cambridge area and there was one single that approached the AM top 100, *Home to You b/w Alfie Finney* that gave the band some notice.

The single got them some promotion and they booked a national tour through the Agency for Performing Arts (APA) in New York. Traveling from the east coast to the west they played venues and clubs starting at The Boston Tea Party in Boston, The Electric Factory in Philadelphia, The Grande Ballroom in Detroit and The Electric Theatre in Chicago. They spent a week in Montreal playing the New Penelope, then to The Black Dome in Cincinnati. All the disturbance and anti-war demonstrations going on driving from city to city throughout the country began to take their toll. It didn't help that they were all on the road wedged into a small van. Peter refers to it as "The Riots and Burning Cities Tour." Finally making it to the west coast they were exhausted. They were paired up with the band West for two nights in May 1969 at The Golden Bear in Huntington Beach, California. Returning home, they managed two shows at The Main Point in Byrn Mawr, Pennsylvania in early October before falling apart for good.

Most of the players returned to the session work that they were familiar with. Pete and Dave decided to pursue their original roots music style.

David Grisman stayed behind in California and hooked up with Peter's brothers Chris and Lorin Rowan. He found a new sound in jazzified mandolin and started his own band The David Grisman Quartet. His services as a mandolin player was and still is in high regard with too many album credits to list.

John Nagy got into the stable side of music, producing bands. He still lives in New England.

Paul Dillon became a studio session musician for bands in both New York and California. He moved back to Philadelphia and got into painting art and portraits. Unfortunately, he left us in Sept 2018.

Bill Stevenson was originally from Canada, he moved back to Ottawa and was involved with an early version of the band Heaven's Radio and has appeared with John Lee Hooker, Amos Garrett, Tom Swift, Colleen Peterson, Hot Toddy and others. The last 40 years has garnered him awards for his works as a Jazz and Blues keyboardist. He also had a weekly national syndicated radio show for CBC.

Peter Rowan was in Nashville and got a call from Richard Greene, former friend and Bluegrass Boys member, to join Sea Train with former member of The Blues Project Andy Kulberg. This band was rock and bluegrass. He joined Jerry Garcia, Vassar Clements and David Grisman for a project called Old and in the Way and then came full circle with players from his past and formed Muleskinner with himself (guitar, vocals), David (mandolin), Clarence White (guitar, vocals), Richard Greene (violin, vocals) and Bill Keith (banjo). He joined his brothers Chris and Lorin performing as The Rowans and they released three LPs on the Asylum label. Peter Rowan has had an extensive career in bluegrass music and is well respected all over the world.

EAST
Capitol

EAST 1972

Aman Ryusuke Seto and Gen Morita were from Tokyo, Japan and were classmates in Middle School during the early 60's. They formed a band called The Four Frogs. Their sound emulated that of another popular band called The Foy Brothers. They were very much into the folk sound of The Kingston Trio and played small clubs where the influential music critic Hiroyuki Takayama recognized them.

He got them a record deal with Polydor, but the band changed their name to The New Frontiers. After the record was released, they began to get more popular and started playing Junior Jamborees and Student Festival Concerts in Tokyo, they were also booked on TV Shows and their songs were played on the radio. In all, four New Frontiers LPs were released *New Frontiers, Jentle On My Mind, Re-Union Live* and *The New Frontiers Sing The Kingston Trio* were released in Japan only and they played many shows at US Military Camps located in the area.

Ryusuke decided that he wanted to attend College in the USA, so he went to New York and then asked the other members to join him there. It was early 1964 and The New Frontiers came to the USA, played shows in New Jersey and it went very well. They got some real confidence and thought they might be able to make a living playing music in the USA. But then Ed Sullivan debuted The Beatles on his variety show. It changed history and bands like The New Frontiers could not compete with the new sound and music of the British Invasion.

They all went back to Japan to finish College. The days were long with class and studies during the day, but they still played clubs after hours. The long hours were tough, but The New Frontiers were still immensely popular and Ryusuke and Gen still had the passion to continue. Members changed over the next few years and so did their sound, which went from traditional folk to more of a Beatle's influence. But playing music in Japan did not satisfy their dream of being a world contender. They needed to go back to America to give themselves a chance.

A demo tape was made and sent to several different US labels where they had hoped to land a US record deal. Ken Nagano heard the demos. He lived in California and convinced a radio personality working at a station in San Jose that they should invite The New Frontiers to the USA. They got a temporary (6 month) U.S. VISA to stay in the US.

So, Aman Ryusuke (aka Ruese) Seto (guitar, piano), Gen Morita (vocals, traditional instruments, guitar), Noboru Asahi (bass), Tadahide Yoshikawa (traditional instruments, guitar) and Fumio Adachi (drums) traveled to the US and settled in the town of Milpitas, California on the outskirts of San Jose. Ken Nagano became their Manager and Booking Agent and they began playing local clubs.

The unusual sound of traditional Japanese instruments, guitars and drums made a significant impact on a lot of people. The psychedelic scene was still present in the Bay area and their sound fit right in. Their big event was a one week stay at The Boarding House on the campus of the University of San Francisco. The buzz was on about this band and they didn't disappoint. The San Francisco Examiner gave them a very favorable review. After this they were asked to play at The Troubadour on Santa Monica Blvd which is where acts like Carly Simon, James Taylor and Tom Waits frequented. This was a showcase for the band to impress an assortment of record label representatives. A bidding war took place and Capitol Records offered them the US record deal they were looking for. They were eager to sign just to get notice in America.

The New Frontiers name was changed to Light from The East which was simply shortened to East. The self-titled album *East* was recorded at Crystal Studios located at 1014 Vine St in Hollywood and then released. What evolves is a genuine uniqueness in sound that compares favorably to Stone Country but influences of Arthur Lee and Love is also heard. A wonderful band. Capitol kept them busy with shows on the West Coast, but they overlooked their VISAs and they didn't get extended. They were extremely popular in Hawaii and had a single *Beautiful Morning b/w Black Hearted Woman* in the top 10 at the major radio station there. When they arrived to play some shows in Honolulu, they were surrounded by fans, but they were delayed by immigration officials who told them that their US VISAs had run out and they had to return to Japan.

Ruese Seto and Gen Morita were that close to attaining their dream and it all ended abruptly.

They all went back to Japan and East dissolved.

Noboru Asahi did not continue as a musician.

Tadahide Yoshikawa (alias Chuei Yoshikawa) returned to Japan and played as a session musician for various artists remaining in music as a producer, arranger and composer. He has collaborated as a respected guitar player with several bands and has released over twenty solo LPs including five instrumental LPs in the 1990's with his band R.E.M. Swimming Club. Chuei is a national treasure in Japan with a Sears SJ-R Chuei Yoshikawa Model guitar named after him as well as the Honkane Shuzo Sake brewery naming a certain blended bottle of alcohol as *Sake Chuei*.

Fumio Adachi became a studio drummer and joined Chuei Yoshikawa for his second studio album entitled *Street Corner.* He also played drums for Akiko Asuge and her album release *Hello Mickey!*

Gen Morita became a holistic healer, promoted organic foods and got famous for his environmental stands against converting forests into Golf Courses. He formed the Global Anti-Golf Movement (GAGM) represented in 10 different countries. He and his wife Yumi Kikuchi also developed The Harmonics Life Center and they traveled the world giving concerts and promoting the cause.

Ruese Seto started writing solo material and built a studio on the coast of Japan in the town of Hayama. He has released six solo albums over the years, produced and recorded other local bands. He records and produces music that his daughter Hanayo writes and has released a few albums (CDs) by her.

Eastfield Meadows
VMC
RECORDS
VS 133
Cover by Sunshine Lake
STEREO

STEREO
INTENSITY
EASTFIELD MEADOWS
VMC
RECORDS
VS133
TREBLE
BASS
REVERB

EASTFIELD MEADOWS 1968

Dwight Payne and Wayne Grajeda developed a friendship while attending Santa Monica College located near Venice, California and the famous Muscle Beach. Dwight was a singer and, soon to be, drummer who formed a band called The More playing church socials. Wayne joined the band although he had never sung in public. Jim Whittemore played guitar and was an accomplished singer and song writer in a band called The Luved Ones. He was already playing the college and party circuit. The two bands crossed paths and got to know each other. Jim folded his other band and after The More called it quits, he wound up joining Dwight and Wayne. They auditioned players and found John Bierer and Dave Carpenter to complete the lineup.

The official members were Wayne Grajeda (vocals, harp, guitar), Jim Whittemore (guitar, piano, organ, vocals), Dave Carpenter (bass, vocals), John Bierer (6 &12 string guitar) and Dwight Payne (drums, vocals). The influential bands were The Beatles, The Buffalo Springfield and The Byrds. It was Dave Carpenter who came up with the band name Eastfield Meadows. Dwight was dating the daughter of Wendell Corey who was a famous actor in the 40's and 50's with A-list films and top Hollywood stars. As former president of the Academy of Motion Picture Arts and Sciences and having had a bid in for the US Congress, he took a real liking to Dwight and the band and they practiced in the basement of his mansion. They were all seasoned musicians and a steady stable of weekly gigs occurred at special events, college dances, the teenage fair at the Hollywood Palladium, The Mirage and others.

Tony Harris saw them and became their manager. A record deal was signed with Steve Vail's Vance Music Corporation otherwise known as the VMC Record Label. Because Tony had been involved with production of The Limeliters and their current LP *Time To Gather Seeds*, he set them up at a studio facility inside the home of Alex Hassilev a former member of that famed folk band. Many songs were composed by Jim and Wayne as they assembled here up in the Hollywood Hills. They completed the final sessions for an album at Hollywood Sound Recorders located at 6367 Selma Ave in Los Angeles. Session musicians included Mike Botts who was the drummer for Bread and Kent Henry who played guitar with bands Pacific Ocean, Genesis (LA) and later Blues Image.

In the brief period at the end of the 60's it was the album cover art that sold many of these unknown bands from distant places. The first rendition for the self-titled *Eastfield Meadows* album cover was the very first "air brush" picture to be designed for an LP. With lots of Pink and Lavender coloring, there was a child like Cowboy with hat in hand stepping over the clouds in a great big valley. Incredibly unique and inventive but the band members saw the picture as childish and thought that it would turn everybody off who had thoughts of purchasing the LP. The band members were dissatisfied with this first of its kind abstract deco art painting and rejected the cover settling for a makeshift quick and dark picture of the studio sound board with knobs & buttons and their faces blended in. In retrospect they realized that this was a mistake.

With three-part harmonies, countrified rock, fuzz guitar and slight special effects the music is reminiscent of The Byrds at times, Michael Nesmith of The Monkees, Yellow Hand and The Buffalo Springfield. Two singles were released from the LP *Silent Night b/w Loves Gone* and *Travelin' Salesman b/w Helpless Is a Feeling*. The song *Silent Night* was their signature tune with great harmonies and fuzz guitar representing more of how they sounded as a live band. This was not the traditional Christmas tune.

Their first gig after the sessions were complete was at Pandora's Box located on a triangular land island at W Sunset Blvd and Crescent Heights Blvd. This place was a big, converted house originally owned by someone who refused a buy-out from the city to give up their home when the roadway came through. It became a coffee house in the late 50's featuring jazz artists before being bought and converted to a teen club by the host of TV's *"Shindig!"* Jimmy O'Neill. Burned down and now gone it is famous for inspiring Frank Zappa to write the song *Plastic People* for The Mothers of Invention and for being the meeting place and start of the Sunset Strip Riots which inspired Steven Stills to write the famous hit song *For What It's Worth* for The Buffalo Springfield.

They branched out to other LA Strip clubs like The Troubadour, The Trip, The Hullabaloo and The Aquarius Theatre which was a bigger concert venue. Never gigging far from the general local area, they were content playing in the clubs each weekend for consistent income. By this time, they had been together for nearly five years and got a terrific rating by the local critics. Things were going well, but the album sales weren't happening as they had hoped.

Dwight felt the band had run its course and realized there was no pot of gold at the end of this rainbow, so he moved on. Chet McKraken, who later went on to play drums for The Doobie Brothers, came in to replace him. Wayne's sister was married to Steve Ihnat, a successful and recognizable film and TV actor. Trekkie fans would know Steve as "Garth of Izar" in the original Star Trek series. He was putting together his first feature film called *Do Not Throw Cushions into the Ring.* Wayne was asked if he could compose a few songs for the movie and he and Jim agreed to do so. They wrote three songs that were also orchestrated as the instrumental soundtrack music throughout the movie. The songs were recorded at Sunset Sound Studios in Hollywood but there was no soundtrack LP released for the movie that was here and gone.

One more non-album single was recorded by the Eastfield Meadows, *Friends of Unequal Parallel b/w Love All Men Can Share* and the band continued to play shows including open air events as far north as San Francisco. A few months passed and the band officially split apart.

Jim Whittemoore had a father who was a well-known architect who designed and built churches all over the Los Angeles area. After the band was done Jim left music and worked with his dad in building and design.

John Bierer did well in the real estate industry.

Dave Carpenter disappeared from music into a stable life elsewhere.

Dwight Payne continued to play in bands on and off throughout his career. He toured with Bobby McFerrin, was involved with the theatre musical *"Always Patsy Cline"* starring a young Sally Struthers and played with blues great Guitar Shorty. He was and still is a respected session drummer for hire that has maintained and prospered playing with many bands for over 50 years.

In November 1970 Wayne Grajeda traveled to Europe, eventually landing in Berlin where he ended up joining a musician's commune called The Hagelberger's. The club scene there was raging and he wrote 100's of songs. Towards the end of the 1970s Wayne returned to LA. and began a lengthy career in television production. In 2002 he returned to Berlin where he played in his own band. Unfortunately, he departed us in September of 2020.

STEREO ABCS-624
EDEN'S CHILDREN
abc
RECORDS

ABCS-652 STEREO
EDEN'S CHILDREN
SURE LOOKS REAL
abc RECORDS

EDEN'S CHILDREN 1966-68

Richard Schamach grew up in Denver, Colorado at a time when rock music was just beginning to be heard on the radio, and he not only wanted to hear it; he wanted to play it! With a rented guitar and basic instruction book, he began learning how to do just that. At age 14, he gave his first guitar performance with a solo version of Duane Eddy's song "*The Lonely One*" at a school talent show.

In the early 60s, Richard was one of a young generation discovering blues and R'n'B on late night broadcasts from WLAC and XERF, a station that featured Wolfman Jack before going commercial. He liked what he heard and began to favor these styles. As a developing player, Freddie King and Lonnie Mack were significant influences, and soon, he joined some like-minded friends at Thomas Jefferson High who had been playing together after school. They became The Chaparrals, with matching outfits, guitars and amps, playing rock, R'n'B and Brit hits. In the already competitive world of teen bands, they were able to play at school dances and make various appearances in the South Denver area.

After graduation, he left for Colorado State University in Fort Collins and joined The Nocturnes, a band that included Dick Whetstone, who formerly played with Rich in The Chaparrals and later played drums and sang for psych-rockers The Electric Prunes. This band played at a club called The Green Onion just off campus. It was in direct competition with The Red Garter, located across the street, as the top collegiate hotspot. The Onion had the distinction of having a stage supported by chains, accessible by ladder only. It was no easy task to load amps, drums, and a Hammond organ up the ladder, but once situated, they became the house band. Fortunate for them, because no one was in a hurry to take that equipment back down again. At this point, the attraction of music was great enough that Rich put college on hold.

The Nocturnes got a summer job in Estes Park, Co., a college resort town, and then got booked at Betty Reilly's A Go-Go in Waikiki, Hawaii. Taking their cue from the way the press had received The Beatles on their arrival in the US the previous year, the Honolulu press was there to greet The Nocturnes and photograph them as they came off the plane. The group's photo then appeared in the newspaper with "The Nocturnes Arrive In Honolulu" in bold print. A TV interview on Good Morning Hawaii announced their presence on the island.

The gigs at Reilly's were played to Army and Navy servicemen who would often square off for some rowdy dust ups but the band played on. The schedule called for performances seven nights a week, and the original two week run was extended as the group continued to be a draw. The island had its charms, but the gig was a grind, and the band was glad to get back to the mainland at the end of the engagement.

Upon returning home to Colorado, Richard met fellow musician Bill Glasser who was looking to put a band together and persuaded him to come out to Boston. Along with his girlfriend and his guitar, he was able to catch a ride with some friends who were conveniently driving straight through to the east coast. The trip to Boston was not a trouble-free one, as, midway through it, the car was broadsided going through an intersection and had to be replaced. Fortunately, there were no injuries. The only immediately available car that fit the budget was a '56 Chevy that they named "The Turtle" due to its inability to exceed 40 mph.

Once in Boston, Rich met up with Bill Glasser and Bill Robar who were roommates in a dormitory at Boston University. They had a friend with a place near the campus where the new arrivals could stay, and with that taken care of, they were able to begin the process of making some music together. All three played guitars and sang, and with drummer Jimmy Sturman and bassist Larry Kiely, they began rehearsing in the basement of the dormitory. Originally playing music by The Stones, The Kinks, The Yardbirds and others, their first gigs were in the dormitory lounge and at recently constructed George Sherman Union which was the student union building on campus. Borrowing from the title of a Stones album, *December's Children*, Bill Glasser came up with the name Eden's Children, and that was the one that stuck.

Their first club gig was at The Rathskeller Club located at 528 Commercial Ave in Boston. This club featured Barry and the Remains who were the leading band in the area. They were the house band here but opened for The Beatles in several cities during their last national tour of the states in 1966. After several months Eden's Children pared down from five pieces to three, with both Bill Glasser and Bill Robar departing. They became a high volume power trio and Richard now went by the moniker of "Sham".

The Boston scene was rife with music and local rock bands like The Lost, Phluph, The Front Page Review, Ill Wind, The Hallucinations (who later became The J Geils Band) and others. There were many smaller clubs where all these bands played including The Unicorn, The Catacombs, The Crosstown Bus and The Psychedelic Supermarket. Eden's Children also played the Ivy League College circuit on the east coast. They were called upon to play in Providence, Rhode Island to substitute for The Cowsills, who were becoming a hit making AM radio pop group. The other group on the bill was The Shades of Blue, a vocal group from Michigan with matching cardigan sweaters. This was an odd pairing of bands, with kids' mouths wide open it was kindred to the unlikely matchup when Hendrix opened shows for The Monkees.

A large venue in the area called The Boston Tea Party would feature bands that had little airplay on the radio prompting a local classical radio station WBCN-FM, through DJ "Mississippi" Harold Wilson, to change its format to "underground music" and spotlight these bands on air. College students were turning away from the AM radio 3-minute ditties and turning on to the experimental psych bands that were so prominent.

Alan Lorber had a vision of Boston becoming the next Hippieville Hotbed in the US based upon all the newsworthy interest thrust upon San Francisco, the Haight Ashbury district and all the rock bands that brought worldwide attention. He was a record label promoter who chose MGM records out of New York to sign as many bands in the area as possible. "The Bosstown Sound" was the name he gave to the project. His strategy was to market the bands native to Boston and promote the psychedelic music scene on the East Coast. But it was a marketing plan that met with music media rebuke.

Several bands were caught up in the storm of signing contracts with Orpheus, The Beacon Street Union and Ultimate Spinach being the first to sign contracts for the MGM record label. However, "Rolling Stone Magazine" planted the seed saying that the Boston bands were pretentious and boring and the underground newspapers released an outburst of protracted controversy. It didn't help that Mike Curb, who was just hired by MGM, was cleaning house of all the bands he felt were promoting drug use through their songs. Any bands on the list, Chamaeleon Church, Phluph, Orpheus, The Beacon Street Union, Puff, Ultimate Spinach, The Front Page Review and Eden's Children were all considered "damaged goods".

Eden's Children chose not to participate in the hype. They were managed by Jonathan Whitcup who arranged for them to record a 4 song demo at RCA Studios on 24th St in New York. He shopped it around and ABC Records took interest. The label had them come over to audition in a small room at their offices on W 66th Street. The record executives had not experienced a loud band of this sort before, but the group was signed to ABC as one of the first hard rock bands on the label.

The studio sessions for the first album started at Columbia Studio B located at 49 E 52nd St in New York with Bob Thiele producing the band. The high volume levels at which Eden's Children were accustomed to playing were something of a challenge to deal with, in the control booth. It turned out that the sessions were not nearly completed in the time allotted, so ABC scheduled them to fly out to California along with Bob Thiele and finish recording. They were set up at United Western Recorders in Hollywood with Eddie Brackett behind the controls. After some adjustments on both sides of the glass, the band's sounds were committed to tape.

The self-titled *Eden's Children* album rocks heavy with psych fuzz guitar, echoing, rotund bass runs and wild drums. Rich plays hard and fast, much like Alvin Lee in the band Ten Years After at times. The softer tunes have intricate guitar runs with overdubbed vocals by Richard, their only voice. The band fits right in with other power trios like Cream, Hendrix, Chariot and Blue Cheer. The only single released was *Goodbye Girl b/w Just Let Go* that made the local charts in the east and the LP made the top 200 on the Billboard and Cashbox charts.

With the album completed, they came back home and opened for Howlin' Wolf at Steve Paul's The Scene. A plethora of who's who folks in rock 'n' roll were there including Mitch Mitchell (The Jimi Hendrix Experience), Jim Capaldi (Traffic), Gene Cornish and Dino Danelli (The Rascals), The Chambers Brothers and more, all to witness the blues legend. During their opening show Jimmy Sturman's hi-hat became disengaged and Mitch came up to make the repairs while they continued to play. After the show, Larry, Sham and Jimmy went across the street with The

Chambers Brothers to have coffee. However, instead of finding a quiet corner for swapping stories, they found plates and cups being thrown around the room by a deranged individual railing against the world. At that point, it seemed there had been enough camaraderie for one night, and they scattered for the exits.

The recording for a second LP occurred at Century Sound Studios on W 52nd in New York. Owner Brooks Arthur was behind the controls and lent a contrasting character to the sound of this recording by plugging the instruments directly into the board, without the use of amplifiers. The result of this production choice was a clean and spacious sound that differed from the heavier sound on the first album but added sonic dimension. Steve Schaeffer engineered the sessions. Final additions for the album *Sure Looks Real* took place at Rudy Van Gelder's Studio in New Jersey. A historic place where many of the early Blue Note Label jazz artists had created legacies. After completing the Van Gelder sessions, the group paid a visit to the Ampeg manufacturing facilities in nearby Linden, NJ ,where they were offered an endorsement deal to promote their amplifiers.

There was little promotion for either LP by the label but the albums were sent out and played all over the country on underground radio. Their support team was Jonathan Whitcup who set up the gigs and co-produced the second album, road manager Jack DiGiovanni and multi-tasker David Glaser would arrange for rental PA's and a van to tour and set up the equipment. They mostly played at small east coast venues, including those in Greenwich Village, within a six state area and the big concert halls The Boston Tea Party and The Electric Factory in Philadelphia opening or headlining for the likes of Bagatelle, The Yardbirds, The Growth, The Rascals, The J. Giles Quintet, The Velvet Underground and others. Interviews occurred during their travels on WBUR radio in Boston, The Ed Baer Show on WMCA radio in New York, with Jazz and Pop magazine in New York, with the Boston Avatar and with Teen Scene Magazine.

The band was kept busy playing clubs and festivals, including the Spring Sing, held on the Boston Common, a park in the central downtown area. This festival was a peaceful cultural meeting of hippies, food, drugs and bands that spotlighted such acts as The Front Page Review, The Third World Raspberry, Tangerine Zoo, The Freeborne, The Colwell Winfield Blues Band and Eden's Children along with the headliner Van Morrison's Controversy. In fact, when

Van came to Boston, he didn't have a band but found some players and when he needed a place to run over some tunes, it was suggested that he use the house where Eden's Children lived and rehearsed in Weston just 20 minutes east of Boston. Sham and the boys were witness to a first-hand private rehearsal from a celebrated rocker. However, when finished, he was gone without a word, taking the entourage along with him.

Another highlight was the Brown University Spring Weekend, sharing the bill with The Rascals, Jimmy Page and the Yardbirds, along with The Shangri-Las and James Brown in front of a crowd of 6000. Soon after this event, Larry Kiely left Eden's Children and bassist Rusty Marcus was brought in to finish the scheduled dates. The band then decided it had run its course and separated.

Original member Bill Glasser moved to Los Angeles and worked for a telecommunications company.

Bill Robar moved to Florida and became a tour boat captain.

Rusty Marcus had a short run with the band but remained a part of the family and operates a commercial lighting company in upper Massachusetts.

Both Larry Kiely and Jimmy Sturman had strokes and were no longer able to continue musically.

Richard Schamach maintained his connection to music and has continued playing guitar and keyboards as Richard Lee. He was briefly associated with the first edition of Edgar Winter's White Trash and The Moonrakers before joining forces with the rock horn band Swallow, who put out two albums in the early 70's. He then disappeared into a variety of local country, rock, 50's and blues bands over the years. Few people knew the history of "Sham", a great guitarist who now lives a good life in Scottsdale, Arizona.

GOOD VIBRATIONS

PLAYABLE ON STEREO & MONO PHONOGRAPHS
5123
ETERNITY'S CHILDREN
tower

ST 6302
PLAYABLE ON STEREO & MONO PHONOGRAPHS
ETERNITY'S CHILDREN/TIMELESS
Capitol
RECORDS
THE
6000
SERIES
EMI

ETERNITY'S CHILDREN 1968

Eternity's Children was made up of members from two popular high school bands in Cleveland, Mississippi, The Phantoms and The Lancers. Bruce Blackman played organ and sang with The Lancers along with Johnny Walker on guitar. Charlie Ross was the bass player and singer with The Phantoms. Bruce left the Lancers to join The Phantoms and they were known to back up Charlie Rich, B.J. Thomas, Dallas Frazier and others at the VFW clubs whenever they came through town.

Bruce was attending summer school at Delta State College where he met Roy Whittaker who wanted to start his own band. Bruce initially said "No" to the offer because he was still playing with The Phantoms. But Roy said he had a "Voice of the Theatre" PA system, which was state of the art at the time, and Bruce couldn't resist. The Phantoms only played sporadically, so he talked with Johnny Walker and Charlie Ross and they all saw an opportunity to play music full time for a living. Roy had already picked out a name he envisioned as Eternity's Children and the four-piece band was born.

They moved to Biloxi, Mississippi and got a one night audition at The Vapors, a club every band wanted to play at because it was the most popular. Owned by Gene Jernigan, it was located on Beach Blvd right on the Gulf coastline. Gene wasn't impressed with their audition but he did arrange for them to play at a new club he opened in the basement of the Biloxi Hotel for his brother Frank. They played there and were between gigs when Roy Whittaker discovered Linda Lawley singing at another local after-hours folk club. He encouraged her to join the group. The formal band now consisted of Bruce Blackman (keyboards, vocals), Linda Lawley (vocals), Johnny Walker (guitar, vocals), Charlie Ross (bass, vocals) and Roy Whittaker (drums, vocals). They practiced at the hotel during the day and had free rooms to stay in at night.

Covering songs by other vocal groups like The Beach Boys, The Hollies and The Mamas and Papas they developed a stunning live act with four-part harmonies and Linda's powerful voice. Their shows were packed and they became the number one group to see in the gulf coast area. Frank booked two 2-hour shows each night to a standing room only crowd of 300 people. With line-ups extending for blocks trying to see the band at The Biloxi Hotel, Gene Jernigan realized his error in letting them go and asked them to come back to The Vapors at twice the pay to become the house band there. So, they moved out of the hotel and leased a 3 bedroom house near the club in Biloxi to stay and practice at. They split sets with bands like The Music Machine, The Blues Magoos, The Cyrkle, The Turtles and others. As the hottest band on the rise, they were eager to launch their recording career.

Branching out playing other venues like The Sands in New Orleans and Independence Hall in Baton Rouge, a few record labels sent representatives to the clubs to witness and sign the band including Dick Holler who worked with Phil Gernhard. He was behind the super hit songs *Snoopy Vs. The Red Baron*, *Abraham, Martin & John*, *Spider's and Snakes*, *Me and You and a Dog Named Boo* and many others. But they were naïve and unsure, and turned down this and many other offers. After a few months Raymond Karl Roy and Guy Marion Bellelo of Crocked Foxx Productions out of Baton Rouge, Louisiana happened upon them playing back at The Vapors club. Determined to finally get representation, Eternity's Children gave in and signed a management deal.

Moving to Baton Rouge the deal reduced their weekly pay to $50 for the entire band but they were able to record their first single *Can't Put a Thing Over Me b/w Time and a Place* at Capitol City Sound Studios on Convention Street. Released on the Apollo record label, it got some local radio airplay in the Gulf Coast area but nowhere else. Keith Olsen, a former bass player with The Music Machine, was producing bands now and made a deal with Ray and Guy. Meeting up in Dallas, Texas at a small "jingles" studio Keith engineered and recorded a few demo songs by the band including *A Taste of Honey* and the song *Rumors* written by Bruce.

Bruce then flew to Los Angeles with Ray and Guy to shop the demos around. Staying at Gene Autry's Hotel Continental on Sunset Blvd, Guy and Ray met Kevin Deverich at his office who was managing The Who and Eric Burdon & The Animals at the time. Bruce was not included and stayed behind while Ray and Guy were at the meeting. He spotted a pamphlet in the hotel lobby listing record companies and headed over to A&M Studios which was only a mile away with a demo tape in hand.

He walked into the office of Gil Friesen, the active president at that time, who just happened to be there and he listened to the demo tape. When he found out Keith Olsen had produced the taped recordings, he signed a contract with Bruce then and there. The next morning Bruce told Ray and Guy the exciting news and they went ballistic. They had already made a deal with Deverich and had to renegotiate a deal with A&M for only one recorded single. The deal favored Ray and Guy with only 10% of any royalties going to the band minus 40% for management fees. In retrospect, a complete and total loss for the band.

Rumors was remastered and recorded at A&M Studios on the lot. It was released as the single *Wait And See b/w Rumors* through A&M with an option for a full LP recording if more than 100,000 copies were sold. It was at this point that Bruce was beginning to see the dark meanderings of the record business. The song *Rumors* was the B-side to the single and had a 50/50 split in writing credits between him and Keith Olsen, although Bruce clearly wrote the song before they even met. Bruce had real concerns about this but was told that this was how the business worked, a 50/50 split between producer and writer. The A-side to the single *Wait and See,* although credited to Eternity's Children, was written, sung and recorded by session players with David Gates who was a rising star that later formed the band Bread. There was no involvement from any of the Eternity's Children players.

The rest of the band had by now migrated out to California waiting for the single to be released. Living on barely enough to pay for meals in a ten-unit complex, they would practice vocals around the pool. Terry Melcher happened to be staying there and overheard them. He was behind many hits by The Byrds and Paul Revere & The Raiders. His offer to record them had to be turned down because of their contractual obligation to Crocked Foxx Productions. They played gigs at the Continental Ballroom backing Three Dog Night with Country Joe and the Fish and the Cheetah backing The Hook with Howlin' Wolf. They also performed on *"Hullabaloo"* and *"Where the Action Is"* on TV. But Ray and Guy were pocketing all the money they made from the gigs and TV performances. The single did okay but nowhere near what was needed. By this time the A&M record deal, which could have been sweet, fell through. Eternity's Children headed back to Baton Rouge. It was here that Bruce wrote the song *Mrs. Bluebird* and, because of industry distrust, he had studied up on business practices and relationships and copywrote the song.

Shortly thereafter a deal was finally made with Capitol Records and their subsidiary Tower Records. Again, Keith Olsen was tabbed for production duties along with Curt Boettcher. Eternity's Children headed back to California and recorded their first album at Columbia Studio D at 6121 Sunset Boulevard in Hollywood. At the time, Keith and Curt were the hot studio commodities, coming fresh from the sessions with Sagittarius and The Millennium. Curt was known for presenting perfectly blended harmonies as probably the ultimate sunshine pop producer in the country. He was used to molding bands to get his sound out there to the public, but Eternity's Children already had perfect harmonies and had been together professionally for a while vocalizing songs. Curt was a little frustrated during the sessions because he was used to being in control.

It got to a point where Kevin Deverich and the management tandem didn't see eye to eye and Kevin dumped the band. It was time to go back to Baton Rouge but they had to sell or pawn their equipment to drive home. Once there, they played one-nighters in Mississippi, Louisiana and Florida to sellout crowds. But Bruce was tired of all the work for no pay, frustrated with his managers, angry for not getting full credit for the songs he wrote, at odds with the record companies and unhappy living in squalor while on the road. Riding with Guy and Ray between gigs, things came to a head over a contact issue that went bad. Bruce bolted from the car leaving his clothes, books, demo tapes, song tablatures and equipment behind. With Bruce gone, Johnny Walker left one week later.

The self-titled album *Eternity's Children* finally came out on the market and the featured single was of course *Mrs. Bluebird b/w Little Boy* that nearly hit the top 50 on the Billboard charts nationwide. But because Bruce had left the band, Ray and Guy decided to combine their middle names to chronicle Karl Marion as composer of *Mrs. Bluebird* to absorb full songwriting credits for themselves and reap the profits. Fortunately, Bruce had copyrighted the song, took them to court and after a couple years received full benefits.

With the band split apart, the album only credits the players as Linda Lawley (vocals), Roy Whittaker (drums), Charles Ross (bass) and newly acquired Mike McClain on (keyboards). Johnny Walker's guitar playing is all over in the music but there is no mention of him playing. Musically the album ranks up there with the best vocal flower-pop groups. The Sunshine Company, Spanky and Our Gang, The Pleasure Fair and The Association come to mind.

Wonderful harmonies and Johnny Walker stand's out on psych guitar. Tower Records flooded the market with three singles from the album trying to get something out of the band. But they were dying as a label and Capitol Records was throwing dirt on the grave. Although the single sold well peaking at #54 on the national charts, the album tanked.

On July 27th, 1968, they played *Mrs. Bluebird* on *American Bandstand* with Dick Clark. The live video has since been removed from YouTube but they looked awkward lip syncing to the hit song with Charlie Ross playing air guitar for the hot solo. After a short while Roy Whittaker had had enough and left the band. Ray and Guy brought in Bo Wagner as a replacement on drums, but he only lasted a couple of weeks. He was eager to join because of who wrote *Mrs. Bluebird* but had no idea that the key song writer, Bruce Blackman, had already departed the band.

Eternity's Children tried to play the club circuit promoting the album as best they could, but nothing worked. They were all set to record a second album but because of previous conflicts with the producers, they chose Gary Paxton. He was formerly with The Hollywood Argyles and produced Bobby Pickett's smash hit *Monster Mash*. They moved over to Bakersfield, California and recorded the album at The Buck Owens Recording Studio. Some songs were written by Linda Lawley and Charlie Ross, but most were written by Gary Paxton and his wife Jan. The musicians were Linda Lawley (vocals), Charlie Ross (bass, vocals), Mike McClain (keyboards, vocals), an unnamed session drummer and (unofficially) Clarence White and Ben Benay both on (guitar). Gary was trying to give them a Fifth-Dimension sound.

Tower Records had by now folded and the second album, with masters completed, was cancelled for release in the US. But Capitol Records in Canada did release the LP *Timeless* based on sales from the *Mrs. Bluebird* single up there. Only about 1000 copies were pressed. The band headed for Memphis and American Studios hoping to find some magic there like The Box Tops did. Their contract was up and Liberty Records saw them as a quality replacement for The Fifth Dimension who had just left and signed a contract with Bell Records. Eternity's Children signed with Liberty Records and thoughts of a third album were in the works, but things fell apart quickly as the label was bought out by United Artists. A few songs were recorded but not released.

They were always a great live act and continued to play venues but finally had to give it up. A band that should have been. With wonderful talent and quality producers, they became another victim of label/management litigation.

Roy Whittaker retired out of the music business and became a successful lawyer.

Linda Lawley toured as back up voice with Carole King and Petula Clark in the 70's. Unfortunately, she passed away in 2007 from cancer.

Mike McClain moved to Dallas, built a recording studio and was director for a children's music company called The Shoebox Theatre.

Charlie Ross played bass on several recordings with hitmaking bands into the 80's.

Bo Wagner had worked with The Lewis and Clark Expedition, The Fifth Dimension and was with Liberace who hired him to play drums in his tour band. They played a show in Atlanta and it was here that Bo finally met up with Bruce Blackman. Together they decided to form the band Starbuck who recorded three albums and four top 50 hits including *Moonlight Feels Right b/w Lash LaRue* which topped out nationally at #3 on the charts. Bo Wagner recorded six LPs on the Statler record label in the 1980's and became a medical doctor before he passed away in Santa Monica, Ca. 2017.

Johnny Walker reunited with Bruce for Starbucks 3rd LP. Sadly, Johnny met his maker in 2007.

Bruce Blackman was proud of Eternity's Children and all his cohorts in the band. They remained close long after the band separated. He has been involved with music as a song writer his entire life receiving several music-achievement awards and is owner of Sports Music, providing jingles for televised sporting events. Additionally, he recently released a CD of new songs called *Is That Your Yacht?* in 2017. Bruce had major songwriting talent. There was always a shining light at the end of the tunnel. His statement "When the art part ends, the hard part begins." is a lesson learned. But he paid his dues, as many had done in the music business, and through Starbuck was one of the few that found a diamond at the end of the rainbow.

STEREO SKAO-363
Hamilton Wesley Watt Jr. and William D. Lincoln
A Gift From Euphoria

EUPHORIA 1967-69

William D Lincoln was primarily a bass player and was with a few bands early on. He and his band would take on gigs wherever they could. At one point, he was playing at a casino in Nevada with a drummer Mike Robinson. Arthur Lee joined them and for a short while the trio played the casino circuit in and around Las Vegas. Johnny Echols had previously been with Arthur in a band called The LAGS. He joined Arthur, Will and Mike and this band became The American Four. They recorded one single called *Luci Baines b/w Soul Food* with the song *Luci* as a reference to president LBJs daughter. After this, Arthur Lee and Johnny Echols formed Love. William and Mike hired John Stewart (not John of The Kingston Trio) to play guitar and they became The Strangers.

The Strangers were the exclusive band that played at a club called Guys and Dolls on Santa Monica Blvd. Another band starring Scott Engle, John Maus and Al "Tiny" Schnieder called themselves The Walker Brothers and they were playing Gazzarri's on the LA Strip. Scott and William were friends and had attended Colin McEwan High School, a private boarding school, together in Hollywood. Scott was also close friends with John Stewart and because of the mutual friendship, both bands The Strangers and The Walker Brothers entered a studio and recorded the single *Tell Me b/w Easy Living*. The band was listed as The Strangers, but included Scott Engles, John Maus, William Lincoln, John Stewart, Mike Robinson and Tiny.

The Bushmen were from Cleveland, Ohio, another band that came out to LA to try and make their mark. This band included Wesley Hamilton Watt (guitar) and Dave Potter (drums). They were managed by Buck Ram who was a big-time producer involved with Count Basie, Duke Ellington, The Penguins and The Platters. They wound up playing the Guys and Dolls club on the nights that The Strangers were not. This is when William met Wesley Watt. Will was asked to be the bass player for The Bushmen. The Strangers broke up after John and Steve were persuaded to go to England and formed The Walker Brothers to great success.

They played several places on The Strip including Gazzarri's, The Sea Witch and traveled up north on occasion to San Francisco, to play small venues there. There was a house up in Hollywood Hills with a small studio where they wrote and recorded some songs. Collaborating as musical partners, Wes and Will recorded under various pseudonyms. One single, *So Little Time b/w Now It's Over,* was released by The Word and two singles *Together Forever b/w War Baby* and *Jeanie's Pub b/w Love Is Love* by The War-Babies. They also performed as a band called The Willy's.

William fell for an English girl who was visiting LA. He quit The Bushmen and traveled back to England to marry her. He stayed there for a while, but the marriage didn't last. Meanwhile while he was gone, The Bushmen (without William) consisted of Wesley Watt (guitar), Doug Delain (rhythm guitar), Peter Black (bass) and Dave Potter (drums). Doug Delain came up with the name Euphoria for the band. The name stuck and they recorded one single in 1966, *Hungry Woman b/w No Me Tomorrow*. But Doug only lasted a couple of months before he moved on.

As a trio Wesley, Pete and Dave went to Houston and played a few gigs during that summer as Euphoria. They shared the stage with Lost and Found, Golden Dawn and The 13th Floor Elevators. LSD was plentiful and it was not illegal yet, but the authorities were putting the pressure on, and had many bands under a spy glass. Lost and Found were the first band to be busted and The 13th Floor Elevators were next on the list. Euphoria went back to LA to avoid the heat.

William had by now returned to the US and reunited with Wesley to begin working on an album project. Several songs were in the works and they refined their tunes at United Western Recorders noted for other hit makers The Mamas & Papas, The Beach Boys and The Fifth Dimension. Wes and Will played all the instruments with overdubs. Wesley (guitar and drums) and William (guitar and bass). Orchestration was added by the LA Philharmonic Orchestra. However, they did travel to Nashville for the country recording embellishments with help from David Briggs (piano), Lloyd Green (pedal steel guitar) and Bobby Thompson (banjo).

Will had been in England and knew his way around, so they traveled to London where the vocal tracks were laid down. This is also where the psychedelic and rock edge was recorded. When they came back home, everything got the final production touches by Nik Venet who was responsible for many other bands including Mad River, Hearts and Flowers, The Stone Poneys and Lothar and the Hand People. It was a high-quality recording released by the

Capitol Label, but the only album *A Gift From Euphoria* was not promoted, no singles from the LP were released and it disappeared to the cut out bins. Musically the LP is diverse with orchestral passages, whimsical voices, psychedelic riffs, backwards guitar, banjo and country rock. The Byrds, Dillard and Clark and Buffalo Springfield would be good comparisons and it does approach near classic status amongst collectors.

Wes and Will never played the songs with a live band in public. They both did side session work.

Wes recorded with Lee Michaels, Bernie Schwartz (aka Adrian Pride) and The Eastside Kids with his friend and drummer Dave Potter. Will played with Genya Raven and Richard Torrence and toured with Dori Previn playing at Carnegie Hall back in New York. This concert recording of *Dory Previn Live At Carnegie Hall* was released as a double album in 1973. Will remarried and recorded another album with his new wife Lynda and other players circa 1970 as Addie Pray entitled *Late for the Dance* also on Capitol records, but it was never officially released. After this both Wes and Will moved back to Minnesota and did work for a while, but Wes joined the army and Will went into hibernation.

Eventually William Lincoln moved back to the west coast, became a teacher and is now happily retired.

Wesley Hamilton Watt wound up in Wisconsin and became a bit of a recluse. He passed on in Sheboygan Falls, Wisconsin in 2015 after a prolonged battle with cancer.

FTS-3053
STEREO
FABULOUS
Verve
FORECAST
FARQUAHR

Farquahr
elektra

The fabulous
Farquahr
The Third Album

THE FABULOUS FARQUAHR 1968-70

The McGowan brothers, Bob, Frank and Dennis, hailed from Branford, Connecticut and started out as a folk group called The Avalon's. One song *Daddy, I Cried* got some local radio notice. After meeting up with Doug Lapham, who was a known songwriter in the area, they were known as Doug Lapham and the McGowan Brothers and were the house band at The Hofbrau House in New Haven. The band liked to tell stories and were a bit of a comedy troupe during the numerous shows they played on the East coast.

It is not known how or why they decided to call themselves The Fabulous Farquahr, but there were several prominent Farquhars (spelling) during that time known as politicians, musicians, in sports and the military. They made up their fictitious heritage and took pseudonyms for names as the Farquahr brothers. Doug Lapham was Barnswallow Farquahr (lead guitar, vocals). Dennis McGowan took the name Condor Farquahr (rhythm guitar, vocals), Frank McGowan assumed Flamingo Farquahr (lead vocals, pennywhistle, fife, guitar), Bob McGowan became Hummingbird Farquahr (banjo, mandolin, autoharp, 6-12 string guitars, vocals), and they were backed by Jack Huber as Mary Farquahr (upright bass). Frank was the spokesman and storyteller for the band during the shows. The songs they wrote had strange titles like *My Eggs Don't Taste the Same Without You* and *Cloud Nine Motel*.

They sold out wherever they played and included audience participation with a huge fan following including "groupies" before the term was even invented. Seemingly they played everywhere frequenting clubs like The Dock & Dine in Saybrook, Connecticut, Charlie Bates' Saloon in upper New York, Fat City in Wilmington, Vermont, The Rocking Horse in Hartford, The Crystal Palace, Christies, Pufferbellies in Cape Cod, Massachusetts and The Land Ho in Orleans, Massachusetts. The Land Ho was housed in a 4-story wood building that was totally engulfed in flames circa 1973 but the club somehow survived the fire. The thought was that the wood floors and walls were so saturated with beer that the place just wouldn't burn. It still stands to this day as an eatery with atmosphere on Main St.

The band was signed by MGM and their Verve Forecast subsidiary label who were promoting psychedelic cutting edge bands at the time. Their first album was recorded at the Hit Factory at 353 West 48th Street in New York and included many studio session players. The studio was owned and operated by Jerry Ragovoy who assisted on (keyboards, piano). He along with Chip Taylor produced the band and added drums, with electric fuzz guitar, kazoo, flute, recorder, horns and three-part harmonies at times sounding like The Jim Kweskin Jug Band. There are dreamy folk sounds and they could rock out with some pleasant flower pop and baroque sounds also with plenty of orchestration, harpsichord and slight effects. A diverse LP entitled *The Fabulous Farquahr* fit the psychedelic times during 1968. The bands Fargo, Bear and Glad also come to mind with a similar sound.

Three singles were released *Sister Theresa's East River Orphanage b/w My Eggs Don't Taste The Same Without You* and *My Island b/w Teddy Bear Days* both from the album plus a non-album single *Hollywood Ending b/w Some Kind Of God.* Verve promoted the band but there was no major radio airplay outside the local area.

As a band they toured the east coast with George McGovern during his presidential campaign. Lost in the shuffle when MGM records sold out to PolyGram, they were forced to switch labels. They were back at The Hit Factory and by the second album they had shortened their name and album title to simply *Farquahr*. There was more of a folk, rock and country sound and this album was released on the Elektra label. They continued to play as either Farquahr in a country, folk, rock vibe or as The McGowan's playing Celtic music for a while after the second LP was released.

Frank worked for Southern New England Telecommunications (the phone company) for 10 years playing with the band on weekends at some nearby location. A third LP called *The Third Album* was released in 1982 in a bluegrass, Celtic vibe. They set up the C. Farquahr Company and the brothers bought and reconditioned antique automobiles and put them up for sale. Frank, Dennis and Bob also owned and operated two nightclubs in Virginia where the band played often. By the mid-1990s they sold the clubs and began to phase out the band playing less frequently. A rare CD of early and later songs called *From the Top* was put out on a limited basis in 1995. Then in 2001 Dennis succumbed to cancer and the band ended officially. Sadly, Frank left us in 2004 and Bobby in September 2021. Those who saw the Fabulous Farquahr in concert have nothing but happy memories about the band.

STEREO
SR 25358
THE
FALLEN ANGELS
ROULETTE
MULTI SOUND

SR 42011
STEREO
THE
FALLEN ANGELS
STEREO
It's a long way down
ROULETTE

THE FALLEN ANGELS 1968

Jack Bryant was a (bass guitar) player who formed his first band in Washington DC during his high school days called The Viscounts. They played the DC area high schools, frat parties and teen clubs for a five year period. When the band broke up, he met Charlie "C.J." Jones (guitar, vocals) and they both joined a band called Steve Charles and the Abstract. But this was short-lived. C.J. wanted to start a band like The Beatles, but with trombones. Then Jack met Jack Lauritsen (rhythm guitar) who was a former member of the Velours. Jack L. really liked a song that Jack B. wrote called *Every Time I Fall in Love* and envisioned the song with strings behind it. Wally Cook (guitar, harmonica) and Ned Davis (keyboards) came on board, who were both from a band called The Disciples. They put together a full band that included Jack Bryant (bass, vocals), Jack Lauritsen (rhythm guitar), Wally Cook (lead guitar), Ned Davis (keyboards) and Richard Kumer (drums).

They stayed as The Disciples and then briefly, they became The Uncalled For. But both names were ones that were already being used by other established bands. Jack Lauritsen told them about a book he was reading called *Paradise Lost* by author John Milton and about the Fallen Angels. That's where the name came from. They started playing at New Mac's Pub, a basement club under The Corral on M Street and other venues around Georgetown like The Dodge Hotel, The Rogue and Sam's Place, establishing themselves as one of the hottest rock bands around.

The local management team of Barry Siedel and Tom Traynor had formed Trayvell Productions. They had brought aboard another local band, The Mad Hatters, for a record deal and wanted The Fallen Angels under their wing as well. Four demo songs were recorded at the small local Rodel Studios *Every Time I Fall in Love b/w I Have Found* and *A Little Love From You Will Do b/w Have You Ever Lost A Love.* Barry shopped the demos around New York and a deal was made with Laurie Records who pressed and released the unaltered recordings as singles but the songs never hit the Billboard charts and Laurie records dropped the band.

They had a long stay at a place called The Keg. This was a club in 1967, not the restaurant that began in the early 70's. Their shows reflected the San Francisco sounds of acid rock. Their stage antics were quite unusual with political satire and they would play their gigs in total darkness except for a strobe light, some black lights and a big aluminum foil ball that was tossed around the room for total mind effect. Mimicking various music styles with diversity and songs by artists like Buck Owens and Bob Dylan or jazz all with an acid psych influence, the stage theatrics were incredible.

They caught the eye of Neil Gilligan who worked with Roulette Records and were signed for a two album record deal. Several songs had already been written and the sessions that occurred at Allegro Studios located at 1650 Broadway in New York only took three weeks to complete. The cover shot for the LP was taken of the band standing in the elevator, laced with paisley cloth, which led to the Roulette offices. Pictured from left to right is Jack Bryant, Wally Cook, Howard Dunchik, Richard Kumer and Jack Lauritsen.

The self-titled LP *The Fallen Angels* was put on the market and although the chosen single from the LP *Your Friends Here In Dunderville b/w Room At The Top* made the radio airwaves, it was not the hit song the Roulette executives were looking for as they were expecting another Tommy James like sound.

However, the album fit perfectly into the FM underground radio weirdness. The special effects, echoes, strange instruments, great guitar playing and odd song arrangements put them in the same pattern as The Baroques, Ford Theatre, The Left Banke, Sopwith Camel and Love. There were favorable reviews of the LP both locally and nationally with major kudos coming from Mike Pearse and The LA Free Press. Plans were all set to promote them on a national tour. But things stalled as the single didn't do as well as hoped. They played a grueling two-night stand at Trudy Heller's in Greenwich Village promoting the album, packing the fans in and the lines extended for blocks.

In Cleveland, they were booked for the nationally syndicated TV show called *Upbeat*. They were to lip-sync to the latest single, *Hello Girl b/w Most Children Do,* and found out that the song *Hello Girl* had been overdubbed without their knowledge, it was completely changed. The new arrangement of the song got under their skin. The band protested and refused to go through with it at first, but then agreed. Jack Lauritsen had found a toy doll and during the video taping of the song, he pulled it apart and tossed the head, arms and legs at the camera. The filming was edited for TV before it was shown, but after finding out what happened, Roulette was unsure how to handle them. The label executives decided to cancel the national tour and stopped promoting the band. The singles were already relegated to the radio stations but promotion to any record stores for marketing or distribution ceased.

Rich Kumer decided to leave the band and they hired John (Thumper) Molloy as his replacement on (drums). Their contract obligated them to record another album. So, they spent six diligent weeks rehearsing for the second LP at Bryant's parent's house where he was living. One gig was played before an audience at T.C. Williams High School in Alexandria, Virginia and then they entered Sound Center Studios Inc. where Roulette only gave them 3-4 days to complete the project. Roulette had washed their hands of the band and didn't want to spend any more money.

They were given complete freedom in the studio but they were rushed. Fortunately, the songs were all well-rehearsed and Max Ellen, from the New York Philharmonic, was able to add some string embellishments to polish the music. But the production was a far cry from what was expected. The second LP *It's A Long Way Down* was completed. The mind melting cover art was drawn by their eccentric friend, Lanny Tupper, who was present during all the sessions and rehearsals and made the intricate illustrations. There is amazing detail for psychedelic effect and if you study the cover, you see the name "Leslie" who was the love of his life girlfriend at the time. The back cover artwork was drawn by Bill Clark. When their masterpiece album with all the right underground radio moves was released, there were limited pressings, no promotion, distribution or attention from the record label and it died a quick death. With no support the band disintegrated.

They stayed apart for nearly 30 years but got back together with renewed interest from fans on the internet. Jack Bryant, Jack Lauritsen, Wally Cook with Larry Willis (keyboards, synth), Kevin Armstrong (bass) and Tom Mansell (drums) recorded a third album, *Rain of Fire,* released on CD in 1998. They were back playing clubs on a regular basis but things fell apart when Jack Lauritsen met his maker in 2009.

The band revived again with original members Jack Bryant, Wally Cook, John (Thumper) Molloy and C.J. Jones along with Brint Hannay and Billy Hancock both on (vocals, guitar) and they continue to play clubs occasionally around the greater Georgetown and Washington DC area.

FANTASY
FANTASY
FANTASY
NAPTHALI
ASHER
GAD
BENJAMIN

YEAR

YEAR
ONE

FANTASY (US) 1970-75

Fantasy was formed in 1967 in Miami, Florida by Bob and Billy Robbins. The band included Bob (bass), Billy (vocalist extraordinaire), Jim DeMeo (guitar), Mario Russo (keyboards) and Greg Kimple on (drums). They began playing teen parties and eventually found themselves as the house band at a club in Miami called Thee Experience. After spending a year refining their sound, they acquired quite a fan following.

Then the club closed down only to be reopened as Thee Image on Collins Avenue at Sunny Isles Beach. Many famous acts came through the club like The Doors, Cream, Steppenwolf and Led Zeppelin. Blues Image was the house band but when they left for California, Fantasy took their place as the main opening act.

Things were going great and their reputation was gaining them notice. Then one evening Billy disappeared, gigs were cancelled and everyone was starting to worry the worst. A month later his body was found in the Everglades. Apparently, a drug deal gone bad. The band was disillusioned and considered calling it quits. But they found a brilliant and beautiful 16-year old female singer. Her name was Jamene Miller and she could sing like Janis Joplin.

Fantasy continued and within months they were signed to a record deal with Liberty records. A self-titled album *Fantasy* was recorded at UA Recording Studios located at 8715 W 3rd St in Hollywood, Ca. The LP has a progressive and symphonic vibe with a couple of long guitar-frenzied jams, baroque keyboards and Jamene's crystalline voice. Comparison's go to Holland's Earth and Fire and Julian's Treatment from London. But the band's claim to fame was the one hit wonder single *Stoned Cowboy b/w Understand*. The A-side was a unique and psychy instrumental piece that was on every radio station's hit list for a few weeks. Fantasy played the big venues all over the US from the east to the west coast and opened for Tamum Shud at the Wonderland Disco in Wollongong, Australia.

But the song had its run its course and they became a real one hit wonder. A forgotten band on the national circuit, Fantasy continued to play gigs and evolved with the nucleus now being Steve Mele (guitar), Jemene Miller (lead vocals), Dane Buxbaum (guitar, vocals), John Simmons (keyboards, synthesizers, vocals), Ross Lawrence (keyboards), John Marcus (bass) and Greg Kimple (drums, vocals).

By 1976 they were back in the studio recording another album as Fantasy on the very obscure Above and Beyond record label called *Year 1.* Recorded at Frank Lindal's Stereo Sound Studios in Miami, it's difficult to say if this LP was ever released to the public or if it was just a test pressing. Fantasy was one of the first rock bands to be featured live at the Grand Canyon on July 7th, 1977, as seen on YouTube. The band was changing into a more progressive sound that Jemene wasn't comfortable with so she left the band. Greg also decided to leave. Steve Mele, John Simmons, Ross Lawrence, John Marcus and Dane Buxbaum briefly joined Burt Compton on (drums) and released a one off LP by Compton/Mele called *Rock 'N Roll Genius*.

Year One was an original concept project developed and written by Greg Kimple and he finished the task with Steve Mele, John Simmons, Ann Holloway, Jim Hilley and others for the self-titled double album entitled *Year One* Including all the songs from the second Fantasy LP plus 6 additional tunes. Over an hours-worth of music there was plenty of hit potential. Musically diverse with prog, rock, jazz, flute, great guitar, fuzz and wah-wah. A lost gem, you could place this album in same box with Big Star and Space Opera. Music with songs so wonderful and hooks that make you cry. If you like the sound of Arden House, Zolder & Clark or early Styx you'll love this LP. Released in limited quantity, the local critics gave the album a wonderful blessing, but it wasn't promoted very well and the public either didn't buy it or couldn't find it on the shelves. With no major label backing the band finally folded.

Most of the former Fantasy folks disappeared and absorbed into a normal livelihood.

Jamene Miller (born Lydia Janene Miller) went on to sing backup with Foxy, Eric Clapton and the Jerry Garcia Band. But she became quiet and depressed towards the end of her life. Alcohol was a problem that she could never overcome and sadly, she passed away in Miramer, Wisconsin in September 2008.

Greg Kimple opened the Power Station nightclub in Melbourne, Florida and introduced many then unknowns like Marilyn Manson, Nine Inch Nails and White Zombie before they became popular. As a respected singer songwriter and 40 years later, he finally released an album with many touted musicians called *Nobody You Know* (circa 2013) and ran a lucrative business called Celebrations DJs before retiring.

RCA
LSP-4178
VICTOR
STEREO
FARGO
I SEE IT NOW

FARGO 1969

The story of Fargo begins with Dean Willden in Salt Lake City where he formed The Maudz Only. They won many Battle of the Bands contests, primarily located at The Terrace Ballroom sponsored by Apple Beer. A cover band at that time, they played several Kinks, Beatles, Stones and Hollies songs. They were extremely popular and gigged at high schools and teen clubs around town. On weekends, they played for the *Hi-Shop* TV show which was a local *American Bandstand* style dance show. The initial Maudz Only broke up but reformed again with Dean on (bass), Tony Decker (guitar), Steve Lubland (lead guitar) and Randle Potts (drums). This lasted a while, then Tony moved to Grand Junction, Colorado to attend Mesa State College.

He joined another band on (guitar, lead vocals) called The Garfield Air Mattress with Bruce Lambert (guitar, vocals), Daryl Cooper (keyboards), Terry Tezak (bass) and Pete Frease (drums) that got some local notice and backing from Ray Ruff and Checkmate Productions in Amarillo, Texas. They became The Tuesday Club and recorded a single *A Godess In Many Ways b/w Only Human* that got heavy radio airplay. Then Bruce and Terry left the band and Tony gave Dean a call to come there and join him. The band now with Tony Decker (guitar, vocals), Dean Willden (bass, vocals), Daryl Cooper (keyboards) and Pete Frease (drums) toured clubs in New Mexico, Texas, Oklahoma and Kansas and finally settled on the new band name of Fargo, which was the shortened name of Wells Fargo representing Dean's love of the west. Their tour schedule kept them one step ahead of the draft, but it eventually caught up to Pete Frease and he was drafted to Vietnam.

The band broke up, but Dean and Tony moved back to Salt Lake and hired Randle Potts and the band became a three-piece trio. They put together some demo tapes and found a production manager, Martin Cooper, who got them studio time in Los Angeles. After signing with Capitol Records, they started spending more time in LA putting an album together. One single was released *Robins, Robins b/w Sunny Day Blue*, but Marty didn't like the Capitol deal. RCA records took over the contract and it looked like Fargo might be on their way.

An album was recorded in Hollywood at Al Casey's Room. Al was a well-known session guitarist and gathered up some of the best in the business to help with the recording. The sessions included Dean Willden (bass, vocals) and Tony Decker (guitar, vocals) with help from session players Dr. John (piano), Rick Chuna (guitar) and Terry Paul (bass) on the song *Round About Way.* Terry and Rick were both from the band Hearts and Flowers. Randle Potts froze up in the studio and only played one song for the album *Lady Goodbye.* They brought in Wrecking Crew member Jim Gordon to drum on all the other tracks. Their lone album *I See It Now* is wonderful, along the lines of The Merry-Go-Round and The Moon with dreamy harmonies and psychy tendencies, a few special effects and sparse floating guitar moments here and there. The aforementioned songs, on the Capitol single, were not included on the LP.

The thought was that they could nominate one song as the "pick hit" of Chicago's WLS, who at the time was the top radio station in the country. But there was little to no promotion of the LP and RCA wouldn't release any singles. Firing Randle Potts, they hired Bob Holman in his place to play (drums) for any live gigs. They never played any clubs in LA, but they did tour the college and high school circuit back in Utah for a short while. Tony and Dean were traveling in different musical directions and they broke up soon after the album was put out.

Manager Marty Cooper wrote several songs with one being *A Little Bit Country, A Little Bit Rock and Roll* made famous by Donnie and Marie Osmond.

Jim Gordon was a well-known session drummer and is credited with the back beat for notable LPs like *Pet Sounds, Bread, The Notorious Byrd Brothers, Nilsson Schmilsson* and many others. He started hearing voices in his head and was wrongly treated for alcoholism. He killed his mother with a hammer. They didn't realize it until his trial that he was truly a mental case with Acute Schizophrenia and he wound up serving his time institutionalized at the California Medical Facility in Vacaville, a psychiatric prison. He has been denied parole several times.

Tony Decker walked away from music and became a teacher.

Dean Willden went to Nashville to do session work for a while, then returned to Salt Lake where he currently writes and records as Dean Wyatt.

FAT WATER
MGM
RECORDS

FAT WATER 1969

Lance Massey played (guitar & keyboards) and was from Florida. He was formerly with the band The Beau Gentry that also included Rick Jaeger (drums), Doug "Chico" Killmer (bass) and Russ DaShiell (lead guitar).

The Beau Gentry had a song on the airwaves *Dream Girl b/w Just in Case* and they were touring the Midwest with great success in Wisconsin and Illinois. Their manager was Steve Sperry and they were booked through Ken Adamany, who became famous as the manager of Cheap Trick. The summer tour went so well that they decided to move there permanently.

The Beau Gentry had a huge following frequenting The Pop House in Beloit, WI and other dance clubs but eventually they fell apart. Russell, Rick and Doug all departed for California and formed the band Crowfoot. Both Doug and Russell got big with Norman Greenbaum later with the song *Spirit in the Sky*.

Lance stayed in Wisconsin. He had unfortunately been in a motorcycle accident and had a lengthy stay in a Hospital recovering from the injuries. After he was released, he played with bands in the Chicago Heights area. He was still being managed by Steve Sperry. One evening Steve asked Lance if he would come out and take a listen to this band with a pretty girl singer who had a great voice named Vicki Hubley. She was with an all-girl group called The Same and Lance liked what he saw.

Irving Azoff also worked with Ken and booked shows for The Same, a band called The Regiment and had also been booking The One-Eyed Jacks. He decided to merge Vicki Hubley (vocals), Lance Massey (guitar, vocals), Bill (Boris) Schneider (who was formerly with The One-Eyed Jacks (bass) and former members of The Regiment, Everett Amundson (keyboards, flute) and Peter Milio (drums). Bill Schneider said that Lance was the best guitarist he'd ever heard and the band clicked very well. They needed a name and Bill remembered a comic strip called "Hey BC" where a caveman saw a snowflake and called it Fat Water.

They frequented and honed their songs at The Illini Brown Jug (still active now as The Clybourne) located on South 6th St in Champaign, Illinois. Steve Sperry also worked with Dick Marx, who was the father of Richard Marx, a real popular 80's and 90's pop musician. Dick had built a sound company, wrote jingles and made commercials for Old Gold Cigarettes, Kellogg's Cereal, Chicken of the Sea Tuna, Colt 45 Beer, Double Mint Gum and just about every other product sold on TV and Radio at the time. He was hugely successful and had a state-of-the-art studio called 8-Track Studios located on North Michigan Ave in Chicago. The band recorded several songs here in the wee hours of the morning.

A photo session occurred and the self-titled album *Fat Water* was put together. Each band member got about $1000 in advance for their effort. Musically the band falls in the category of Yankee Dollar and/or The Love Exchange. Vicki Hubley was heavily influenced by Janis Joplin and comes across like Karen Lawrence of the LA Jets and the band 1994. The *Fat Water* album in general has a San Francisco sound with heavy guitar from Lance, special effects, backward embellishments and female vocals emphasis. This is an album that gets better with each listen.

They went out on the road to promote the record playing several pop and rock festivals, most notably The First Annual Palm Beach International Music and Arts Festival in Florida Nov. 1969. Set up only 3 months after Woodstock, many of the featured bands like Grand Funk Railroad, Rotary Connection, Sweetwater, Johnny Winter, Rockin Foo, King Crimson, etc. were scheduled to play. The opening act was Iron Butterfly and the headliner was The Rolling Stones. This was the largest crowd Fat Water had ever played to with more than 40,000 attendees.

The album was released and then MGM decided to make changes. The company was in trouble financially and sold off the record division. Mike Curb became president and brought in his own acts. They stopped supporting bands under contract and they were no longer being promoted. Mike Curb was anti-drugs and began a campaign of cleaning house and clearing out bands that had questionable song titles and lyrics.

Songs on the Fat Water album like the released single *Santa Anna Speed Queen b/w Amalynda Guinevere* and another album song like *Waiting for Mary* had drug influenced titles, according to the label perception, and because of this Fat Water made the "goodbye" list. Eighteen other bands under contract were dropped by MGM. The list was never made public but bands like The Velvet Underground, The Mothers Of Invention, The Blues

Project, Orpheus, Puff, The Bloomsbury People, Ultimate Spinach, A.B. Skhy, The Beacon Street Union and others suddenly either stopped making records or found another record label for distribution. But it was really an excuse to release the bands that weren't making the label any money. Mike Curb retained The Cowsills, Petula Clark, The Osmonds, and other "bubblegum" bands that were all hit making machines. The one exception was Eric Burden and the Animals who were based in Los Angeles and heavy into the drug experience and experimental psych music at that time, but they had proven clout with top ten chart success in the past and Mike kept them on. Lance saw the writing on the wall and left Fat Water because he knew they were going nowhere.

But the band carried on and replaced Lance with G.E. Stinson. Lance had been the main songwriter along with Boris Schneider and G.E. also wrote music, so he was a good fit. But the music direction changed as G.E. was more into Heavy English Blues. The songs were much more progressive rock oriented and Mr. Stinson felt Bill Schneider wasn't a good fit so Don Cody replaced him on (bass). G.E. was really into the experimentation of John McLaughlin's Mahavishnu Orchestra, Led Zeppelin, Jeff Beck and Miles Davis.

The band continued playing venues and festivals locally and began getting more gigs at bigger venues for concerts backing nationally known bands. They were featured at the first Kickapoo Creek Rock Festival, 1970, located in Heyworth, Illinois along with Canned Heat, Country Joe and the Fish, Paul Butterfield Blues Band, Fuse (soon to become Cheap Trick), REO Speedwagon (before they were nationally known) and The Amboy Dukes. As good as they were and became, there was little interest from any other record labels during this time and the band eventually faded out completely.

As for Fat Water members, Vicki Hubley, Don Cody, G.E. Stinson and Peter Milio continued as session musicians backing Harvey Mandel on his version of a Super Session and the album *Get-Off in Chicago*.

Don Cody then wound up as a well-known recording engineer in San Francisco.

Vicki and Peter were part of the *Bruised Orange* album put out by John Prine and were featured with Steve Goodman for several albums. Vicki was also with a band called Otis and the Elevators for a while.

Peter Milio moved to San Francisco and played with Country Joe MacDonald and David LaFlamme of Its A Beautiful Day for a while.

G.E. Stinson formed the highly influential and successful Shadowfax.

Everett Amundson retired from music and lives in Illinois.

Bill (Boris) Schneider was originally an art major in College before taking up the bass guitar. After Fat Water, he finished college, became a financial adviser and eventually retired to his first love of painting. He is a well-known and respected artist, teaches workshops, has attained several awards and has had exhibitions of his paintings featured at several galleries all over the country.

After he left Fat Water, Lance Massey played with Aorta for a brief period and made music with local bands Horsefeathers and Duck Soup. He retired from music as a living and became a professional Carpenter. He still plays on occasion near his hometown.

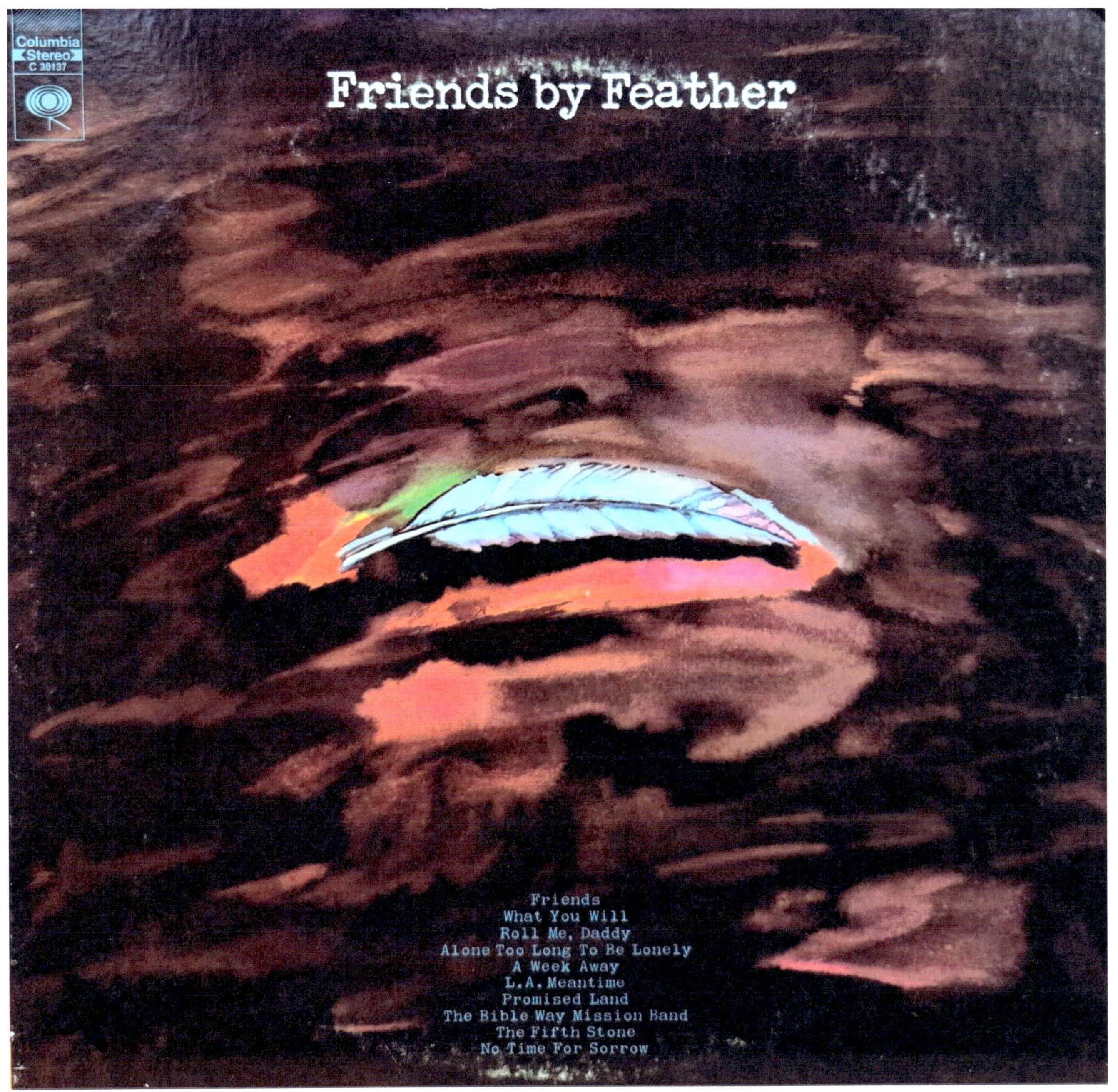
Columbia
Stereo
C 30137
Friends by Feather
Friends
What You Will
Roll Me, Daddy
Alone Too Long To Be Lonely
A Week Away
L.A. Meantime
Promised Land
The Bible Way Mission Band
The Fifth Stone
No Time For Sorrow

FEATHER 1970

Johnny Townsend grew up in Tuscaloosa, Alabama. He found that he could sing and in high school formed his first band The Spector's. They became The Nightcap's and played high school dances and teen clubs for money. Johnny then attended the University of Alabama hoping to become a doctor but focused his studies on Music and Art by his sophomore year. He helped to form a band called The Magnificent Seven with John Wyker who later gained fame with the hit single *Motorcycle Mama b/w Rainbow Road* in the band Sailcat. The Magnificent Seven grew in popularity and they started touring the college circuit and beach clubs in the Southeast.

They recorded some singles that caught the eye of Charlie Calello who worked with Columbia records in New York. He was well known and had produced many singles for The Four Seasons, Lou Christi, Laura Nyro and others. Through Charlie, another single was recorded but they couldn't use the band name because of infringement rights. *The Magnificent Seven* was also a big Hollywood movie and the name was copyrighted so they changed their name to the Rubber Band.

The song *Let Love Come Between Us b/w Charlena* was released by Columbia Records. The record was sent out to the radio stations and it got big in a few cities nationally but was dismissed by Columbia because they thought it was released on one of their subsidiary labels and didn't realize the song was put out on their own label. Very few copies were sold because there weren't enough copies pressed up to fill the stores.

But The Rubber Band did eventually go out on the road and played about twelve cities where the song had reached #1. They had lucrative gigs playing ballrooms and dance halls in Mississippi, Alabama and Tennessee and did quite well. But it all ended and the Rubber Band broke up. Later James and Bobby Purify took *Let Love Come Between Us* to a #15 Billboard hit.

Johnny was between bands and found his way out to California to contemplate his next move. He was no sooner settled in Laurel Canyon when he got a call from his friend, Ed Sanford, back in Alabama who was now with a band called The Rocking Gibraltar's. They were discovered by Bob Hinkle who managed and produced the band. Singles were recorded and the band was getting some real interest but they needed a singer because their lead vocalist was married with children and couldn't afford to travel with the band. Johnny agreed to join and went back to Montgomery. He got familiar with their songs and played some gigs. But he asked the band if they wanted to come out to Hollywood for some steady work and record some backtracks for the latest teen movie soundtrack. So, they all decided to travel to California and live the dream.

The band morphed into Heart. (No relation to the band from Albuquerque or Heart from Seattle). The members were Johnny Townsend (vocals), Ed Sanford (organ), Rusty Crumpton (guitar), Keith Brewer (bass) and Bobby Dupree (drums). Upon arrival they were overwhelmed with the Sunset Strip where on any given night you could see Traffic, Laura Nyro, Muddy Waters and any of several other bands. There were so many dance venues. Through Ed Sanders contact, Bob Hinkle, they started playing clubs and got notice from Russ Shaw who was a promotion man for the Reprise Record label. They signed a deal and recorded a single *The Train b/w Heartbeat*, then were booked to open for Jimi Hendrix on what was called the Pacific Rim Tour. (Bakersfield, Fresno, San Bernadino, etc.)

They were featured at the Shrine Auditorium with Poco, Iron Butterfly, Canned Heat and many others. But after a while, the guys in the band grew homesick and Heart fell apart. They went back home but Johnny loved LA, he knew the ropes and had the backing. Johnny ran into Larry Sims (bass) and Merle Bregante (drums) who were players with The Sunshine Company, a band that had some hit song success and three LPs. Larry was friends with both Roger White (guitar, vocals) and Michael Collings (guitar, vocals) who were with a band called Catch. So, they all got together and found magic and inspiration.

The song *Friends* was written and they were able to get into Gold Star Studios on Santa Monica Blvd to record it. They called themselves Feather. Unbeknownst to the band, their manager J.R. Shanklin shopped the song around and accepted $5000 from the White Whale label. Meanwhile the band moved out to San Bernadino, wrote more songs and played shows here and there. They were unaware that their song had been released and just happened to be driving back from a gig and overheard it on the radio. The single *Friends b/w Salli* shot up the charts and a bidding war began over who was going to sign the band.

J.R. pocketed the White Whale advance and things began to go bad. Larry and Merle decided to leave and eventually they both got on with Loggins and Messina. Feather was not officially signed to any label, but because of their hit song, Columbia Records offered the band a bundle of money. Johnny added Steve Woodward to join in on (bass) and Dan Greer on (drums) to fill the void. The official members were Johnny Townsend (keyboards, vocals), Michael Collings (guitar, vocals), Roger White (guitar, vocals), Steve Woodward (bass) and Dan Greer (drums). One album was recorded at the Annex Studios, formerly Radio Recorders, located at 1032 N. Sycamore Ave. in Hollywood.

The album called *Friends by Feather* sounds like CSN&Y and Loggins and Messina with a slight country rock feel and intricate three-part harmonies. In addition to *Friends*, another single from the LP was submitted to the radio stations *No Time For Sorrow b/w The Fifth Stone*. Johnny's former partner in Heart (Ed Sanford) joined in on (keyboards) when the band hit the road to promote the LP. They toured up and down the west coast, but the band was short lived and eventually called it quits.

Larry Sims had a long presence with Loggins and Messina over the years and was the bass player on tour and played on all their albums. He died in December 2014.

Merle Bregante also toured and played on all the Loggins and Messina LPs and was with The Dirt Band. He settled in Austin, Texas with his recording studio Little Bear Records and now owns and operates Cribworks Digital Audio.

It's known that Steve Woodward passed away many years ago.

Dan Greer worked with Pure Prairie League and The Nitty Gritty Dirt Band writing songs but disappeared into normal life by the end of the 80's.

Unfortunately, Roger White took his own life in 1992.

Michael Collings also moved on due to acute depression and liver failure about 2010. Michael had twin sons and Jason Collings is quite well known as a stand-up comedian in Southern California.

After the breakup of Feather Johnny Townsend and Ed Sanford teamed up and became The Sanford Townsend Band scoring the huge international hit song *Smoke from a Distant Fire* in the mid-70's. They released three LPs and toured all over the nation opening for the likes of Marshall Tucker, Fleetwood Mac and The Charlie Daniels Band.

Ed Sanford has always been a singer songwriter and has played not only with Johnny Townsend but Michael MacDonald, Loggins and Messina, Ted Neeley, Nigel Olsen, Amy Holland, The Dirt Band and others.

Johnny is a terrific singer, has written several songs and played with numerous bands over the years. His last was the TGZ Band out of Virginia Beach.

He and Ed are still lifelong friends.

stereo
MUSICOR MS-3162
MUSICOR
FEDERAL DUCK

OGANOOKIE

FEDERAL DUCK / OGANOOKIE 1968-73

This band initially started at Haverford College located about 15 miles east of Philadelphia, Pennsylvania. Previously as The Stomp Jackson Quartet and then as The Guides, they were only sophomores and included Dave Barry (guitar), Ken Stover (organ), Pete Terry (bass) and Tom Pleatman (drums). Meanwhile Bob Stern, a violin player who was fresh from Juilliard School in New York, attended Haverford and roomed with Rob Stavis who was the younger brother of George Stavis. George, a junior, was a great (banjo, guitar) player and was in a band called The Monks with Tim Ackerman (drums). Bob met George who saw his potential as a (fiddle) player and taught him some bluegrass tunes.

Bob then joined a bluegrass band called The Paoli Locals to hone his chops on fiddle for a short while. He and Rob Stavis were living in the same building in a room near Dave Barry and Ken Stover. They became friends and at some point, became a folk quartet called The J. Edgar Hoover Memorial Jugband. Bob was talked into playing bass guitar and by their junior year they became a rock band adding Huck White on (electric guitar) and Professor Tom D'Adrea on (drums). Huck had a 200-foot guitar cord and during gigs would wander off into the audience or elsewhere in the venue while still playing the chords and guitar licks during any given song. Then they named themselves as Federal Duck.

Many think the band name came about from the duck stamp created as a permanent source of money to purchase and preserve wetlands for The Migratory Bird Conservation Act (commonly known as the Duck Stamp Act) signed by Franklin Delano Roosevelt in 1934. However, the odd name moniker came about when the guys were sitting around a Duck Pond, located on the grounds, passing around a Pakalolo Spliff. Keep in mind the anti-Vietnam War movement was flourishing, with lots of unrest. Some ducks came out of the water and started waddling towards the guys. Paranoia started to set in and they gave an appearance of a duck squadron in the moonlight and imagined that the ducks might be working for the government. Thus, the name Federal Duck.

The band evolved and by their senior year they were back to a quartet with members Dave Barry (guitar, vocals), Bob Stern (bass, vocals), Kenny Stover (keyboards) and Tom D'Adrea (drums). As the best band on campus, Dave purchased a much better amp and speaker then threw his old equipment from a third story window saying that it sounded better hitting the ground than it sounded when he played his guitar. Their manager was Buzz Burger and they played the local college auditoriums. But they were always only a cover band playing hits of the times for dancing boys and girls. Busy every weekend they gigged at Haverford College, University of Pennsylvania, Bryn Mawr College, Villanova University and others in the local area.

George Stavis had a high reputation amongst his peers and did some recording at Down East Studios located at 52 Pitt St in Lower Manhattan, NY. Lamont Johnson, a well-known bass player and jazz pianist produced the session. He had some connection with the Musicor Record label that wanted to enter the pop music market. George said he had some tunes in mind and Lamont told him if he could get a band together, he could make a recording deal happen with the label. So, he called the Federal Duck guys and other players he knew at Haverford and they spent a week in the apartment of George's parents to rehearse. The full band for the LP included George Stavis (banjo, guitars, vocals), Jack Bowers (guitars, dulcimer, recorder), Huck White (guitars, French horn, recorder), Ken Stover (keyboards, tuba), Bob Stern (bass, vocals), Tim Ackerman (drums), Tony Shaftel (lead vocals, bass), Thesha Dow (aka Lamont Johnson) (triangle) and Dave Barry (guitars, vocals). But Dave didn't see himself as a studio musician and decided to leave and continue his education back at Haverford.

They signed a contract with Musicor Records, a label more noteworthy of Gene Pitney, The Platters and George Jones. The practice and pre-production for the album occurred back at Down East Studios. Then gathering at 240 W 55th St in New York at Groove Sound Studios they recorded one album's worth of diverse music, jazz, rock, haunting vocals and fuzz guitar that all blend quite nicely with light paisley psychedelia. Kind of like The Millennium, Circus Maximus and at times The Fallen Angels. The self-titled *Federal Duck* LP has a wonderful, colorful, psychedelic cover that completes the package. There was talk of a single to be released to the radio stations *Circus in the Sea* but it never got beyond the thought process. This band never played live and parted ways after the recording session was complete. Also, when graduation happened at Haverford the formal Federal Duck band ceased. They all moved on with thoughts of post graduate work.

George had graduated the year before, was amid grad work at Purdue University and had an idea for an eclectic concept for an LP. He got together with his old drummer mate Tim Ackerman and recorded some songs for banjo and drums. The Vanguard Record label took on the project and released a groundbreaking instrumental album for banjo and percussion called *Labyrinths, Occult Improvisational Compositions for 5-String Banjo and Percussion* which took the banjo to other heights. On the album, he does a John Coltrane version of *My Favorite Things* which was very unusual and interesting. But although the critics had high accolades for George and the LP the public didn't understand and sales were slim.

After the project and one year at Purdue, George Stavis received a fellowship in Philosophy and moved out to Encinitas, Ca. to attend the University of California San Diego (UCSD) only 14 miles south. The money he received was more than he needed so he asked Tim Ackerman, Jack Bowers and Bob Stern if they wanted to come out to California to start another band. They agreed and came out to stay with George. Tim, Jack and George then played the local clubs as The George Stavis Trio, an acoustic band. Jack stayed home, was writing songs, playing piano and rehearsing with the guys. Bruce Frye had won the San Diego Blues guitarist for the year. He met the guys at a club they were playing and eventually joined in. They spent nine months rehearsing and perfecting new songs. Tim received a scholarship to Santa Cruz University, so the band migrated north. They advertised in the Valley Press as "Four PhD candidates seek study retreat in the mountains." and were offered a big house with a lot of land to occupy. This site was beyond their wildest dreams. They lived communally for over three years rehearsing every day and built up a new band incarnation.

The band became known as Oganookie, a name that has aired in mystery for years. The members here included George Stavis (banjo, vocals), Jack Bowers (piano, mandolin), Bob Stern (fiddle, bass, vocals), Bruce Frye (guitar, bass, lead vocals) and Tim Ackerman (drums). They played many gigs in and around Santa Cruz at places like The Chateau Liberte', The Opal Cliffs Inn, The Catalyst, The Bodega, San Jose State and The Longbranch Saloon in

Berkeley. This was a band that mesmerized folks with their rock and bluegrass sound and had a huge fan following. The *Oganookie* self-titled LP was recorded live and shows a band that had matured and graduated from the psychedelic 60's to a Grateful Dead, Goose Creek Symphony, Max Creek sound. They were the premiere band in the Bay and Santa Cruz areas competing with the band Snail in the early 70's. The band broke apart by 1973.

Dave Barry landed a job with The Daily Local News in West Chester, PA. where he covered very dull local city meetings. He then moved on and wrote a humor column with the Philadelphia Inquirer. He was eventually hired by the Miami Herald and became editor for their Sunday magazine called Tropic. His humorist column was nationally syndicated where he won a Pulitzer Prize, he had a TV show and has authored several books.

Bruce Frye is still in Santa Cruz and became an arborist and photographer.

Tony Shaftel moved to Hawaii for many years and had an auto repair shop. He was last heard from in Los Angeles.

Huck White became a full-fledged Doctor and lives in Massachusetts.

Kenny Stover stayed in Santa Cruz and played for many different bands including Quicksilver. He moved to Hawaii, continued to play music and is or was a property manager.

Tim Ackerman played with Jerry Miller (from Moby Grape) and Bob Stern in a band called Juice, then moved back to New York and worked for Tom & Jerry Boyswear, a children's apparel manufacturer owned by relatives and still did session work and plays for several other local Bands.

Jack Bowers taught school back in Virginia for a year then returned to Santa Cruz and played for Jill Croston (now known as Lacy J. Dalton). But his claim to fame is he was invited to teach a songwriting workshop at Soledad Prison. This led to him developing an Arts for Corrections program for prisons in the state of California, a life changing experience and 40-year career working at penitentiaries teaching music and directing arts programs to those who are less privileged. He still plays jazz piano with local bands on occasion.

Bob Stern also played with bands in California with Jerry Miller and Charlie Prichard (Conqueroo and Cat Mother and the All Night Blues Boys) and did studio work at Pacific Recorders in San Mateo. He moved back to New York, graduated from the NYU College of Dentistry and became a Dentist. Retired, he still plays violin and fiddle at shows with the Gil Gutiérrez Trio.

George Stavis built and ran The Louden Nelson Community Center in Santa Cruz for nine years, graduated from Columbia University back east and became an Attorney. Retired now and living in New York, he is well respected and still plays concerts on occasion. He once met the renowned banjo player Bela Fleck after a show. Bela's immediate response to him was "I know who you are. You're the guy who started all this!"

nasco
Felt
STEREO
NASCO 9006

FELT 1971

Myke Jackson was born Michael Thomas Jackson in Nashville, Tennessee. His dad, Tommy Jackson was a country fiddler and part of the staff band for The Grand Ole Opry. Tommy was also part of the "Nashville A Team," an elite group of recording musicians who played on most of the big country records from the early 1950s into the mid-1970s. So, Mike was fortunate enough to tag along with Dad, watching the professionals in action from an early age.

In 1966, his Mom and Dad divorced and he, his little brother, and Mother moved to Arab, Alabama. Mike had started playing guitar at age 11, but the move gave him a different motivation. By age 13 he had started his own band, The Wanderers. Soon he was approached by two fellow musicians from another band to play lead guitar. So, Mike disbanded his own band and went to work for The Dimensions - for money! This is when he met Michael Neel, the future drummer of the band that they would become.

While at Arab High School Mike took two years of typing to strengthen his fingers. One day he mis-typed his name as Myke Jackson. He thought it was cool and kept it. The Dimensions were forced to change their name, so Myke came up with the band name Everyday Lyfe. Mike Neel moved to Florida within a year. While in Florida he started listening to a lot of original bands. He came back to Arab to visit, contacted Myke and pitched the idea of starting their own original band. They began writing songs and looking for musicians.

Mike and Myke met Tommy Gilstrap through a friend, Waddy Berry, at a free concert on Monte Sano Mountain State Park at the Amphitheater there. The 3 jammed on 2 songs Mike and Myke had written and there was chemistry. They got together for a practice the next week at Mike's Dads upholstery shop and Tommy introduced another guitarist Stan Lee (not of The Dickies). They continued to jam and write songs until one night after an intense jam session Tommy declared, "Man, I felt that!" Myke said, "That is the name - Felt, cause our music can be felt by our listeners." And thus, Felt was born.

One day Mike Neel saw Allen Dalrymple walking in downtown Arab. He stopped and asked if he needed a ride somewhere. Allen's van had broken down and was in the shop. So, Mike brought Allen to rehearsal that night where it took all five guys to unload his heavy Hammond B3 organ. Myke had wanted to stay as a four-piece guitar band, but the organ was cool and Allen became an official member of Felt. So, the players in the formal band were Myke Jackson (guitar, vocals), Stan Lee (guitar), Tommy Gilstrap (bass), Allen Dalrymple (organ) and Mike Neel (drums).

They were busy performing on stage but there were few paying gigs, sticking mostly to hullabaloos, high school dances, outdoor teen events and frat parties as well playing at the Redstone Arsenal which was an Army Post just outside Huntsville. Mychael had written some songs and the band was getting some local notoriety. Lynn McCroskey, a sound guy for a local TV station, overheard a band rehearsal one night. He became their manager and paid for a demo recording at Boutwell Recording Studios in Birmingham, Alabama, which they sent to Bob Tubert at Lookout Music in Nashville.

Some big-time labels were interested (Columbia, United Artists, A&M) but they wanted to single Myke Jackson out from the band. He absolutely refused to break up the band's camaraderie and turned down the offer. Mychael's uncle was CEO of Crescent Corporation that owned Nashboro Records and Lookout Music. Although the label primarily published black gospel and blues, they wanted to try their hand in the pop music business. Bob Tubert was head of publishing and really liked the songs that Myke wrote. So, to keep Felt intact he signed the band to Nasco, part of Nashboro.

They were one of only a few rock bands along with Whale Feathers, Westfauster and The Electric Toilet to be featured on the Nasco label. Preproduction occurred at a studio in Tupelo, Mississippi. Then they moved to the big state-of-the-art Woodland Sound Studios in Nashville, Tennessee to complete the project. This studio was only two years old at the time but has had a long archive with big time acts. Woodland closed to the public in 1998 and again on March 2020 due to Tornado damage but remains a part of rock history recording bands including The Charlie Daniels Band, MacKendree Spring, The Indigo Girls, Neil Young, Michael W Smith, Kansas and more.

There were no singles released to the radio airwaves. But the self-titled *Felt* album was released and had some local airplay featuring the song *Look at the Sun* with voice harmonies like The Beatles. Mychael played way beyond his years here and it is a wonder how he wasn't more known. Some say the band sounds like Twentieth Century Zoo, but rock and heavy guitar throughout put them closer to The James Gang or Help. According to Mychael, the cover of the album was talked about with the cover designers before anything went to print. They said, "We're gonna shoot a naked girl painted with tempera paint lying down on a white colored background." This sounded good as described to the band. But none of the band members saw the cover art until the album was released. To quote Myke, "OH MY GOD! It looks like a Fellini film!" This could be rated as one of the worst LP covers of all time.

Because they had more of a progressive sound, they were put on the list to play The Isle of Wight Festival in England. But this and a promo tour never happened, as Myke was arrested for possession of marijuana. He served eight months during which time the album was released. The band broke up temporarily but after Myke got out, they reunited for some jamming and rehearsing. But drugs were still everywhere and Myke didn't want to be in another "wrong place, wrong time" situation. The band fell apart, but they all parted as friends.

In 1975 Michael Neel and Myke Jackson joined and played with a 50's band called Myron and the Van Dells. While on the road a song publisher named Cliff Williamson, signed Myke to Tree International Publishing. In late 1977 Myke left the band and moved back to Nashville changing his recording name to simply "Mychael". There were jokes about him and the more famous Michael Jackson. He did session work and live gigs, while writing and recording demos of his songs for the Tree Publishing Company. One of his songs, *Walls,* was recorded by Charlie Rich.

Over the course of 1977-78 Mychael and Cliff recorded an entire album entitled *Neon Dreams.* RCA started a rock label called Free Flight and approached Cliff to sign Mychael for the album. One single *Stay b/w Neon Dreams* was put out and the B-side of the single *Neon Dreams* was getting serious airplay in San Francisco spending eight weeks at the top of the local charts. *The Life Sonata*, another song on the LP, was set for guitar orchestra and got accolades from Guitar Player magazine. Mychael went back to session work after this.

Lynn McCroskey, former manager of Felt, repaired guitar amplifiers and started a company called Sonics. They started selling and installing sound systems, PA's, locally for Churches and sound events. Sonics merged and got the contract for Omnimax Theatres back in 1981 which blossomed into the worldwide IMAX subsidiary. Lynn McCrosky was a visionary in sound that sadly crossed the line peacefully in September 2018.

Allen Dalrymple tragically died in a car accident in the mid-70's.

Mike Neel became a session drummer and played with many other bands but eventually settled and worked for R.C. Davis Inc., an Industrial Chemical Manufacturer.

Tommy Gilstrap went to college and became a Physical Therapist and Caregiver. He still plays bass guitar and lives in Florida.

Stan Lee still played guitar with jazz bands but spent 38 years working as a project manager for the Army Corp of Engineers at Redstone Arsenal in Huntsville.

Mychael found religion and released several CDs along those lines. Devoted to his many talents he has done commercials, acted in stage plays, done musical scores for movies and TV and instructed on music technique at local universities. In 1988, after years of bad jokes, Mychael changed his name to Mychael John Thomas officially and had an active life in music. Sadly, he passed away suddenly on September 17th, 2021. He will be missed.

There was/is a lot of interest in the band Felt from collectors and publishers alike. In 2011 Michael Neel, Stan Lee, Tommy Gilstrap and Mychael John Thomas reunited to record a second LP with new songs. The magic was still there and they released *Felt II – Psychedelic Memoirs* on CD circa 2012.

STEREO 73024
fever tree

STEREO 73040
fever tree
ANOTHER TIME
ANOTHER PLACE
©UNIVERSAL CITY RECORDS • A DIVISION OF MCA INC. PRINTED IN U.S.A.
UNI

STEREO 73067
FEVER TREE
CREATION
UNI

FEVER TREE 1968-70

You'd have to start with Michael Knust when one talks about Fever Tree. He picked up a guitar at the age of eight, was dedicated and practiced every day before and after school. He attended Spring Branch High School and started taking serious lessons at Westview Music in Houston, Texas. After a few months, he got surprisingly good at it and was asked to teach others. Mike had been teaching Bud Wolfe guitar chords and asked if he wanted to play bass guitar instead. Meanwhile Dennis Keller who could sing "lights out" was taking guitar lessons from Jerry Campbell who also worked at Westview. The four of them talked about it and agreed to form a band. Mike Knust (guitar), Bud Wolfe (aka E.E. Wolfe III) on (bass), Jerry Campbell (lead guitar) and Dennis Keller (vocals). Don Lampton was hired on (keyboards, rhythm guitar) and Jerry had a friend, John Tuttle, who played (drums).

Dressing in Beatle boots and matching suits they wanted an English sounding name. They saw an ad in a men's magazine for Bostwick Men's Fashion Cologne and thought it sounded English enough so, they decided to call themselves The Bostwick Vines. The first gig was on the roof of Westview Music timed just as high school was done for the day. It was a remarkable success and they started playing local high school dances and Senior Proms in the area. They had steady work for quite a while, then Jerry Campbell got drafted leaving Mike to take over on lead guitar. Then smaller teen club dates came along like The Rose Room at the Beaumont Hotel and The Box, formerly The VIP Club.

They hooked up with Scott and Vivian Holtzman who were successful songwriters and folksters who had played The Jester Lounge along with Jerry Jeff Walker, Townes Van Zant, Lightin' Hopkins and others. By this time, they were columnists for the Houston Chronical covering the San Francisco bands. Scott was also writing radio and TV ad jingles. He and Vivian both took over managing and advising the band. They felt that The Bostwick Vines as a band name wouldn't do and renamed the band as Fever Tree instead. They also felt Rob Landes who had been working with Scott and the commercial jingles, was a better fit for the band, so he replaced Don Lampton on (keyboards).

Rob was a little older than the guys and was clean shaven. He didn't really look the part, so Scott got hair and spirit gum and made a mustache for him. Rob didn't have a real feel for music but could read notes so he wrote the songs down in a notepad that he was to read from during their first show together. He had never seen them play live and wasn't sure what to expect. All the lights blinded him so he couldn't see what he wrote down and the mustache was falling off. It was an awkward and laughable situation.

They played the Gulf Coast area from Corpus Christi to Lake Charles in Louisiana gigging in clubs like The Stardust Rollercade, The Puppy Pen, The Driscoll Hotel, Love Street and The Catacombs in Houston opening for bands like The Moving Sidewalks, Kenny and the Casuals, Zachary Thaks and others. Their first big concert was opening for The Jefferson Airplane at the Houston Coliseum. Scott and Vivian had major connections in the industry and the shows got much bigger wherever they played.

Bob Shad came down from New York and got them a deal with Mainstream records. Two singles were put out *Hey Mister b/w I Can Beat Your Drum* and *Girl Don't Push Me b/w Steve Lenore* and both became #1 hits locally. Both singles were recorded at the Andrus Studio in Houston on Broadway near the ship canal. This is where The 13th Floor Elevators recorded their albums. Suddenly the pay went from $400 to about $1500 per show. The UNI Record label took notice and signed them up. Rob Landes and Mike Knust wrote new music with Scott and Vivian providing the lyrics. They spent two months back at Andrus Studio laying down the basic songs for their first album. Then moved to Los Angeles and finished the songs at DCT Recorders on Sunset Blvd. in Hollywood with orchestral overdubs and special effects.

The first album simply called *Fever Tree* is brilliant with pipe organ, harpsichord, flute, cello and baroque sounds from Rob, Dennis Keller's wonderful voice and sounds of wah-wah, sustain and fuzz from Michael's guitar that left folks in wonder. The single *San Francisco Girls b/w Come With Me* put them on the national charts and they toured relentlessly to all parts of North America and Canada. Sound comparisons go to SRC otherwise known as The Scott Richardson Combo but the hard edge they were noted for in their live shows was not present on the LP and this soured the sales a little bit.

The critics didn't help their cause, stating that the band was holding back. The second album *Another Time Another Place*, recorded at Andrus Studios with finishing touches completed at Summit Sound in Dallas and United/Western Studios in Hollywood, was put out with the same effect. By the third album entitled *Creation*, UNI was starting to lose interest. The band moved to California and continued to "woo" the audiences at The Avalon Ballroom, The Fillmore and The Kaleidoscope on the LA Strip where they opened for The Mamas and Papas. For this performance the atmosphere was hazy purple with pot smoke and after the show Mama Cass was awaiting her stage entrance on an elephant. They were touring all over the US opening for Love, The Velvet Underground, Spirit, Blue Cheer and were the headliner when The James Gang (with Joe Walsh) opened for them.

But the band was bumbling and grumbling over drug addiction and their booking manager Ron Sunshine was taking half the tour money to book hotels, air flights, truck rentals and equipment and was in general control of all the expenses. He wound up pocketing everything when they got home after the US tour. Ron disappeared and they found they owed over $13,000 to the record label. Trying to pay off the debt, they played as many gigs as possible. Their final tour gig was scheduled for the City Auditorium in Colorado Springs but they were stuck in Casper, Wyoming due to weather and couldn't drive the 350 plus miles to get there. It's noted that the Colorado concert promoter Tony Spicola hired somebody to fly up in haste to get the band and bring them down for the show. The local backing bands played for 6 hours waiting for the star attraction to show up. Without their own guitars, organ, drums or amps, Fever Tree used the supporting band's equipment to play the concert and then broke up.

But they still owed UNI an album recording as part of the 4-album deal they initially signed. Dennis had already left the band in frustration and the guys weren't talking. But to honor the contract they all decided to get back together one more time and record a final LP. Knowing they couldn't emulate the excitement of their live performance on record, at least in UNI's eyes, it was decided to record a final live concert. Recorded at Mt. Carmel High School in Houston, this show was memorable and had all the excitement missing from the studio LPs. This was the last time they formally played together as a band. But UNI passed on the recordings and dropped them like a lead brick.

Instead, the UNI label executives decided to put together outtakes from the former studio sessions and reworked them with well-known session musicians Hal Blaine (drums), David Cohen from Country Joe and the Fish (guitar), Joe Osborne (bass), Larry Knetchel (keyboards) and others at United/Western Recorders in Hollywood. The album *For Sale* was released by the newly formed Ampex Record label but was not promoted. Sales for all Fever Tree albums were disappointing. However, in England they were over the top, viewed as intellectual rockers experimenting with songs and sounds pushing the psychedelic envelope. But they never toured overseas. Three years together and they were done.

John Tuttle sold his drums and became a home builder.

Bud (E.E.) Wolfe left music behind and was last heard from in Philadelphia.

Michael Knust retained the rights to Fever Tree and revived different incarnations of the band. He tried to keep the band together but was the only one left as an original. Gigs were set up and played but the magic was gone. He was in a couple of horrible car wrecks that left him in a lot of pain, but he survived and worked his way back as the only remaining original member eventually releasing a live album (CD) by Fever Tree (circa) a 1978 concert. He was on constant painkillers during his later years and in 2003 his life passed on.

Dennis Keller left the music business and became an executive in the car and motorcycle industry. After 30 years without his voice, he got the bug again and reformed the band as Fever Tree Rising. They were quite successful at cloning the sound of the original band, especially with the original voice of Dennis.

Rob Landes shaved and cut off his hair, played jazz piano at nightclubs and then formed The Rob Landes Trio (a jazz band). They landed a local morning TV show in Houston that got them enough money and exposure through name recognition to select shows and private gigs. They are still active as of this writing playing about 30 concerts a year. Rob was solely responsible for getting the original tapes of the final live Fever Tree concert proposed and rejected for the 4th UNI album. Entitled *Live 1969,* the performance included the original five members and their final show. It was put together, remastered and released in 2011 on the Sundazed record label.

ABCS-661 STEREO
TOM WILSON
abc
RECORDS
FIRE

FIRE (US) 1968

Paul Glanz formed Fire. He started his music career as an acapella singer. His first rock band was The Unluv'd who recorded a few singles on the True Love record label. This band lasted a little over a year. Paul was a singer, songwriter and played a Hammond B3 organ playing with other bands. He then formed Fire with Barry Sandler (drums), Wayne Morrison (guitar) and a bass player who wishes to remain anonymous. They based themselves in Manhattan and were all seasoned musicians. The bass player had already done some studio work with Tom Wilson who was THE production Guru at the time. Tom was behind the likes of Bob Dylan, The Velvet Underground, Simon and Garfunkel and The Mothers of Invention among many, many others during this time.

Fire got an immediate record deal, were signed by ABC Records and were all ready to record at The Record Plant in New York under the keen ear of Eddie Kramer. But before things started Wayne Morrison got cold feet and quit the band. Hugh McCracken was a well-respected session guitarist and stepped in for most of the guitar parts on the record. However, before the recording was completed, they found another (guitarist) in Jeoffrey Richardson who became an official member of the band. He was from England but was not the same Geoffrey Richardson of Caravan. He added the final changes to the album.

Musically, their style, although unintentional, is very much like that of The Young Rascals. Some nice soul influenced sounds that is organ based with some trick guitar. Paul Glanz certainly comes close to sounding like Felix Cavaliere. The self-titled *Fire* album is more noted for the trick cover jacket as it looked and opened like a giant book of matches. Although no singles were released, there are nice AM radio ditties that probably didn't get airplay too far out of the general New York area.

Fire was dispatched out on the road to promote the album touring the east coast, mid-west and southern states. A whole book could be written about the clubs they played in and the hard, dreadful road. They had little money, had road trip breakdowns, wound up sleeping in the truck on the side of the highway, got in bar fights and the general hatred of hippies in the south saw a few bullets whistling by. They rarely got paid and Jeoffrey Richardson, who had had enough of the madness, quit and went back to England before the tour was done.

Seth Connors was hired as guitar replacement to complete the shows. But, when they were in Wichita Falls, Texas, Seth made an unfortunate pass towards the wife of a club owner. Payment was the least of their worries. They had to skip out on the hotel bill and left the truck behind with all the equipment. With extraordinarily little money they found a sweet young receptionist at the airport and talked their way into the flight home for student fare. Paul had his Hammond B3 shipped (uncrated) back to New York COD. It took him 3 months to gather enough money to retrieve his beloved monolith organ only to find it in bits and pieces where it was being stored. The band had only been together for maybe a year, but they were done. No hard feelings and the members all went their separate ways.

Paul Glanz moved onto a stable music career in other bands playing with The Critters and their last album output on the Project 3 label, he was also with the Soul Survivors and toured with Arthur Brown. But he got his kudos with Carly Simon when she hit it big with her *Anticipation* album. Afterwards he was busy with Meatloaf, Roy Buchanan, Garland Jeffries, Flo and Eddie and over the years was with many other well-known bands. The lifestyle was rough and Paul decided to find peace through religion. He became a born again Christian and changed his name to Paul Gene to remove any thoughts about his former life on the continuous road.

FLAT EARTH SOCIETY
WALEECO

FLAT EARTH SOCIETY 1968

The Flat Earth Society were from Lynn, Massachusetts. Before they formed as a band, Rick Doyle played (guitar) and Jack Kerivan was a classically trained (piano) player. Both had been playing in bands at high school dances and at coffee houses in the area. They decided to form a rock band and asked Phil Dubuque (guitar, vocals) to come to Jacks house for a rehearsal session. Rick and Jack had already determined that the name of the band would be The Flat Earth Society. The name was based upon Samuel Birley Rowbotham who took a literal interpretation of passages in the Bible and developed Zetetic Astronomy stating that the Earth was Flat, centered at the North Pole and bounded at the edges with a wall of ice. Man! The books we read in the 60's. The imagery!

Phil Dubuque had known Rick and his reputation as a great guitarist. He had already been playing the coffee house and folk circuit for about 2½ years. The three of them rehearsed at Jacks house and were using Jacks left hand on his keyboards for the bass parts but they wanted a real bass player and hired Paul Carter in on (bass guitar). He had been in a few garage bands and was also a (lead singer). Curt Girard was the last to join in on (drums). So, to be clear the players for the formal band were Jack Kerivan (piano, organ, vocals), Phil Dubuque (rhythm guitar, recorder, lead vocals), Rick Doyle (lead guitar, vocals), Paul Carter (bass, vocals) and Curt Girard (drums).

Jack Kerivan was the main composer for the lyrics. Phil and Rick would arrange the songs. They were a covers band but played some of their own compositions and after they got comfortable, they played high schools, teen dances and places like the Rubicon Coffee House in Providence, Rhode Island and The Unicorn which was a small coffee house used for solo acts and folk music in Boston.

The advertising firm of Quinn and Johnson sought a group of musicians and bands to record a "jingle" for The F.B. Washburn Candy Company and their Waleeco Candy Bar. There was a competition set up amongst several bands in the area and the jingle chosen would be used for commercial radio airplay to promote their candy bar. The payoff was whichever bands jingle got the nod they would get free time to record an album at a local studio. Phil wrote three different short songs to submit. They went to Fleetwood Studios at 321 Revere St. Revere, Massachusetts to record the ditties and as luck would have it, Phil's jingle was chosen. The deal was that each wrapped Waleeco Candy Bar purchased included a coupon and if you bought six candy bars and sent six wrappers plus $1.50 to the F.B. Washburn home office you would receive an album by The Flat Earth Society. The campaign was like finding the golden ticket in the Wonka Bar in the *Willie Wonka* movie.

They only had a week to complete the project. The Fleetwood studio was small and, short of the demos they made previously, none of the guys really had any recording experience. Russ Hamm was the recording engineer, but the band pretty much produced the songs themselves. The bass amp was too overpowering, so they had to set it up in the bathroom with porcelain tiles. There were no overdubs and the reverb was exaggerated to highlight the music. Some songs were already written but not enough to fill a full album, so Jack would write lyrics on the spot. Phil and Rick came up with the notes to accompany the words.

The album master tapes were in stereo but Russ, during the final master, mixed everything together, so the album came out in MONO form. It wasn't until later, in 1993, that the true stereo effects were brought out through a reissue of the original master tapes on Arf Records. The stereo effects were crude but effective. On the first song it starts as MONO and about halfway through it sounds like a jet airplane flying through the speakers right to left. But to get the jet flying sound effect it was just a can of paint being sprayed into a bucket.

Local artist Jerry Pinkney made an elaborate illustration for the album cover with lots going on and vivid coloring reflecting the psychedelic times. The album was notably called *Waleeco* after the candy bar. What a recording! This was a band that was into dreamy folk music, echoed with psychedelia, their harmonies chilling, the guitars like bells on the slower numbers and hard-core fuzz guitar on the rockers. All but one song was composed by Jack Kerivan and/or Phil Dubuque. The songs had an overall mysterious sound so prevalent during this time. They were experienced players that appeared to be only about 14 years of age. But they made wonderful flower psych like the pros. Ultimate Spinach, Liberal Religious Youth and West Coast Pop Art Experimental Band are good comparisons.

As a result of radio advertising and the jingle expounding on the airwaves, the band played at The Psychedelic Supermarket which was a much bigger venue located in the alley behind Kenmore Square right next to Boston

College. They also played at the fairground concerts that summer in front of 2-3000 people. It's not known how many candy bars were sold for the promotion or how many records were mail ordered as a result but by the end of 1968 the promotion period had expired. The studio closed its doors in 1974. And with it, boxes of albums left behind were thrown in the dumpster. What a shame. The Flat Earth Society played a few venues over the next couple of years but never outside of the local area. By 1970 the band had split up.

Phil Dubuque moved to San Francisco and met Pete Axtel. They formed a duo and played some of the clubs in the area. It was decided they should move to Europe and they did get some interest from Chrysalis Records. Phil got hold of Rick Doyle to see if he would come overseas to help. He did and they put together a band called Cottonwood and played the college circuit there, but nothing panned out with a record deal and no songs were ever recorded. He lived in Europe for 15 years and played the club scene as a solo act. He returned to Boston and started a guitar instruction service through Facebook.

Rick Doyle moved back to the states and settled down in Salem, Massachusetts.

The whereabouts of Curt Girard is unknown.

Paul Carter moved to Boston and hooked up with a band that toured for four years in the southeast states. Small recordings occurred in the early 80's with The Infliktors, Radio Hearts and The Young Jacques. Then he was a roadie for Aerosmith and later became the lead road manager for Ted Nugent. He finally broke away and settled into a family life in Seattle.

Jack Kerivan got heavy into electronic music and played his last live performance with The Indianapolis Community Orchestra.

THE
FLOATING
OPERA
STEREO/SD 730
EMBRYO

THE FLOATING OPERA 1971

Steve Welkom was in high school when he was asked to join a local band calling themselves Them (unrelated to Van Morrison's band). They had a big following in Cincinnati, Ohio. He decided to attend college at the University of Michigan (UM) and during his freshman orientation met John Nemerovski who was a piano player known as Nemo who was familiar with Steve from his days in a band called The Port Clinton Four before Steve moved to Cincinnati. Together they formed The Long Island Sound (aka The Fox) that included Steve Welkom (guitar, vocals), Greg Hayward (guitar, vocals), John Nemerovski (organ), Gary Munce (bass) and John Briegel (drums).

This band played college parties and clubs around Ann Arbor, Michigan like The Canterbury House and The Roostertail in Detroit. They also played a homecoming for UM and opened for The Doors at the Intramural Sports Building. Long Island Sound finished a great set but when The Doors hit the stage, Jim Morrison was so inebriated that he began dropping F-Bombs at the audience. The Doors, Ray Manzarek, John Densmore and Robbie Krieger had to leave the stage with a staggering Jim in tow. The audience was dumbfounded and angry. The promoters of the dance became desperate and asked Long Island Sound to come back on stage and play another set. They won the crowd over and everybody was happy to have a band they could dance to and bail out the event. Inexplicably, Morrison did sober up and, later, The Doors came back out to play a flawless show. But very few of the spectators remained as, by this time, most had disappeared. However, John Osterberg (otherwise known as Iggy Pop) was still in attendance and credited this one particular show as the inspiration for him to form The Stooges.

Then Steve and John started to write original material and they decided to rename themselves as Floating Opera. Steve suggested the name, which was a short novel written by John Simmons Barth. One single was recorded, *Gotta Find A New Baby b/w It's A Great Day*. After they all graduated from UM, Greg Hayward and John Briegel left the band. As replacement players they added fellow UM alumna Carol Lees (organ) and invited Artie Alinikoff (drums, vocals) who was a seasoned older drummer from Cincinnati to come up and add some experience and punch to their sound. They played dance clubs, colleges and larger venues like The Michigan Union Ballroom and The Hill Auditorium in the local area, adding more original material according to the crowd response.

Confident with their original songs and having enough new material they contacted another friend, Sandy Nassan in Cincinnati. He had signed with Herbie Mann's record label, Embryo, and had released a jazz guitar album entitled *Just Guitar* one year earlier. Sandy convinced Herbie to sign Floating Opera as another rock band, along with the band AIR, to expand his jazz name into the pop music mainstream. The album was recorded at A&R Studios in New York and the music is very keyboard oriented with heavy harmonies much like another Michigan band, Savage Grace, and San Francisco's It's A Beautiful Day without the violin. The album cover pictures the band running clockwise from the bottom Carol Lees, Gary Munce, Nemo, Artie Alinikoff and Steve Welkom.

The band promoted their self-titled album *Floating Opera* traveling in a big orange van they called Easy Rider playing venues in the mid-west plus The Village Gate in New York and The Fillmore West with Tower of Power in San Francisco. One single from the album was released, *The Vision b/w Song Of Suicides* but the album and single wasn't really promoted by the Embryo label and Floating Opera went their separate ways after about a year.

Carol Lees wound up in Hollywood and was involved with writing, arranging and producing movie scores for many years. She had notable production duties for *Original Sin* starring Anglie Jolie and Antonio Banderas as well as *Happy New Year* with Peter Falk. She also worked with Madonna. But regrettably passed away sometime in 2018.

Gary Munce played with The Cadillac Cowboys and spent his career as head of Computer Security for UM.

Steve Welkom traveled back to San Francisco and became part of Bill Graham Presents. He was in partnership with Gregg Perloff and ran Another Planet Entertainment which as of this writing is still a promotional group for many of the mega players and bands in the world who come through the San Francisco area.

John Nemerovski and Artie Alinikoff got heavy into Apple Computers and were deeply involved with an internet publication that promoted much of the new technical devices related to MAC computers. They wrote for the MyMac website focusing on music and photography. John is now actively teaching and playing music in Tucson, Az.

Artie Alinikoff also played in The Don Kelly Band, a "hot" country/rock band, for over 20 years at the well-known club Robert's Western World in Nashville. He's since retired and living the good life.

ABCS-658 STEREO
abc RECORDS
FORD THEATRE
trilogy for the masses

abc RECORDS
STEREO ABCS 681
12
9
3
6
FORD THEATRE
Presents
TIME CHANGES
A New Musical

FORD THEATRE 1968-69

Initially these guys started out in 1961. They were known as The Continentals and hailed from Milford, Massachusetts. Members were John Mazzerelli (organ, vocals), Art "Butch" Webster (guitar), James Altieri (bass, vocals) and Robert Tamagni (drums, vocals). They had been playing frat parties around the Boston area. A couple of acetates were recorded in hopes of landing a record deal, but it didn't pan out. Songs had been written and although they were basically a covers band, they would throw in some of their own compositions.

They played weddings, bar mitzvahs, fraternity's and college dances. Fred Cenedella was an event and dance coordinator at the University of Massachusetts who got familiar with the band and would book gigs for them at the college. After a while, it was made clear that The Continentals as a band name was not a good fit. Times were changing and someone suggested The Joyful Noise as a name update. This band included Butch Webster (guitar), John Mazzerelli (keyboards, vocals), Damon Hollenger (guitar), Jimmy Altieri (bass, vocals) and Bob Tamagni (drums, vocals). Meanwhile Harry Palmer was a composer from New York who was well known as a songwriter. He had written at least one song that was the B side to a single that was out there on the airwaves by Sandra and Gayl *The One You Love b/w Step It Up*. The Continentals had also played some songs he had written.

Harry had put together some other songs and was looking for the proper band to bring his ideas to light. He had a meeting with Fred Cenedella and they were talking about music and bands. The subject of The Joyful Noise came up as they were one of the great bands in the area. He, Fred and the band then met and they were impressed by the tunes they heard from Harry. Joe Scott came on board as a singer they had known playing with another band. Damon Hollenger departed and Harry Palmer became a full-fledged member. Fred became their manager and began booking gigs for them.

By now the members were Joe Scott (lead vocals), John Mazzerelli (organ, vocals), Butch Webster (guitar), Harry Palmer (guitar), James Altieri (bass, vocals) and Robert Tamagni (drums, vocals). Harry took over all the song writing duties. The music got more intricate and lyrically sophisticated. Participating in Battle of the Bands contests against other bands like The Rockin' Ramrods, Thunder Train and others, they usually won first place. Harry's songs were written and derived a few years earlier when President Kennedy was assassinated. They were dark and ominous and full of deep meaning, so it was decided to rename the band as Ford Theatre, based on the dark days where President Lincoln was shot and killed.

They played the New England college circuit and gigged in the local area playing clubs like The Lakeview Ballroom, The Ark, The Escape Lounge and opened for Procol Harum on their first US tour at the Unicorn Coffee house in Boston. It was on this night that they were approached by Dick Summer, a well-known DJ who was famous with the Boston radio station WBZ and introduced them to Bob Thiele at ABC Records who signed a record deal with them. Bob requested that they record a demo and they spent two hours playing with no breaks on what was to be a concept song. They set up at Fleetwood Studios located in Revere, Massachusetts and recorded their first LP *Trilogy for The Masses*. All done in one take, it was one of the first concept LPs and predated The Who's *Tommy* by a year. FM underground radio was starting to play these long songs and full album sides.

With lots of excitement and artistic meandering, the record labels hated this kind of stuff at first. A band without a 3-minute AM radio ditty, just didn't make it on the radio stations. This album is quite good, has lots of guitar jamming, organ passages, orchestration and some minor effects. A step out from the norm, but it was a little too progressive for the pop hits on AM Radio and the songs were too long. It also didn't help that the songs all ran together with no breaks in between. However, a single was released with a 3-minute excerpt from the 14-minute instrumental song *From a Back Door Window (Search)* backed with *Theme For the Masses*.

Ford Theatre was sent on tour to cities in the mid-west like Detroit, Chicago and Cleveland. On August 9th, 1968, they were featured in St Louis playing in front of 10,000 people at the Kiel Auditorium with local bands Truth, Good Feelin' and The Aardvarks along with Iron Butterfly, The Hourglass, Spirit, and the headliner Big Brother and The Holding Company. The big FM radio station there, KSHE, was playing full albums on air and were noted for playing "concept" rock albums. Ford Theatres *Trilogy For The Masses* was one such LP, but the album wasn't available at any of the record stores for purchase. This was similar in most of the outer regions where they played and it hampered their chances for any real public notice. Jim Altieri then left the band. Joe Scott remained as lead vocalist and took over on (bass).

A second album was recorded at The Hit Factory in New York, the first rock band LP produced by Bill Szymczyk. This second release called *Ford Theatre Presents Time Changes A New Musical* was still a concept album but was much more AM Radio friendly. The cover pictures left to right are Harry Palmer, Art Webster, Bob Tamagni and Joey Scott standing with John Mazzerelli in the forefront. A couple of singles were released *Wake Up in the Morning b/w Time Changes* and *I've Got the Fever b/w Jefferson Airplane*. But the label provided little to no support and although they were local heroes regionally with lots of press, nationally they were a figment of everyone else's imagination. ABC dropped the band, but they were picked up by DECCA Records and went to a recording studio in Winchester, Massachusetts to complete a third LP but it is still sitting on the shelves. Eventually the band broke apart.

Jim Altieri stayed in Milford, formed his own band, The West River Band, and sustained his music career playing on weekends with other bands in the local area. He bought a truck and owned a transport business hauling non-hazardous materials to the general area. The last known band he was with was a local band called Goldrush.

Joe Scott took up guitar, sang and played in bands then spent many years teaching guitar at the Cape Cod Conservatory located in West Barnstable, MA. before retiring.

Bob Tamagni taught at The Berklee School of Music in Boston. He was also in a jazz band with John Mazzarelli called Impulse for a while.

John Mazzarelli was a keyboardist who played in many jazz ensembles and still lives in Milford.

Butch Webster stayed in the music industry playing in local bands. He worked with Muzak and DMX Inc. and then moved up to regional director of Mood: Media North America providing background music and video with sight, sound and scents (the total package) for large stores and office buildings.

Harry Palmer settled into the business end of music and became an executive for various record labels (Sony, BMG, Polygram, Atlantic) securing deals for other bands like Euclid, Nektar, Peter Myers, Melissa Manchester and others.

MERCURY STEREO SR-61256

PLAYABLE ON MODERN MONAURAL EQUIPMENT

Mercury

THE

FORT MUDGE

MEMORIAL

DUMP

FORT MUDGE MEMORIAL DUMP 1970

Richard Clerici (guitar, vocals), Dan Keady (guitar, vocals), Caroline Stratton (vocals), James Deptula (drums) and David Amaral (bass) formed this band in Walpole, Massachusetts. Richard had some former experience with Yesterday's Children and The Crusaders (no relation to the more famous bands of that name). Dave was Richard's cousin. Caroline was from Norwood, the next town over, and was dating Dan Keady. She came up with the name for the band Fort Mudge Memorial Dump from the Pogo comic strip in the newspapers that ran from 1948 through 1975.

They practiced in the basement where Dan Keady lived and drove his folks nuts because of how loud they played. When they were ready, they started playing local teen clubs and dances. Ron Beaton, a part time actor, took a liking to their music and became their manager. They spent all they had and made a demo tape for Ron to shop around. He hitch-hiked to New York with the tapes and got interest from Simon Hayes who was an A&R man with Mercury records.

They were signed and traveled to Boston to record an album at Petrucci & Atwell Studios located on Newbury St. This is where many of the Vanguard Label artists recorded. One story is that upon arrival the band was shown a safe that had one cassette tape inside. This was a demo tape that had been rejected by the Vanguard label. The tape had been submitted by Bob Dylan and had been left there as a reminder to executives that hasty decisions can lead to big mistakes. Of course, Dylan was absorbed by Columbia Records.

Michael Tschudin (The Listening, Cynara) did the production for the Fort Mudge recording session. The record is heavy with dual guitar assaults, ripping bass lines, wah-wah and fuzz abound. The best comparison goes to Leigh Stevens and his *Red Weather* album in spots. Caroline doesn't sing on every cut and has been compared to Grace Slick, but although the album has a west coast feel, I believe she has a sound of her own falling in with the gals who fronted Art Of Lovin and Lacewing. Richard Clerici has a deep passionate voice like Michael Kac of Mandrake Memorial.

To promote the LP entitled *The Fort Mudge Memorial Dump*, they played The Electric Circus and The Fillmore East in New York and every major college town around the greater northeast US and opened for the likes of Albert King, Aerosmith, The Flock and others. But it seems wherever they played the album was not available in stores. Apparently, Simon Hayes was let go from Mercury Records upon the album's release and his replacement didn't know or care about Fort Mudge. There was no support for the band, no singles were released and the money ran out. Disillusioned, Richard and Dave left the band to form Brother Ralph. Dan and Caroline hired other players for Fort Mudge and continued. The fans adored this band for their live shows and they had enough staying power to last until about 1973.

Unfortunately, Jim Deptula passed away some years back.

David Amaral made a career of playing bass touring with Bobby Whitlock and Peter Wolfe. He opened a recording studio in Walpole, Massachusetts and as of this writing was with a band called wiki3 playing local gigs in Boston.

Caroline Stratton toured with Dan Keady as a duo in the aftermath of Fort Mudge but then she decided to sing solo. But there were no known recordings of her music.

Dan Keady moved to Florida where he has been a member of several bands over the years.

Richard Clerici married and he and his wife have a clinic in Boston that helps people with sleep disorders. He is still passionate about his music and plays with his band Raven.

The Fort Mudge Memorial Dump record was relegated to obscurity in the cut-out bins nationally, but it is worth every penny if found.

FREAK OUT

PEAK IMPRESSIONS / THE FREEBORNE
monitor

YS-2048-RM
PEAK IMPRESSIONS / THE FREEBORNE

THE FREEBORNE 1967

The Freeborne got their start in Brookline, Massachusetts. Dave Codd and Nick Carstoiu had both grown up around classical and opera music. Nick was a cellist and Dave a violin player. They played together in a string quartet at Brookline High School and paid little attention to the pop music being broadcast over the radio until that world changing night when The Beatles played the Ed Sullivan show. Nick and Dave were sucked right into rock and roll. Trading their classical instruments in for guitars, they formed as The Missing Links and played high school dances and teen clubs.

Meanwhile guitarist Bob Margolin had formed The Indigos that included a great drummer Lew Lipson. Both bands were playing popular songs and blues on the teen circuit. Nick and Dave were writing their own songs and grew tired of playing the same radio hits night after night. A more creative and experimental sound was needed and they were looking for other players that felt the same. Bob and Lew were thinking likewise and they managed to jam together one evening and everything just clicked. They all had heard of this terrific keyboardist Mick Spiros who also played trumpet and when he came aboard The Freeborne was formed. The band name was inspired by the hit movie *Born Free* and they felt their music was very free form.

Looking for this musical challenge, three members were multi-instrumentalists with Nick Carstoiu (vocals, rhythm guitar, piano, recorder), Dave Codd (vocals, bass, guitar, harpsichord), Mick Spiros, (organ, trumpet, guitar, chimes), along with Bob Margolin (lead guitar) and Lew Lipson on (drums). They played the college circuit and each gig brought out a different sound, they never knew where the music would go. Barry Richards became their manager. He owned the local Brookline Music Store and knew someone at Monitor records. The record label was noted for Orchestral, Baroque and World Folk music from other countries. The Freeborne was their endeavor into pop music. They were the only rock band featured on the record label.

The sessions occurred at A&R Studios and were finalized at CBS Studios. Their only album called *Peak Impressions* is full of special effects and weird sounds throughout, soft in nature with a little fuzz guitar and a haunting, echoed sound like the Flat Earth Society, only more mysterious. Inventive use of trumpet, recorder and chimes in unsuspecting places. Very melodic with some freak out jams. The perfect underground psych band and the stunning album cover illustration was drawn by Richard Smith, a well-known NY artist. One single was released from the LP *Land Of Diana b/w Images*. The LP was also released in Japan on the Columbia Ltd. record label with a more vibrant and stunningly colorful album cover with a full set of song lyrics printed on the inner sleeve.

They opened for such acts as The Velvet Underground, The Left Banke and Canned Heat in clubs near the Cambridge area of Boston like The Crosstown Bus, The Psychedelic Supermarket and were paired with The Velvet Underground at The Boston Tea Party. They were also featured with other bands at an event called Spring Sing in Common Park with Eden's Children, Tangerine Zoo, The Front Page Review, The Van Morrison Controversy and others. But the band never made the big time and fired Barry Richards. With no promotion from the record label the band fell apart. They were all high intellectuals and moved on to other colleges studying the music field.

Dave Codd traveled to North Texas to study composition and became a session musician and bluegrass player with the likes of Ricky Skaggs in Nashville. He released some very experimental mind music in 2007. Mick Spiros put together The Incredible Two Man Band with Bob Lichtenfels on drums and percussion releasing two albums and touring all over the country until the 90's. Lew Lipson became an avid Hamm Radio enthusiast and was known nationally amongst a legion of peers. He met an untimely death due to pancreatic cancer in October of 2009.

Bob Margolin played with Luther "Snake" Johnson and then formed The Boston Blues Band. He was a huge fan of Muddy Waters in 1973 and was asked to replace longtime guitarist Sammy Lawhorn after he was fired for being too drunk for too many gigs. Bob is seen playing right next to Muddy during the filming of *The Last Waltz*, a noteworthy film of The Band's last concert together. Bob remained with Muddy Waters until his passing in 1983. He then played and toured with Johnny Winter's blues band.

Nick Carstoiu attended Berklee School of Music and continues to write otherworldly music. Lew Lipson's unfortunate passing prompted the band to merge again and they wrote a song called Lew's Blues dedicated to his memory. Some pictures of The Freeborne playing live 2014 are here: www.punkblowfish.com/Freeborne.html

ENOCH LIGHT PRESENTS
3
Project
TOTAL SOUND STEREO
THE NEW GROUP
THE FREE DESIGN
KITES ARE FUN
MAKE THE MADNESS STOP • NEVER TELL THE WORLD
AND 9 OTHERS

Enoch Light presents
The Free Design
Heaven/earth
Project 3 Total Sound Stereo

ENOCH LIGHT PRESENTS
PR 5045SD
free
design
Project 3
Total Sound
Stereo

THE FREE DESIGN 1967-72

From Delavan, New York near Buffalo this vocal group would not normally be considered for inclusion on a list of psychedelic bands. They were brother and sister siblings whose Dad (Art Dedrick) was chief music arranger and trombonist for Vaughn Monroe's big band sound in the 1940's. Their Uncle Rusty Dedrick was a trumpet player who was with many big bands and released albums on his own and with jazz great Don Elliott. The music influenced all the siblings. Chris Dedrick and his sister Sandy attended the Manhattan School of Music in the early to mid-60's and they each attained master's degrees in music education. Chris was a master at guitar and trumpet, Bruce played guitar, bass and trombone and Sandy played keyboards.

Moving to New York after graduation they practiced in Sandy's apartment located in Queens. Their voices were pitch perfect and as a three-part harmony trio Chris, Bruce and Sandy began singing mostly folk songs emulating Peter, Paul & Mary in Greenwich Village. The name Free Design came about because of the intricacies of the songs. The point and counterpoint vocalization was different. The term Free Design fit their music and jazzy style.

Chris had a real knack for writing interesting melodies and admits influence from the Hi-Los in the 50's. Their unique vocalizations prompted Chris to pen several songs that could fit their magic style. He reworked cover songs from The Beatles, The Mamas & Papas and Simon and Garfunkel that blossomed with new life. Dad, who had started a publishing company, was impressed and sponsored some demo recordings that he got out to his friends in the industry. Record labels were clamoring to sign them, but Dad and Chris ultimately chose Enoch Light's Project 3, an audiophile label known for high quality sound recording and packaging. Chris and Dad felt that the small record label would eliminate competition and garner more attention to the group.

The first album sessions occurred at A&R Studios in New York. This was high quality audio with sound recording film rather than recording through audio tapes. This removed most of the wow and flutter which was a mechanical imperfection affecting the pure sounds of voice and instruments. The high-end session musicians were Jay Berliner (guitar), Russ Savakus (bass) and Gary Chester (drums). As a band they recorded the songs in only a few takes. Chris was given creative freedom and inspiration by Enoch Light. Except for an overdubbing of a recorder, which Chris played during one song, the entire first album called *Kites Are Fun* was done completely live in studio.

A single was released *Kites Are Fun b/w The Proper Ornaments.* The song was a fresh and bright pop sound that was the only song that ever charted by the group. Out on the road they hired Bob Paplioni to keep the beat so the road band was Chris Dedrick (guitar, vocals), Bruce Dedrick (bass, vocals) Sandy Dedrick (organ, vocals) and Bob Paplioni (drums). When the youngest sibling (Ellen) graduated from high school, she was immediately added to the mix and joined on (vocals). As a five-piece band they played teen clubs and college dances around New York and saw time on *The Tonight Show* with Johnny Carson and *The Mike Douglas Show*. There was a tremendous following on the east coast where they were also booked to play with orchestras such as The Rochester Symphony and The Buffalo Philharmonic.

These four siblings had such pure crystal-clear voices. Add to it wonderful and flawless jazz influenced pop tunes, they fit right in with the best of the flower-pop and flower-psych bands of the era ala The Fifth Dimension, The Rotary Connection, Sergio Mendes and Brazil '66, The Association and The Carpenters. The one difference that sets The Free Design apart from others is that their music is truly timeless. Six albums were put out with the Project 3 label *Kites Are Fun, You Could Be Born Again, Heaven/Earth, Sing For Very Important People, Stars/Time/Bubbles/Love* and *One By One*. But distribution was sparse, airplay was limited and sales were poor. This was all due to competition and focus that had changed in the music industry from pop sounds to bands like Cream, Led Zeppelin, Jimi Hendrix, The Doors and other hard rock guitar driven bands.

Chris had to get away from the hustle-bustle of New York and wound up in Canada. Bruce had left the band, but Chris, Sandy and Ellen recorded one more album *There Is A Song* released on the small-time label Ambrotype out of Rochester, NY. On this LP all but one song was recorded at Manta Sound Studios in Toronto, Canada.

Then Chris, Ellen and Sandy helped to form The Star Scape Singers under the direction of Kenneth Mills. They developed into a ten voice acapella group with intricate and complex harmonies accompanied by some instrumentation. Ellen didn't stay long but her youngest sister Stephanie joined and had a dynamic voice as well.

They were busy. They toured Europe and the states well into the 90's, with Chris, Stephanie and, initially, Sandy as the stable base of the group. Several LPs were put out on the market with *Sing Unto Me A New Song,* The *Star-Scape Over Europe* series, *The Heraldic Message, The Fire Mass,* The *Tonal Persuasions* series, *Sound Voyage, Watch* plus two Christmas LPs *The Heart Of Christmas* and *Flame On The Hearth*. Chris helped to produce and arrange the songs. These LPs and CDs can be found on Discogs, at Kenneth G Mills website or downloaded at the Apple Music website.

It was with great sadness that Stephanie Dedrick died of Lou Gehrig's Disease in 1999.

Sandy Dedrick left Star-Scape, married and was a music teacher in the Ontario School District in Canada for many years and has retired.

Ellen also stayed in Canada but had little to do with singing or vocalizing.

Bruce Dedrick stayed in New York, he was a session musician and vocalist and was a music teacher as well.

Chris Dedrick resided near Toronto and had won several awards for TV and Film scores. But we lost him due to Cancer in 2010.

There was a total of seven studio albums released by The Free Design between 1967 and 1972. All are dynamic and wonderful. Because of renewed interest in their airy style of music, they were persuaded to re-enter the studio for yet another album on (CD). Released in 2000 *Cosmic Peekaboo* has newer songs that are just as fresh as the earlier albums.

PSYCHEDELIC STATE

STEREO/BN 26502
FUSE
EPIC
STEREO
CAN ALSO BE PLAYED ON MONO EQUIPMENT

FUSE 1970

Rick Nielson was from Rockford, Illinois. His folks were both musicians and they owned Nielson's Music, the premiere music store in town. So, at an early age he lived and breathed music and had his choice of guitars, thus the vast collection that he's now known for. His first band of any significance was The Grim Reapers. Rick played (guitar & organ) with Joe Sundberg on (vocals) and Jim Zubiani on (drums). They were in competition with another Rockford band called Toast and Jam which included Tom Peterson (bass), Craig Myers (guitar) and Chip Greenman (drums). The Forest Hills Country Club would have periodic Battle of the Bands contests with The Grim Reapers, Toast and Jam plus another great band called The Esquires. The Grim Reapers always seemed to win the contest, but at some point, Rick proposed a merging of his band with Toast and Jam to form a super group of sorts. Craig, Tom and Chip agreed to the collaboration, Toast and Jam broke apart and they continued as The Grim Reapers.

Craig Myers had primary (lead guitar) duties and his folks had a room built on their house that was set up for practice and rehearsals. Rick Nielson, Craig Myers and Joe Sundberg wrote the songs and the practice sessions shook the neighborhood. They hit the clubs with the new material and were gathering new fans everywhere they played. At the age of 17 Chip Greenman was still attending Guilford High School and was involved with both the band and the orchestra. Tensions grew between himself and the instructor due to his long hair. He was basically kicked out of the high school band and orchestra and received unjustified failing grades in both music classes. The grades were later reversed.

The Grim Reapers were a hot commodity and their manager Ken Adamany was trying to get some music industry interest in the group. The members were Rick Nielson (guitar, keyboards, vocals), Joe Sundberg (vocals), Craig Myers (lead guitar), Tom Peterson (bass) and Chip Greenman (drums). They recorded a single on the local record label, Smack, called *Hound Dog b/w Cruisin' for Burgers.* By 1969, they got big venue gigs in Chicago and were billed with Wilson Pickett at The Factory in Madison, WI. Picked up by CBS and EPIC Records for an album deal, it didn't take long before they were in the Columbia Studios at 630 N. McClurg Ct. in Chicago recording their first album.

Chip was still in high school, commuting to Chicago afterwards and doing studio sessions until the wee hours of the morning. After the sessions were completed, EPIC wanted a name change for the band stating that The Grim Reapers name was just too dark. So, the band scrambled trying to come up with a new name. Monikers like Man's Nuts and The Fleetwood Turks were thrown about, but EPIC finally came up with the name Fuse which fit the heavy sound of the band. The previously mentioned non-album single *Hound Dog b/w Crusin' For Burgers* was reissued by the EPIC label for mass distribution. The self-titled album *Fuse* was released and you can hear the influences of The Yardbirds and Jeff Beck, a guitar hero of both Rick and Craig. No psych or special effects were present and their sound emulates the likes of Uriah Heap and Deep Purple.

During the record release and just after the positive vibes of Woodstock, rock festivals were popping up everywhere. Fuse opened at a number of these in the mid-west. They kicked off "The Kickapoo Creek Rock Festival" in Heywood, Illinois. Another show was at "The Galena in Wadena" which was a festival scheduled for Galena, Illinois, but moved to Wadena, Iowa. Apparently, the city of Galena ran the promoters out of town not wanting to deal with 40,000 hippies and they relocated to Wadena 90 miles west. This is where Chip got major heat exhaustion during their first song and had to be attended to medically before finishing the show. Never lacking for excitement Fuse played "The People's Fair under the Sign of Cancer" in Steven's Point, Wisconsin, where bullets were flying and they were rushed off stage. There was no crowd control and folks were entering the site for free. A dispute occurred with a motorcycle gang after some fans set some bikes on fire and then the guns started blazing. Three folks sustained gunshot wounds but none were fatal.

Having access to all the latest sound equipment, Fuse had a real Wall of Sound, before the term got popular, with double tall HiWatt speakers, Sound City cabinets and Fane speakers with Ampeg bass amps. They went back to the studios and completed some tracks for their second album. But a major riff occurred between Ken Adamany and the sound engineer. Ken was fired and threatened to sue everybody, the label, the studio and the band members. As a result, CBS dropped the band like a brick and they were left with no booking agent, no record deal and no representation. This pretty much spelled doom for the band and they fell apart.

Craig Myers, Joe Sundberg and Chip Greenman formed the band Silver Fox for a short while. But they were just a weekend club band with no original material.

Chip Greenman then joined the Army and was stationed in Germany. When he returned, he got into ECM Solutions for business management.

Joe Sundberg moved to Los Angeles and tried to mold into that scene but things didn't work out. He became a senior executive with a 30 year career for a sales and marketing group.

Craig Myers stayed in music playing with various bands for maybe 10 years, he married and eventually settled into managing an automotive dealership out of state.

Rick Nielson and Tom Peterson hired drummer Thom Mooney and keyboardist Robert Stewkey Antoni, both formerly of The Nazz with Todd Rundgren, and toured around as Fuse or The Nazz depending upon what town they were playing in. Calling Philadelphia as home they became a band called Sick Man of Europe.

This band fell apart and after hiring Brad Carlson (aka Bun E. Carlos) (drums) and Randy Holden (aka Xeno) (vocals) they became Cheap Trick. Ken Adamany was back on board and when Robin Zander replaced Randy, Cheap Trick was set and gained worldwide fame.

FAITHFUL VIRTUE
STEREO FVS-2003
Game

game
long hot summer
Evolution

GAME 1969-71

This band started out in Southern Florida and was the combination of two bands. The Proctor Amusement Company (PAC) included Chuck Kirkpatrick (guitar, vocals) and George Terry (bass, vocals). Another band called Bridge starred Chucks brother Scott Kirkpatrick (drums), Les Luhring (keyboards, vocals) and Eddie Keating (guitar, vocals). PAC had a little better following because they were seen on a local weekly TV dance show. When PACs drummer got drafted to Vietnam, Chuck asked his brother Scott to help. Bridge broke apart and Les and Eddie followed. PAC did very well as a hot covers band playing steady gigs for good pay. But a turning point occurred when the band realized that playing for drunken high school kids was as good as it would get unless they moved to a higher level and wrote their own tunes.

Chucks day job was as engineer at Criteria Studios in Miami. The band renamed themselves as Game and hired Steve Goldberg to oversee management duties. Chuck, Eddie Keating and Les Luhring put together enough new original material for an album and recorded the sessions at Criteria. Chuck and Steve produced the songs and found Koppelman/Rubin Enterprises out of New York and their label, Faithful Virtue Records, for representation and distribution. Charles Koppelman and Don Rubin were noted for signing The Lovin' Spoonful to great success.

The self-titled album *Game* along with a single *Stop, Look and Listen b/w Fat Mama* was released locally. The LP was dedicated to Mack (Max) Emerman, founder of Criteria Studios. The music has heavy guitar riffs throughout along with great hooks, jazz-a-blues moves and wonderful three-part vocal harmonies. To me they mimic other Florida bands like Steel and Katmandu.

Game promoted the album at high schools and the college circuit. They played at several beach clubs in Florida including Thee Image extending throughout the Panhandle down to The Keys and opened for The Allman Brothers at the Jai Alai Fronton in Miami. They were also invited to showcase at The National Entertainment Convention in Kansas City. With all the notoriety the Evolution Record label bought out Faithful Virtue Records, picked up the band and re-released the first album on their own label for national distribution.

A second album called *Long Hot Summer* was put together and released with much of the same sound. Pictured on the cover left to right is George Terry, Ed Keating, Scott Kirkpatrick, Les Luhring and Chuck Kirkpatrick. Frustrated about all the hard work and reaping very little, if any, money, dissention began to set in. They were bickering over production credits and song writing which spelled the beginning of the end of Game as a polished unit. Trying to salvage the vision that they had when they started initially, they decided to move to California and make a go of it there. Scott Kirkpatrick chose to stay behind in Florida forcing the band to hire a replacement drummer Dave Robinson (no relation to The Cars drummer).

Over the next two years they played the clubs in Southern California and recorded enough new material to put out another album, but they made no splash and there was no record deal found. Disillusioned, the band returned home and broke apart. George Terry toured with Eric Clapton for a while. Les Luhring became a big time painting Contractor. Scott Kirkpatrick drummed for former Byrds members McGuinn, Clark and Hillman.

Chuck Kirkpatrick went back to Criteria Studios as sound engineer. He did sessions there for Eddie Money, Aretha Franklin and Eric Clapton and traveled to Abbey Road studios in the UK as sound engineer for the likes of America, Peter Frampton and others. Many major rock bands came to Criteria to record and Chuck was there for them all.

In 1976 he recorded a solo album that included brother Scott (drums), Les Luhring (backing vocals) and Ed Keating (bass). This was supposed to be a Chuck Kirkpatrick solo LP but he was anonymous to the public. Capitol records determined that selling the LP would benefit the marketing strategy more as a band LP rather than as an unknown solo act so the album came out as *Crane*. The name was taken from his brother Scott's middle name.

Then, in 1982, Chuck and Scott got their calling with the resurging band Firefall, who were on a comeback, and they toured with them for over five years. But tragedy happened when Chuck pulled over with a flat tire on his car. Hailing help, he was victim of a drive by shooting. They never caught the culprit who shot him. Chuck recovered but it nearly ended his playing career. After this he spent years writing jingles for TV and radio advertisements. He currently plays 60's favorites with his band Orange Sunshine.

File under Rock
ST 121
Capitol
Stereo
GANDALF

GANDALF 1969

Gandalf began its infant stages with Peter Sando and Bob Muller in Tenafly, New Jersey. Peter started playing guitar when he was 13 years old and Bob knew how to play several instruments. Bob had his own band and was a decent drummer already established with The Clef Tones (not the known doo-wop group). Members included Bob Mueller (drums), Michael Nouri (guitar), Richard Garrett (guitar) and an unnamed (sax) player. Bob and Mike were in competition over the same girlfriend and because of this Bob decided to fire and replace Mike in the band. He asked Peter if he wanted to join their group on (rhythm guitar) and he agreed.

Their first practice rehearsal was in Bob's basement. After that, the sax player left and they became a three-piece band. By this time Bob had changed the band's name to The Thunderbirds. Pete and Bob both worked at a restaurant called *Hot Dogs etc.* owned by Pete's Dad and they eventually moved the practice sessions there as it was located at the Mall which was closed on Sundays. Tenafly High School had a few notable bands to play the teen dances. One band, Willie Nelson and the Dukes, was led by Ricky Nelson's cousin. Another, The Impalas, was headed up by Gary Wright, who later went on to sing for the UK band, Art, who eventually evolved into Spooky Tooth. Actor Ed Harris also graduated from Tenafly High School.

The Thunderbirds were a great band as well, but they had to break up because Bob's Dad was transferred to California and the family had to move. However, after a couple years, Bob was back. He hooked up with Pete and they decided to reform the band as The Rahgoos, named after Bob's favorite spaghetti sauce. The new band included Peter Sando (guitar, vocals), Bob Muller who now played (bass, vocals), Paul Venturini (organ) and Bryan Post (drums). They played at several New York clubs in and around town, The Phone Booth, Scott Muni's Rolling Stone, The Electric Circus and others. Paul left the band and wound up with The Soul Survivors who had one big national hit single *Expressway to Your Heart b/w Hey Gyp.* He was replaced with Frank Hubach on (keyboards). But Bryan Post also left, signed with The Naval Reserves and went to Vietnam. He was replaced by Dave Bauer on (drums).

Shows occurred at The Night Owl in Greenwich Village with two bands playing each night. The Rahgoos were paired on stage with such notables as James Taylor and The Flying Machine, The Lost Sea Dreamers, with Jerry Jeff Walker, The Myddle Class and others including The Magicians who included Garry Bonner and Alan Gordon. These two later became hitmaking songwriters with highlights of songs like *Happy Together* and *She'd Rather Be With Me* sung by The Turtles and *Celebrate* sung by Three Dog Night. Bonner & Gordon knew Charles Koppelman and Don Rubin who were Columbia Records representatives. They were formerly behind the comedy team of Dean Martin and Jerry Lewis and the songs they sang together. As Koppleman/Rubin Associates, they had just signed a big record deal with The Lovin Spoonful, had formed their own record label as the Hot Biscuit Disk Company and decided to sign The Rahgoos.

The band went to Century Sound Studios located at 135 W 32nd St. in Manhattan to record an album engineered by Brooks Arthur. The Rahgoos had a pretty big fan following, but K&R insisted on a name change. The band liked the name they had, but the executives continued to press the issue with name changes that didn't sit well with the group. They continued to play shows and gigs as The Rahgoos but finally gave in and decided that getting some album distribution with a major record label would get them better recognition. During one of their shows Dave Bauer was reading J. R. Tolkien's *The Hobbit* and suggested the name Gandalf and the Wizards and the other members thought that band name might work.

Meanwhile, the Hot Biscuit Disc Company fell apart. Koppelman & Rubin had produced several bands for Columbia records but were at odds with the label. Finally, an agreement was made. Koppelman separated from Rubin and sold the Gandalf and the Wizards master tapes to Capitol Records. Almost a year had passed since the completed album sessions and before things had settled the band had grown frustrated and broke apart. Ultimately Capitol did release the LP but had shortened the band name to simply *Gandalf*. Minimum copies were pressed and went directly to the cut-out bins. With no promotion and no band to back the record, the LP disappeared into obscurity. The songs emit a laid-back sound with acid psychedelia much like that of Flat Earth Society, The Bach's and Complex, a band from the UK. This LP is rare and much recommended.

Dave Bauer traveled to California and hooked up with Chris Flinders who had been with a second incarnation of The Chocolate Watchband. Peter followed him there at Dave's request, but the band never happened. He eventually wound up with the tour band for Albert King. Regrettably Dave died in 2007.

Frank Hubach had a long career as a recording engineer for several bands including Lou Reed, Deodato, Alice Cooper, The Allman Brothers, Lynyrd Skynyrd, Frank Zappa and others.

Bob Muller wound up with a band called Skyhook for a while, but eventually got out of music for a living and built custom homes. He and Pete remain great friends.

Peter Sando recorded a couple of singles written by the two that discovered the original band, Alan Gordon and Garry Bonner, with studio musicians including Dave Bauer on drums. The band was called Barracuda and the singles charted locally but only briefly. After he returned from California, Pete married and settled down. He worked in the restaurant business and continued to write songs along with Jack McMahon and continued to play with several cover bands and as a solo artist. A few solo albums and CDs have been released over the years.

There was great interest amongst record collectors about Gandalf and a second album and CD *Gandalf 2* was put out by Sundazed Music that consists of outtakes and live music from back then. There was a recent third LP/CD released called *Tears of Ages* available through Peter's website.

STEREO/BN 26374
EPIC
STEREO
GENTLE SOUL

GENTLE SOUL 1967-1969

Pamela Polland was an aspiring singer/songwriter who grew up in Los Angeles. Her parents didn't like pop music to be played in her family home, so she would write songs privately in her room from a young age. She met Ry Cooder when they were both teenagers, and for about two years they played as a duo, mostly at the famed Ashgrove Coffee House. Pamela gives Ry credit as the first person who taught her how to sing, because he taught her how to **listen**. She was working as a waitress at Bob's Big Boy in Costa Mesa, Ca. helping to pay for College when a friend who knew Jackson Browne, who was only 14 years old at the time, wanted her to meet him. Pamela agreed and Jackson showed up with his friend and poet Greg Copeland. They talked and she brought them over to her house where he played her the song *Flying Thing*. He wasn't known yet, but Pamela knew Jackson was going places after she heard that song.

Pamela eventually married Greg Copeland, and they moved to Echo Park where her neighbors were Jackson Browne and Glenn Fry. Joni Mitchell and Linda Ronstadt were friends who lived in nearby Laurel Canyon. They knew The Byrds, Buffalo Springfield, The Association and others. This was an amalgam of the best bands and singers in the country at a time when rock and pop music were taking off. In 1967, Pamela was introduced to Rick Stanley who got his influence from The Everly Brothers, Jim Kweskin and Bob Dylan. Because Pamela was also influenced by Bob Dylan and the Everly Brothers, they found that their voices complimented each other very nicely. Billy James, who met Pamela a year earlier, introduced her to Terry Melcher who was a producer for Columbia Records.

Terry then signed them up to Columbia Records and set them up in a home just off the Sunset strip. A Hispanic fellow named Bobby (last name forgotten) came in and played (contra bass). Then Terry hooked them up with Riley Wyldflower (guitar). The story goes that Riley was lying in a back room toking away on a doobie and blowing the smoke on her cat. Normally that cat was skittish, but she just laid there and wouldn't move. Pamela thought there might be something wrong and Riley said "Nope, she's just a gentle soul". With that, he ultimately provided the name of the band.

A single was recorded at Columbia Studio D located on Sunset Blvd *Tell Me Love b/w You Move Me* and there was some regional radio airplay. They began playing at The Golden Bear in Huntington Beach followed by a few other local clubs on the strip including the famous Troubadour. After a year, Bobby was replaced with Bill Plummer (electric bass) and Sandy Konikoff (drums) was added to the group on stage. It was a little intimidating for them at first as they were an acoustic band, but soon they accepted the fuller sound.

They recorded another single *Our National Anthem b/w Song for Three* which had all the wonderful harmonies and hooks. A great Mamas and Papas feel about this one with jangling guitar that still stands the test of time. Their hopes were way up, but the singles went nowhere. They recorded all the basic tracks for the album then Rick left for India for few weeks. Terry still had to polish the recording and give it a few studio embellishments. Additional players on the LP included Ry Cooder and Mike Deasy (guitar), Paul Horn (flute), Van Dyke Parks (harpsichord), Larry Knechtel (organ), Joe Osborne (bass) and others. Once all the recording was completed, Pamela took off for Greece with her husband Greg.

When Rick got back, he was overwhelmed with the studio production that Terry completed. Pamela returned and thought the album was great, but she didn't care for the 4 ½-minute overture that opened the album. She felt there were other songs that could have been used. The album *Gentle Soul* was released on EPIC Records and sounds a lot like The Stone Poneys with wonderful harmonies and minor psych effects. Unfortunately, they were a total so-called "tax write off" for the Record company. The promotional stage shows weren't set up, there was no radio promotion and no support for the band or the LP. Billboard Magazine mentioned the album just once.

They played a few LA clubs, but that was all. Terry set them up to play the Monterey POP Festival, but they would have been on a side stage away from the main headliners, so the band decided not to play at all and participated only as audience witnesses to the historic event.

Afterward, Riley Wyldflower (Riley Leon Cummings) was a session guitarist at the time and played with Rick Nelson and The Stone Canyon Band until Rick passed. He also played with Barry McGuire and Jim Valley. Unfortunately, Riley was killed in a car accident (Hawaii) 1983.

Bill Plummer was a renowned session bass player who was featured with The Rolling Stones, Gabor Szabo, Judee Sill, Tom Waits, Paul Horn and too many more to list.

Sandy Konikoff had been playing with Ronnie Hawkins and Bob Dylan and after this, drummed for Joe Cocker then continued session drumming. Last known, he was back in New York playing with his old Rockin' Rebels pals The Kipler Brothers.

Rick Stanley hooked up with Kenny Edwards, formerly of The Stone Poneys, and played the LA clubs. He found his way back to India as planned and wrote quite a few songs while there. He eventually became enamored with Celtic music and currently builds Celtic Harps and plays on occasion.

Pamela Polland joined Joe Cocker and was part of the Mad Dogs and Englishmen tour featured on the album and film of that concert tour. She released a couple of solo albums in the early 70's with studio friends and musicians and recorded an album in London with Elton John's producer Gus Dudgeon. Then she got hooked on the jazz vocals of Billie Holiday, Sarah Vaughn and Ella Fitzgerald and put together *The Melba Rounds Show* on stage in San Francisco complete with 1930's era costumes. She depicted herself as Melba Rounds, a character likeness to that of Barbara Streisand playing Fanny Bryce in a presentation of song and dance. She moved to Mill Valley, north of San Francisco, and spent 8 years with Dick Oxtet's Golden Age Jazz Band then moved to Hawaii where she still resides as a vocal coach, ukulele teacher and performs in the Hawaiian music duo "2 Tūtū". Pamela is also featured in the 2021 film *Learning To Live Together,* a documentary spanning from the original Mad Dogs & Englishmen tour of 1970 to the 2015 reunion concert hosted by the Tedeschi Trucks Band at the Lockn' Music Festival located in Arrington, Virginia.

A GIANT CRAB COMES FORTH
STEREO 73037
GIANT CRAB
UNI
PRINTED IN U.S.A.

Cool It...Helios
Giant Crab
STEREO 73057
UNI
©UNIVERSAL CITY RECORDS • A DIVISION OF MCA

STEPPENWOLF
BIG
BROTHER
ALL
AMERICAN
STEREO
ERNIE
JOSEPH

GIANT CRAB 1968-69

The roots of Giant Crab began in 1962 at Santa Barbara Junior High School in California and started with the three Orosco brothers. Dad and Mom billed themselves as Joseph and Esther and they played shows themselves up and down State Street. They were well-known local entertainers but gave up musical events to raise a family and completely backed their sons as rock and roll musicians. Joe had a charismatic personality; he was proud and made sure the boys had every opportunity to do well as musicians. He took them to downtown Los Angeles looking for new instruments and a wardrobe and this is where they saw a Fender Stratocaster sitting in the window of Schierson Brothers Music store. They still make tribute to Stan Schierson as the one who helped to give them their start. They were able to buy the Strat and all the other equipment through him on credit with a monthly payment coupon book.

Calling themselves Ernie and the Emperors, the band consisted of Ernie Joseph Orosco (guitar, vocals), his brothers Brian Rueben Orosco (drums), Raymond Cory Orosco (guitar) and a schoolmate Randy Busby (bass). They practiced and rehearsed every day at home in the garage with full support of friends and family. As players they got quite good and dad began to schedule gigs at places for them to play. They started with junior high school dances and special events but worked their way into teen dance venues at places like The Dolphin Club, in Solvang, The Rose Gardens, in Pismo Beach and Surf's Up, in San Luis Obispo.

The Earl Warren Showgrounds was a new area (85 acres) set up just outside Santa Barbara as an Equestrian park. Pioneer promoter Chris Sugish was the first to book rock shows in the area. Ernie and the Emperors was one of the first "rock" bands to be scheduled by him to perform there at the "Dome". He also sponsored a Battle of the Bands and after they won the contest, he took them under his wing and featured them as the house band for over 5 years. Sharing the stage and supporting such acts as The Chantay's with *Pipeline*, The Safari's with *Wipeout*, Bobby Vinton, The Isley Brothers, Sam the Sham, Sonny and Cher and many others. Branching out to other areas they were popular in LA at The Hullabaloo, The Hollywood Palladium, The Cinnamon Cinder, owned by Bob Eubank, The Beverly Hilton, The Ice House and Pacific Ocean Park. Other places outside of LA like The Bing Crosby

Hall, in San Diego, The Anaheim Convention Center, The Orange County Fairgrounds, The San Bernardino Civic Auditorium and The Sawtelle Veterans Hospital were also memorable venues.

The band got notice from the Reprise Record label and they recorded a nice jangling guitar Beatles and Searchers like single *Meet Me at the Corner b/w Got a Lot I Want to Say*. There was heavy radio airplay for the song that made it to #1 on the local charts in the central coast. The Reprise executives felt highly about the band and wanted them to go out on tour nationally. This had the boys on top of the world, but they were young and still in high school prompting Dad to put the old kibosh on that idea, dashing their dreams of glory. Randy Busby then wound up leaving the band to go play drums with The Dover's. Being a multi-instrumentalist Brian took over on (bass) and Dennis Fricia, who was a close friend, and his brother Kenny Fricia were asked to join in on (drums and keyboards) respectively. Ernie and the Emperors had a huge following in Santa Barbara and nearby areas.

The radio DJs, concert promoters and recording producers had the band as "go to" guys for any projects they had to promote for public events and recordings. They would do one-off recording projects for radio producers at various studios and they were open to changing band names for any assignment. One such name was Ernie's Funny's for Hanna-Barbera Records producer Tom Ayers. Another was for a Corby Records recording project where they called themselves Giant Crab. A combined effort by the band and producers Steve Walter, Dennis Hardesty and Doug Cox generated three singles on this label including *It Started With A Kiss b/w The Answer Is No, Day By Day (It Happens) b/w King Of Funny* and *Listen Girl b/w Soft Summer Breeze* all of which were recorded at San Gabriel Studios. *Listen Girl* got well into the local top 40 singles spot. They decided to keep Giant Crab as the official name for the band.

Enter Johnny Fairchild as an influential program director for K.I.S.T. radio in Santa Barbara. He had a passion and belief in many bands, especially the local bands that came through his airwaves. Ernie and the Emperors had already proven their worth and as Giant Crab they were no different. It was Johnny who introduced the band to Bill Holmes. He had formerly discovered Thee Sixpence who had changed their name to The Strawberry Alarm Clock and charted the national number one hit single *Incense and Peppermints b/w The Birdman of Alkatrash*.

Bill signed Giant Crab to the UNI Record label and a five-year contract. Traveling to Hollywood they recorded their first album at Original Sound Studios located at 7120 W. Sunset Blvd. Bill Holmes produced the sessions along with Gary Woods who arranged the horns. The session players included members of The Strawberry Alarm Clock Ed King (guitar), Greg Munford (backing vocals) and Gary Lovetro (bass), along with members of The Ensenada Brass Band Greg Ellis (trumpet) and Tom Cormier (trombone), with Jimmy Valves and Greg Grindle both on (trumpet) and John Dodero and Ron Hurd along with Brian himself all playing (saxophone). However, other than Brian these players were uncredited on the LP.

The album called *A Giant Crab Comes Forth* was dedicated to Johnny Fairchild who verbalized a narrative introduction about Giant Crab to start the record. Unique at the time, the narrative included all the song titles on the LP in a long oratory to begin side one. The cover artwork was done by famed artist Bob Masse. Musically it was full of special effects, psychedelic guitar and great harmonies by the Orosco brothers. The horn arrangements and orchestrations were added effects. They approached the sound of The Young Rascals, The Dream Merchants and at times Hamilton Streetcar.

Promoting the LP, Wolfman Jack featured them on the radio at XERB with his screaming howl echoing through the speakers “The-Gi-Ant Craaaaaab!” and he would promote the gigs where they would be playing. The band joined his Fantasy Fun Fair at Devonshire Downs in Northridge, California and were paired on the road at college concerts with The Lovin' Spoonful, The Zombies, Strawberry Alarm Clock and others. Sharing the stage with The Count Five who were from San Jose, they also traveled north and played concerts at many of the San Francisco venues.

Most of the music was written and arranged by both Ernie and Cory. Ed King and Greg Munford joined the band on the road. Many venues were played in the mid-west states and up and down the west coast. Pat Mason was a key concert promoter in Northern California, Washington, Oregon and Idaho and booked the band to play there. Greg Munford normally drove the tour van and near Bend, Oregon disaster nearly took them out when the trailer they were hauling began to swing and sway and they began to spin out of control with a semi-truck heading straight for them. Fortunately, their van as the target was averted and nobody was hurt.

Bill Holmes had them back in the studio for a second album called *Cool It Helios.* This appeared to be his idea to exploit Giant Crabs' talents to play the songs penned by staff writers Claus Ogerman, Martin Seigel, Larry Weiss and others. The Orosco brothers had no song writing credits on this LP but it started the same with a different oratory by Johnny Fairchild at the beginning of the record. Musically the album was very much as the first, but you can sense much more studio control of the songs. One more single *E.S.P. b/w Hot Line Conversation* was recorded and released. As a song *E.S.P.* was a non-album cut that was a great psychedelic phase shifter, but this was the last song that they recorded as Giant Crab.

Shows were sold out wherever they played but UNI wasn't promoting the band or distributing the LPs. Giant Crab was a frustrated lot and they got out of the 5-year deal they made with the record label. The Vietnam War was the demise of many bands and the band began to feel the strain. Dennis and Kenny Fricia both had left with Dennis enlisting in the army. Brian attended college at UC Santa Barbara and Cory joined the Marines. But the Orosco brothers were able to take leave and still play gigs. Greg MacDonald was a jazz/rock drummer they knew who filled in for Dennis, but he didn't stay long and Dennis came back.

After playing a few shows to promote the 2nd album Dennis suddenly retired from touring. Giant Crab was in a pinch as they were scheduled to play at The Bing Crosby Hall in San Diego that night and needed somebody to pound the skins in a hurry. The promoter for the show suggested Bob Forrester who was the best-known drummer in San Diego and he was available. Big and tall, he sounded like a Ginger Baker clone. But when he met the guys before the gig there was only a couple of hours with the band to learn the songs before they hit the stage. How fortunate it was that he had an amazing ability to absorb a feel for their music and the show came through without a hitch. Ernie was the oldest of the brothers and was always known as Big Brother, so it was then that they decided to rename as Big Brother featuring Ernie Joseph. They became more of a hard rock band and played the college circuit during the summer of '69.

Back at Original Sound and American Recording studios they recorded another album on the All-American Record label called *Confusion*. Again, produced by Bill Holmes who owned the record label. A few songs were put to tape but during the sessions Bob Forrester left. Steve Dunwoodle (drums) had formerly been on board as a tour member with The Grateful Dead. He previously was asked to join Big Brother and turned them down but eventually he became part of the band to finish the recording session. Steve was a flamboyant drummer and was a vision to behold as he would light his drumsticks on fire while playing. So, this became the stable version of Big Brother which finally included the oldest brother Ernie Joseph (guitar, vocals) and the others with pseudonyms, Brian (The Jet) (bass, sax, vocals, percussion), Ray (Cory Colt) (keyboards) and Steve Dunwoodle as (Stevie D) on (drums).

On the latest LP you can still hear Giant Crab in their sound, but the special effects were traded in for some very heavy guitar assaults. Two singles *Heart Full of Rain b/w My Love* and *ESP b/w Brother, Where Are You* were both released. *ESP* was a rerecording of the earlier Giant Crab version and both singles had non-album B-sides. It was the song *ESP* that hit the FM airwaves on the underground radio stations and Big Brother featuring Ernie Joseph got a real surge as a noteworthy band. They did a short tour promoting the album at several colleges including an east coast stint, but the band was minus Brian who was back at school. The tour band here included Ernie (guitar, vocals), Cory (guitar, vocals), Stevie D (drums), Jake Robinson (bass) and Bill Davis (backing vocals, percussion).

Clearly Bill Holmes was true to details and kept the band busy with constant shows and gigs all over the country. They traveled east to promote the LP but on their way to Atlanta had another mishap with loss of control on a mountainside in the middle of winter that nearly cost the band again. With help they were able to reassemble and trudge their way through the snow and ice to make the show on time. But two near misses changed the band. Something or somebody was watching over them as they avoided catastrophe twice and they became a real force to be reckoned with on stage. It was during this tour of the oncoming Christmas season in Spartanburg, South Carolina that Stevie D announced he was going to take a few weeks away from the band, but they never heard back from him after that meeting. He was replaced on drums with Danny Eller who was from North Carolina.

With the short tour over they were back home. Brian was already gone at school and Cory was back in the military. The band was in transition and Ernie was eager to travel back to Atlanta, Georgia. He left by himself and when he got there, gained a great reputation as a guitarist guesting with other bands. It wasn't long before he found players to bring back home to California and re-establish his own band. The players Bill "Randy" Holt (bass), Wayne Iradi (guitar) and Danny Eller (drums) were on board for practice and rehearsal until together they perfected songs for another east coast tour.

Ernie, Cory and Brian all gave credit to the folks who made a lasting impression and helped with the tours. During their travels, the band included Bill Davis and Jake Robinson from California along with many Atlanta area musicians who joined them on the road and on stage during their performances. Players like Bill Hoyt from Atlanta, GA, Wayne Iradi from Wilson, NC, Danny Eller from Ashville, NC, Larry King from Hendersonville, NC (drums) and a Rod Stewart look-a-like Gary Pelfrey from Dallas, TX (drums).

There were many notable performances including The Nashville Music Festival with Bruce Springsteen and Roy Orbison, The Love Valley Festival in North Carolina with the Allman Brothers Band and The Hickory Speedway Festival in N.C. with Blue Oyster Cult. They were also invited to a ceremonious tribute given for the guitar GOD after he passed, The Jimi Hendrix Memorial Concert at The Middle Georgia Raceway was the site of the famous Atlanta Rock Festival.

Bill Hoyt later became the stage manager for The Allman Brothers and Dickie Betts & Great Southern. He currently is tour manager for The Nitty Gritty Dirt Band.

Sadly, years later they heard that Steve Dunwoodle had met his maker.

In 1977 Dennis and Kenny Fricia recorded one more LP as The Fricia Brothers called *A Song for Everyone* and then sustained a stable life in California, both are married and have children.

Coming back to their roots in Santa Barbara, Ernie, Brian and Cory evolved into The Brian Faith Band featuring Brian on (lead vocals, drums, sax, bass), Ernie Joseph (guitar), Cory Orosco (keyboards, bass, vocals) and Karen Perry (vocals). A well-respected band that sounded much like Canada's Headpins, they opened for The Missing Persons, Jackson Browne and many others during the 80's.

Cory and Ernie then set up SRS Studios in Santa Barbara and helped to launch the careers of Alanis Myles, Jewel, Katy Perry and Beach Boy (Mike Love's) son Christian Love. But ultimately it cost more to operate the studio and keep it active than to generate income. SRS studios closed in California.

Cory Orosco passed away in 2017.

Big Brother Ernie Joseph and Brian were keeping the Faith as The Brian Faith Band with other players and were still active playing shows and events. Their last show together was on September 24th, 2021, at The Grapes and Hops event on Main Street in Ventura, California.

Ernie had been playing guitar in a band since he was 10 years old. He was truly a pioneer in the rock music industry with a passion for doing what he loved for 65 years. Sadly, Ernie Joseph Orosco will be missed as he passed away on November 3rd, 2021.

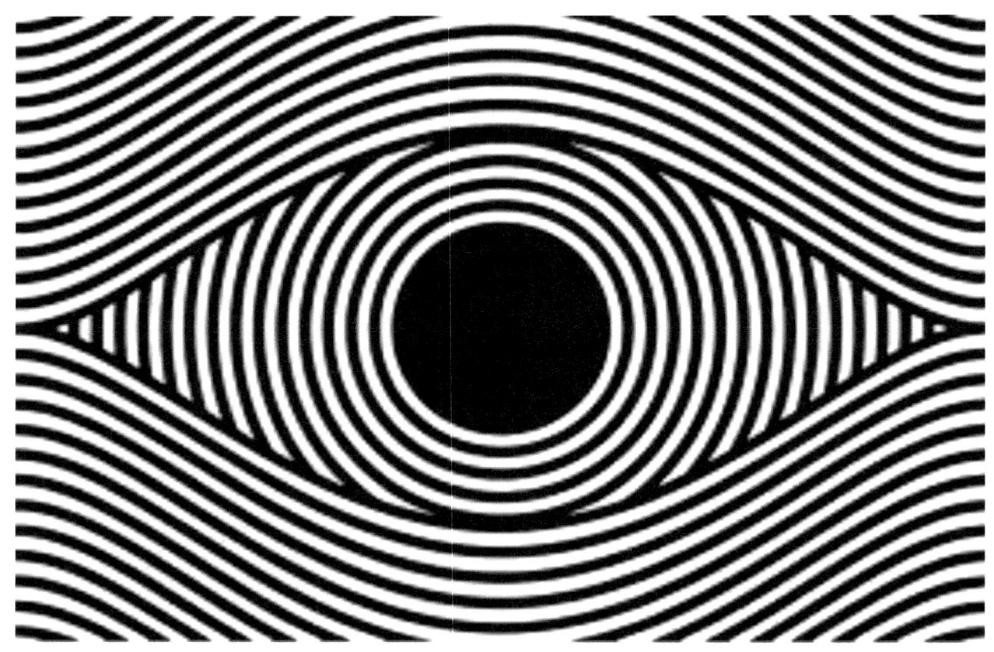

STEREO
THE
GLASS FAMILY
ELECTRIC BAND
1776
PRINTED IN U.S.A.

THE GLASS FAMILY 1968

Ralph Parrett was a student at UCLA and was a member of several bands that played frat parties, beer busts and dances. With names like The Carpetbaggers and The Soul Survivors (not the Chicago group), they played surf and rock 'n roll with songs like *Money* by Barrett Strong, *Snatch & Grab It* by Julia Lee, *What'd I Say* by Ray Charles, and *Big Boss Man* by Jimmy Reed for some real fun times.

The Glass Family formed (1965) in Topanga Canyon just north of Hermosa and Redondo Beach, California. At the time Topanga Canyon was a mecca where artists like Canned Heat, Spirit and Neil Young lived. Original members of The Glass Family were Ralph Parrett (guitar, vocals), Charles Lamont (keyboards, vocals), Jon Bongiovanni (bass) and Gary Green (drums). Their name was based upon J.D. Salinger's two novellas about The Glass Family: *Fanny and Zooey and Raise High The Roof Beam, Carpenters and Seymour: An Introduction*. There was a run of shows at underground clubs like The Topanga Corral on Canyon Blvd, The Flying Gib in Redondo Beach, Brothers Galley in Santa Barbara and The Cheetah in Santa Monica. They recorded a song for Mike Curbs Sidewalk record label called *I'm Losing It* released on the *Freakout USA* various artists LP. Later, a promotional double-sided single *Teenage Rebellion* was put out as a theme song for the teen flick of the same name.

Then Charles Lamont left and helped to form Alexanders Timeless Bloozband. Enter David Capilouto on (keyboards, vocals) to replace him. Jon Bongiovanni then got into some heavy drug problems and left the band as well. David, being classically trained, was able to fill the void by playing (keyboards) and (bass keys) much like Ray Manzarek did for The Doors. Then they expanded out to clubs on the LA Strip like The Whiskey A Go Go, Gazzarri's, The Third Eye in Rancho Palos Verdes and most of the bigger colleges in California (USC, Cal State, UC Santa Cruz) opening for the likes of The Grateful Dead, Lee Michaels, Black Sabbath and many more. They also opened for Deep Purple on their very first tour of the US at UCLA.

At the time many labels were seeking out those bands that were into experimentation and psychedelic music. The band had been together for quite a while and were managed by American Entertainment. Their manager at the time was Don Podolor brother of Richard Podolor who produced Steppenwolf, Iron Butterfly, Three Dog Night and many others. Don introduced them to Joe Smith who was the executive at Warner Brothers Records and The Glass Family signed an album deal.

Their only album *Electric Band* was recorded at the original location of American Recording Co. in Studio City. Being a seasoned concert band, the songs they had written and recorded were longer extended versions during their live shows. The song *Agorn* found on the album was normally about 15 minutes long, but it was cut way short for the single *Guess I'll Let You Go b/w Agorn (Elements Of Complex Variables)* due to record labels seeking AM radio hits limiting songs to 3 or 4 minutes of maximum playing time for airplay.

The cover of the album shows left to right David Capilouto, Gary Green and Ralph Parrett in the foreground of a communal setting. The house was located near Silver Lake in Los Angeles and belonged to Dave Capilouto. He's holding a Raggedy Anne Doll in the cover shot of the band. The significance is that his girlfriend was out of the country and Dave told her that Raggedy Anne, her favorite doll, would represent her for the picture. Fans and friends were always hanging out at the house, so they gathered around for the picture shot.

Musically, comparisons go to Quatrain. The band was disappointed with the recording because of the overdubs and over production. They were a hard core three-piece rockin' band and felt the recording didn't really show them in their true form. The LP sold very few copies and The Glass Family really weren't expecting much. They continued to play venues as before including The Fillmore in San Francisco with gigs also in Reno and Las Vegas, but they never branched out onto the national scene. Drummer Gary Green left shortly followed by Dave Capilouto. After the psych scene ran its course, the band went into hiatus.

Dave Capilouto was a landscaper for a while, but he never stopped playing keyboards and music. He was a member of several other bands afterward. He currently teaches keyboards.

Gary Green worked for the local phone company and to anybody's knowledge never played drums again.

To make ends meet Ralph Parrett got into production and engineering duties for Hollywood Sound Recorders. He didn't get a lot of work initially and figured it was due to his name, Ralph, which in the day meant hurl or vomit. He decided to legally change it from Ralph Parrett to James Callon with Callon being the name of the street he lived on at the time. In the mid-70's he got primary engineer and production duties for the band Funkedelic and produced many of their LPs starting with *Tales of Kidd Funkedelic*. On this album he is listed as Ralphjim Callow. It was because of his work with Funkedelic and the song *Shit, Goddamn, Get Off Your Ass and Jam* that he got interested in disco music.

Ralph attended a dance club in Los Angeles that had a big booming sound system where he was witness to 100's of people dancing, mesmerized by the music and the hard driving beat. The energy reminded him of the venues in the 60's with light shows where people got up and danced. The Glass Family enjoyed making people dance and Ralph (now Jim) was sold on making that kind of music. He formed JDC Records with his wife Dale, then hired some musicians and recorded a single *Smoke Your Troubles Away b/w Mr. DJ You Know How to Make Me Dance* which had considerable airplay. The B-side starred Taka Boom, the sister of Chaka Khan.

A full disco album followed entitled *Mr. DJ You Know How To Make Me Dance* and it had unexpected success prompting a follow up LP. Jim wasn't sure he could get the same players back. Taka Boom had moved on, but The Glass Family made their final LP circa 1978 called *Crazy!* Their sound here was nothing like the psychedelic music they played previously. Hereafter, Jim's company took off and was committed to vinyl Extended Plays (EPs) for the disco scene and R'n'B. JDC Records was a major player in the disco industry with recording and distribution of those EPs worldwide and is still thriving today. Jim Callon, Dave Capilouto and Charles Lamont along with others still see each other and "Jam" in Jim's studio twice a month.

Another Glass Family album *Invisible World* was recorded recently with Jim Callon, Dave Capilouto and others and is now available through JDC Records on vinyl and CD at Amazon, eBay and other places on the net.

GO WITH THE FLOW

GLASS HARP
STEREO
DL 75261
decca

STEREO DL 75306
GLASS HARP
SYNERGY

STEREO DL7-5358
GLASS HARP
IT MAKES ME GLAD

GLASS HARP 1970-72

Phil Keaggy and John Sferra had known each other as 8th graders at St. Christians grade school in Youngstown, Ohio. In 1965 they fancied themselves as The Beatles with Phil looking a little like Paul McCartney and John a little like John Lennon. They would get together and sing a lot of Beatles and Peter and Gordon songs. John was a drummer, but he also played a little guitar. They remained friends, but never formed a band at that early age.

By 1966 Phil refined his guitar skills with The Keytones, The Vertices and then The Squires where he recorded the single *Batman b/w I Don't Care Anymore*. Then Phil's family moved to California along with him. His eyes opened wide to all the great bands he saw and his chance meeting with Dick Dale got him his first Fender Stratocaster. He had a real inspiration from Mike Bloomfield and The Electric Flag and wanted to form a band just like that.

He came back to Ohio with that in mind but wound up joining The Volume VI which had more of a Rolling Stones vibe. But because he was a Paul McCartney clone, they did a Beatles thing complete with Sgt. Peppers uniforms. Tom Page was a producer from Canfield, Ohio and wanted the guys to record some singles, so he got them signed to the Date Record label and into the Cleveland Recording Studio. They decided to change their name and became The New Hudson Exit after the popular teen club in Canfield. The records did well locally and the band was able to expand their gigs outside the state.

A Pittsburgh agency liked the band well enough to pair them up with The Grassroots, The Turtles, Vanilla Fudge and other nationally known touring acts. Phil was a hot guitar player, only 17 years old at the time and the band was making $1000 a gig. But he still had dreams of forming his own band, so he quit, found his old friend John Sferra drumming for The Jokers and asked him to join. Steve Markulin joined on (bass) and they called themselves Glass Harp which was a knockoff of the Truman Capote novel The Grass Harp.

Playing the teen dances around Youngstown, they became one of the big draws with fans. Geoff Jones became their manager and got them some studio time to record an album for United Audio. When it was finished Geoff sent the tapes to Apple Records in England in hopes that the band would be signed by The Beatles Record label, but they were rejected. One single from the session was released *Where Did My World Come From b/w She Told Me* which had some airplay, but the rest of the proposed album remained as an acetate. After the sessions were done Steve Markulin left to join his cousin Ting Markulin with the Human Beinz. This band had a big national hit single with *Nobody But Me b/w Sueno*. Bassist, Dan Pecchio, was available after his band, The Poppy, fell apart and replaced Steve.

They began to expand their music into long improvisational jams on stage playing places like Kent State University and The Ludlow Garage in Cincinnati. The Warner Brothers record label was interested, but after winning top prize at the Meyers Lake Battle of the Bands contest, they were signed to a multi-album deal with DECCA Records. Lewis Merenstein was fresh from producing Van Morrison's *Moondance* album and brought Glass Harp to New York and Electric Ladyland Studios to record their first major label record. This was Jimi Hendrix's preferred studio and they had the album completed within a week. Jimi died just before they finished the session.

The best musical comparison to this first album *Glass Harp* would be Glory Road with real nice guitar (heavy at times) and airy vocals. The band had been toying with religious themes. The album was great, but mellow sounding when compared to their live shows. They went on tour and backed the likes of Yes, Traffic and Chicago. Phil was a wizard guitarist and some of the songs would jam on for 20 to 30 minutes. The band seemed to be blessed with good fortune, but during the tour Phil's Mother got in a terrible car accident and died soon after. It hit Phil real hard, but he credited his growing religious faith to get him through. He became what was then known as a Jesus Freak and started speaking Christianity to the audience between songs and after the shows.

They recorded their second album *Synergy* and then were asked to play for a PBS Special that was one of the first to be simulcast on TV and FM radio at the same time. A plan for the third album was made to record them live at Carnegie Hall, this was the chance of a lifetime. They were a little intimidated opening for the Kinks who were less than gracious and the crowd was Kink friendly. But they started playing and put on their usual great show. By the end of their hour, the Kink fans were honoring this unknown band and cheering for an encore. The concert was recorded but DECCA decided to ask for one more studio recording and shelved the Glass Harp Live performance.

The third album *It Makes Me Glad* was recorded and released, but Phil was drawn to Christianity. John and Dan knew he was leaving for a solo career and it happened right after the album was complete.

Phil traveled to California and joined Chuck Girard and the band Love Song, who were heavy into the Jesus Movement at the time. Dan Pecchio and John Sferra continued as Glass Harp with Tim Burks on guitar, but the magic was gone and they all parted ways a year after Phil had left.

Afterwards Dan Pecchio recorded and toured with The Michael Stanley Band for 6-7 years.

John Sferra played on and off with other bands and opened his own home studio writing and recording songs for over 30 years. He currently maintains the Glass Harp website.

Phil Keaggy went on to do quite well as a Contemporary Christian Music musician releasing more than 50 albums over the years. He has become a legendary guitarist, is very well respected, has achieved several Dove awards and a Grammy Nomination.

The 1972 Carnegie Hall show was finally released to the public both on CD and DVD in 1997. This concert really highlights the virtuosity of Phil as a guitar player. He may have been underappreciated but to hear him play at this time, oh my, he was good.

Phil, John and Dan have reunited several times over the years for shows and CD releases. They managed to release four additional CDs between 2001 and 2004 with *Hourglass* having nearly 80 minutes of new material and *Stark Raving Jams* a 3 CD set covering over 30 years of live recordings circa 1970 through 2003.

The original members are all still active and still play live shows booked through their website.

PEACE, LOVE AND HAPPINESS

RCA
LSP-4201
Poe through the
GLASS
PRISM
VICTOR
STEREO

RCA
LSP-4270
ON JOY AND SORROW
GLASS PRISM
VICTOR
STEREO

GLASS PRISM 1969-70

Tom Varano was a blossoming guitarist in Wilkes-Barre, Pennsylvania. He had been involved with a few bands back when car names were cool. His friend George Fox had just moved to Berwick, PA and found that there were auditions for backup bands for some of the big names that came through town. This was in the day when the headliners like Elvis, Jerry Lee Lewis, Chuck Berry and others would travel from town to town with a sidekick to teach the house band the latest songs. At George's beckoning, Tom showed up and formed a band with himself on (guitar), George Fox on (piano, vocals) and Steve Bond on (drums). They went through a few rhythm guitarists and sax players until they found the right mix with Carl Siracuse (guitar) and Jim Shrader (bass, sax).

Steve Bond named the band The El Caminos he took from his High School Spanish Book. The translation means The Way or The Road in English, but it also was the name of a car, a Chevy El Camino, which was immensely popular during those times. They were the best band around and had a solid following for a few years. The place they played the most was The West Side Ballroom in Berwick. They were up on all the latest trends in sound and when the Beatles hit with the British Invasion, The El Caminos were one of the first bands to clone that sound. In 1965 they traveled to Bell Sound Studios in New York to cut a single *Storm Warning b/w We Stand Alone* that emulates their English influences.

George Fox decided to move on and attended the Berkeley School of Music in Boston to study music theory and composition. The end came in 1966 when Steve Bond, on his way to a show at the Scranton Masonic Temple, lost control of the car he was driving and was killed. Details were never known as to what happened. Things were not going well for the band. The West Side Ballroom was a huge dance hall that dated as far back as the 20's. Famous big bands like Les Brown, Harry James, Sammy Kaye, Cab Callaway and The Dorsey Brothers all played there, but that year The West Side Ballroom burned to the ground.

With two El Camino members gone Jim Shrader headed off to college as well. His replacement was a former Henchmen player Augie Christiano on (bass) who says he faked his way through the audition. Rick Richards, formerly with The Kingtones and The Treasures, came along on drums and Carl Siracuse took over on (keyboards).

The Psychedelic times were in full effect and they decided to try something a little different. Augie was a poetry buff and it was at his suggestion that they put music to the verses of Edgar Allan Poe. Word spread about the project and soon they found themselves with a two album RCA record deal and a recording session at the Les Paul Studios located at 201 Franklin Turnpike, Mahwah, New Jersey. Their concept album was produced under the watchful eye of Gene Weiss and engineered by Les Paul himself. It was necessary that the band change its name to fit the theme of the record. Carl's sister was a nurse and was thumbing through a physics book when she saw a picture of a Glass Prism. The name was perfect and they called their first album *Poe Through the Glass Prism*. They appeared on the cover dressed in Victorian attire for full English looking effect and are pictured from left to right Carl Siracuse, Rick Richards (holding the Raven), Augie Christiano and Tom Varano.

The album was a hit locally and had some national interest due to the macabre curiosity, the mix of psychedelics and verses by the horror master Edgar Allan Poe. The single *The Raven b/w Eldorado* got into the top 50 nationally. With dark meandering organ, intricate fuzz guitars and a voice like that of Allan Springfield, they come across somewhat like the Last Ritual without horns.

There was a big push to pair Glass Prism up with Blood, Sweat and Tears, but it fell apart and promotion of the record waned. They still owed RCA a second album. It took 3 days to come up with new tunes and a day to record another album in New York, at RCA Studio A, which was put out as an obligation record. Called *On Joy And Sorrow*, Tom Varano turns up the fuzz guitar here and hits the territory of Richard Schamach in Eden’s Children.

Mort Lewis was their manager. He had direct handling of jazz greats Duke Ellington, Ella Fitzgerald and Nat King Cole along with Dave Brubeck in the 50’s. Additionally he had control of Simon and Garfunkel throughout their career together. After the release of the second Glass Prism LP, he disappeared and the RCA label promotion stopped. It was a mystery as to why he left the business but it affected sales for marketing of the band.

Not long after the release, Carl Siracuse helped to form another Scranton band called The Buoys. Rupert Holmes had written a song called *Timothy* and specifically chose Glass Prism as the perfect band to record it. A Scepter Records representative, Michael Wright, came to Scranton hoping to sign Glass Prism but the band was still under contract to RCA Records. So, Tom Varano suggested The Buoys who he also booked and managed at the time. They were signed and put out the international hit single *Timothy b/w It Feels Good*. Of course, the A side song was noteworthy and eventually censored from airplay at many radio stations because of its morbid reference to cannibalism.

The band as Glass Prism was no more. Tom Varano, Augie Christiano and Rick Richards then became the rock trio Shenandoah, playing a cloned version of Grand Funk Railroad, Cream and Hendrix. They were together for a year before Augie left and was replaced by Louie Cossa on (bass, vocals). Shenandoah entered the studio and recorded an album in 1973 but it sat on the shelves. They continued playing through 1976 then disbanded into normal lives. The Shenandoah album was not released until 2011 on CD as part of a double Glass Prism release called *Resurrections*.

Lou Cossa joined the band Dakota that evolved from the original members of The Buoys. He recorded and toured with them and later became a touring member of The Box Tops. He currently owns a music store.

Augie Christiano became a truck driver for Pepsi Cola and plays with other New Jersey bands.

Carl Siracuse did Government work after The Buoys.

Rick Richards is the owner of an electrical company, a banker and works with other local music projects.

Tom Varano is busy as a producer, arranger and songwriter and is the owner of a booking agency, a management company, an employment agency and an insurance company.

Tom Varano (guitar, vocals), Augie Christiano (bass, vocals), Rich Richards (drums, vocals) and Lou Cossa (bass, keyboards, vocals) reunited for periodic concerts in 2007 in Philadelphia at The Edgar Allen Poe Historic Site for the EAP Society, releasing a live concert on DVD as well as a documentary *On Joy And Sorrow: The Glass Prism Story.* They continue to play for their adoring fans showcasing as recently as 2021 which took place at The Theatre at North in Scranton, Pennsylvania.

first edition
DYNOVOICE
STEREO
DY 31905
the
glitterhouse
color blind

THE GLITTERHOUSE 1968

This band was formed in New York with members from Great Neck on Long Island. Great Neck was an area that saw many people like The Marx Brothers, W.C. Fields, Alan King, Paul Newman and most notably F. Scott Fitzgerald's rise to fame. Hank Aberle (guitar) attended M&A, a high school of Music and Art, located in Manhattan. Notable for graduates like Laura Nyro, Janis Ian, Felix Pappalardi, Elliot Randall, Bela Fleck and others who went on to some notoriety in music. Renée Fladen was also a student there and was the focus of Steve Martin (Caro) who was the voice behind the top 5 hit song *Walk Away Renée* for The Left Banke. The school was specialized for young students that had real talent and wanted to make it in the music industry.

Alan Lax (bass) although two years older than Hank lived nearby and the two would skip school and go play pool downtown and hang out at The Gaslight Café in witness to performances with Tom Paxton, Bill Cosby, Ed McCurdy and others. Hank and Al decided to play electric guitars and form a surf band with a couple other guys and called themselves The Outsiders (no relation to the band from Ohio with the hit song *Time Won't Let Me)*. They played various coffee houses and folk venues in Greenwich Village. One evening The Outsiders were playing a high school party up on the West Side of New York and met Mike Gayle. He was a black man who played guitar and was a prolific song writer.

Mike sat in with Hank and Al and they seemed to fit well together. He shared an apartment in New York with Bob Gruen who was just beginning to gain interest in Photography. Bob became famous later in his career for candid pictures of well-known music personalities, specifically members of Kiss, Lou Reed, Debbie Harry and John Lennon. The trio started rehearsing there at the apartment. They hired Tom Weiner on (drums) but because of the noise ordinance decided to move back to Great Neck for practices in the basement of Toms parents' house.

Renaming themselves as The Justice League, they played high school parties and teen clubs in the Great Neck area. A steady fan following occurred and they decided to hire a manager, Alan Nevins, who got them gigs and drove them around to the various venues in The Village. Another Great Neck musician, Mark "Moogy" Klingman, was a young keyboard player. He had attended the Newport Folk Festival in 1965 when he was only 15 and met Bob Dylan after his famous "going electric" thing on stage. He was in a band called The Living Few and at 16 had a one-night stand playing with Jimmy James and the Blue Flames starring a yet unknown Jimi Hendrix and Randy California who later was a guitarist who formed the band, Spirit.

Moogy had attended many Justice League gigs and was determined to become a member. He was hired but started out as the Justice Leagues "roadie". After a while Tom Weiner departed and was replaced by Gary Reems on (drums). Gary was well into abstract paintings and art and did some work with Ad Reinhardt and his Black Paintings. Gary offered up a new name for the band and they became Pop Art. They hired Bob Slater to manage the band and he booked them through the Premiere Talent Agency owned by Frank Barsalona. Premier was the first booking agency in the USA to promote major English rock bands like Herman's Hermits, The Who, The Rolling Stones, The Yardbirds and others. But he also encouraged emerging bands around the country to come aboard and Pop Art was kept busy. Soon Moogy was on stage with the band playing his Hammond M1 organ.

Bob's brother Alvin Slater worked for Columbia Records and got them some recording time for a single that was recorded at CBS Studios in New York. It was released on Epic Records and called *Rumpelstiltskin b/w Ode to an Unknown Girl*. The single got some moderate airplay on local radio WMCA. They played the Village clubs like The Café Au Go Go, The Night Owl, The Bitter End and became the house band for both Scott Muni's Rolling Stone and Joel Heller's Eighth Wonder. They were playing at a club called Arthur, a place owned by Sybil Burton, the wife at the time of mega movie star Richard Burton. This club featured many of the British groups (The Yardbirds, The Who, etc.) The single was getting notice, so they traveled to Cleveland, Ohio to play on *Upbeat*, a syndicated TV show. Billed as "Straight from Arthur's in NYC" they had a one week stay at Cleveland's Otto's Grotto.

About 1 1/2 years together and Pop Art was pretty much done as a band. Mike Gayle and Moogy Klingman both left, but Hank, Al and Gary hired Dave Heenan to replace Mike Gayle on vocals and this band was called the Dave Heenan Set. They recorded one single *Alice In Wonderland b/w So Many Roads* again on Epic records and stayed together for about 8 months.

Mike and Moogy reunited the original band back together which included Moogy Klingman (keyboards, vocals), Al Lax (bass, vocals) and Hank Aberle (guitar, harmonica, vocals), Mike Gayle (lead guitar, lead vocals) and they hired a friend of Moogy's, Joel O'Brien on (drums, vocals) who was formerly with James Taylor and the Flying Machine. Joel's friends just called him Bishop. Moogy was a big movie buff at the time and he suggested that the band should be called The Amazing Dr. Glitterhouse which was based upon a 1938 movie starring Edward G Robinson called *The Amazing Dr. Clitterhouse*. It's certain that the name Clitterhouse would not have been too well accepted even during the "daze" of free love and sex. It sounded too much like a house of "blue lights". So, they shortened the name to The Glitterhouse and the new band was born.

They didn't play any clubs of note but practiced for a few months getting their sound exactly right. Mike Gayle was coming into his own as a song writer, he could write 10 songs in a week and with Joel's drumming the band had potential to be a hit making machine.

They were hired to play a book publication party via Moogy's Dad. He worked for a public relations company in charge of releasing a new coffee table book called *The Birds of Britain*. This was John Green's book exploiting all the Hot models and actresses in 1960's Britain. The cover picture was of Patty Boyd (George Harrisons wife at the time and Eric Clapton's wife later). Others pictured in the book were Jane Asher, Twiggy, Diana Rigg (Emma Peel in *The Avenger's*), Honor Blackman (Pussy Galore in the movie *Goldfinger*), Julie Christie, Sandy Shaw, Lulu, Dusty Springfield and many other known British female stars. Bob Crewe was a top song hit maker and production genius at the time. He happened to be in attendance, heard the band and was inspired to hire them for $500 a week. He made a handshake deal then and there with the band and they signed a formal contract in his offices.

Bob got them rehearsal time at his office space located at 1841 Broadway. They shared the space with Mitch Ryder & the Detroit Wheels. The album was recorded at A&R Studios located at 799 7th Ave in New York. Roy Cicala and Shelly Yakus, who worked with The Four Seasons and all their hits, engineered the sessions. Bob began to focus on the band and dedicated himself to the production of the album adding his own vocals and studio embellishments wherever he felt they were needed. Bob really had big plans and thoughts of many potential hits.

During the process they also had a choice to do a soundtrack recording for either a movie called *Greetings* (starring an unknown new actor Robert De Niro) or a movie called *Barbarella*. They choose *Barbarella* because of Dino DeLaurentis involvement as a well-known producer, Roger Vadim, a well-known director/screenwriter, and the main star, Jane Fonda, who was Roger Vadim's wife at the time. The movie was to be a guaranteed hit. They recorded some songs (voice only and harmonica by Hank). Bob Crewe's thought was to give the public a taste of Glitterhouse through the movie and then hit the public with a full LPs worth of tunes.

The band showed up for the premiere of Barbarella in a Limousine at The Murry Hill Theatre on Lexington Ave. It was a big thing to meet Dino DeLaurentis in person. But things didn't work out as planned. The movie kind of bombed, the single *Barbarella b/w Love Drags Me Down* didn't climb the charts as was thought and the *Barbarella* album didn't sell well enough to give the band any focus.

The recorded LP by Glitterhouse was called *Color Blind* and Bob had a vision of creating a 3-dimentional faux Wedgewood Pottery album cover, but he settled for a simple picture of the guys. Moogy wasn't present for the photo shoot so the silver foiled cover shows Mike on the left, Al Lax, Hank in the middle, Bishop (with the beard and peace sign) and Moogy's fill-in for the picture (a studio guy) on the right. When the album was finally released, the single *Tinkerbell's Mind b/w I Lost Me a Friend* was chosen as the hot song and although it had interest in New York it died everywhere else.

Then Bob Crewe put all his focus on other projects, the album was not promoted and the band was dismissed. This was the usual empty promises made and visions of grandeur unfulfilled by record company moguls. The Glitterhouse had played their last gig together before the album was even recorded at the party where Bob Crewe took them under his wing. Under wraps for a year without sight or sound, the public never saw Glitterhouse perform live as a band. The album went directly to the cut-out bins and they broke up.

The LP is full of psychedelic decoration courtesy of Bob Crewe toying with the songs and there are some real pop-psych gems found in the grooves with three-part harmonies and hooks galore. Some compare the sound to The Band and The Rascals in their later days of progressive experimentation. It seems they would have been the perfect band for Paul Rothchild and Elektra Records who were signing other different acts like Ars Nova, Earth Opera, The Doors and Renaissance.

Afterwards Mike Gayle played with several local bands, but he pretty much retired from playing live and opened a small recording studio called Open Sky. He married well and lives in The Berkshires, Massachusetts.

Al Lax quit the music business and built furniture for a living. He moved to China, learned the language and marketed furniture through his Import/Export business there. When he came back to the US, he became a successful Stockbroker.

Joel O'Brien went back to playing with James Taylor, joined the band Jo Mama and played with Carole King's backup band before retiring to Woodstock and becoming an artist. Unfortunately, he passed away in 2004. There is currently an elaborate website featuring his biography, music, paintings and pictures.

Moogy Klingman helped to form Todd Rundgren's Utopia, he played on the first two Utopia LP releases and the first six Todd LPs. He also recorded two albums under his own name and had a successful career in music up until November 2011 when he unfortunately lost his life due to cancer.

Hank Aberle started building classical guitars and gave classical guitar lessons. But for income and stability he got into sound production and worked for Gotham Recording Studios. Eventually he opened his own sound production company called Aberle Sound where they do voice overs, commercial work and help Internationally with voice and sound engineering. The company is still active as of this writing.

ESP–1037 STEREO
CONTACT HIGH WITH THE GODZ

GODZ 2

THE THIRD TESTAMENT
GODZ

THE GODZ 1967-70

Jim McCarthy (guitar), Larry Kessler (bass) and Paul Thornton (drums) all worked at Sam Goodies Record Store in New York. They all had previous recording experience. In the early 60's Larry released a single *Wonderful Days* under the aka of Miles Standish. In 1964 Paul and Jim were members of The Dick Watson Five that had put out an album called *Baker Street* based upon the Broadway musical Sherlock Holmes. Larry was asked to become a salesman for the newly formed ESP label by Bernard Stollman. One night the three of them experienced The Fugs on stage at a club which started them thinking about music expression rather than current covers of popular songs.

Jim was then kicked out of his girlfriend's flat and moved in with Larry. Paul came over one evening. The three of them were all sharing a joint at the apartment and began banging away with various percussion instruments on furniture, tables and anything that made noise in frustration of the current personal events. It was all weird and strange. Then Larry suggested that they audition for the ESP label. He already had a part in hiring The Fugs and the label was focused on hiring bands that were way out of the mainstream as far as music goes.

They called themselves The Godz. Larry thought Bernard would love this sound but he didn't like the idea that one of his top label representatives wanted to be a musician and refused to hire them. Meanwhile the art director for the ESP label, Jay Dillon, was persuaded to come aboard, they practiced their unique madness in sound and after a while Bernard was persuaded to listen. They were outrageous and totally experimental with no song structure, using odd sounds as more of an experience for the audience. Bernard was floored and agreed to sign them up. He set them up for a two-hour session at A-1 Sound Studios located at 234 West 56th St. in New York. This is where all The Godz recording sessions for the ESP label took place. But for their initial session the band spent six hours and recorded 11 songs. The non-album recorded single was *Lay In The Sun b/w I Want A Word With You*.

Bernard was furious because of the time it took, but after he heard the product, he agreed that a full album would go out. *Contact High* was a very experimental LP with yelps and noises and absolutely no direction. They may as well have been banging on pots and pans, almost unlistenable. The records were sent to every underground

College radio station throughout the US and at first it was assumed that they were like all the other weird bands. But as the songs found their way to the FM radio airwaves, everyone realized that these guys were way out there.

Their reputation grew and they began to get more club dates, but the audiences weren't sure what to expect. They came out with all sorts of strange instruments, cheap acoustic guitars, autoharp, large drumsticks, a plastic flute and would spend 30-40 minutes just tuning up. This would infuriate the crowd who were expecting a show. The freaks loved it. Frequent gigs occurred at The Scene, The Café Wha? and Gerde's Folk City. They were asked to play The Miss Greenwich Village pageant, but musical anarchy occurred when they tried to get the band off the stage and The Godz refused to leave. Understand this was back in 1966-67, way before punk and the Sex Pistols. So, this band could truly be called The Godz of punk and anarchy.

For their second album they got some regular instruments with Jim McCarthy (electric guitar, vocals), Jay Dillon (keyboards), Larry Kessler (bass) and Paul Thornton (drums). The album *Godz 2* was a little more structured, but still very strange. The publishers of the legendary Eye magazine, Michael Soldan and Judy Parker, took a real liking to the band. They hired the Pablo Light Show for their stage performances and promoted their records heavily in England. Things looked incredibly good, but tragedy stuck in 1968 when Mike and Judy lost their lives in a boat accident off Long Island. It was a blow to the entire band. Jay Dillon was completely devastated and quit.

Larry, Jim and Paul collaborated for a third album called *Third Testament* with other friends whooping it up on sound effects and adding solo songs by each to complete the record. The album cover shows left to right Jim McCarthy, Larry Kessler and Paul Thornton. Some call this one the most accessible and listenable to date with some psychedelic studio effects, the noises and effects became a pleasant addition instead of an irritation. Shortly after this Larry broke his neck in a diving accident which effectively ended the band.

But when he recovered and got his old job back in sales for ESP, he began singing in a regular rock band called Seventh Street. Paul Thornton formed another band with Leslie Fradkin who later, in 1976, was a key player with the original Broadway rendition of Beatlemania. By 1971 Lester Bangs published a big article about The Godz in Creme magazine that regenerated interest in the band. Bernard Stollman wanted another recording of The Godz.

He approached Larry to try and form the band again, but the others didn't want to go there. Instead, a compromise occurred.

Jim McCarthy helped with the sessions along with Paul Thornton, Larry Kessler and members from Seventh Street for the fourth Godz album called *Godzundheit.* A-1 Studios was now relocated to the basement of the Opera Hotel on 76th and Broadway. The record was more of a standard folk-rock format and disappointed their hard-core fans. A single with *The Wiffenpoof Song b/w Travel'n Salesman* was originally recorded in 1967-68 but released about this time. All four albums sold well more as a curiosity, but the band members didn't see a dime in royalties. There were thoughts to reunite The Godz, but it never officially happened.

Jim McCarthy released one LP through ESP called *Alien* as a follow up to *Godzundheit.* He had help from Steve Martin Caro and George Cameron, both from The Left Banke, and other studio musicians for this one. He later became a highly respected photographer.

Paul Thornton was a member of a musician's society called The Multitude and played with other bands but notably with Thornton, Fradkin, Unger and the Big Band. One LP was released *Pass On This Side,* a folk psych album that is an unknown gem, with great vocals and string arrangements that is surprisingly quite good musically. Paul and Les Fradkin tried to involve Jim and Larry in an updated version of the Godz for the LP *Godzology* that was eventually released in 2000 but they both bailed on the project. Paul Thornton passed away in April of 2019.

Larry Kessler held all the rights to the Godz music and never authorized a rerelease of the official catalogue. He drove a taxi in Baltimore for a living and was resident father of wrestling champions, as his sons led Owens Mills High School to 8 state championships. Sadly, he passed away in March of 2022 due to being hit by a drunk driver.

Jay Dillon, who disappeared after Mike and Judy had the boat accident, was the most mysterious member. After he left, he went back to painting and displayed his artwork in a few fine galleries from New York to Philadelphia. In 2005 he was completely off the radar with Larry, Jim and Paul as they thought about reuniting. They hadn't seen or heard from him for years and couldn't find him. According to his niece he had survived as a painter and those who knew him back in the day were surprised to hear he had passed on in 2001 nearly 4 years earlier.

abc RECORDS
ABCS-702 Stereo
GOLIATH
Patti

GOLIATH 1969

Goliath started its infancy in Manhattan, New York. Dennis Jason and Steve Jason were brothers of a Navy family who grew up in Hawaii. They moved to California and found an outlet of music. Both played guitar and when they were old enough, they moved to New York because in the early 60's that's where all the record labels were and that's where you went to get discovered. Starting out as a duo they called themselves The Jason Boys. Not a terrific band, but they somehow found steady work playing the coffee houses and clubs.

Meanwhile, another group called The Solitudes were playing around town that included Ted (Butch) Barbella on (bass guitar). They were a solid R'n'B outfit, but the work wasn't steady. Butch was a good bass player and talked some of his band mates into merging with The Jason Boys. It wasn't a good move at first. Steve Jason had a great voice, but he couldn't sing and play guitar at the same time. Butch had all the mental chops to mold players into something worthwhile and saw potential in the group. Steve dropped guitar playing and after a few months they got rather good as a quartet with Dennis Jason (guitar), Butch Barbella (bass), Jerry Gilbert (drums) and Steve Jason (vocals). They called themselves The Young Savages and frequented the major clubs around town like Scott Muni's The Rolling Stone, The Crystal Room and The Cheater Club.

During this time, the Hammond B3 organ was the big new instrument in pop music. It cost almost as much as a house to buy, but those who had one and knew how to play it, could write their own ticket musically. They found a young organ player who was already playing clubs with a band called The Sons of Jesse James. His real name was Jerry Guida, but he went by the stage name of Gerard. His added keyboards brought a real dynamic to The Young Savages and they became the hottest band in greater New York.

Notice came in haste from Roulette Records and they recorded two singles in 1968 *Could I Be Dreaming b/w Can't Get Over You* and *Sitting On A Plane b/w Wait A Minute.* The guitar work especially on *Wait A Minute* is pure psychedelic bliss. These two singles really show a band that had lots of energy. But it wasn't long before Gerard left. They were playing The Rolling Stone one evening opening for another New York band called Group Therapy.

After the show, Gerard was swayed to join that band and traveled to California. It was an abrupt move that upset The Young Savages big time.

They still had a schedule to keep at the Rolling Stone, a venue whose manager was a real Mafia Wise Guy. He emphatically explained to Butch that the people who showed up to see their show expected to hear that terrific organ sound and it would behoove him to be sure that it would happen. Butch had no choice and decided to learn the instrument himself. He borrowed a Hammond B3 initially and spent about 3 days with no sleep relearning the tunes. Norm Conrad was hired to fill in on (bass). Fortunately, the shows came off better than expected and the cement shoes weren't needed.

They expanded their shows along the east coast down into Florida as well as into Detroit, Chicago and Cleveland. A large fan base followed them and some real momentum was happening for possibilities into the big time. When they hit Philadelphia, they had sellout crowds and ABC Records offered them an album deal. The times indicated a name change and someone suggested they had a real big sound, so they decided on the name Goliath.

The sessions were recorded at Sigma Sound Studios in Philly. Their self-titled album *Goliath* was released on ABC Records with high expectations. It was quite theatrical and had a nice underground feel about it with flute, spooky organ and a sound approaching hints of The Collectors on a few songs. Steve Jason had a powerful voice and was the focus of their sound since the band's inception five years prior. However, he sounded a whole lot like David Clayton Thomas of Blood Sweat and Tears. This band had just released their second album a few months before. Al Kooper left after the first album and the band revamped. David Clayton Thomas was unknown up until this point and they had the push and the backing to put them at the top of the heap. B,S&T burst on the music scene and where the hottest thing going at the time.

Fans and critics turned on Goliath and accused them, especially Steve Jason, of being a copycat. For Goliath it was just bad luck and poor timing. They were not happy with the album, feeling that it lacked the energy they portrayed on stage and there was a serious lack of the guitar madness from Dennis Jason. They were in the process of recording a second album, but things fizzled out and they broke apart. The band gave it their best shot, but like so many others they saw the dream fade in a hurry.

Norm Conrad, Dennis Jason and Jerry Gilbert all left music for a normal life.

Steve Jason toured around the country showing up here and there with other bands of little significance. He had always sung the same, but after the B,S&T debacle, could never really live down the fact that he sounded like David Clayton Thomas. One must wonder, who cloned who here. He later collaborated with actor Chazz Palminteri, who wrote songs at the time, and Butch Barbella who wrote most of the songs for another LP by Steve Jason & Ruby J entitled *It's About Time* released in 1983. Steve Jason died in 2004.

Ted (Butch) Barbella went on to the stability of playing the oldies backing such 50's bands as The Earls, The Duprees and played with Dion for several years touring all over the world. He was forced into learning the organ which in retrospect provided him with a 50-year career in music. He wrote the sound score for the movie *A Bronx Tale* (starring Robert DeNiro and Joe Pesci) and now fronts his own band Streets of the Bronx.

V6-5062
STEREO
The Gordian Knot
Verve
NOT FOR SALE
DJ
MONAURAL

THE GORDIAN KNOT 1968

Jim Weatherly grew up in Pontotoc, Mississippi and grew to love music. He was a big Elvis fan and in high school formed a band called The Empaladors. Chuck Berry, Jerry Lee Lewis and other Sun Records artists were the theme. They played the current hits at sock-hops and school assemblies. Jim was also a star athlete and got a football scholarship to the University of Mississippi (Ole Miss). He was part of their only undefeated season in 1962 and as a sophomore helped quarterback them to the 1963 Sugar Bowl win over Arkansas. He was also an honorable mention All-American and 2nd team All-Southeastern Conference quarterback. He could have gone on to the NFL, but his first love was music.

Outside of football at Ole Miss and during the summers he played clubs and dances with his band, Jim Weatherly and The Vegas. The band included Jim (guitar, vocals), Pat Kincade (lead guitar), J.D. Lobue (keyboards, piano), Leland Russell (bass) and Johnny Miller (drums). A popular band, they wanted to branch out. In 1964, they played at the New York World's Fair and other clubs up that way, but no thoughts were put into recording records. However, during that summer they wound up in Erie, Pennsylvania and found a booking agent. Johnny Miller left the band and was replaced by Dulin Lancaster on (drums).

They recorded one single *I'm Gonna Make It b/w Wise Men Never Speak* and Jim also performed on Shindig! in LA. The band was not with him, but when he returned, he talked them into traveling to California. The band decided on the groovier Gordian Knot name during their travels there. Once they got to LA, they had no idea how to make their mark. They were living in a one room flea bite motel on about $3 a day. After a few weeks, they found John Babcock who got them a residency at The Mystery House club on Hollywood Boulevard.

Then Carl Brent befriended the band. He was a player in Hollywood who knew all the stars. He got the band to play at house parties for Connie Stevens, Eddie Fisher, Richard Harris, Sammy Davis, Tony Curtis and others. Like you see in the movies, they would set up a stage by the pool, play music and watch the stars dance away. They were part of Hollywood's elite and got to play in all the hot star clubs around town. They opened The Factory which was an exclusive club for movie stars only. This was an early version of Studio 54 where (the story goes) Richard Burton and Elizabeth Taylor were turned away at the door because the club was full.

The Gordian Knot got their big break after Nancy Sinatra saw them playing at a party. She fell in love with the group and took them on a 17-day USO tour of Vietnam. Camps were set up in haste for entertainment. Jimmy Boyd started with a comedy routine, The Gordian Knot would play their set and then back Nancy for all of her hit songs. Fortunately, no war incidents occurred while they were on stage. When they returned home, they had appearances in movies and on television. Things were good.

It was only natural that they go into the studios to record an album. Verve records signed them. Clark Burroughs became their producer. He had arranged the vocals for the huge hit songs *Windy* and *Never My Love* for The Association and worked with Jim Weatherly and the Gordian Knot. They went to United Western Studios in Hollywood and the sessions included a who's who of musicians with Hal Blaine, Mike Deasey, Larry Knechtel and others. When completed the cover showed the band but didn't list who was who. The cover photo shows from left to right Dulin Lancaster, Pat Kincade, Jim Weatherly, JD LaBue and Leland Russell in that order.

The self-titled album called *The Gordian Knot* was superb, full of magical vocalizations right up there with The Millennium and The Association. Best described by a fan "They were a fusion of sunshine pop and gentle psychedelia geared towards accenting all things melodic." It was certain that the hits would come. Two singles were released. The dreamy *If Only I Could Fly b/w The Year of The Sun* and *We Must Be Doing Somethin' Right b/w Broken Down Old Merry-Go-Round*. But neither single charted.

They toured San Francisco, Seattle and Dallas, but the album did nothing. Things in the music industry were changing so fast. The focus was now on Led Zeppelin, Jimi Hendrix and heavy guitar. Their sound was a year and a half too late. Disappointed, Dulin Lancaster left. The Verve record label dropped the band. They added a couple of new musicians, revamped the band and auditioned for Columbia records who wanted to sign them up. But terms were not reached or agreed to. That was the end of The Gordian Knot.

Dulin Lancaster moved back to Mississippi and played for others like Dan Penn, John Hambrick, Barefoot Jerry and Billy Swan but little else is known. He lived out his life there until his passing in 2014.

Pat Kincade managed used car sales for nearly 20 years and then became a franchise owner of Jersey Mikes Subs in Ventura, California.

J.D. Lobue became a TV director for several weekly shows. Among them *Soap, Soul Train, Newhart, Its A Living and Two and a Half Men.*

Leland Russell was a session musician for a while and played with some local bands before establishing a consulting group for the betterment of different business groups. He founded GEO Virtual Leadership and is a noted and well-respected advisor for business leadership and development in a fast-changing world.

With the band now defunct, Jim Weatherly was ready to go back home and coach football, but he hung around in LA for a while longer and was playing flag football with Lee Majors, star of the hit TV show, *The Six Million Dollar Man*. Through Lee he met Jim Nabors who gained notoriety on *The Andy Griffith Show* as Gomer Pyle. He wound up writing songs for Jim Nabors and his TV variety show, saving enough money that when the show was cancelled, he was ready to go back home again.

But fate wanted Jim to be in music. He happened upon Gary Usher who hooked him up with noted publisher Larry Gordon. He then wrote several songs for Gladys Knight and The Pips. She recorded 13 of his compositions with five being top ten hit's including the single *Neither One of Us b/w Can't Give It Up No More* and the number one national hit *Midnight Train To Georgia b/w Window Raising Granny*. Jim Weatherly's accomplishments throughout the years in the music industry are unparalleled. He currently lives in the suburbs of Nashville with his family.

Far Out!!

ABCS 663 STEREO
abc
RECORDS

GRAFFITI 1968

Graffiti was formed from the remnants of The Hangmen who released several singles, recorded one full album and had a great run for about 5-6 years. At this time, the band included Tom Guernsey (guitar, vocals), George Daly (rhythm guitar), Tony Taylor (lead vocals), Paul Dowell (bass) and Bob Berberich (drums). They were from Washington D.C. and psychedelia was the name of the game at this point. The band began a transitional period where the members came and went.

George Daly moved on and they found Jorge (George) Strunz who was playing in a band called The Seldom Scene. A band that evolved from Joe Corey and the Bristol Singers but was not the famous bluegrass band that started in that area and went national later. This band frequented a place called The Brickskeller near Georgetown when he was asked to join the band. Paul Dowell moved to San Francisco and was replaced with John Cyr on (bass). Tom Guernsey left a month later with Ralph Bryan replacing him on (lead & rhythm guitar). Then Alan Fowler, who was with The Mad Hatters, came aboard replacing Ralph who had left. Alan was a known bass player but was also surprisingly gifted on guitar, playing a Fender Telecaster and sounding like Roy Buchanan.

Arnold Aaron Stahl had been The Hangmen's manager for years. He was a known attorney in the DC area and during this time, some members of the band were living at Arnold's house located on Church St. near the Dupont Circle. The band changed with the times now calling themselves The Button and were featured at New Mac's Pub located in the old Georgetown area of DC. The Hangmen had a huge fan base, so to keep the house full they were billed as The Button (featuring former members of The Hangmen). The band at this point now included Tony Taylor (vocals), Jorge Strunz (guitar) Alan Fowler (guitar), John Cyr (bass) and Bob Berberich (drums).

Jay Senter came aboard to help with managing duties and there was talk of moving to New York to make their mark. Alan came to New York but had a change of mind and decided that he wanted to go back to DC. When the band got there, they were able to play Steve Paul's The Scene, a place where on any given night the patrons included big time movie stars or rock stars. One evening Keith Moon got up on stage and kind of took over the drumming which didn't set well with Bob at all. Soon after Bob left the band and by now all the original Hangmen had departed. A guy named John Z filled his place temporarily.

Jay set the band up a few blocks from Greenwich Village at the Albert Hotel which was the place where all the bands from out of town were accommodated. The hotel desk clerk knew about a big drug bust that was happening that night and warned George and Tony about it. Both took heed and made themselves scarce, but the other band members, girlfriends and acquaintances had arrived earlier and were up in the two suites. There was no indication that bad vibes were about to happen. They were all "busted" and hauled off to the local jail. Fortunately, it was only a temporary stay. Jay was able to bail them all out.

He then secured some recording time at RCA Records in Studio A located at 155 E 24th St. between 3rd and Lexington Ave in New York. It was suggested that the band change their name and they became The Collection. One single was recorded *A Paper Crown of Gold b/w Aquarius*. Side one was a nice pop psych song that fit the times. The B-side of the single was the first recording by any rock band of the song *Aquarius* which was one of many featured songs from the Broadway musical *Hair*. This was 1968, before The Fifth Dimension took the song to number one on the charts in several countries worldwide a year later.

The band evolved again with John Cyr leaving, a new drummer replaced John Z and they added a second guitar player. So officially the players now included Tony Taylor (vocals), George Strunz (lead guitar), Jon St John (rhythm guitar), Steve Benderoth (bass) and Richie Blakin (drums). There was a basement in China Town and a loft in the Tribeca area near the Holland Tunnel where they practiced and rehearsed. They played the clubs in and near Greenwich Village, The Café Au Go Go, The Rolling Stone, The Café Wha and back at Steve Paul's The Scene, where Jimi Hendrix came up after one of their shows, joined them on stage and played a few of his songs with George's right-handed Les Paul SG. Hendrix was clearly ambidextrous.

One album was recorded at The Record Plant located in Manhattan. It was then that Jay Senter came up with a name change from The Button to Graffiti as another update for the band. Eddie Kramer had just flown in from London to engineer the *Electric Ladyland* LP project for Jimi Hendrix and took time for the Graffiti sessions with overall production from Jay Senter and general observance by Bob Thiele. Because both bands were sharing time at the studio, Hendrix witnessed one Graffiti session and asked George if he could borrow his Marshall Stack, since it was already set up, to finish a song or two on the Electric Ladyland recordings.

The self-titled LP called *Graffiti* was finished and has all the right moves, special effects, dreamy vocals and echoes reminiscent of a heavy Chamaeleon Church and approaches Jasper Wrath territory at times. The cover picture was a double exposure of the band standing near the Hudson River with another picture of them in a public restroom (two members at a urinal) superimposed over the river shot for a psychedelic textured affect. George (Jorge) was originally from Costa Rica and was listed as George on the inside cover, but his last name was misspelled as Stunz. A small promotional tour was set up playing several times at The Electric Circus, opening for The Doors at Westbury Fair on Long Island, sharing the stage with Blood, Sweat and Tears in Central Park, supporting The Jefferson Airplane at Asbury Park in New Jersey and then following them up to Thousand Island Park on Wellesley Island by the Canadian border for a gig there.

On the way to this show, they were spotted by a police car who put the lights on and motioned for them to pull over. Thinking they might be in trouble Jon St John quickly wrapped all the Hippie Lettuce he could find in tin foil. But rather than hiding it in a convenient concealed spot, he threw it out the window. All the guys were giving him a look and a tone, yelling "What the....!!!". Of course, they pulled over, the cop got out of his car and walked directly to the wad of foil, picked it up and carried it to the "hippie" van apparently looking for an explanation. What could they say? They were dragged to the local Justice of the Peace, mentioned that they were on their way north as the opening band for Jefferson Airplane and after some discussion and persuasion with the judge, he gave them a warning and bid them farewell.

A single was released *He's Got the Knack b/w Love in Spite* with the non-album A-side getting some regional radio airplay but sales and distribution of the LP was not as desired. It was pressed in limited quantity and Graffiti only played gigs locally. Jorge was the first to leave and it wasn't long before they all separated. They had only been together for maybe one year.

Of note Bob Berberich, Paul Dowell and George Daly, previously with The Hangmen, formed a band with Nils Lofgren called Dolphin. This band never recorded and fell apart but Nils and Bob stayed together forming a new band called Grin for four LPs and then Nils became a semi superstar with Bruce Springsteen.

Arnold Aaron Stahl had a celebrated life as a Korean War veteran and practicing law. He traveled the world after his days with The Hangmen and the band who became Graffiti. Then he wrote a book after returning to New York about his experiences and became a City Law Administrative Judge. He is in his 80's and still resides in New York.

Jon St John disappeared for a while. He was a bit of a drifter but he showed up at Jorge's place who years later had relocated to Los Angeles. He stayed for a week, departed and hasn't been heard from him since.

Richie Blakin stayed busy behind the scenes of the music industry and spent over 35 years mixing, editing and as sound engineer for various artists like James Taylor, Paul Simon, Rod Stewart and others in several New York studios.

Tony Taylor moved to Destin, Florida where he still lives and became a Physical Therapist.

Steve Benderoth stayed in music mostly doing session work and writing songs and jingles for products like Clairol, Eastern Airlines, 7-Up and Folgers Coffee. He was part of the band formed by Michael McKean as *Lenny and the Squigtones* releasing one LP back in the late 70's and wrote one notable song *This Boy's on a Roll* sung by Robert Palmer for Brat Pack actor Rob Lowe and his hit movie *Oxford Blues*. Unfortunately, Steve died due to kidney failure March of 2007.

Jorge Strunz continued playing guitar eventually forming the well-known and respected jazz fusion band Caldera releasing four LPs. He met Ardeshir Farah, another fabulous guitarist, soon after and the two as a duo have been together for more than 40 years. Credit Arnold Stahl and his connections for helping them get their start. They have played all over the world and have released more than 20 albums with over one million units sold. They received a Grammy nomination for Best World Music Album of the Year in 1992 with their album *Américas.* Strunz and Farah are noted for their virtuosic guitar technique, intricate sounds and great backing band.

DOT RECORDS
STEREO
DLP 25939
HAMILTON
STREETCAR

HAMILTON STREETCAR 1969

Tom Fannon was from Glendale, California and he aspired to play guitar. He took lessons but got frustrated and quit. His cousin Rick stayed with the family for a while and got Tom re-interested in playing. Together they started a surf band playing various Ventures, Wailers and Dick Dale tunes, but with The Beatles and Rolling Stones changing rock music forever, surf music was falling by the wayside. By this time Tom could sing and play at the same time. Rick graduated from college and moved away.

Tom and Bart Conway (bass) were school buddies and were both taking guitar lessons at a Glendale music store to further their skills. It's noted that Spencer Dryden, future member of Jefferson Airplane and Moby Grape, was a drum teacher at this place. Auditioning several players, Tom and Bart hired John Burge (keyboards) and Barry McGuire (drums) both from the town of La Canada to complete the aspiring group. They called themselves The Regents for a while and then became The Chosen Few. (Note that this was not the popular Midwest band that put out an album on RCA). Daily rehearsals took place at Johnny's house. Tom put an ad in the local paper seeking a lead vocalist and got a call from Ralf Plummer who was not only a seasoned singer as front man with several other bands but had written a few original songs and became their main song writer.

They began playing teen dances and frat parties. Barry moved on and they went through a few different drummers before settling on Greg Hart. He was a character and they changed their name to The Rollin' Machine inspired by Greg's recreational habit. Forrest Hamilton met them at a frat party and took a real liking to the band. He offered to manage them but they were skeptical at first because he appeared to be just another drunk. As it turned out his dad was Chico Hamilton, a well-known jazz drummer, and Forrest proved to have some real clout knowing all the right people in the industry because of his father.

Changing their name to Hamilton Omnibus based on their new manager and a local coffee house they frequented, they eventually renamed as Hamilton Streetcar. Hamilton because of Forrest and Streetcar as a tribute to San Francisco and the band that inspired them, The Jefferson Airplane. Forrest got them signed up with the William

Morris Agency and their first show was at the Santa Monica Civic Auditorium opening for Gabor Szabo and The Association in front of 2000 people. Promoting their own shows at certain venues, they billed themselves as second act to any band established on the national charts.

Recording a demo, Forrest shopped it around and got them signed up with Lee Hazelwood and his label LHI. A single was recorded *Invisible People b/w Flashes* at T.T.G. Studios located at 1441 McCadden Place just off the Strip that did well locally. Tom left temporarily to start a family and the band filled his spot with Michael Georgiades who later teamed up with Bernie Leadon of the Eagles for one LP. One more single was recorded and released *Confusion b/w Your Own Comedown*. Both singles were psychedelic gems that fit right in with the sounds of Jefferson Airplane, Big Brother & the Holding Company, The Mystery Trend, Gold, Moby Grape and other San Francisco bands at the time. Shortly thereafter Bart Conway left for College and was replaced by Jay Alan on (bass). Tom returned to the band and they recorded a live set of songs in the studio that was potentially set to be released for an album called *Silver Wing*s. But nothing panned out.

They frequented Bido Lito's at 1608 North Cosmo St. in Hollywood. This club was small but was noted for featuring bands like Love, The Doors, The Seeds and The Byrds to name a few. They would close North Cosmo Street between Selma Ave and Hollywood Blvd and place huge speakers to blare out the sounds of whichever band was playing live to the overflow crowd outside who would literally dance in the street.

By this time, the official band included Tom Fannon (guitar, vocals), Mark (aka Ralf) Plummer (vocals), John Burge (aka Ian Hamilton) (keyboards, organ), Jay Alan (bass, vocals) and Greg Hart (drums, vocals). Playing clubs along the LA Strip and becoming the house band at The Cheetah Club in Santa Monica, they established themselves as a band to watch. Venturing out to bigger venues they opened for The Doors and Steppenwolf at the Las Vegas Convention Center, played with Spirit (their first big concert), The Strawberry Alarm Clock, The Hour Glass (soon to evolve into the Allman Brothers Band), The Sunshine Company and Jefferson Airplane for the 1st Annual Sacramento Pop Festival at Hughes Stadium and they were added to the list of bands with Country Joe and the Fish, Canned Heat, Things To Come, The Hook, Smokestack Lighting and Buffalo Springfield for their farewell concert at the Long Beach Sports Arena on May 5th 1968 billed as The Electric Carnival. Hamilton Streetcar was written up in Teen Life magazine covering their show with high praises.

They got an album deal with DOT records. Produced by Richard Delvy, who was a former drummer for The Challengers, he wanted a different sound from the band and had a desire to change things. Creative differences between him and the band caused Tom, Jay and Greg to leave the recording sessions before they really started. Ralf and John stayed on board and they laid down tracks at Sunset Sound Studios located at 6650 Sunset Blvd. in Hollywood. Engineered by Brian Ross-Myring and Pete Ramano, the sessions included Buzz Clifford (guitar) and John Boylan (from Appletree Theatre) who were asked to be part of the project along with studio musicians. Originally proposed for the *Silver Wings* LP, only one song written by original band member Ralf Plummer was included. All the other songs were penned by staff writers Buzz Clifford, Lee Michaels, John Boylan, Tim Buckley, Carol King and others.

Although not a true representation of the band and how they sounded, the self-titled album *Hamilton Streetcar* nonetheless was quite good. Somewhat overproduced with horns and orchestration, the album had echoing vocals, special effects, fuzz guitar and a mysterious vibe. It wound up as a conceptual piece much like a rock musical. The songs would fit well into theatre productions like Hair or Jesus Christ Superstar. Assimilating a studio produced band the LP had no mention of the players involved in the project. It sounded nothing like the original band. Those who didn't know dismissed the LP as a fake band studio product. Fans of the band were surprised and disappointed. Three singles were released *I See I Am b/w Silver Wings, Brother Speed b/w Wasn't It You* and *Honey and Wine b/w Now I Taste the Tears.*

Hamilton Streetcar with the original members continued to play live dates after the album was released but played few if any of the songs from the LP onstage. They were frustrated with the final product and the album languished. Over time, the record has become a favorite of psychedelic enthusiasts, but the band to this day has grown sour grapes over the whole recording. Rightly so, with only Ralf and John involved on a limited basis there was no promotion for the LP and royalties? Forget about it.

Because of the disillusionment with the record industry Hamilton Streetcar soon broke apart.

Former member Bart Conway became a furniture/cabinet maker and still plays guitar with local bands near Denver, Colorado.

Barry McGuire never left the area where he grew up and was in a band called Maggie that did some recording in the 70's. He eventually owned and operated a pool construction business in Southern California. He still plays with bands.

Greg Hart moved to Sacramento and still plays drums with his son's band.

John Burge joined the military becoming a career service veteran. He retired as a Colonel and lives in Washington State.

Jay Alan became a sound engineer and producer in California.

Mark (Ralf) Plummer went back to school and became a freelance graphic designer and art director for several companies near Seattle, Washington before retiring to Cape Cod, Massachusetts.

Tom Fannon moved to Colorado and is in the banking industry.

As mentioned before there were several songs recorded in studio before the DOT debacle and Jay Alan has the master tapes. About 10 years ago there was real interest in the band and a good possibility that these tapes could have been remastered and released but legal issues occurred with the Lee Hazelwood estate so things were put on hold.

LOOK 11000 • STEREO

KS 1119 • STEREO
have a heart
KING
K

HEART

HEART 1969-72

We can start this band circa 1965-66 at Highland High in Albuquerque, New Mexico with Bob Barron (bass), Jim Callaham, (guitar), Jerry Beardsworth (vocals) and David Goodenow (drums). They initially called themselves The Agents but later became The Pallbearers. The Pallbearers and Lindy Blaskey & the Lavells were two of the hottest high school bands on the local teen scene playing frat parties and dances at the University of New Mexico. Lindy & the Lavells had already recorded and released at least 6 singles and Carl Silva, who was a member, was a multi-instrumentalist playing harmonica and percussion with this band. But he left and became lead singer and drummer for The Striders. The Striders released a single in distribution *When You Walk Into a Room b/w Sorrow* that had a local label release but was picked up by Columbia and released as *Say You Love Me b/w Sorrow* for multi-state distribution.

The Pallbearers eventually broke apart and Bob Barron joined The Striders as well. They moved to Laurel Canyon in California for some big-time recognition, then hired Arnold Bodmer, a keyboard wizard from Switzerland. As they couldn't find any major label interest, the band broke apart. Carl Silva (drums, vocals), Bob Baron (bass, vocals) and Arnold Bodmer (keyboards) all moved back to Albuquerque and they hired Danny Burnett on (guitar). Three or more years as a band in the music business, they were seasoned musicians that could all write songs and eventually hooked up with John Wagner Recording Studios located at 806 Lomas Blvd NE in Albuquerque, the best studio in town.

Their first album, simply called *Heart,* had all the right moves with rock, soul, psych and enough hooks to keep things interesting. Promotion of the band occurred locally with two singles from the LP *Now b/w Give Me A Happy Day* and *Love b/w I Love You* that were released to the airwaves. Little happened sales wise, but they had enough material to record a full second album called *Have A Heart.* More of the same as the first album, but with a little more guitar. Afterward and with no public interest in either album, Danny Burnett left along with Arnold Bodmer who joined the high fledging band Mud. This band cooked and put out two albums on the UNI label.

Trying to keep Heart together, Carl and Bob hired David Butterfield, ex player from The Eternals on (guitar, vocals) and Bob Mora (drums). They spent a year or more playing at several venues around town highlighting at a biker bar, The Thunderbird, in Placitas, NM. Meanwhile Mud had a quick breakup because their leader and singer overdosed on drugs. So, Arnold Bodmer returned on (keyboards). Ex-Mud and former Eternals guitarist Steve D'Coda (aka Steve Miller) also joined. Bob Mora left and was replaced by drummer Dave Goodenow.

A 3rd self-titled *Heart* album was recorded and released on Motown's subsidiary label Natural Resources with only Bob Barron and Carl Silva listed as band members but all the others, although uncredited, were on board. Again, there was truly little promotion, although the album seems to be the most available on the marketplace.

Eventually they all separated. Danny Burnett was last seen in 1972 near New York trying to make it to England to team up with Richie Blackmore, but he never made it there, and unfortunately, it's confirmed that he took his own life. Arnold Bodmer continued with Steve D'Coda in a band called Fingers and played in other bands (The Sox, Rampant Egos, Kobiyashi Maru) and then teamed up with Justin Parker and formed a band called Solid Ghosts for some very mystical ambient sounds. He was fronting The Entourage Jazz Trio with Susan Corley (vocals) and Mark Tatum (bass) and had a long and well-respected career in music. He currently has a guitar and keyboard instruction website called Albuquerque Guitar Lessons. Bob Barron currently plays with the long running and established band Combo Special.

Carl Silva remained a musician and fronted several bands during his career. Not only Heart but The Planets, Street Talk, The Pink Flamingos and The Carl Silva Revue, where this band was sought after by major nationwide corporations for entertainment at national events all over the country. Although they didn't play any Heart tunes, the band had high energy from start to finish playing popular hits from the 50's through the 90's. A self-taught musician, Carl was an amazing instrumentalist playing (drums, guitar, bass, piano, keyboards, harmonica, saxophone and accordion) and he could sing. The best example of his talent is found on YouTube where he filmed and produced a video for NASCAR that was nominated for an EMMY award. Sadly, he will be missed as Carl Silva passed away in November 2019.

DL 74920
STEREO
THE HOBBITS
DOWN TO
MIDDLE
EARTH
DECCA

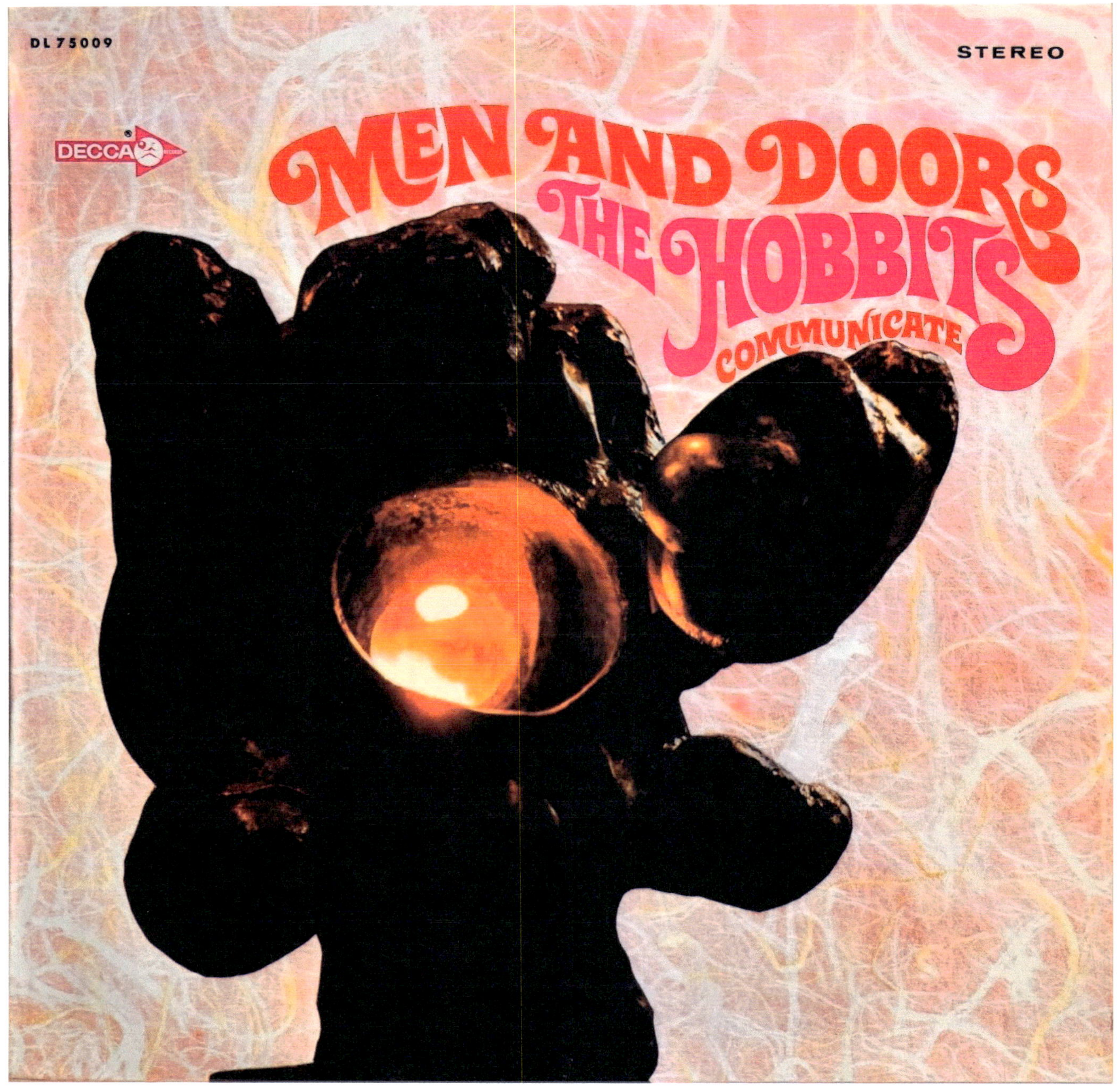
DL 75009
STEREO
DECCA
MEN AND DOORS
THE HOBBITS
COMMUNICATE

STEREO
PLP10
THE NEW HOBBITS
BACK FROM MIDDLE EARTH
Perception
RECORDS
INC.

THE HOBBITS 1967-69

Jimmy Curtiss was from Queens, NY and was part of the doo wop combo The Enjays. He knew someone in the business in New York and managed to get the group recorded for a couple of singles. There was some local airplay but no interest in the group itself. However, Jimmy had a voice and he could write songs. Don Costa was an A&R man for the recently formed United Artists record Label. He noted Jimmy's vocal ability and after recording his first solo single, *Without You b/w Simple Things,* thought he might become the next Bobby Vee or Paul Anka. A second single was put out there as well but neither one took off, so Jimmy and UA Records separated.

Jimmy then spent the next five years in the advertising industry. He always had a guitar, never stopped composing music and would go home each day after work to write and record songs on tape. There were quite a few record labels in New York and he was always presenting his songs to those who would listen to see if there was any interest. Some of his songs were recorded by other groups. Music was his first love and he saw that he could make a living at it. So, he quit advertising and teamed up with Ernie Mareska at the Laurie Records label.

Ernie was notable for writing a lot of Dion's biggest hits along with Eliot Greenberg. Jimmy had a specialty for writing great melodies with that special hook that could grab the listener. He would sit in the recording sessions and play guitar. Eventually he recorded a couple of his own tunes that were released on the Laurie label. One single *Psychedelic Situation b/w Gone But Not Forgotten* took off in Germany. But Laurie didn't treat him very well, he wasn't getting paid for what was agreed to for his efforts and he wanted to be put on retainer. But they refused so he had to move on and left.

Terry Philips, Jerry Vance and Marcia Hillman worked with Decca Records and were putting together an album focused on J.R.R. Tolkien's "The Hobbit". It was basically an in-studio effort. They had the idea and the concept for the album including the name of the band, The Hobbits, and the album title called *Down to Middle Earth.* Marcia Hillman was an in-house song writer and three Decca session vocalists (Heather Hewitt, Tony Luizza and Zok Russo) were on board. But they wanted a lead vocalist and another song writer, so they called on Jimmy to come in and suggest some ideas.

The team of Vance, Philips and Hillman helped Jimmy complete the project. The recording sessions took place at A&R Studios located at 112 W 48th St in NY on the 4th floor of the Mogall's Film and TV building. The album included Jimmy Curtis (vocals), Heather Hewitt (vocals), Tony Luizza (vocals), Zok Russo (guitar, vocals), Danny Mahony (bass, vocals), Jay Savino (guitar), Joe Di Marzo (keyboards) and Al Esposito (drums) Of note here is that Danny, Jay, Joe and Al were the house band for Decca Records and were the session players for other Decca artists.

The first Hobbit album *Down To Middle Earth* has weird special effects, echoes, flute, wah-wah guitar, organ, strings and sitar. A good effort, but the songs had nothing to do with the actual Hobbit story as the novel reads. It was more of a psychedelic exploitation album with songs about groovy flowers, sunshine and happy dreams. Wild colorful cover art and songs that were ready-made for AM radio made the album a perfect sales project for Decca Records and the times. Musically The Cowsills and The Sunshine Company come to mind.

There was heavy distribution for the album and it was well received. Jimmy, Heather, Tony and Zok ventured out to play live at The Bitter End located near Greenwich Village on Bleeker Street and a few other clubs. They traveled to California and were paired up with Sandy Bull at The Western Front in San Francisco September 1967. There's also a rare video on YouTube of them playing live 1967 at a club in New York singing the song *Daffodil Days*.

Milton Rackmill was president of Decca at the time. He had just returned from Spain and wanted Jimmy to record another Hobbits LP. But Milt wanted a Spanish feel for the music. Jimmy objected but had to go with his wishes. The band included the same players, but Gini Eastwood was added in on (vocals) and Marius on (flamenco guitar). The second album called *Men and Doors: The Hobbits Communicate* was released and the music was more of the same pop-psych, but it did have a Spanish guitar flavor.

Jimmy then launched Perception Ventures Inc., a production company, and became Vice President and creative director. As mentioned before Dan Mahoney, Jay Saving, Joe Di Marzo and Al Esposito were the house band for

Decca records. They became an official band called The Bag and recorded one album released on Decca entitled *Real* produced by Jimmy starring themselves. He put together a solo LP simply called *J. C. Life* with him on vocals and guitar and help again from members of The Bag for the first Perception Records label album release. No three-part harmonies here, the songs are an introspection of his life in general.

The Perception record label distributed LPs from other artists that recorded sessions from odd rock bands like The Albert, Fat Back, Pendulum & Co., Bartel, J.J. Jackson's Dilemma and others. The band Would put out a notable psych album although it was in very limited quantity. Would re-named themselves as *Velvet Night* and had a later repressing of their LP with a different album cover and different song order sequence on the Metromedia Record label. King Harvest also released an album on Perception and had a hit song written by the band Boffolongo in 1970. *Dancing in The Moonlight b/w Marty and the Captain* was a huge hit and made it to #17 on the national Billboard charts. Boffolongo later evolved into the band Orleans that was quite successful in the 80's and 90's.

A third Hobbits LP was recorded with The Bag and other session players and Jimmy renamed the band as The New Hobbits. Entitled *Back from Middle Earth,* only a few copies of this album were pressed up and are impossible to find. They never gigged or toured and had all but separated. The New Hobbits LP *Back From Middle Earth* was reissued on CD only back in 2010.

Gini Eastwood and Heather Hewitt went to Hollywood and were featured in a few movies basically because of their looks. Gini recorded a single *With The World At My Feet b/w Everything I Do, I Do For Love* on Tower records.

Dan Mahony was elected to the American Society of Authors Composers and Publishers in 1968. Then got heavy into music theory and advanced sound techniques at City College of New York and Juilliard. He spent a few years in Ireland playing festivals and theatres, but became a full-time music teacher frequenting New York, Boston and Albuquerque.

Jimmy Curtiss grew disenchanted with the business side of the recording industry, went back to graphic design and became an advertising executive. He wrote commercial songs for Ford Motor Company, Bumblebee Tuna and others. A lifelong career in Advertising and Music, he passed away on February 2nd, 2022.

PHILIPS
PHS 600-252 STEREO
H.P. LOVECRAFT
PHILIPS

PHILIPS
HP
Lovecraft
PHS 600-279 STEREO

6419
LOVECRAFT VALLEY OF THE MOON
I would rather be ashes than dust!
"...I would rather that my spark
should burn out in a brilliant blaze
than it should be
stifled by dry rot.
I would rather be a superb meteor,
every atom of me in magnificent glow,
than a sleepy and permanent planet.
The proper function of man
is to live, not to exist.
I shall not waste my days in trying
to prolong them.
I shall use my time..."
—Jack London

H.P. LOVECRAFT 1967-70

George Edwards grew up in Chicago. He started to sing in choirs and musicals and by the time of high school he was singing and playing banjo and guitar. Two high school friends joined him and they formed The Coachmen as a folk trio. They played at the high school and at coffee houses that were becoming popular. Realizing that his calling was in music he packed up and traveled to California. Finding a steady job with other musicians playing an upright bass at The Golden Bear in Huntington Beach, he played with Ian & Sylvia, Hoyt Axton, Doug Dillard and any other band or artist that came there to play.

Writing his own songs, he followed his path to Florida and at The House of Pegasus he played with Jerry Jeff Walker and discovered Fred Neil. Fred was a huge influence on his life in music. In New York he played the clubs in Greenwich Village, specifically The Bitter End and The Café Wha?, gaining a reputation as an accompanist on bass and 12 string guitar and as a solo act. His first recording experience was at Prestige Records playing bass and 12 string for Len and Judy Novy on their album *Folks Songs, Sweet and Bittersweet.*

He ventured back to the mid-west and booked himself into clubs and coffee houses in Philadelphia and Cleveland and then was asked to write a jingle for Kellogg's Raisin Bran for the Michigan cereal company that was faltering at that time. Back in Chicago he befriended George Badonsky, Bill Traut and Eddie Higgins who had just started the Dunwich Records label recording *Norwegian Wood b/w Never Mind I'm Freezing* with himself on (guitar) and Eddie Higgins on (harpsichord). This song also included a young guitarist named Steve Miller who became a huge star a short two years later. The single had some airplay in the Midwest states and on the East coast radio stations. This led to a tour of a few clubs locally and in New York and he also toured in Europe. After completing that journey, he began singing backup vocals with The Will Mercier Trio back in Chicago.

The Philips Record label then hired George and he recorded the song *Any Way That You Want Me* written by Chip Taylor who had a long history of writing hits including *Wild Thing* for The Troggs and *Angel of the Morning* for

Marilee Rush, two worldwide hit singles that each sold over 1 million units. Chip was also the brother of actor Jon Voight and an uncle to Angelina Jolie.

After George recorded and heard the initial recording of the *Any Way...* song, he asked to have David Michaels come in and add his high voice to the mix. David had formally attended Northwestern University and was previously in a college trio with David Sanborn (the famous jazz saxophone player). Dave Michaels and George were both in The Will Mercier Trio singing nightclub songs to a dinner audience. Dave's voice was a perfect blend with George. The single *Any Way That You Want Me b/w It's All Over For You* hit the airwaves and gathered interest but there still wasn't a formal band.

Dunwich Records, owned by George Badonsky and Bill Traut, was interested in producing local Chicago rock bands. Dave and George met at George Badonsky's apartment and were discussing names for a proposed band but couldn't come up with anything. The conversation turned towards George B's Yorkshire Terrier that was just lying there. His name was Yuggoth. George E asked where he came up with a name like that. It was the name of a planet listed in one of the stories written by the author H.P. Lovecraft and that was it. It turns out Bill Traut knew August Derluth, who handled the H.P. Lovecraft estate and he got permission for the band to use the name.

They were able to hold auditions at The Mother Blues Club located directly below George B's apartment during the day when they were closed. Several guitar players came through and when Tony Cavallari played, he fit the bill. The three of them started rehearsing acoustically and things were coming together. But Tony was a rock musician and it was decided that the band should go electric, so they went out and bought electric guitars and amps. They found a vacant fourth floor at an office building in downtown Chicago and then 16-year old Michael Tegza was brought in on drums. Tom Skidmore initially came in on (bass) and H.P. Lovecraft began playing clubs around town including The Celler and The Cheetah in Chicago where they were paired with Neil Diamond.

Their sound and songs were unique because they were the only band playing their own song compositions while other bands were still doing cover versions of popular songs. The harmonies of Dave and George together is what made the distinctive sound of H.P. Lovecraft. After a few live gigs it became clear that Tom was not going to work out. The Shadows of Knight was another band under contract with Dunwich Records. George Edwards had played in studio sessions with that band. He knew that Jerry McGeorge, their bass player, was rumored to be leaving and asked him if he wanted to join his band.

He agreed and about a week later they began recording their first album at Universal Recording Studios in Chicago located on East Walton St. The band was set, with George Edwards (bass, guitar, vocals), David Michaels (keyboards, vocals). Tony Cavallari (lead guitar), Jerry McGeorge (bass, vocals) and Michael Tegza (drums, vocals). This studio was huge and recorded stars like Frank Sinatra, Vic Damone, Dinah Washington and others with the backing of a full orchestra. They also had all the latest recording gadgets and techniques. The studio was the first to use isolated vocal booths and multi voice overdubs.

The band came in and took full advantage of the resources. The engineer, Jerry DeClerk, had been used to big orchestras but was open to listening to the band and experimenting with sound effects in recording. Many songs on the album were the ones that George Edwards had been playing as a solo folk artist in the coffee clubs, but they were rearranged and reworked for an electric sound and the psychedelic times. The studio was a real playground for the band. The first album, simply called *H.P. Lovecraft,* was full of harpsichord, ocarina, guitar, some orchestration, echoes, meandering spooky passages, haunting vocals and special effects. The band Wizards from Kansas would be a close clone to their sound, at least to these ears. Two singles were put out *The White Ship (edited) b/w The White Ship (complete version)* and *Wayfaring Stranger b/w The Time Machine.*

When the album was done, they got a spot opening for The Who outside of Chicago. This led to gigs at bigger venues in the mid-west. They wore an unusual wardrobe for the shows and put drummer Mike Tegza at the front of the stage. George Badonsky knew Bill Graham and they headed for The Fillmore in San Francisco. Once in California, they found constant working gigs at all the big clubs up and down the west coast and decided to relocate to San Francisco where all the music was happening.

Then they were on the road constantly for about a year touring all over the country. It was the best of times and the record company wanted another album output. George Edwards hadn't really written any more songs and bassist Jerry McGeorge left the band. They hired Jeff Boyan on (bass, vocals), who had formerly been with the hot Chicago band Saturday's Children, to take his place. As a live band HP Lovecraft would improvise the songs they were playing and come up with new ideas to work on.

They went to I.D. Sound Studios, a studio owned by The Beach Boys, in Hollywood to do the sessions and thought they could do the same improvisations for their second LP. But the band was so discombobulated from touring it was obvious that they needed rest. George would stay up at night writing lyrics and composing as best he could. They fumbled their way through the songs in the studio making things up as they went along. Fortunately, Chris Houston was overseeing the production and added a lot of special effects which carried the songs through. As an audio engineer he had been responsible for the sounds of Led Zeppelin, The Who, Eric Burden & War and many others. The result of his technique was a real utopia of psychedelics.

The band was tired, but the album *H.P. Lovecraft II* was a perfect sophomore edition follow up to the first LP. In retrospect George Edwards felt the album was rushed and could have been so much better. They toured for a little while longer, but dissention began to set in and the band was burned out. They had been together without a break for over two years and the disagreements were festering. The partnership of George Badonsky and Bill Trout had also soured and everything fell apart.

All the guys went back to Chicago. But George wanted to reform the band and went back to Los Angeles with Bill Trout to work out a deal with Warner Brother Records. He knew James Vincent (Donlinger) (guitar) and brought back Michael Tegza on (drums). James brought in Mike Been on (bass, vocals). Mike and Jim had both been with the band Aorta and The Rotary Connection. Mike was the spitting image of and had the voice of David Michaels, who chose not to participate with the new band. They also hired Marty Greeb on (keyboards) who was formerly with The Buckinghams.

The new band was renamed as Lovecraft and they found a big house with acreage for rehearsals and practice and lived the communal life. Songs were written but the personalities clashed. George Edwards departed before things were fully completed. The album was recorded at Wally Heider Studios located on Hyde St in San Francisco. Even without George the album called *Valley of the Moon* was rather good with great guitar work and three-part harmonies but there were none of the weird studio special effects that made the band's sound so eerie and unique. Released on Warner Brothers Records, George was not part of the band and because of this there was no support or promotion from the label. They played a few gigs on the west coast but it all fell apart before the album was even put out to the public. They all went their separate ways.

Jeff Boyan didn't record anything else but had a successful career as a solo artist for many years until his passing in May of 2013.

Tony Cavallari never connected with any other bands as an artist afterwards. However, he did tour with The Grateful Dead for many years as part of the road crew and then managed a lumber mill in California.

Jerry McGeorge wound up as a session player in Nashville for many country stars. He got into the auto industry and became an executive for Volkswagen and Jaguar.

Michael Tegza paired up with the band *Bangor Flying Circus* for one album before the Lovecraft project. By 1975 he reformed the band again with disco singer Lalomie Washburn calling it Love Craft but none of the other original players were there. The AOR album *We Love You (Whoever You Are)* was nothing like the beauty of their former selves. As a rock album it's not bad but it sank like a rock. Michael reportedly lives in Texarkana.

David Michaels finished his degree in music theory & composition. He sang and played piano at Max's Opera Café in San Francisco for years.

George Edwards discovered that he was adopted and found that his real name was Charles Ethan Kenning. He built hand remodeled houses for a while, then partnered up with a friend and wrote a lot of commercial jingles for Levi's. Taco Bell, Chevy Trucks and other products earning him two CLIO awards. He worked as an independent producer of folks like Doc Watson, Leon Redbone and others and still plays solo gigs on occasion.

ABCS-641 STEREO
FLASHES
THE ILL WIND
A RASPUTIN PRODUCTION BY TOM WILSON
abc RECORDS

ILL WIND 1968

Ken Frankel and Carey Mann met at (MIT) the Massachusetts Institute of Technology in Cambridge near Boston. They were both highly educated graduate students. Ken played guitar but was also versed in several other instruments and had been playing in a rock band during his high school years in Los Angeles. At Berkeley he played in bluegrass bands with Jerry Garcia and others in San Francisco. Carey was also playing piano and guitar in bands at high school and at MIT. Ken met Norman Gan at a party. Norm had a folk duo with Judy Bradbury and Ken offered to accompany them on guitar and banjo. They played at a club in Boston called The Loft for about six months. Carey joined in on bass and it wasn't too long before Ken and Carey decided to form a rock group. Judy had a great voice so she sang (vocals). Ken (guitar) and Carey (guitar, vocals) hired friends at MIT to play bass and drums.

Ken had been writing songs and the band rehearsed but they couldn't get gigs because they weren't playing cover tunes. It didn't help that Ken and Carey both had long hair and beards. They were a little intimidating. It wasn't long before the fellas they hired to play bass and drums left. They advertised locally for replacements and found Richard Griggs who was a singer, song writer and played rhythm guitar. Dave Kinsman also responded to the add as drummer. Both had been in rock bands for a few years and liked the songs Ken had written. The nucleus of the initial band became Ken Frankel (lead guitar), Judy Bradbury (vocals), Richard Griggs (rhythm guitar, vocals), Carey Mann (bass, keyboards, vocals) and Dave Kinsman (drums).

They decided to call themselves The Prophets because of Ken and Careys long hair and beards, but they soon realized that The Prophets was a name used by too many other bands. Ken had written a song called Ill Wind, so they chose that as the band name. They tried to get gigs through the local club booking agency but there were no takers because they didn't play any of the popular AM radio hits. It was only a stroke of luck that they played in some teen dance clubs. The summer of 1966 and the psychedelic 60's was hitting the Boston area. The dances were terrific and word of mouth got out about the band.

A guy named Terry Hanley had sold them their sound equipment and had just built a studio, so he agreed to have them come in to make some demos there. The band's popularity was high but Judy decided that she couldn't commit full time and decided to leave. They put out another add for a vocalist and after several auditions Connie DeVanney became their new female on (vocals). They finished the demos and shopped it around.

The gigs began to pour in, so they hired Kens brother, Tom Frankel, to be their manager and R. Berred Oullette to handle the road equipment and get them to the venues. They played the colleges and east coast resorts and frequented The Boston Tea Party, Boston's equivalent to The Fillmore in San Francisco. Capitol records showed some interest, but things fell through when the label realized that they were not a "pop music" band. However, they knew that Tom Wilson, the big-time producer for bands like Bob Dylan and The Mothers of Invention, was looking for new talent so they sent the demos to him and he signed them to ABC Records right away.

The recording sessions occurred at The Record Plant in New York. Things were completed and the band had a great idea for an album cover but the ABC executives, in haste to get the record out, rejected that, took a boring picture of the band, and used that for the cover instead. After all that, the album wasn't put out on the market until six months later. The back-cover pictures of the band were so dark that you couldn't see the players and one of the songs had a repeated ending due to a tape flaw. They just threw the package together without any real thought.

Only 1000 albums called *Flashes* were pressed and it was quite good musically but they were difficult to come by. Beautiful west coast female vocals and harmonies like The Neighb'rhood Childr'n and great wild psych guitar jams on a couple of cuts. There were only minor special psych effects and it had a nice melodic vibe throughout. Wonderful vocals from Connie with the notable song *People of the Night*. For me, this song is the anthem for guitar psychedelia. It's just a beautiful euphoric guitar solo that transports those who lived the 60's to a different level and brings on real tears of joy. *Walking and Singing b/w In My Dark World* was released as the single.

They toured a lot, opening for the likes of The Who, Fleetwood Mac, Moby Grape and others. Ken put a small studio together in the basement where he was living near Wellesley College and was hoping to record more demos to inspire Tom Wilson and ABC Records to give them a second chance for national recognition. But then Carey

Mann decided to leave the band. Michael Walsh came in as his replacement and they continued to play in the big venues. More demos were recorded at the basement studio, but nothing happened beyond that.

Ken wound up marrying Judy Bradbury (the original female singer) and they both moved to San Francisco. The band reunited without Ken as a covers band. They were busy but no more official recordings occurred and by mid-1973 Ill Wind finally gave it up.

Judy Bradbury and Ken separated amicably and she became an internationally known singer releasing several CDs of Jewish Sephardic songs. She passed away in 2008.

Connie DeVanney opened a booking agency called CoCo that became well-known and continued singing with Dixieland and Big bands.

Dave Kinsman played in other bands for a while but gave it up, moved to Maine and started a bicycle parts company. He ran that successfully for 20 years and is now retired.

Richard Griggs went back to school and got his Ph.D. in composition and music technology. He created the Ill Wind website and was responsible for putting together the Ill Wind CD with all the outtakes and unreleased session work including the Wellesley Basement Recordings. Sadly, Richard died in 2005.

Carey Mann formed the band *Dirty John's Hot Dog Stand* and released one commendable self-titled LP. He played a few instruments and was always modifying the circuits and pickups on his equipment. He finally quit and made a career in computer technology.

Ken Frankel got his Ph.D. in psychology. He sold real estate and owned a music venue, The Cotati Cabaret, near Sonoma State University south of Santa Rosa, Ca. This place featured the likes of Huey Lewis and the News, The Tubes, John Lee Hooker and so many more. He does psychology research and formed The Electric Guitar Quartet that performed classical songs. He has been and is still involved with several bands playing banjo, mandolin, guitar, acoustics, et al.

A Compatible Stereo Record
FOR NOW

A Compatible Stereo Record
FOR
NOW 2

INDELIBLE INC. 1970

The mystery about this band can finally be told. The ministry of The Lutheran Church-Missouri Synod (LCMS) located in St Louis, Missouri has been established since 1847 and is still strong today. In the 1960s and early 70s, the US was going through an upheaval in race relations, with anti-war demonstrations against the US involvement in Vietnam and with a revolt against authority on college campuses. In the church, there was also a growing division between the youth and the adult ministry. The Resources for the Youth Ministry Board of the LCMS saw a need to address these issues in the church, so, in collaboration with the church's publishing company, Concordia Publishing House (CPH), they collected Christian folk and gospel music to involve the youth of the church in the LCMS with the issues swirling around them in the secular world.

Through CPH, music was recorded and sold through the Church and at religious events. Reverend Victor Growcock was the main man that all the music went through. He had produced many Christian records, but none were upbeat or in the rock genre. Dave Dister worked with Communico Inc., a division of Maritz Inc., who assisted Victor and Concordia Publishing to design and create ideas for products to be sold. Regarding the music, they would design a record album cover, write liner notes and then help market the final album through the church. Dave represented Rev Growcock with his musical endeavors and one day they met to discuss the latest trend of Religious Rock.

The Reverend had never heard of such a thing but was willing to listen. Dave had a copy of Norman Greenbaum's song *Spirit in the Sky* which was way up in the Billboard charts at the time. After hearing the song, Reverend Growcock was intrigued. Dave and he discussed the possibility of traditional hymns being presented in a more modern format and how this could gain a broader audience, especially with the younger generation. Victor wanted to hear a test recording before he committed to anything, so Dave contacted one of his workmates Frank Whitman.

Frank was a former drummer who had played a few gigs with Wayne Young. Wayne was a well-known and established rock musician in Louisville. He started at a young age in the late 50's playing guitar for Jimmy Decker and then The Carnations. He founded Soul Inc. and twice, traveled the country with Dick Clarks Caravan of Stars included with Paul Revere, Lou Christi, The Tradewinds, We Five, The Byrds, Bo Diddley and many others.

This seasoned the band and they began writing their own songs and recorded them at SAMBO Sound Studios located at 9912 Taylorsville Road in Louisville, Kentucky during their off time. The studio was owned and operated by local DJ Jack Sanders along with Ray Allen and Hardy Martin, both former members of The Carnations. SAMBO stood for "Sanders Allen Martin Booking Office". Wayne was the constant with Soul Inc. Members came and went, but specifically Marvin Maxwell (drums), Jim Settle (vocals, bass) and Frank Bugbee (guitar) who branched away and formed the band Maxwell, Settle & Bugbee. They preferred performance in the studio over playing live.

Signing with Imperial Records they entered the studio and recorded a single *Kind Of Man b/w Alone On Your Doorstep*. The label asked them to change their name to keep with the times and they became Elysian Field. Member changes occurred and they released a few more singles for Imperial. Eventually the most well-known lineup was Jim Settle (vocals), Mark Miceli (guitar), Dennis Lile (guitar), Dennis Ledford (bass) and Marvin Maxwell (drums). The single *Strange Changes b/w 24 Hours of Loneliness* was released nationally and had favorable reviews from Billboard.

However, Elysian Field's music became more hard rock and psychedelic. They were one of the best bands in the area, but Imperial Records was pushing the band to have a more pop oriented sound. The contract was unfortunately cancelled. They did audition for Capitol records, but it didn't work out.

Meanwhile, Frank Whitman contacted Wayne about this studio project because Wayne was somewhat religious and Frank knew he would be serious about the recordings. Wayne gathered some of the hottest players in Louisville for the project. The players consisted of Elysian Field members Mark Miceli (guitar, vocals), Dennis Lile (guitar, vocals) and Marvin Maxwell (drums). Wes Scott, who was still with Soul Inc. (bass, vocals) and Ronn Bedenbaugh, a session guy with SAMBO Studios (keyboards) were both included. Wayne, Mark, Dennis, Ronn and Wes all shared lead vocals depending on the song.

These fellows were no angels by any means, but they were highly professional musicians who knew the studio and were familiar with the process of recording. The initial test recording was a song called *With Joy*. Rev. Growcock was impressed with the song and hired Dave and Frank to select some tuneful hymns to be used for an album. His intent was to take traditional hymns and give them a rock feel.

The songs chosen were written by the likes of Ray Repp, Peter Scholtes. Robert Edwin, Joe Wise, Sydney Carter and others who were Folk Songwriters credited with introducing Contemporary Christian Music to the Christian youth of the times. The songs were mostly folk and choir tunes. Some of the songs were written by Norman Habel and Richard Koehneke and taken from a show that was presented at the Missouri Synod called *For Mature Adults Only.* Ronn Bedenbaugh was responsible for reworking and rearranging most of the songs submitted by Dave Dister.

The recording session spanned over a three-week period, but they were long hours. Two albums were planned. The first album took over 100 hours of recording time. A week off in between and then the second album was recorded. When everything was put to tape and the final mix was completed, the players returned to what they were doing previously. The band name was put out there after the sessions were done. In the rush to get the album cover printed, Dave called Victor and said, "The band should have a name". In the discussion, Victor commented that the music would have an indelible impression on the youth. That was it. Dave said he'll call the band Indelible Inc. He never told Wayne and the session players had no idea that a band name had been attached to their effort in the studio.

Until recently they had not even heard the final product. Two LPs were available *For Now 1* and *For Now 2*. All the cover photos for both LPs are of Mark Miceli except for the center photo on *For Now 1* (inside the "O" of Now). That photo is of Dennis Lile. There was no domestic release of the records to any stores locally or nationally. Very few were pressed and they were only handed out or sold at Lutheran Church Events through the church store, Concordia Publishing House. Musically the albums have a hard rock, psychedelic feel with vocals sounding at times like Allan Springfield of Last Ritual. You will find lots of wild fuzz guitar, some wah-wah, echoes, bells, piano, bass and drums along with great vocal harmonies like Crosby, Stills & Nash on some cuts. Overall, they are somewhat like Giant Crab and Merchants of Dream and some compare them to Rare Earth. Dave Dister admitted he harmonized on some of the tracks and keeping with the religious requirement Reverend Victor Growcock recited the Nicene Creed on one cut.

Although the members had played live with each other in Soul Inc. and Elysian Field, as Indelible Inc. they never played these songs live anywhere, no religious shows or Jesus Freak concerts. After the three week session was over, the guys moved on and had pretty much forgotten about the recordings. The religious rock albums were complete. However, Rev Victor wasn't quite done. He realized that there may be folks that weren't into the hard rock sound and believed he could reach even more people by presenting another set of albums that were less electric sounding.

Located up in the county outside St. Louis, there was a small 4-track studio, a converted garage, owned by Jim Wright. James Bottom was brought in to coordinate a lighter sound for the very same tunes previously presented to the rock musicians. Victor felt that the songs held the same meaning no matter how they were presented. Friends, neighbors and family members of the LCMS all showed up and sang the songs like they were sitting around a campfire. It was just a little 4-track studio, so the sound isn't quite as refined as the two albums recorded at SAMBO Sound. Banjo, acoustic guitars and clapping made for a very folk-like recording session. The albums called *Hymns for Now 1 How* & *Hymns for Now 2 How* were pressed and delivered as previously.

A third religious rock album was then recorded in Glendale, California at Whitney Studios later in 1972 *For Now 3* with a different set of songs and other rock musicians who were named The Coalition. Please note that these were not the same players that backed Carolyn Hester on her two rock albums. This album was followed by a corresponding folk album *Hymns for Now 3 How*. But the Indelible Inc. LPs are the definitive religious psych rock records everybody needs to hear.

Unfortunately, the good Reverend Victor Growcock found his maker after years of devotion to the church and dedication to getting the message out to as many young folks as he possibly could through the enlightenment of music.

David Dister was dedicated to this project and believed that music was a bridge to fulfillment. He's the one who planted this seed and his devotion to these sessions made them special.

Wayne Young continued producing and engineering bands at SAMBO studios, played with many other bands and has won several awards as a Louisville music icon. He currently fronts his own local superstar's band The Louisville Legends.

Ronn Bedenbaugh remained a session keyboardist, producer and songwriter throughout the 70's releasing one extremely rare LP *Swingin' Bridge – Simply.*

Marvin Maxwell started Mom's General Store for Musicians (now called Mom's Music) in Louisville over 35 years ago. Still thriving, the business provides new and used instruments, instrument repair and music lessons for those who wish to create. He still plays drums with Wayne Young in a reincarnated Soul Inc.

Dennis Lile formed the band Otis and then played with Puddinfoot. He recorded his own self-titled LP at SAMBO studios which was a real unknown classic, comparable to Neil Young's Harvest LP. Waylon Jennings took one of his songs *Fallin' Out* to a top 10 country hit. But times caught up with him and he succumbed to alcoholism in mid-1995 at the early age of 44. His brilliance was finally noticed and a dual CD-DVD music documentary of his life *Hear The Bang: The Life and Music of Denny Lile* has recently been released. It's stated that "While he may not have been quite the musical genius that many proclaimed him to be, he deserved much more success than he enjoyed."

Mark Miceli co-founded the band Jake with former Elysian Fields member Dennis Ledford and continued in music and studio sessions with several bands. He then founded and composed the music for the band Easter Island. The self-titled *Easter Island* LP released in 1979 is highly regarded among record enthusiasts. He still travels to Chicago twice a month to perform his variations of pop, rock, blues, mystical and electronic compositions. He has his own in-house studio and has released about 10 albums over the years, all found on the Bandcamp website.

Several songs were recorded by *Elysian Field* that were never released but their full catalog of songs (21 in all) was put out on a self-titled CD from Akarma in 1999. Most of these songs were in the same time frame as Indelible Inc.

STEREO
PLAYABLE ON STEREO
& MONO PHONOGRAPHS
Capitol
RECORDS
The Insect Trust The Insect Trust The Insect Trust

STEREO

THE INSECT TRUST 1969-70

Nancy Jeffries met Evan Flavell at Monmouth University in New Jersey. She was more into the folk scene and singing and decided to quit school to focus on a music career. Evan had a 12-string guitar and was heavy into Bob Dylan at the time. As a duo they played some coffee houses for spare change and decided to travel to San Francisco where the things were happening. They bought a VW Bus and headed on the road west. Money was non-existent so to fund their way back they would stop from city to city and play coffee houses for food, gas, a bed or change in a hat. They called themselves The Solip Singers.

Arriving in Memphis, Tennessee they enjoyed the strange hippie folk rock music scene and decided to stay for a while. The trip to California was cancelled and Nancy met and started dating Bill Barth. Bill had formerly played acoustic country blues as a solo artist on the folk circuit up in Greenwich Village but when he got to Memphis, he was playing electric guitar and had formed the Memphis Country Blues Society, a non-profit group focused on preserving and promoting Delta blues.

He joined Nancy and Evan. Jerry Lee Lewis became their booking agent for a short while. They played at some small clubs and coffee houses including Levy's Coffeehouse in Little Rock, Arkansas. Bob Palmer met them while they played there. He was at Little Rock University working as an editor for their College Paper. The instruments he played were, recorder and alto sax, and he joined in. They continued to play the small places for about six months but went back to Memphis to promote the Blues Festival.

While there, they went into The American Sound Studio owned by Lincoln "Chips" Moman located on Thomas Street and recorded a single *A Woman's Blues b/w He Was A Friend of Mine*. Shortly afterwards Evan left and The Solips broke up. Nancy wanted to form a rock band and Bill knew some other unnamed players who could help. Calling themselves The Primitives, this band only lasted a short while but they honed their skills and wrote songs.

Bill was the main promoter for the Blues Festival and was always in attendance over a 5-year period. Peter Stampfel, of The Holy Modal Rounders, happened to be attending one year and saw The Primitives playing. He knew Bill Barth and asked if they wanted to come up to New York and play in his band. The Holy Modal Rounders included among others Pete Stampfel (fiddle, banjo, violin), Barbara & Wendy Antonia (vocals), Steve Weber (guitar) and Sam Shepard (drums). Sam, as we all know, became famous as a playwright, screenwriter and actor best known for his portrayal of Chuck Yeager in the movie *The Right Stuff*. The Primitives disbanded and Bill, Nancy and Bob followed Pete to New York and lived at his house.

Luke Faust had been part of the Village scene playing with Jerry Rasmussen for a few years. He was friends with Peter and had been playing occasionally with The Holy Modal Rounders. He came over to visit and after meeting the new guests, asked Bill, Nancy and Bob to come live at his place in Hoboken, New Jersey. It was an apartment house with cheap rent only across the Hudson river, ten minutes from the Village scene. They set up there and would practice. Luke played banjo and wound up joining the band.

But they continued to travel to the Blues Festival back down in Memphis every year. It was here that they met Trevor Koehler who played baritone sax, piccolo and other instruments. He joined and suggested that they be called The Insect Trust, which was a term used in William S. Burroughs book *Naked Lunch*. So, the band was official with Nancy Jeffries (lead vocals), Bill Barth (all acoustic and electric guitars), Bob Palmer (alto sax, alto soprano recorder, clarinet), Trevor Koehler (baritone sax, piccolo, upright bass) and Luke Faust (all banjos, mandolin, harmonica, guitar, vocals). An unusual combination of instruments with diverse songs ranging anywhere from Appalachian Bluegrass, Folk, Country and Rock to Jazz.

Bob Palmer had a side job working for Robin Leech's *Go* magazine and had connections with people in the music industry. So, he, Nancy and Bill were invited to a party in New York that Steve DuBoff was hosting. In the mid-60's Steve and his partner Artie Kornfeld had written quite a few top 10 hits for The Cowsills, Crispin St Peter, Jan and Dean and others.

Steve became their manager, advanced the band $25,000, an unheard-of amount at the time, and got them scheduled to record at Capitol Studios located at 151 West 46th St in New York. Practicing at the apartment back in Hoboken trying to blend the different styles into one, they had no rhythm section, but Trevor knew Pharaoh

Sanders (sax) and Elvin Jones (drums) and they were able to join the studio sessions. Capitol also brought in Chuck Rainey (bass), Hugh McCracken (rhythm guitar) and Bernard Purdie (drums) to fill the sound. Folk, Hillbilly music, jazz horns, banjo and Nancy's voice filled an amalgam of ebb and flow on the first LP *The Insect Trust*. Somewhat like Kaleidoscope for the diversity, and like Peter Stampfel's band The Holy Modal Rounders.

Two singles *Been Here And Gone So Soon b/w World War 1 Song* and *Special Rider Blues b/w Miss Fun City* were released. The album was complete and distribution happened nationwide. Things were looking good but a national tour was out of the question. They still didn't have a permanent rhythm section for the road however, they were able to pick up players in New York for the clubs there. They got gigs around town opening for the bigger bands, The Doors, The Mothers of Invention, Santana and others at bigger clubs including The Electric Circus.

When they went back to Memphis, they would hire session players from that area to play gigs. They did find an unnamed drummer who was quite good and he showed some promise. But he was only 16 and heavy into LSD. The band would partake but would start every morning in a haze. The shows were interesting and they had a hard-core fan base but unfortunately, he didn't last.

Eventually the advance money ran out and the LP did well enough to have Steve DuBoff bring them back for a second album recording session. This time at Century Sound Studios with owner Brooks Arthur on the sound board. Session musicians were used again with Joe Macho, Bob Bushnell or Bill Folwell on (bass), depending on the song with Charlie Macey and Ralph Casale playing (rhythm guitar). The second album *Hoboken Saturday Night* was released but may as well have been sent directly to the cut out bins. A great album that didn't get noticed.

By the end of the sessions Bill Barth had had enough. He was always an arrogant so and so and got into a huge argument with Nancy. He wound up being fired from his own band. Ed Finney came in to replace him on (lead guitar). Then they hired an official bass and drummer (names not mentioned). They finally had a real band and things were going great as they finished the last leg of the current tour on an upbeat note with high aspirations. But then it all crashed when they got home. Steve DuBoff called and said things weren't working out. No support from the label or the manager and having no money meant the end of the band.

Luke and Nancy tried to keep things together but that didn't work either. They all went their separate ways.

Trevor Koehler continued to play in jazz bands locally but was heavy into drugs and was always looking for attention. He was constantly staging suicides trying to find a friend to come and rescue him. He finally succeeded in ending his life in 1976 via asphyxiation in a gas oven.

Bob Palmer was always a writer and became an editor for Rolling Stone magazine and then had a featured weekly column in the New York Times. He passed away in 1997.

Bill Barth continued to play the Blues and was based in Memphis. He relocated to Amsterdam and then moved to The Hague in The Netherlands where he died suddenly due to a heart attack in July of 2000.

Luke Faust married, moved to Texas and played in a few bands, then quit music completely and "worked for the Man" for about 10 years. He finally came to his senses, left his job and his wife, returning to the place where he grew up, in Hoboken, New Jersey where he still lives. Living his dream of a free life he still plays in bands. The most recent as a (jug bottle) player in The Carolina Jug Stompers. He is 84 years old as of this writing.

Nancy tried to make a living as a singer. It just didn't work out but still wanting to stay involved with the music business she went to work for the RCA record label and became a talent scout. Then she left RCA and worked for A&M, Virgin and finally Elektra Records. As an executive in the industry, she was responsible for signing several bands including Suzanna Vega, Iggy Pop, Lenny Kravitz and others. Against her ideals, she worked in the corporate world but had all the street smarts to know what it was like being poor and starting out trying to make a living in music. With no regrets "Working for the Man", her life is happy and fulfilled.

MAKE LOVE NOT WAR

JAIM 1968-69

What little is known of this band is they were formed in Santa Barbara, California. It started with Jerry Cronin and Martin Hall. Martin was the son of a Presbyterian Preacher and was noticeably quiet and reserved. But he was also a creative force behind music and he wrote a lot of songs. Jerry was the party animal and was much more outspoken. Although Martin was a year younger than Jerry, they both attended San Marcos High School together and formed an acoustic duet. They played school parties and High School sock hops.

After graduation, Jerry got involved with KIST radio as a part time DJ and knew all the right people who had connections in the industry to possibly record the songs he and Martin had written together. The two hired a backup band to support their music from a selection of local session musicians. So, the original band started out with Jerry Cronin (12-string guitar, vocals), Marty Hall (6-string guitar, vocals), Fal Oliver (drums), Gary Woods (bass) and Paul Bishop (organ, piano, keyboards). The name JAIM had no religious connections or hidden mystical meanings. It was a play on the names of Jerry and Martin which was only known to themselves. The band played Weddings, Restaurants, Hotels and Colleges locally and traveled up the coast to the Hyatt Hotel in Monterey for a gig or two. They also were known to play the Hungry I in San Francisco.

But they were too light and folk driven to back up any of the psychedelic bands that played any of the more-wild clubs in San Francisco or back on The Sunset Strip in LA. Jerry had all the drive to promote the band, he was full of tall tales and would play to the audience during the gigs. Eventually he and Marty formed their own Ethereal Record label and put up all the money for a recording session.

Initially they recorded at the small Sound Recorder Studios behind the Record Rack store located in Santa Barbara. Fritz Ashauer owned the store and had a studio in the back where he designated himself as recording engineer. Fal Oliver remembers laying down some instrumental tracks for an LP early on, but he never heard any more about these sessions and they were assumed shelved or lost.

JAIM continued to play gigs to improve these songs, write new songs and eventually wound up at Sunset Sound Studios in Hollywood. This is the same studio that Walt Disney financed and is where all the great movie soundtracks came from (*Mary Poppins, Bedknobs and Broomsticks* and music for most of the Disney cartoons). Bands like The Doors, Elton John and other infamous players recorded there and it's the studio where The Beach Boys *Pet Sounds* LP was recorded.

Jerry and Marty hired the help of session horns, strings and vocals to get a big full sound for the tunes the band recorded. The album has a homemade sound of dreamy soft rock and a light feel throughout, but it is a quality recording. The songs sound somewhat like early America and have similar Curt Boetcher meanderings, but Curt was not involved here. The innocence pours out of the grooves, but the music is so infectious, you can't play the songs just once. The album was called *Prophesy Fulfilled*. This was probably Jerry's dream recording. He oversaw everything for the band and tried awfully hard to get some local airplay.

The single *Ship Of Time b/w Running Behind* was distributed and this 45 with along with *Back in Circulation Again* and *Sunny Dawning Morning* from the LP hit the radio airwaves through KIST radio station where Jerry worked. The cover for *Prophesy Fulfilled* is very eerie and very dark with only a candlelight glow reflecting from the faces of the two showmen. Jerry is in the wired spectacles on the left. There is no cover lettering, so it draws you in for pure curiosity.

For years it was thought that only the one album was recorded, which is true. However, some of the *Prophesy Fulfilled* album covers had another album inserted and included. The album was unofficial and other than Jerry and Marty none of the current band members knew it existed. At some point strings, organ and piano were added to that first recording session that occurred at the studio behind the record store along with vocal arrangements. It included eleven songs, the album was pressed and entitled *The Preservation of the Hereafter.* The label number sequence is next in line on the Ethereal label, so it was pressed after Prophesy Fulfilled. But the songs, however incomplete, were taken from the first sessions at the Record Rack back in Santa Barbera and completed later. Fal

Oliver confirmed that he was indeed the drummer on these songs after he heard the music. There was no album cover and very few of these "ghost" pressings exist. The songs complement *Prophesy Fulfilled* with more of the same wonderful tunes. So, there were two full albums with different songs recorded and pressed.

As stated previously, Gary Woods, Fal Oliver and Paul Bishop were essentially session musicians and were the nuts and bolts behind JAIM. But occasionally they were asked to back Sergio Mendes whenever he came through town. Little riffs would occur between Jerry and the guys when this happened and he tolerated it. But one evening, JAIM was scheduled to play at another venue on the same night that Sergio was playing in town elsewhere and the guys wanted to play for the nationally known act.

Jerry went ballistic. So, Gary, Fal and Paul were all asked to leave for good. Other players came aboard. Paul Bishop was replaced by Mike Bono who was classically trained and felt a little frustrated with the simplicity of the music they were playing on stage. He wanted to play a little more rock & roll during the shows. Mike also attended San Marcos High School and remembers Jerry very well. He said that JAIM never really felt like a band that was together after he was involved. Players would come and go and became the backdrop to the stars of the show, Jerry and Marty. But JAIM still played the shows.

Jerry was still promoting the band and doing his day job at KIST. One day he mentioned over the airwaves that Mike Bono played with Simon and Garfunkel. This was a complete fabrication used to entice folks to come and see the band. At the time, the song *Bridge Over Troubled Waters* was Billboards number one song in the country. He said that JAIM was playing at The Santa Barbara Firehouse that night and that everyone should come out and see JAIM and the famous Mike Bono. That evening at the show Mike was hounded by groupies wanting to know about Simon and Garfunkel, wanting autographs and offering illicit favors. Jerry was always promoting the band any way he could.

Towards the end of the group, Mike says he just stopped getting calls to come to the gigs. As far as he knows Jerry and Marty just faded out.

Mike Bono owns an Electrolysis Clinic.

Afterwards, Fal Oliver got big in the Real Estate industry and still lives in Santa Barbara.

The whereabouts of Paul Bishop is not known.

Marty Hall as of this writing is still alive but is not reachable and is believed to be living in Palm Springs.

Unfortunately, Gary Woods passed away in 2015.

Jerry Cronin also sadly died of an intestinal problem years ago. He was only 53.

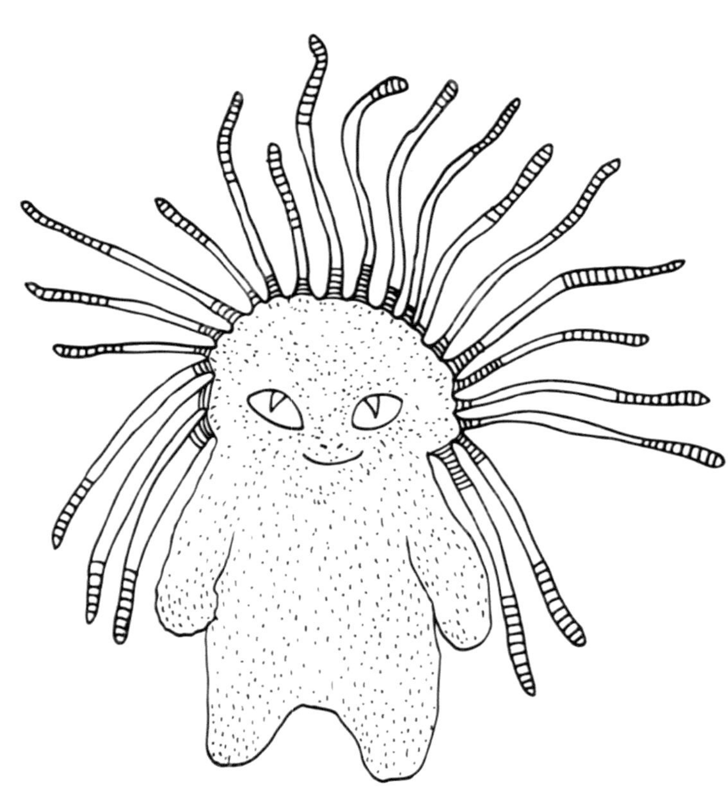

J. K. & Co.
Suddenly One Summer
WHITE WHALE
STEREO

J.K. & CO. 1969

Jay Kaye was the son of the famous 1950's recording artist and singer named Mary Kaye. He was also grandson to Johnny Ukulele who was Mary's Dad. Mary was a major part of The Wrecking Crew who were the studio artists that backed all the famous bands and their top hits. Songs like Sonny and Cher's *The Beat Goes On*, Richie Valens *La Bamba* The Beach Boys *Help Me Rhonda* and their subsequent albums Pet Sounds and Smile showed her guitar and bass licks. She was known to have been on more than 10,000 recordings over the 50-year span throughout her career as a session musician and was known as the First Lady of Rock and Roll.

In the 1950's she performed in Las Vegas with her band The Mary Kaye Trio that included her brother Norman Kaye and Frankie Ross. They were noted for changing Las Vegas into an all-night town. Vegas used to open at 6:00 am and close down at 1:00 am every night. The Trio finished up a 4-week show on the main stage at The Frontier Hotel. Afterwards the owner, Jack Kozloft, asked if they wanted to extend their stay. Mary agreed but only if they built a small stage in the bar area to accommodate her band. She called it The Lounge.

The Mary Kaye Trio began playing almost every night between 1:00 am and 6:00 am and was the first Lounge Act to start it all. The first week that they played, Frank Sinatra and his cohorts dropped $120,000 and became the dusk 'til dawn crowd. Then the all-night parties began. All the big stars including Dean Martin, Marlene Dietrich, Loretta Young, Buddy Hackett, Sammy Davis Jr., Peter Lawford, Vic Damone and all the other movie stars would show up. The other hotels followed suit and Las Vegas became the town that never slept.

In 1957 Fender Guitar asked Mary to promote one of their Stratocaster Guitars. This was a custom-made ash blonde guitar with a maple neck and gold hardware. A promo op of the Trio and Mary with the new Fender Stratocaster were taken and things flourished. The thing was, she played through Fender Amps but never played a Fender guitar in the early days. Her preferred guitar was a specially designed D'Angelico Archtop with electric pickups but her name being associated with a Fender Stratocaster is the guitar that all the guys wanted to play. She was eventually inducted into the music Hall of Fame.

Her son Jay was born in 1953 and was by her side for the first year being attended to in her dressing room during the scheduled shows wherever the Trio appeared. On Jays tenth birthday he got a small record player and his first single by The Beatles *I What to Hold Your Hand b/w I Saw Her Standing There*. From that early age he was hooked and was determined to become a guitar player and singer. Mary lived in Las Vegas and because of her endorsement of Fender Guitars she always had another Fender Guitar, Fender Amp or other equipment delivered to her doorstep free of charge.

She began to teach Jay the basics of guitar playing and he started singing. By age 12 he formed his own band called Jay Kaye and the Loved Ones. They didn't last long and over the next two years Jay got heavily influenced by the cultural shock of psychedelia, the "love-ins", the Hippie scene and the music of Jefferson Airplane, Jimi Hendrix and The Beatles *Sgt Pepper* album. By now he began writing his own music.

In 1968 his Mother was offered a job in Vancouver, Canada and Jay, then 15, traveled up there with her. When the gig was done, Mary went back to Vegas. Jay stayed behind and hooked up with Robin Spurgin who produced and recorded many local psych bands, The Collectors, The Painted Ship, Spring and others, in his Vancouver Recording Co. Ltd studio. There was no formal band per se but with the help of multi-instrumentalist Robert Buckley, who arranged the songs with members of the band Mother Tuckers Yellow Duck, Jay recorded a wonderful psychedelic album called *Suddenly One Summer.*

The LP is full of hooks, backwards guitar, phasing, echoes and dreamy acid drenched lyrics. Jay seems to be floating on a cloud throughout the entire vinyl disc. Songs like *Fly, Speed, O.D.* and *Dead* were part of a basic concept album where he wrote about a man's life from birth to death. Very mature lyrics from such a young person. There are many special effects that seem to be very acid influenced, but the music is full of pleasant melody.

The White Whale Record Label in the USA released the album to high kudos in California. Especially on FM underground radio. He never performed in Canada and left for LA where he reunited with his family. There he formed a band with his cousin John Kaye and different players and began to play clubs to promote his album, but with all the studio effects, it was clear that those songs could not really be duplicated live on stage.

The White Whale label was trying to take advantage of the psychedelic effects and released the double sided single *Break of Dawn*. An anomaly, the song was literally 32 seconds in length and was just a precursor at the very beginning of the LP to any of the great songs that followed. With echoing bells, water flowing and general weirdness this was supposed to be the big draw for the psychedelic fans to buy the album, but you didn't hear any music. It turned folks off and backfired. The LP had a very enticing colorful album cover that drew your curiosity. But based on the single it may as well have been a sound effects album. Nobody bought it.

The band he put together fell apart, but Jay continued to excel at playing guitar. He played in various bands, The Rush Hour, Champion, Masterplan and his reputation gained as he absorbed a Cream and Hendrix-like guitar sound. He fronted a band called Shotgun and played all over California. But by the 80's he had moved to Cardiff, Wales and then settled in Mallorca, Spain. He formed a trio called The Jay Kaye Band with Braham Heidl (bass) and Toby Taylor (drums) and toured all over Europe as well as putting out a few CDs.

Jay Kaye suddenly got quite sick with terminal brain cancer and was unable to overcome the illness. He passed away, February of 2015.

LACEWING
MAINSTREAM
S/6132 STEREO

LACEWING 1970

The story of Lacewing is really the story of The Measles and starts with a band audition ad in the Kent Stater, a college newspaper published through Kent State University located in Kent, Ohio. There was a request to start a new rock band and several players showed up with instruments in hand at a small student rooming house hoping to show off their talent. Chas Madonio was a bass player who played a few licks for the organizer and then decided to stay afterwards to hear the competition. A short while went by as several try-outs occurred.

Then, after his trial on guitar, this skinny blond-haired guitar player found an empty seat next to Chas. He introduced himself as Joe and said he and his friend Buddy, who played drums, were both looking for a bass player for a band they were starting up. Joe said he overheard and liked what he heard from Chas and invited him to come up and jam a little where they were staying. They piled into Chas's new Chevy Corvair and drove to Joe's dorm at the Eastway Center.

They formally introduced themselves as Joe Walsh and Buddy Bennett. Joe originally hailed from Wichita, Kansas, but his dad relocated to Ohio and then the east coast. Joe and Buddy had been together at Montclair High School in New Jersey and started a high school covers band. After graduation in 1965, Joe wanted to go back to Ohio. He and Buddy wound up at Kent State. Chas listened as Joe picked up a 12-string guitar and he was astounded as Joe played the songs flawlessly. He could play better than anyone Chas had ever known. The three decided to start practicing the next night, but Joe was also looking for a second guitarist, so Chas suggested Larry Lewis and just like that the band came together.

The initial band started with Joe Walsh (lead guitar, organ, vocals), Larry Lewis (rhythm guitar, vocals), Chas Madonio (bass) and Buddy Bennett (drums). The practices occurred several nights a week on campus at a large storage room in the Eastway Center. Meanwhile Chas was married and had car payments. Gigs started out few and far between with little to no money coming in, so he chose to vacate the band early on and defect to The Majestics who were playing 5-nights a week. Their bass player was drafted to Vietnam and they offered Chas the job at $125 a week. The guys understood the situation and the parting was amicable. Chas said he knew another bass player that would fit in, so Joe and Buddy went to see Bobby Sepulveda who was playing with some guys at a college party.

He could play (bass) and sing at the same time. Bobby didn't know these two guys from a hole-in-the wall and initially said "no" to their offer to join, but he was eventually swayed to come to a practice session. With his voice the band developed 3-part harmonies and Bobby was hooked. They tossed around a few band names, but it was when Joe's dorm roommate got a letter from home about his sister being sick that they decided to call themselves The Measles.

They played college dances and high schools. The clubs in town were brimming and full of patrons. The Kove, JB's, The Deck, The Blind Owl and The Dome were the clubs they played at. But when Joe Shannon opened The Fifth Quarter on Depeyster St. in Kent, that's when the band found it's calling. The building was an old, converted Ford Dealership that could house about 1000 people. All the big acts that came through town would play there and the lines were four blocks long just to get in. The Measles were the house band that opened for all the national bands.

Joe bought a Farfisa Organ that he was starting to play during the shows. Larry was not really a lead guitarist, so they hired Richie Underwood who could play (lead guitar) while Joe was playing organ and Richie could also sing. He was the former guitarist for the Majestics, now called Styx (not the Chicago band). The Measles had a manager Joe Basile who was an electronics wizard and built amps and a sound system specifically for The Measles to perform. He booked the band and they started writing their own songs and played venues out of state.

The Measles gained notice from Jeffrey Katz and Jerry Kasnetz who wanted them to be the kings of the bubblegum music craze. They recorded some songs in Philadelphia, but Katz/Kasnetz didn't like what they heard. It was way too heavy! When the boys turned down the song *Beg, Borrow & Steal*, Katz/Kasnetz let them go and offered the song to another band, Sir Timothy and the Royals, who later became The Ohio Players. Two songs that were part of The Measles audition *And It's True* and *I Find I Think Of You* were written and credited to Bobby Sepulveda and Joe Walsh respectively and featured on the first album release by the Ohio Players *Beg, Borrow & Steal.*

The Measles band members became frustrated with the business of the music industry and Vietnam was looming heavy for the draft. Bobby Sepulveda was drafted, Larry Lewis and Rich Underwood enlisted into the Navy. Joe Walsh had a deferral and eventually wound up with The James Gang. Buddy Bennett joined another band temporarily but was determined to keep The Measles going.

He hired Dave Andress (keyboards), Bill Lohr (guitar), Fred Weber (guitar), Mary Sterpka (vocals), original player Chas Madonio (bass) with himself Buddy Bennett on (drums). They continued the local Kent college and club circuit, but musical differences occurred and the band changed players several times. They started playing more underground psych music and wanted to travel the country. Chas left again because he had a family and a day job. Jeff Curry replaced him. Soon after, Buddy Bennet also left and was replaced by Joe Vitale on drums, but only for a short time. Joe Vitale went on to drum for Joe Walsh in the band Barnstorm. He was replaced by Mark Frazier.

They finally got the record deal they wanted, but none of the original members from The Measles were present. So, the band now consisted of Mary Sterpka (vocals), Bob Webb (guitar, vocals), Dave Andress (keyboards, vocals), Jeff Curry (bass) and Mark Frazier (drums). This was the band that went to Florida and recorded the album at Criteria Studios in Miami on the Mainstream label. Buddy still had the rights to The Measles name. The label wasn't happy with their name as a marketing ploy and wanted something different. So, to keep with the times, they became Lacewing.

The self-titled *Lacewing* album has a very west coast sound with baroque harpsichord, great female vocals, nice fuzz psych guitar and outstanding harmonies. Bob Webb puts out some great Joe Walsh guitar licks as heard on the first standout cut *Paradox*. This song was sent to the radio stations as a promo and pressed as a double-sided single in mono and stereo with both sides abbreviated from nearly four minutes to about two and a half minutes. It went nowhere. The album is like all the best from the other Mainstream groups Growing Concern and Art of Lovin, only a heavier guitar sound is mixed in. The cover art was an early painting by Gary Jackett who was a local artist.

The band went back to Kent and sort of fell apart. But Buddy refused to see The Measles die, so he reformed the band again with other players including Mary Sterpka and Bobby Sepulveda, who had by now returned home having fulfilled his Vietnam duties. They got big again in the general Kent, Ohio area, but tragedy stuck on May 4th, 1970, when students at Kent State gathered to protest the Vietnam War and a recent Cambodia bombing by the US. The Ohio National Guard was sent in to break it up, but things got out of hand and unarmed students died. The event got some serious national attention. A student strike occurred all over the country. Colleges and High Schools closed. The City of Kent basically shut down for roughly 2 months. The clubs were closed, activities ceased and the nightlife died. All the fun was gone.

The Measles faded out for good.

As for those involved with the original band, we all know that Joe Walsh became a superstar with The James Gang, Barnstorm and The Eagles.

Buddy Bennett went into the restaurant business in Florida.

Larry Lewis moved to Connecticut after the Navy and got an engineering degree.

Bobby Sepulveda continued playing music but didn't land with any famous bands.

Lacewing members Dave Andress, Mark Frazier and Jeff Curry absorbed into a normal life outside of music.

Mary Sterpka sang with Joe Walsh & James Gang for their *Thirds* studio album.

Bob Webb joined The James Gang on guitar and vocals for their last studio album *Jesse Come Home.* There are obvious influences of Joe Walsh. He also played and toured with Jay Ferguson in the 80's, an original player with the band called Spirit.

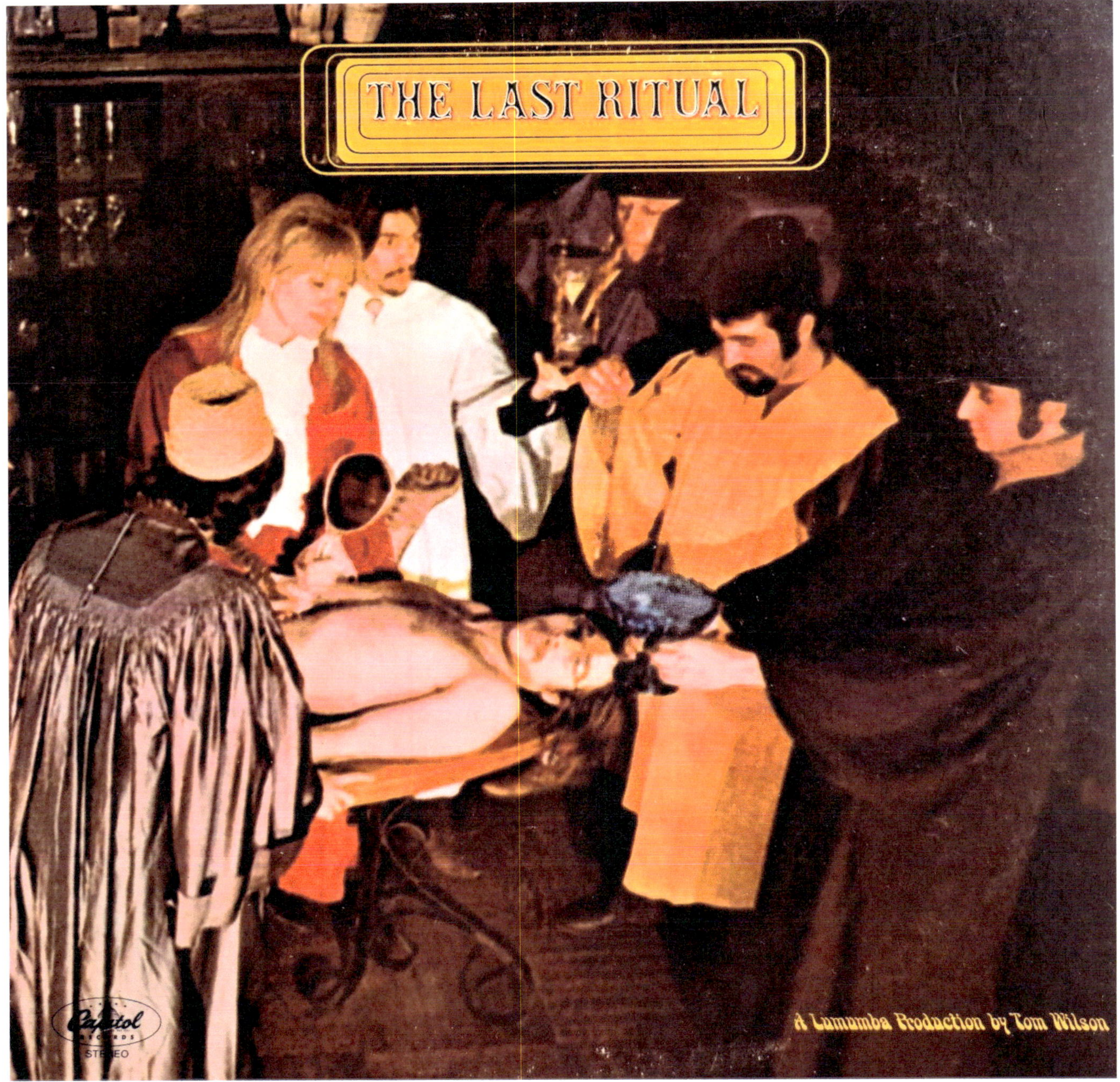
THE LAST RITUAL
Capitol RECORDS
STEREO
A Lumumba Production by Tom Wilson

THE LAST RITUAL 1969

Michael Beskin and Allan Springfield were close friends from childhood and grew up in Riverdale, Bronx, New York. Allan Springfield's parents were actual survivors of the Holocaust. Mikes parents owned a coffee shop and he and Allan would meet there each morning for breakfast before heading to DeWitt Clinton High School. Mike had been studying piano since he was four years old. Allan became a great song writer and lyricist and together they formed a band called The Cast Aways and played frat parties and high school dances. The band evolved and they hired Mikes friend Chris Efthimian on drums. The man could play.

They renamed as The Take Five and were a basic rock band that played the current hits. Their name came from the famous Dave Brubeck song which was an up-tempo jazz number that became their signature song. The band was comprised of Allan Springfield (vocals), Billy Gera (guitar), Billy Thornhill (bass), Mike Beskin (organ, piano) and Chris Efthimian (drums). Allan would come over to Mikes house and they would write and compose songs on Mikes piano. Their manager, Alan Rice, was a guy who was great at keeping the band busy.

Their shows took place all over in Greenwich Village at clubs like The Rolling Stone, Ungano's, The Wagon Wheel, which was formerly The Peppermint Lounge, a classy topless club, and The Gaslight Café, which was run by Betty Smyth. She was Patty Smyth's mother who fronted the band Scandal in the 80's and married John McEnroe. Other clubs they played were The Eighth Wonder and Trude Heller's. Both clubs were owned by Trude Heller, who was a hardcore lesbian, that demanded hard rocking and dancing, no ballads in her club. Six 45-minute sets per night and if the music slowed down, she would be in the back flicking the lights on and off to let you know she wanted rock 'n' roll. She wanted people to bounce and move!

There was no record deal for this band. As they evolved, Allan Springfield couldn't get along with Billy Gera, so he was replaced by Joe Gabriel or Gabe, as he was known, on (guitar). He had formerly been with The Novae Police that was a well-known band playing the New York club scene and included Buz Andrews (lead guitar), Eddie Rabin (keyboards), Randy Monaco (bass) and J. Kevin Lally (drums). It should be noted that Randy Monaco and Kevin

Lally joined Micheal Kac and Craig Anderson to form Mandrake Memorial. Gabriel only wanted to be known by one name and was kind of freaky, but he could play the hell out of a guitar. Billy Thornhill and Allan also had disagreements, so Billy T. left and was replaced by Robert Lichtig on (bass). Mike Beskin changed his name to Mickey Davis because Allan and he thought it would be a cool stage name.

A change in musical direction occurred. Mickey and Allan had written some well-orchestrated songs and wanted to add horns to the mix. At first just a sax and maybe a trumpet, but they were innovators and wanted to change their sound to something unheard of at that time. So, they advertised for more horns and the players they found were all top-notch graduates of The Manhattan School of Music, Juilliard and The Berklee College of Music in Boston. The new members hired on to show off their talents in a band that was already established and had proven musical clout. By this time their manager Alan Rice had become too demanding and changed things constantly, much to the dislike of the band, so they replaced him with Bill Sute, a music manager wannabe who happened to be the Executive Vice President at Texaco Oil headquartered in Harrison, NY about 30 minutes north of the East Village.

The band now had a full horn section and continued to play all the venues. Members were now Allan Springfield (vocals), Gabriel (guitar), Mickey Davis (piano, organ, harpsichord), Robert Lichtig (bass, flute, sax), Chris Efthimian (drums), Sharon Moe (French Horn), Kenny Lehman (sax), John Scarzella (trumpet) and Tony Salvatore (trombone). They made some demos and Allan and Mickey shopped these around to several record labels. The Take Five were tearing up the club scene. Enough so that they finally got notice from Capitol Records. The label told them to get with Tom Wilson who was the visionary behind all the early works of Bob Dylan, Simon and Garfunkel, The Mothers of Invention and The Velvet Underground. He took chances on bands that were different from the norm (Harumi, Fire, Soft Machine, Central Nervous System, etc.) and had the power to stand toe to toe with the big wigs in the record industry.

A deal was made and Tom initially set them up to practice at Sammy Davis Jr's New York penthouse. After a few weeks there, they wound up at the Hog Farm, a hippie commune run by Hugh Romney aka Wavy Gravy. It was a huge space that occupied a 40,000 square foot building. They could practice, crash, eat and sleep. A big stage was set up for bands to perform.

They eventually found themselves at The Record Plant recording their first album. Tom produced the band and Jack Adams engineered the sound. The session musicians were the best around and Kenny Lehman showed his horn arrangement talents at an early age. Tom Wilson renamed the band as The Last Ritual. This was all a marketing ploy to sell as many records as possible. The album cover photo shows the band dressed in robes and gowns and they were pictured surrounding Allan, lying down, ready for the sacrificial taunt.

The Last Ritual album was released and had some underground radio airplay, especially the 16-minute *Bugler's Reveille,* their epic magnum opus. One single was released from the LP featuring two of the shorter songs *Talk About Time We're Wastin' b/w Delighted, Strung Out and 25*. The band played at The Electric Circus, formerly The Dom and briefly The Balloon Farm, which had been open for about a year and they were LOUD. Some of the horn players said they couldn't hear themselves play during the shows. The Last Ritual was one of many local acts that opened for some of the nationally known headliners touring and playing at the Fillmore East.

Their album sounded somewhat like Blood Sweet and Tears or England's Greatest Show on Earth. Yes, there are horns, but they are added as spice and not the main entrée. Lots of heavy guitar with moments reminiscent of the classical works of Aaron Copeland and the echoed sounds of Phil Spector. The album is almost perfect and fits nicely in every psych enthusiast's collection. Unfortunately, the band did not last long after the album came out.

Allan Springfield had earlier befriended a guy by the name of Mike Barton, a drummer that had been vying for Chris Efthimian's job. He never got the spot, but he and Allan got close. Mike was heavy into drugs and Allan got sucked in. Allan's drug habit eventually turned to heroin. The band was on the verge of breaking up. Little spats occurred amongst some of the players that exploded into huge arguments. Not only that, but the lack of promotion and money from the sales of their Capitol Record album became a frustration. The band finally did split apart.

Nobody knows where Joe Gabriel went afterward.

Sharon Moe had a long career on and off with Philip Glass and is still an on-demand artist for several classically orchestrated recording sessions.

Tony Salvatore moved onto Jazz and was involved with Gato Barbieri for a while. He was much older than the other players and at last recollection was fighting Alzheimer's disease.

Robert Lichtig joined Seals and Crofts and they scored big with their national hit single *Summer Breeze b/w Hummingbird*. They both had heavy beliefs in the Baha'i faith. Robert toured and recorded two top ten albums with them, but he felt pressure to join their religion, so he quit. He then joined Bob Winkleman's band called Bonaroo that was somewhat of a super band in California with well-known players for a great AOR album. He later was involved with the band In Transit before retiring out of music entirely. He passed away on June 2, 2012, after complications from a motorcycle accident.

Former Take Five mate Billy Thornhill enlisted in the army and was shot three separate times in Vietnam, but he survived. He was sent home to New York then got into a little trouble with the law and served jail time. A hard luck story for sure, but he's still around.

Billy Gera started hitting the bottle and sadly succumbed to alcohol in the late 80's.

Allan Springfield, Mickey Davis, Chris Efthimian, Kenny Lehman and John Scarzella remained together and with others reformed as Chelsea Beige.

But Mickey Davis (aka Mike Beskin) didn't last long and left the band. He continued his skills backing B.B. King, was with James Brown for a while and played organ for a song or two while Ron "Pigpen" McKernan sang at Woodstock with The Grateful Dead during their set. Mickey now owns and operates a digital advertising agency.

STEREO/E 30413
EPIC
Chelsea Beige
Mama, Mama, Let Your Sweet Bird Sing
SAYS

CHELSEA BEIGE 1971

Formerly this band was The Take Five and recorded one previous album as The Last Ritual. After the band fell apart, Allan Springfield (vocals), Kenny Lehman (sax, winds), Chris Efthimian (drums) and John Scarzello (trumpet, flugelhorn) hired in Stafford James (bass) and Billy Schwartz (aka Billy Cross) on (guitar). The band name became Chelsea Beige based on the current blend of marijuana that was floating around on the streets of New York.

As with Last Ritual the horns continued, but again you would not consider them a horn band as per the usual. But Chelsea Beige had a harder edge about them with heavy guitar from Billy Cross. They rehearsed for the better part of a year and became the exclusive house band at The Electric Circus (formerly the Dom) where the Velvet Underground refined their Incredible Plastic Inevitable show. The venue had an over the top psychedelic light show for each band that performed and a circus act (trapeze, etc.) that occurred when the bands weren't playing. This was the only club Chelsea Beige played outside of one show at The Electric Factory in Philadelphia.

Their former reputation as Take Five and Last Ritual followed them. As a killer hot band, they carried on and were all set to be signed. But Allan's drug problem got beyond bad. On the evening that EPIC Records sent their stable of executives to The Electric Circus to preview the band before signing the contract, Alan had taken an overdose of heroin and became so discombobulated that they had to stop the concert. The band lost the deal.

But Chelsea Beige, as with The Last Ritual, were the top of the heap at the time and Allan was great when he wasn't out of it. Eventually EPIC did sign the band. They went to Columbia's 30th Street Studios known as The Church to record the LP. The building was designed and dedicated in 1875 as a Presbyterian Church. It was a huge wide-open space with 50-foot ceilings. Sound engineers Don Meehan and Jim Reeves gave high accolades to the sound they could get here. It was acoustically inspiring. Additional horns were added to help with the sessions with players Dominic Aloi and Lloyd Michaels (trumpet) and Earl Ford (trombone).

The album entitled *Mama, Mama, Let Your Sweet Bird Sing* was completed but it was with little enthusiasm from the top floor label executives. No singles were released. EPIC had fulfilled any obligation to the band and turned their backs. Chelsea Beige slipped into oblivion and the band broke apart.

Chris Efthimian still lives in New York and fronts his own band.

John Scarzello went on to perform with Blood Sweat & Tears for a while and performed with Joe Battaglia and the New York Big Band.

Kenny Lehman became a renowned disco producer working with Robin Beck, Roundtree and Chic where he helped write the song *Dance, Dance, Dance* with Nile Rogers and Bernie Edwards elevating this band along with Nile and Bernie to superstardom. He has been active on numerous other recordings throughout the years.

Stafford James played with Pharoah Sanders, Sun Ra, Albert Adler, Dexter Gordon and so many other known jazz artists. He moved to France, became a world-renowned Contra-bass player and has toured the world with many jazz greats and currently fronts the Stafford James Project.

Billy Cross (real name Billy Schwartz) remained close with Jerry Brandt who sold The Electric Circus and discovered Bruce Wayne Campbell who had previously fronted the band called Pidgeon. Bruce renamed himself as Jobraith Salisbury. Billy was hired as guitarist backing Jobraith with The Creatures in the studio and on tour. The huge campaign to promote Jobraith as the next big glam rocker failed, which is another story. Billy remained faithful to the music business, starring on guitar with Topaz for one LP, touring with Meatloaf, Link Wray, Bob Dylan and producing many other bands. He moved to Copenhagen, Denmark in the mid 70's, has written two books and released six albums, the most recent being *The Prettiest Train* in 2021.

Allan Springfield was a brilliant song writer, but he was a troubled soul. He wound up at The Phoenix House in the Bronx trying to beat his drug habit. It is said that he had a spot interview broadcast on TV circa 1978 when *60 Minutes* came to the facility to film a segment. Unfortunately, Allan could never overcome his drug dependency and sadly moved on sometime in 1982.

Columbia
Stereo
C 30686
MICHAELANGELO
one
voice
many
West
300 Watt Music Box
Come To Me
Son
(We've Kept The Room
Just The Way You Left It)
Okay
Half A Tap
It's Crying Outside
This Bird
Medley: Take It Bach
Michaelangelo
One Voice Many

MICHAELANGELO 1971

This album is somewhat of a classic amongst collectors. Growing up in the New York area, Angel Peterson fell in love with music at an early age and wrote songs in her head. In grade school she began playing music and took 4 years of lessons playing Violin, but she always wanted to compose her own tunes. She tried to show her violin instructor some of these tunes but was dismayed to hear her teacher say that "The Violin is for the classics. The instrument you write music on is a Fiddle." She was discouraged and put down the Violin.

She taught herself to play the Piano, but when she got to college with all the small dorm rooms the Piano was not an option. She discovered and was intrigued by the Autoharp because it put out a unique sound and was easily portable. The Autoharp was such an unusual instrument and she wanted everyone to hear the wonderful sounds emitting from the strings. Angel wrote a few songs and she began playing the coffee houses in Greenwich Village. It was there that she discovered John Sabastian and The Lovin' Spoonful. John also played Autoharp, but it was amplified with a large pickup under the strings.

She proceeded to get her Autoharp electrified and tried out several different amps until she found a Magnatone that had a swirling Leslie Speaker sound affect. She played her instrumental songs and catered to the crowds at clubs like The Gaslight Café and The Café Wha? for a couple of years. Then Bob Gorman happened onto one of her shows and was floored by the sound. He was a bass player and joined Angel. The two became a duo and continued to play the coffee house circuit. One night, Earl Carter was witness to one of their shows and was interested in representing them. He worked for Columbia Records and introduced them to Walter Carlos and Rachel Elkind, who were involved with the early stages of electronic music and especially the Synthesizer.

Both were inspired by the unique sound of Angels Autoharp. Taking on the project, they agreed to produce an album. The times as they were, it was decided that Angel and Bob should have the backing of a full band. Bob worked at a music store in town with Steve Bohn who was a guitar player. Steve knew Michael Hackett who was a drummer. So, the band was born with Angel Peterson (autoharp, vocals), Bob Gorman (bass, vocals), Steve Bohn (lead guitar, vocals) and Michael John Hackett (drums). Angel decided to name the band Michaelangelo based upon the name she gave her Autoharp.

They set up at the Record Plant and recorded all the instrumental parts there. Walter and Rachel were early pioneers in the electronic sound movement and had moved to a Brownstone House located on W. End Ave and 79th St in New York City. They built a small studio in the basement of their home that they called the MOOG Studio where Walter Carlos recorded the albums *Switched on Bach* and *Well-Tempered Synthesizer.* It was here that all the overdubs and vocalization for the Michaelangelo album occurred.

Angel had written poetry for years and had composed her own lyrics for the songs she wrote, but she and Bob never sang when they played the coffee houses. During the vocal sessions Angel was placed on the spiral staircase of the basement studio for the perfect natural sound for her voice. She was nervous about singing anything, but with Steve and Bob adding their voices the three of them together matched harmonies quite well. Mixing the Autoharp with a rock band was completely different. The album was completed and had a west coast sound, echoes with baroque qualities and choir like vocals. It is a blessing to listen to. The production was great and the album was ready for the market.

However, Walter Carlos and especially Rachel Elkind were at odds with Clive Davis, the owner of Columbia Records at the time. Rachel was a female in the record industry trying to be worthy in a man's world. She was a producer independent of Columbia Records. Walter Carlos had befriended Robert Moog and bought one of his Synthesizers to experiment with. The album *Switched on Bach* was a showcase for what could be done on a Synthesizer. The album was self-produced by Walter and Rachel and was a major national hit. Clive had no part of that album and missed out on the monetary benefits, so he was a little jealous.

Clive had no control and he made it exceedingly difficult. He and Rachel seemed to be arguing all the time. She was a strong-willed woman who was calling all the shots and because of their conflict, very few albums were pressed and there was little if any store distribution. The single *300 Watt Music Box b/w Half a Tap* started getting some airplay on the radio but Clive made efforts to block any movements of the song climbing the charts. He did not want to see another "hit" album involving Rachel Elkin. The album called *One Voice Many* was unique and with proper promotion the band could have gone on to bigger things, but it never happened.

The band played the college circuit for a while, but nobody could find an album in the stores and the band made no money. There were great expectations and so much effort was put forth towards something that could have been. They never saw any money and that was the deciding factor for the band to break apart.

Walter Carlos was in the middle of Transgender Treatment during the recording process for the Michaelangelo album and completed the final stages in 1972 officially becoming Wendy Carlos. She was a major pioneer working with Robert Moog to bestow the sounds of electronic music and the synthesizer.

Rachel Elkind worked with Walter (Wendy) Calos singing on several LPs through a vocoder. She was co-writer for the film score of the huge hit movie *The Shining*. Eventually she relocated to France with her husband in 1980.

The whereabouts of Michael John Hackett is unknown.

Bob Gorman always wanted to move to the west coast, so he moved to California.

Steve Bohn did studio work in New York for a while, then moved to Cologne, Germany towards the end of the 1980's. He formed The Mavericks, a band that was popular for over 20 years. He was known for his pedal steel guitar and loved playing on the stage in front of an audience. After The Maverick's he formed Steve Bohn's String Theory with Dirk Bell, (guitar) and Alex Morsey (bass) playing various jazz numbers. Becoming quite ill circa 2011, he could no longer perform on stage. Still alive as of this writing he left a legacy for peer musicians to follow.

Angel Peterson married her road manager and moved to Florida. She played her Autoharp in clubs down there, but music was changing and it just didn't work out. She reluctantly retired and gave up her dream of playing music to the masses and started her own business.

FREE LOVE

AUDITION
MONO
LP
NOT FOR SAL
a product of Liberty
IR
IMPERIAL
RECORDS
THE MOON
WITHOUT EARTH

STEREO LP-12444
THE MOON
IMPERIAL

THE MOON 1967-68

Starting out Matthew Moore had formed a band at his Rupert, Idaho High School which he called The Matthew Moore Plus Four. His older brother Daniel had written some songs and Matthew wanted to follow in his brother's footsteps. His band played high school dances covering the hit songs of the day, but Matt also wrote songs as well. Two singles were put out, *Codyne b/w You've Never Loved Before* on the White Whale record label, and *I've Been Lonely Before b/w I Know You Girl* on GNP Crescendo.

Daniel was older and had established himself in Los Angeles and asked his brother if he wanted to move down there. So, Matt and his band mates went to LA and played various Hollywood clubs including Ciro's on The Strip. Matthew wanted to stay in LA and it wasn't long before the other guys got homesick for Idaho and left. Matt had been writing songs all along and had them ready to go, but he needed a band and a studio to do some recording. Daniel was in thick with Mike Curb who found some seasoned players to assist Matt and then found time to put them up at Continental Sound Recorders, a new recording studio. The players in the band were Matthew Moore (guitar, vocals), David Marks (guitar, vocals), Andrew Bennett (bass) and Larry Brown (drums).

David Marks was a neighbor of Brian Wilson and was an original member of The Beach Boys and their first recordings. Andrew Bennett was with Davie Allan and the Arrows who had released several albums and did movie soundtracks as well. Larry Brown was also with Davie Allan but did not want to tour, opting instead to produce and be a sound engineer behind the boards. He was the one who designed and built Continental Sound Recorders with Mike Curbs money.

The studio time was free, so they could elaborate on the songs and they spent many hours making them just so. There was a three-track recorder, so they could overdub and enhance the tunes and there was a lot of Marijuana Haze helping to spin the audio and studio effects. A small string ensemble was hired and added. The sessions were grueling, but Matthew was dedicated to the songs that he wrote and wanted the music to reflect the times. All told, it took one month to record the first album alone. The band lived in the studio until it was finished.

Mike Curb absorbed all the costs for production of the record and hired John Eastman to do the cover artwork. A dreamlike pictorial with vivid colors. Imperial Records was going through label changes and were trying to stay afloat, throwing all their money towards The Classics VI who had the big hit single *Spooky b/w Poor People* at the time. The product was finished and surprisingly Imperial released the album called *The Moon Without Earth* nationwide.

Three singles from the album went out to the radio stations *Someday Girl b/w Mothers and Fathers* with *John Automation b/w Faces* and *Pirate b/w Not To Know*. There was high praise from the few critics who listened to the record, but it didn't get very much radio airplay other than on the underground FM stations. It has become a psychedelic masterpiece of sorts with backwards effects, phase shifting guitars, stereo spanning, three-part harmonies, warped vocals, overdubbing and all else that completes the perfect psych album.

The Imperial label was in trouble at the time and many of the bands and artists who had signed with the label were left behind. The band thought there might be some promotional live dates and they wanted to go out on the road, but nothing happened. Upon the release of the album the band went back into the studio to record a second LP. Andrew Bennett was disappointed and had left. He was replaced on (bass) by David Jackson, who was previously with Dillard & Clark. Long hours took place and the second LP was completed. The cover art for this album, simply called *The Moon,* won an art graphics award in the industry but there was no promotion whatsoever and the Imperial record label was eventually sold off to Liberty records.

The Moon as a band were disillusioned and fell apart right away. There wasn't even a showcase and they never played any clubs. They put so much time and studio effort into both albums and nobody paid attention.

Afterward, David Jackson became an in-demand studio musician and voice-over artist. He is known for his infectious enthusiasm and humor and has wowed audiences across the country with his prowess and versatility on bass, piano and accordion.

David Marks grew tired of the LA scene and relocated to Boston where he studied jazz at The Berklee College of Music and The New England Conservatory. He too became a great session guitarist and eventually rejoined The Beach Boys replacing Carl Wilson.

It's assumed that Andrew Bennett opted to go into engineering and sound as there are no other details about him continuing as a performer.

Larry Brown continued playing, producing and arranging for such artists as Andy Williams, Al Jarreau, The Fifth Dimension, George Harrison and too many more to mention. Continental Sound became The Producers Workshop where bands like Steeley Dan, Coven, The Plimsouls, Billy Thorpe, Firefall, Ted Nugent and others recorded. Pink Floyd recorded *The Wall* here. The studio is also where the Sheffield Lab occurred for the first direct to disc recordings. Then Larry got into TV and Film where all three main TV stations ABC, NBC and CBS along with HBO and Showtime became clients. He's had a long and lucrative career.

Matthew Moore went on to do production work and continued as a songwriter. He wrote the song *Space Captain* which got attention from Joe Cocker. Because of this Matt went on tour with Joe, Leon Russell and others during the Mad Dogs and Englishmen tour which was filmed. Six more of his songs were recorded by Joe Cocker and he released two other albums as a solo artist on the Columbia subsidiary label Caribou Records. He also toured with David Cassidy and Yvonne Elliman. Matt continues to write songs living on the royalties.

Years later in 2007 original members of the band Matthew Moore, David Jackson, David Marks and Larry Brown performed live for a small audience in Santa Monica for a book release party about David Marks life called *The Lost Beach Boy*. At least four songs from The Moon album were played and videoed, the only time the original members played live on stage featuring the songs they wrote 40 years previous. It was only a one-off show at a small venue in California. This stage show was filmed and posted by an amateur on YouTube for a while.

A reissue of both albums including previous songs written by the Matthew Moore Plus Four was released 2010.

THE NEW YORK ROCK & ROLL ENSEMBLE
STEREO
ATCO
SD33-240

new york rock & roll ensemble
Faithful Friends...
ATCO
SD 33-294
STEREO

Columbia
Stereo
C 30033
The New York Rock Ensemble · Roll Over

The New York Rock & Roll Ensemble 1968-73

The New York Rock & Roll Ensemble formed in New York at the Juilliard School of performing arts. Known alumni included such famous actors as Kelsey Grammar, Adam Driver, Robin Williams and so many others. Dorian Rudnytsky was in a rock band with Brian Corrigan and Clifton Nivison called Invicta. Michael Kamen and Marty Fulterman were in another rock band named Emil & the Detectives. Michael, Marty and Dorian were all classically trained multi-instrumentalists. At a friend's suggestion the bands merged to try something different in the form of Classical music and rock music together as one. An unusual challenge but one that could possibly work.

They honed their skills together and named themselves as The New York Rock & Roll Ensemble incorporating classical instruments with guitars and drums. Band members were Michael Kamen (keyboards, oboe, synthesizer, English horn, lead vocals), Dorian Rudnytsky (bass, piano, cello, trumpet, French horn), Clifton Nivison (lead guitar, vocals), Brian Corrigan (rhythm guitar, vocals) and Martin Fulterman (drums, oboe). Their first performance was at a Juilliard Halloween dance 1967.

Shortly thereafter a management deal was set with Adrian Barber and Bruce Tergesen, the owners of the ABBT Music Company. Bruce arranged a one hour recording session at A-1 Studios at 234 West 56th St in New York that resulted in an all-night stay. A promo single *Kiss Her Once b/w Suddenly* was put out for radio distribution. Ahmet Ertegun heard the session tapes and signed them to a record deal with Atlantic records. He told them, "You play all the right notes on all the wrong instruments."

As seasoned musicians all members were the principal songwriters. They had a real different sound perfect for the psychedelic music scene so prominent at the time combining the two music genres together. The first album was recorded at Ultra-Sonic Recording Studios located at 149 North Franklin St. in Hempstead, NY owned and engineered by Bill Stahl. He recorded other oddball psych bands here like Spirits and Worm, Ram, Space, Sir Lord Baltimore and other known bands like The Vanilla Fudge and Cactus. The self-titled LP *The New York Rock & Roll Ensemble* had short classical interludes dispersed between rock songs, like the band Ars Nova. One single was released from the LP *Pick Up In the Morning b/w The Thing You Do* that had some local airplay but national airplay for the album only occurred on FM underground rock stations.

Promoting the album on the local college circuit and at various Greenwich Village clubs like Trude Heller's, The Bitter End and Steve Paul's The Scene got them notice. The stage shows were out of the norm as they dressed formally in renaissance white ruffs and tailcoats. The performances were much like their album release with rock songs from the full band and then an intimate performance as a small trio ensemble that featured oboes and cello with Dorian, Marty and Michael. Bach's *Brandenburg Concerto* and Thomas Morley's *Aria* were a delight for the audience but they could also rock with the best them covering a Hendrix song *Wait Until Tomorrow* and others.

Meanwhile they entered Atlantic Studios at 11 West 60th Street where the boys began recording their second album. But before it was completed Greek composer Manos Hadjidakis, who was famously known for writing the film score to the movie hit and theme song *Never On Sunday,* happened to see them at one of the clubs and was visiting Atlantic Studios. He collaborated with them on a newly proposed film score he was working on and they accepted his offer. *Reflections* was the remake of a successful Turkish film entitled *Dry Summer* and the producers asked Manos if he would write an American version of the film score with music by an American band. They made the recording that included lead vocals by Manos himself on the introductory song *Orpheus*. The music was a slight deviation from their rock roots and sounded much like the Dutch band Ekseption. There was rock music with much more of a classical influence. However, the movie was not completed and the LP was set on hold.

Completing the sessions for their initial second album called *Faithful Friends* it was put on the market which was more in line with the first LP. Pictured on the cover, left to right, is Dorian Rudnytsky, Marty Fulterman, Brian Corrigan, Michael Kamen and Clifton Nivison. They promoted the album in New York, the surrounding states and traveled to the Midwest. Playing larger venues like Carnegie Hall in New York, The Crosstown Bus in Boston, Psycus in Buffalo, NY, The Grande Ballroom in Detroit and The Kinetic Ballroom in Chicago.

There were television performances on *The Tonight Show* with Johnny Carson and *The Steve Allen Show*. As a result of the classical numbers they played, Leonard Bernstein, a well-known orchestra conductor, invited them to play a *Young Peoples Concert* with the NY Philharmonic Orchestra. This was a televised program broadcast on PBS introducing young ears to what would be considered the rock stars from the past, three to four centuries ago, like Mozart, Bach, Beethoven, Strauss and others gaining a real interest in the complexities and the joy of music then as it was now.

They continued to tour the second LP with stints at the Fillmore East and The Boston Tea Party but the media had difficulty placing them into any bracket of rock music. They were gaining a fan following but Atlantic Records began to lose interest. They had already signed a three album record deal and rather than record another album Atlantic released *Reflections* as their third vinyl output but it dampened their popularity. It was only later that *Reflections* became their biggest selling LP when it was re-released in Europe in the mid-1970's.

Brian Corrigan left after this and as a four piece band they shortened their name to The New York Rock Ensemble. Meanwhile they were asked to become players in an unusual movie that takes place as an electric western in the 1800's with rock bands. Entitled *Zachariah,* the movie included bands like The James Gang, Country Joe and the Fish, Doug Kershaw, White Lightning and The New York Rock Ensemble. They had the distinction of playing the song *Gravedigger* as Belle Star's Band. You won't see this on YouTube but towards the end of the song they appear to be nude. The censored YouTube footage only shows the upper bodies. In the original theatrical movie release, they're playing fully nude distorting the pertinent parts through clear-plastic instruments, guitars, bass, drums, etc.

The movie helped their cause and by now they had signed a contract with Columbia Records and released their magnum opus fourth LP called *Roll Over*. Recorded at CBS Studios located at 49 East 52nd St. in New York, this album is a genuine rock gem LP with wah-wah guitar and inventive songs written by Michael Kamen and Clifton Nivison. Every song was a potential hit from the LP with the singles *Ride, Ride My Lady b/w The King Is Dead, Running Down The Highway b/w Law and Order* being promoted everywhere. The MONO b/w Stereo single *Beside You* that was the promo sent to all the radio stations should be recognizable to most everyone.

The fifth album *Freedomburger* was recorded and it is an underrated rock LP but shortly after its release, the band fell apart. Everyone moved on except Michael Kamen and Dorian Rudnytsky. After a short hiatus Mike and Dorian hired Hank De Vito (steel guitar, dobro), Larry Packer (lead guitar, violin) and Dennis Whitted (drums) for one last go at it. They re-signed with Atlantic Records and went to Intermedia Sound Studios in Boston to record an album called *New York Rock*. But the artist was billed as Michael Kamen. This LP was a little bit different as it had string arrangements, sax and woodwinds. Michael's voice is unmistakable and it has that New York Rock Ensemble quality. They played some clubs locally but there was very little national attention. After this they all departed and went their separate ways.

Brian Corrigan left music all together.

Cliff Nivison and Marty Fulterman joined Scepter records and Opal Productions. They wrote material for other artists, did production work, recorded demos but nothing worked and after two years there they separated.

Marty Fulterman moved to Los Angeles, changed his name to Mark Snow and wrote TV and movie scores too many to list. The most notable was writing music for *The X Files* TV and film series.

Cliff Nivison moved to Florida and developed a music publishing company.

Dorian Rudnytsky moved to Los Angeles and became a session cellist and bass player for TV and movie scores. After 25 years there he moved to Europe and spends time composing music for theatre productions and splits his time between Calpe, Spain and Seigen, Germany.

Michael Kamen was probably the most successful writing film scores for the *Die Hard* movies series, *Mr. Holland's Opus, Brazil, The Highlander*, the *Lethal Weapon* movie series and too many more to mention. Sadly, he died in 1997 at the early age 55 in London from Multiple Sclerosis.

Note: After Marty and Cliff left Opal Productions, the demos they recorded were sold off and released in 1977 on the "tax scam" labels Vibration and Tomorrow Records. An LP called *Former Members Of The New York Rock Ensemble* was put together from recording sessions that included both Cliff Nivison and Marty Fulterman. These songs were demo rock songs but are completely different sounding from anything The New York Rock Ensemble put out. More of a pop sound like 10CC. But it is a rare piece that did include former members of the band.

STEREO
A-38004
acta

THE OTHER HALF 1968

This band started in Venice, California with Tom Lennon and Jeff Pasternak. Tom was related to The Lennon Sisters who sang every Sunday on TV on *The Lawrence Welk Show.* Jeff's dad, Joe Pasternak, was an MGM Hollywood Producer. Tom Russo was also one with parents who worked in the movie industry. They all worked in MGM's mailroom personally delivering notes and letters to those who managed the stars of the time. It was Tom Lennon who planted the seed for starting a band with himself (guitar), Tommy Russo (drums) and Jeff Pasternak (vocals). They began to practice in Venice in the family room of the house where Tom Lennon's parents lived and through Jeff, John Branca (keyboards) and David Lucey (bass) came aboard for a full band. They weren't particularly good but had a passion to play. Tommy Russo is credited for conceiving the formal name of the band as The Other Half.

They got good enough musically to play cover tunes by The Yardbirds, The Animals, The Kinks and The Rolling Stones. Their thought was that the Beatles tunes were too mellow. Tommy's girlfriend made up a blank 3x4 foot poster board with The Other Half painted in "cool" script lettering planted on an easel. They played their first gig at a party and it was obvious that Jeff Pasternak, as a singer, was not going to work out. He knew it also and left the band. They brought in Jeff Nowlen on (vocals) who also worked in the mailroom. They would all venture down to the LA Strip to catch the bands playing in clubs like Love, The Byrds, The Buffalo Springfield and The Sons of Adam. Their first paying gig was at The Brave New World paired up with The Doors, who were yet unknown.

Tommy Russo had reached his limit on drums and wanted to leave the band. Dan "Woody" Woodward was a seasoned drummer who had serious drum lessons from some respectable musicians. He joined and it made the difference of night and day when he played. Their sound was inspired and elevated, but they hit another snag when they were booked to play the Reseda Bowling Alley lounge. John Branca was only 16 years old and this place had a strict rule, "No one underage". So, he had to go. Jeff Nowlen knew Geoff Westen who was constantly hanging out at Gazzarri's, where they also played, so he was asked to join the band.

Geoff's dad, Al Westen, worked as a producer and assistant director for the weekly TV western episodes like *Sky King, My Friend Flicka, The Rifleman, Cheyenne, Rawhide, Rin Tin Tin* and others. Geoff was known as an extra whenever they needed a kid (or kids) to sit in for filming. This occurred until his early teenage years when he got interested in rock bands and learned how to play guitar. His dad owned a house in Palm Springs and got the band time to play in a lounge at one of the Hotels there. The band was still trying to find a vibe and putting things together, but as luck would have it, Don Otis and David Lawrence just happened to be there and really liked what they heard. They were both higher ups with KHJ TV and radio.

David Lucey was let go and through an advertisement for a bass player they hired Larry Brown. So, the band members were now Tom Lennon (guitar), Jeff Nowlen (lead vocals), Geoff Westen (rhythm guitar) Larry Brown (bass) and Dan Woody (drums). Don Otis set them up at his ranch house in an area called Palmdale that, four years previous, had just incorporated. The house had power and water but there was no nearby town, no vehicle for travel, no store, no food, no nothing. They could rehearse and practice without any distractions. Don did this purposely for them to focus on writing songs and getting their best sound musically together as a band. Don would drop by once a week to give them enough food and supplies and monitor their progress until he was satisfied.

After a month Don saw the improvement and set them up in clubs like The Salty Cellar, The Golden Bear, Ciro's, The Classic Cat, The Rain Room, The Hullabaloo and they lip synced to a song they recorded on a TV dance show called *9th Street West* hosted by Sam Riddle that was conveniently broadcast on channel 9 KHJ TV.

Then Tom Lennon got drafted and just like that he was gone. The band went into a tailspin, but it didn't last long. Randy Holden was the ultimate rock guitarist for The Sons of Adam. Fans would line up out the door where his band played just to see him and they were loud. But there was a difference of opinion between Randy and the other guys in The Sons of Adam so he quit.

He sat at home contemplating his next move. Rumor had it that he was offered a job to replace Jeff Beck after he walked out on The Yardbirds who had a date to play at the Santa Monica Civic Auditorium. There were always groupies hanging around Randy at his house. They knew all the bands, they knew about Jeff Beck, they knew that

Tom Lennon was drafted and they knew that The Other Half needed a guitar player. Randy didn't believe their story about the great Jeff Beck leaving The Yardbirds, so he chose to pay a visit and see The Other Half.

He was a guitar God to the players and was playing all the known Hollywood clubs. The Other Half had attitude and passion and were playing songs from the bands that inspired him. They were also playing through Dual Showman amps which was what Randy used. He was the draw that the band needed. The first thing Randy did when he came aboard was to turn up the volume on all the amps, they weren't playing loud enough.

Both Jeff Nowlen and Geoff Westen had been writing material. It had only been six days since the time Tom Lennon left before the band was in the studio recording a song. There was a quick deal made through Don Otis and Dave Lawrence with the GNP Crescendo label to get the band some recording time. A small place between KHJ studios and Paramount Pictures called Nashville West is where they recorded *Mr. Pharmacist b/w I've Come So Far* as the first single recording the band released. There were obvious drug connotations to the song but Dave and Don along with Randy who was drug free didn't mind. It had reasonable airplay locally and got the band some notice outside the minor clubs they were playing.

Once the single was out there, they parted ways with Don and Dave because they were pressuring the band to focus on the next big pop radio hit and this wasn't what Randy or the rest of the guys wanted. Randy was married and they practiced at his wife's Mothers house located in Altadena, Ca. Randy was the drive behind the band and took over the reins from Jeff Nowlen who was the main songwriter. Randy had all the chops and knew what the crowds wanted to see on stage.

At some point they were up in Laurel Canyon at another house practicing. Things were loud as always and they could be heard everywhere. Larry Goldberg and Hank Levine were visiting someone nearby and couldn't help but hear the rock music. They literally climbed in the car and drove all over trying to find who was playing and where the music was coming from. Larry and Hank had been with Hanna & Barbera Records and worked with Kim Foley finding record labels to release new material. Now they were seeking a band to promote for the psychedelic phaze that was happening. They found the house and signed the band on the spot. A new management deal happened and they were on their way to San Francisco at The Avalon Ballroom competing with the bands up there.

Back in LA another single was recorded at Western Recorders in Hollywood *Wonderful Day b/w Flight of the Dragon Lady*. It was thought that this would put the guys on the charts, but it went unnoticed. They headed for Elysian Park, an area that basically surrounds Dodger Stadium in LA, on Easter Sunday for the first "Love-In." Joining an assortment of noted psych bands The Daily Flash, The Rainy Daze, The Peanut Butter Conspiracy, Fraternity of Man, The Steve Miller Band, Clear Light, The Flaming Groovies, The West Coast Pop Art Experimental Band and others. It was a day amongst 15-20,000 hippies of mostly peace and love, music and getting high.

Branching outside the LA area they were playing other clubs and then more frequently in San Francisco at The Fillmore and The Avalon Ballroom. The venues here were bigger than in LA and the sound was superb. Chet Helms took a real liking to The Other Half and the band played much more in San Francisco than LA so they wound up moving north. Randy felt Danny was almost too good for the band. He was a jazz drummer, not a good fit and was suddenly let go. His replacement was Ron Saurman who was from Michigan and formerly of The Jayhawkers.

The album deal they were seeking finally happened and they went to Golden State Recorders in San Francisco to finish the sessions on a full LP. The deal was kind of shady but very typical with money movement between the record company, the studio and Larry Goldberg, their producer. The Acta label fronted the money to the studio and the advance was split between Larry and Golden State Recorders. The band was never in the picture as far as benefiting from the dollar factor. They had already recorded some tracks in LA at Western Recorders and only needed a few more to complete enough for an album.

The recording sessions here went badly from the start. Larry Goldberg and Hank Levine as producers were sight unseen. Normally they used a splitter to be sure there was some tone and quality to the sound but Leo De Gar Kulka didn't want them playing through their amps, he wanted them to plug into the sound board directly. Randy was really upset with David Tonelli who engineered the sessions and thought Golden State was like a "dead room" in comparison to the LA studios. The songs came out thin sounding according to the band.

The band members had a vision of how they wanted the album cover to look. A photo shoot was set up and showed the band dressed normally and then also dressed in drag. Two different visual looks for the band showing them as one half and as "the other half". This was inspired by a picture of The Rolling Stones dressed androgynously for the cover of their *Have You Seen Your Mother, Baby b/w Who's Driving Your Plane* (LU 26.086) single pressed and released in Belgium. They played around with an LP titled *The Other Half of The Other Half.*

The guys presented the idea to ACTA who rejected the photo and thought the whole thing was immoral. Instead, cartoon versions of their faces were drawn up with vivid bright colors. There was no mention of who was in the band anywhere in the credits. Country Joe MacDonald was credited for writing one of the songs *Feathered Fish,* a song that the band enjoyed playing during their shows, but a song that was written by Arthur Lee, from the band Love, and given to Randy as a courtesy when he was with The Sons of Adam.

Musically there is a real resemblance to The Yardbirds, The Stones and maybe The Electric Prunes. Although the critics found *The Other Half* album favorable, it was not promoted. There was one other single released *Morning Fire b/w Oz Lee Eaves Drops* and then the ACTA label moved on to the next victimized band. Through Geoff Westen's dad, The Other Half was then seen playing a club, the Spectrum 2000, formerly known as Ciro's, during the opening credits of the very first episode of the weekly TV series *The Mod Squad*. There is minor film footage of the band playing their song *Oz Lee Eaves Drops*, maybe all of 3 seconds in total. But the full song is heard during the action sequences and dancing which is mostly of Go-Go Girls and the chicks dancing on the floor.

Randy and Geoff both had had enough and left the band. It was shocking to the others but Larry, Ron and Jeff decided to keep it going. They asked Ron Saurman's ex mate and former guitar player with The Jayhawkers, Tom Hundley, to come out for a try on guitar. He was good enough, but they only played a handful of clubs before he went back home. The band moved back to LA and they were looking for guitar players.

Its significant to note that they were staying at The Landmark Motor Hotel located at 7047 Franklin Ave in Hollywood, a known place catering exclusively to rock musicians. Larry, Ron and Jeff had been partying that night with members of other bands including Janis Joplin. She retired to her room and they were down by the pool when they heard the cry "Help! She's not breathing!" Janis died that night of a heroin overdose.

Shortly after that, the band fell apart for good.

Original members Jeff Pasternak joined John Branca and formed a band called The Mustard Greens. They renamed as The Pasternak Progress and released a single *Cotton Soul b/w Flower Eyes*. Jeff Pasternak's livelihood kept him active as a songwriter and he lived in England for a while. Back in the US he currently lives in Scottsdale, Arizona.

John Branca, the 16-year old who was basically fired, became an entertainment lawyer and manager representing The Beach Boys, ZZ Top, Fleetwood Mac, Aerosmith, The BeeGees and too many more to mention. He also partnered with John McClain as head of the music division of the entertainment law firm Zifferan Brittenham LLC and is currently co-executor of the Michael Jackson estate.

Tom Lennon stayed stateside all the while he was drafted. He never saw action, came back to LA, married and had a normal life. He played music in his spare time and released a CD called *The Other Half* of his own music in 2011.

David Lacey and Tom Russo absorbed themselves in normal life outside of the music industry.

Dan "Woody" Woodward played with Hearts and Flowers, Louis Prima, Johnny Tillotson, Fats Domino and others. He hit a low spot winding up in a Mexican jail for a 3-year stint due to drugs but he found his real dad. Verdi Woodward was the one he never knew and realized the similarities they both had with music and drugs. Verdi was a formidable sax player with some of the greats during the 40's & 50's. He had written a book about his life in music, heroin and the life of crime to feed his habit. He recognized Dans dilemma right away and took him to Westside Rehab. Clean and sober, Dan credits his father for saving his life.

Jeff Nowlen also hit rock bottom but sadly never recovered and succumbed in April 1997 due to a heroin overdose.

Ron Saurman continued to play with other bands but eventually settled in Marin County Ca. and opened a studio called Marin Recorders. The studio went defunct and Ron moved on as an electrician and project manager in San Francisco.

Larry Brown hooked up with Peter Kaukonen, Jorma Kaukonen's brother, the guitarist for The Jefferson Airplane, and recorded the album *Black Kangaroo*. He stayed playing music with other local cover bands over time and was last heard playing with a band called Illegal Sweedes.

Geoff Westen helped to form the band *C.K. Strong* with Lynn Carey and Jefferson Kewley. One self-titled LP was recorded then Geoff and his wife Patricia Mitsiu established Oz Studios and Zo Concepts to record and market rock 'n' roll music. Their clients on the design side of things included Iggy Pop, Fanny, David Bowie, Pink Floyd, Queen and others. Geoff began writing music again and has released six LPs.

After he left the band, Randy Holden joined Blue Cheer replacing Leigh Stevens and toured nationally with them for about a year. They began recording their third album *New! Improved!* but Randy realized that he wasn't under contract and wasn't going to be paid, so he packed up his equipment and left in the middle of the session. Deciding to go out on his own he hired Chris Lockheed who was the former drummer in Kak. He could play keyboards and bass with a drum sequencer and the duo recorded an album called *Population II*. Randy was sponsored by Sunn Guitars and Amplifiers and had all the power wattage he wanted and more showing off their equipment. But things fell apart in a hurry. The album contract with Hobbit Records had no guaranteed release clause, so it sat dormant for a while. Then Sunn amps pulled the plug.

Randy went bankrupt and became a painter and went into game fishing. He was gone and out of music for over 25 years. But he came back after a rabid fan refused to let his hero die. He has since re-mastered many of his previously recorded works and released new material available on his website.

STEREO
Pacific Ocean
VMC RECORDS
VS135

PACIFIC OCEAN 1969

Joey Zagarino was a bit of a heart throb at Montebello High School just east of LA in California. He played (guitar), had formed a band called The Upsets and had already been playing high school dances at the age of 15. The drummer had just left the band, so Steve "Rusty" Johnson was asked to fill in. Rusty had witnessed Joey and the Upsets and really wanted to be in the band so he ceased the opportunity. Mike Hoops was the (bass) player and Ed Winn played (saxophone). The band sounded mostly like The Ventures with occasional vocals.

Joey had written a few songs and he aspired to get them recorded for a record album. Joey would sing, but he wasn't a great singer. Rusty was a vocalist and he could play and sing at the same time. However, he was reluctant to be the main voice for the band. Still, he had a much better voice than Joey. They played some of the self-written songs at the gigs and were a well-known established band playing almost every weekend. Having recorded more self-written songs together, Joey was shopping the demo tape around trying to find interest from a record label. A year went by and devastation was about to hit.

They were seniors in high school and Joeys family wanted to move back to New Jersey where they originally were from. One evening, they were playing The Plush Bunny nightclub and Joey, being so depressed, was having a terrible night. Eddie James Olmos witnessed the show. He was a friend and classmate at Montebello High as well and was a lead singer in another band. Rusty noticed him and asked him to come up to sing a few songs with The Upsets. Eddies stage presence, voice and moves swayed the crowd.

Eddie initially wanted to be a baseball star. He joined the L A Dodgers farm system at age thirteen as a catcher and became the Golden State Batting Champion for his age group during this time. But his passion was music and, against his father's wishes, he was determined to make his living that way. During this performance, Joey was in a better mood for that evening, but he wasn't old enough to be on his own and there was no way out of moving to the east coast with his parents. To make matters worse, on the day they were all packed and leaving, Joeys Mother handed a note to Rusty, written to Joey and the Upsets, stating that there was great interest in the band.

Surf Records wanted to sign them to a contract. Joeys Mom had opened the letter, but never showed it to Joey. The kid with all the dreams and effort to become a big star faded and the band broke apart. A few months went by and a chance meeting between Rusty and Eddie occurred. Eddie James, as he now called himself, fronted his own band called The Left Hand and asked Rusty to come over for practice and just sing. The two voices expanded the song repertoire and they began to travel south to the Hollywood club circuit.

The travel wore on the band, getting them back home at 3 or 4 in the morning, so Eddie and Rusty moved to Hollywood and formed another band. Members were Eddie James (vocals, keyboards), Kent Henry (Plischke) (guitar), Freddie Rivera (bass) and Rusty Johnson (drums, vocals). They called themselves Pacific Ocean. The name came about because they had a big explosive sound and the Pacific Ocean was the biggest thing on the west coast. Playing six nights a week at Gazzarri's on the Sunset Strip, they became the house band and were trying to get interest from a big-time record label. But it didn't happen and the frustration set in.

Kent and Freddie left and joined a band called Genesis (not the famous English band). This band from Los Angeles had signed a deal with Mercury Records and seemed to be on their way to something special. Kent was offered $1000 a week with concerts at big venues and all the perks included. Eddie was dejected, but Bill Gazzarri assured him that he and Rusty were the heart of the band and good things would eventually happen. Ronnie Hensley (keyboards, bass) and Toney Carruba (guitar, vocals) were brought in as replacement players.

Pacific Ocean was managed by Rick Marcelli and he finally had some good news with interest from Capitol records. All they had to do was record a couple more demo songs for them to hear and the big label would decide. A few weeks went by and unfortunately Capitol passed. But all was not lost. Tony Harris took an interest in them. Tony had a long history in the LA music industry writing songs, releasing singles and producing bands. He was involved with Steve Vail who ran the VMC label and helped produce radio singles and albums by bands like Eastfield Meadows, Dennis Oliveri and The David.

It's certain that Pacific Ocean had more than a few original songs written. There would be no reason for a record label to sign a "covers" band for a full album. But with the departure of Kent and Fred, new band members, little time to rehearse and the urgency to get the band in the studio, many cover song versions were rehashed quickly with only two original songs both written by Tony Harris. Even so, their only album called *Purgatory* is quite good.

Again, most of the songs were cover versions of familiar hits done in an R'n'B style. Eddies screaming vocals with lots of fuzz guitar helped. The album came across like the blue-eyed soul of The Rascals and others during a time when psychedelia was exploding on the scene. There was no phase shifting or weird studio effects. The album was recorded at TTG Studios on Sunset Strip and had a limited release.

Steve Vail did sign them to a one-year deal. An extended contract would happen if the single they released took off. Steve was all about marketing. The album was completed and distributed, but the single was hardly played. The boys decided to go off on their own, visit as many radio stations as possible and do their own promoting of the single *Can't Stand It b/w I Want To Testify* to get some airplay. There was little interest, but on a whim Eddie and Tony decided to travel down to radio station XERB and visit "Wolfman Jack" directly. It all paid off as The Wolfman was caught in a rare "weak" moment. He decided to interview the boys right then and there on air and play their 45. Wolfman loved the song that featured Eddies screaming voice. He promised to play the song every hour for a week.

There was "on air" promotion for the band still being featured at Gazzarri's and Wolfman wanted to showcase them on a tour of High School and College dances over the next few months in LA. So, for that summer, they became part of Wolfman Jacks Traveling Rock and Roll Show. It was great and got them some serious exposure, but the single never took off and the album did likewise. As good as the band was and with all the energy of the live shows, they could have been big a few years earlier. But timing is everything and it passed them by.

Meanwhile Joey Zagarino called from back east to catch the guys up on what he was doing. With visions of a previous life Eddie filled him in on the new band and asked him to come out and join them on guitar. Joey turned the offer down because of commitments to his wife and he worked at The Hit Factory in New York. But he said he would come out and visit soon. Pacific Ocean was offered an open-ended agreement at Gazzarri's and continued to play sold-out shows.

A really wasted Jim Morrison was sitting at a table with Bill Gazzarri for one of the gigs. The boys went over to meet the "superstar" hoping to see if he could influence Elektra Records to take notice. Jim mumbled his way through the conversation spewing obscenities about all the record labels and the industry in general and Eddie knew there would be no hope of Jim remembering anything the next day. Their stay at Gazzarri's had run its course.

A new club was opening called The Factory. A huge building that was literally a steel fabrication area built in the 1920's. It was being converted to a private club for movie stars and the rich and famous. Pacific Ocean was touted to be the house band there. They also lucked into a gig tabbed for The Jefferson Airplane. Robert Francis (Bobby) Kennedy suddenly announced his campaign for the presidency in March of 1968.

In California, Kennedy's campaign headquarters organized a campaign with Hollywood's elite for support. Andy Williams chaired the "Hollywood for Kennedy" committee that included many well-known stars and entertainers. Two star-studded "Kennedy For President" galas were televised. One on May 24th at the Los Angeles Sports Arena and the other on June 1st at The San Francisco Civic Auditorium. These events were used to give RFK the needed exposure to win the California primary and the Democratic nomination to run against Richard Nixon.

Featured performers Included Mahalia Jackson, Milton Berle, Trini Lopez, James Brown, The Jefferson Airplane and a host of others. JA had to cancel their performance for the June 1st event and Pacific Ocean were chosen to take their place. Lots of influential people and well-known stars were there in attendance. There were about 30,000 people in all with Bobby and Ethyl Kennedy sitting in the front row. Afterwards the band and the Kennedys conversed over a catered meal for the masses. Four days later, just before midnight on June 5th, 1968, Bobby was fatally shot at the Ambassador Hotel in Los Angeles. He was pronounced dead early the next morning.

Pacific Ocean's year at The Factory ran its course. They worked hard to find anybody and any big-name label to make a record deal, but it never worked out. The thoughts of not signing with a big record label ate at them. They took a hiatus. Then Eddie got a call from Joey Zagarino who said he was being transferred to LA to work out there.

He had become a well-respected producer and engineer and worked with Jimi Hendrix and too many other stars to mention. He traveled back with his wife and kid, bought a house in Laurel Canyon, schmoozed with the other famous rock stars and built an in-house studio. Eddie and Rusty thought they might reform the band again and make another go at it. But then, Joey died of a drug overdose and that was that.

Kent Henry (Plischke) hated his last name and for purposes of acceptance became Kent Henry. He recorded an album with Genesis (from LA) called *In the Beginning*. He then replaced Bob Wall in a band called Wrinkle that was formerly called Houston Fearless. Then he went on to star with Steppenwolf and Blues Image. Unfortunately, he died in 2009.

Freddie Rivera was in the middle of the recording sessions for the Genesis LP yet to be completed. He was drafted into the Army and went to Vietnam. It was a very traumatic experience being at war but even worse, when he returned to the US, he suffered from Post Traumatic Syndrome (PTSD) and had horrible bouts of depression. But he survived and wrote a book about his life called "Raw Man" detailing how he coped with the post war despondency. He became a leader of the cause to fight the disease.

There are no details about Ronnie Hensley or Toney Carruba.

After Joeys death, Steve “Rusty” Johnson had a chance to play out on tour and did just that to remove the memory and pain of Joey’s demise and the dreams of what could have been. He finally wrote a book called "Walk Don’t Run" that detailed the Pacific Ocean story and healed a lot of the sorrow.

If the name Edward James Olmos sounds familiar, it’s because he has become a noted character actor in several movies and TV shows. He starred in the TV series *Miami Vice, Dexter* and *Battlestar Galactica* and has received many awards i.e. The Hugo, an Emmy and the Golden Globe.

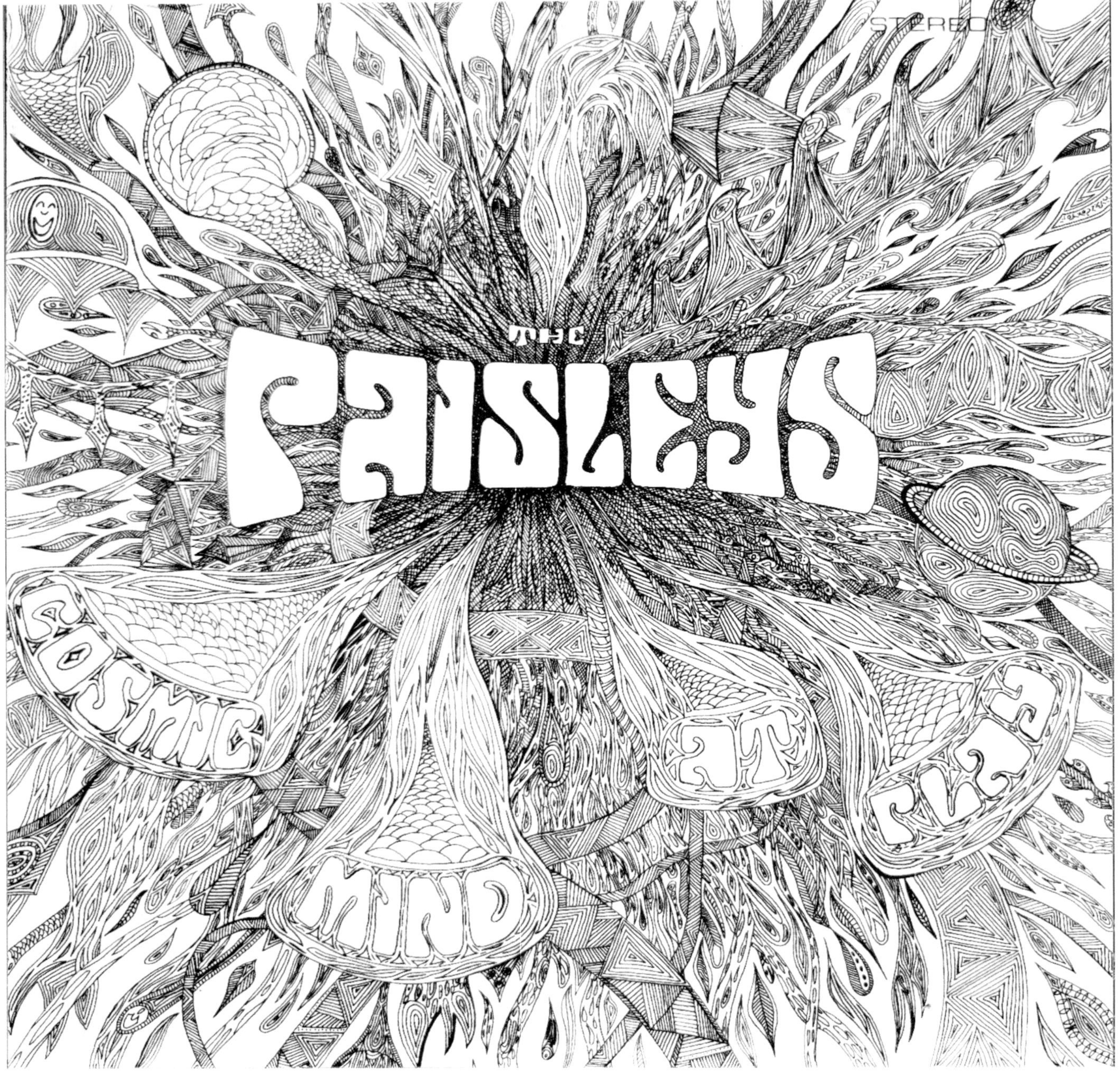
STEREO
THE
PAISLEYS
COSMIC
MIND
AT
PLAY

THE PAISLEYS 1970

Richard Timm and Bill Smith were both high school students at Robbinsdale Senior High School in Minnesota. Neither had really known each other and both graduated and moved on. Bill attended the University of Minnesota (UM) and Richard was called up for active duty in the Naval Air Reserve just before he was set up to attend college. He learned guitar while on his own in the military and eventually formed a band with other players calling themselves The Purple Pythons. He was stationed on the Aircraft Carrier *Midway* and the band would play in the ships' mess hall and ports of call in whatever city or seaport they happened upon in the world.

When his military duty was completed, he moved back to Minnesota and formed another band called The Pied Pipers. A chance reacquaintance with Bill Smith occurred. Bill had been playing keyboards in bands back in high school and college and both had been writing songs. They got together and combined a sequence of songs they had each written into a suite called *Musical Journey*. Bill knew Paul George who was a graduate student from the UM. He was impressed by what he heard at a jam session and became their manager.

They began auditioning players for a formal band and found Rick Youngberg who was fabulous on guitar. Richard decided to play bass and they jelled quite well. Rick knew a drummer at the music store he worked at called Traficante Music in St Paul and Peter Larson joined on drums as the first incarnation of the new band. The store's owner, Ralph Traficante, supported the band. They honed their skills and refined their sound at Bill Smiths house. There were so many cover bands in the area that they decided from the start to present themselves with only new material that they had written. The prevalent fashion of the times was Paisley, which had variations of printed material and clothing incorporating the Yin/Yang symbol in numerous colors and intricate design. It was decided to name themselves as The Paisley's.

Richard lived only a block away from Dania Hall, located at 427 Cedar Ave S. in Minneapolis. This place was a community center where people would gather and the surrounding area became known as The West Bank. The building itself had a wide open third floor auditorium and stage with high ceilings and balconies to overlook the activities. Richard always heard bands playing there whenever he walked by and was able to establish The Paisleys there for dances and shows that they called Happenings. The balconies were set up to feature light shows for the bands that played. Light Fantastic was the exclusive light show for the Paisley's but Charlie Campbell's Community News light show was also used at the venue.

Paul George promoted the band and knew people at the college where the band played dances, protest gatherings and any other events where a band was the entertainment. The Paisleys were the inspiration for what became known as the "Circle Dance" where a couple would start spinning joined by others until it evolved into tens of hundreds participating in unison. This seemed to be a ritual for the fans of The Paisleys only.

As the Vietnam war grew, the West Bank area became the site for demonstrations and war protests. It was the focal point for imagination and discovery with record stores, head shops, hippie beads, coffee houses, wild clothing, dress shops and imaginative arts expressing all that was unique. Music became the bedrock of interest for all activities including bands like The Litter, The Pepper Fog, Noah's Ark, Jokers Wild, Lightning, The Pandemonium Side Show and others. Herbs, LSD, mescaline, MDA (the 60's version of the love drug Ecstasy) and alcohol where the drugs of choice and experimentation.

The Paisleys were the first rock band to feature Marshall Stacks for amplifiers in the Twin City area due to their inside connection to Traficante Music. This upgraded their sound to an already powerful stage presence. They had a basis of songs they played but each night was different as it became more of a feeling for what direction the song would go. No show was the same. Branching out to other places they played an outdoor gathering at Powderhorn Park and other venues like the New City Opera House and the Hullabaloo. The local media was taking notice and favorable news articles took place in The Minneapolis Star and the local magazine Connie's Insider.

At this point Pete Larson left to join the Army. He was replaced by Greg Payton on drums. The war draft was somewhat worrisome to the band members so they decided to pack up and move to Canada. The band members, the road and stage crew, wives, girlfriends and kids, about 20 in all settled in Vancouver, BC. Greg Payton got sick and headed back home. His replacement was Bob Belknap who formerly drummed with a band called The Yellow

Brick Road in Vancouver. They played the University of British Columbia, Simon Frazier University and some smaller clubs like The Village Bistro but the money just wasn't there. The band took a hiatus.

Paul George and his wife had already applied for immigration and had intentions to make permanent residence in British Columbia. But things didn't go well up north for the rest of the band, they were falling apart. Rick Youngberg and his wife headed back home to the states. Richard Timm hired on short term at the Boeing Plant in Everett, Washington for the construction of the 747. Bob Belknap and Bill Smith stayed in Canada for a while and wrote songs but after about a year most everyone was back in Minnesota.

By this time Rick Youngberg had joined another band called Cottonwood and didn't want to leave that band, so Richard, Bob and Bill Smith put the word out and hired Brad Stodden to replace Rick on guitar. He knew all the licks and was a good fit. Officially the band included Richard Timm (bass, vocals), Brad Stodden (guitar, vocals), Bill Smith (keyboards, vocals) and Bob Belknap (drums). They gigged at all the old haunts. But many of the clubs were changing to top-40 dance venues and The Paisleys, having their own sound and not being a "covers" band, were being passed over as psychedelic hippies. They couldn't find enough gigs, but they hooked up with Marshall Edelstein who loved the band and owned his own production company, Marsh Entertainment Productions. He had some clout, represented them and was able to book the right places to feature the band.

Warren Hendrick was a local engineer and the label owner of Hexagon Records who had produced singles and recorded albums for local bands The Litter and White Lightning. He was expanding his small studio and told the guys if they would help him do the physical labor to enlarge the building, he would trade time to record an album. This was a deal that happened because of their involvement with Ralph Traficante. About two months later the Audio City Studio was complete, located at 3009 East Lake Street in Minneapolis.

It was Summer 1969 and by this time outdoor concerts were the happening thing. The Paisleys were featured at most of the Love-ins, Be-ins and Hope Festivals in the area promoting peace and love. The band was recording songs at the studio and provided tapes directly to Alan Stone at KQRS who happily played the songs on their FM underground radio station. During this time, Bob got married and headed back to Canada for a short honeymoon with his new wife. But the trip resulted in a major delay upon returning to the States due to VISA problems. It took nearly a year and a half to straighten things out with the paperwork before his return to the US. Mike Cornelius filled in for him on (drums) during his absence, finished the studio sessions and was part of the band for the shows. Mike had parents who were very well to do and the band rehearsed at their house on Lake Calhoun.

The hope was that Marsh Edelstein would take the master tapes to New York and try to schmooze his connections for big label interest there, but it never happened. Warren decided to form a new record label to release the LP with hopes to expand interest nationally. The label name, called Peace, was suggested by Richard Timm. The album was pressed in limited quantity, about 2000 copies, and the wild cover sketch was drawn by Bill Smith. There was no mention of Bob Belknap and the picture on the back cover shows Richard Timm, Mike Cornelius, Bill Smith and Brad Stodden in that order. There was no specific photo shoot and the picture of the band was just a snapshot taken at the studio during one of the sessions. The album called *Cosmic Mind At Play* was released while Bob was still in Canada.

Musically the LP is full of special effects, phase shifting, echoes, moans and groans, warbling vocals and psych guitar. *Musical Journey* is the sidelong song on side two that was their showcase for the live shows but it was shortened to only 19 minutes in length for the LP. They took full advantage of the psych scene and mind experimentation both musically and visually to expand the senses. No singles were released but the band and the song *Wind* was spotlighted locally on KQRS FM underground radio and on KUOM, the college station at the University of Minnesota.

Their reputation grew even more due to radio airplay. They played a newly established venue, The Depot, opening for the Joe Cocker's Mad Dogs and Englishmen Tour along with The Flying Burrito Brothers. The Peace Festival at The U of Wisconsin featured them along with Mandrake Memorial, Pepper Fog, Thundertree, Zulu and others. So many other shows and festivals happened. There were Earth Day Events, Arts Showcases and several War Protest gatherings at the University, The Fair Grounds and The Capitol Building throughout 1970-71.

Bob Belknap was finally able to return to the states and rejoined the band. But by the end of August that year they played their final performance. They were busy playing every weekend and more for nearly five years and began to wear down musically and physically. The Paisleys ended.

But the parting didn't last long. In 1974 they reformed, began writing new songs and went to Moon Sound Studios located at 2828 Dupont Ave South in Minneapolis to record. With other talent involved, musicians and vocalists, they called themselves The Minnesota Family. There were no live shows or gigs but by 1980 they had recorded about 30 new songs. Thoughts of another LP were in the works but issues occurred between the building property owner and Chris Moon, the studio owner. The Landlord locked everybody out and confiscated all the master tapes of the sessions. Presumed lost or destroyed, the only remnants of these sessions were found on a few cassette tapes that were made.

It was decided to play one last Paisley's reunion show for the fans so Richard, Bob, Bill and Rick Youngberg had one final bash on April 11th, 1980, in the Great Hall located at The University of Minnesota. They all separated into normal lives after this.

Bill Smith played with various bands locally but was the first to find the glory road in 1998.

Brad Stodden was living in White Fish, Montana when he passed away in 2009.

Rick Youngberg departed us in 2014.

Michael Cornelius had a relatively high IQ and became an accounting wizard last heard from in North Carolina.

Richard Timm stabilized himself with various jobs over the years and is alive and well living in Minnesota.

Bob Belknap played with The Jake Labue Band for a while then settled as an accounting Specialist and Quality Engineer for Reynolds Food Packing Inc. until he retired. He lives in Wisconsin.

Of note, there are several unauthorized reissues of The Paisleys only album. But the Sundazed Music record label has the only sanctioned re-release, and re-established Bob Belknap as an official member of the band.

STEREO
PLANT AND SEE

STEREO R-2003
OVERDOSE
ALBUM & GAME
LUMBEE
RADNOR RECORDS
IN ASSOCIATION WITH NANTICOKE PUBLISHING CO., INC.

PLANT AND SEE / LUMBEE 1969

The focus for this band starts with Willie Lowrey. His parents were sharecroppers in Robson County, North Carolina and Willie picked cotton during his childhood. They were of full Lumbee Indian heritage and quite poor living in a truly diverse area. Willie admitted hearing music in his head always, even though he didn't play any instruments. But when his sister married, his new brother-in-law gave him a guitar and taught him some basic blues riffs. Over time he got rather good at playing guitar and decided to try his hand at playing live.

Initially he played for a traveling carnival, he then joined a band called The Corporate Image and eventually formed Plant and See, the band name was based on the verbiage "Plant a seed and see it grow." The band was ethnically diverse with Willie a Lumbee Indian on (guitar, vocals), Scottish born Carol Fitzgerald (vocals), Latino Ron Seiger (bass) and from Africa Forris Fulford on (drums). Carol was attending Methodist University in Fayetteville and had been singing with other rock bands noted for her stage antics and showmanship. Plant and See was based in Fayetteville, North Carolina and gained a reputation.

They traveled up to Baltimore to play at The Baltimore Civic Center. Plant and See was represented by Charles Koppleman and Don Rubin who had signed the Lovin' Spoonful and another unknown psych band, Gandalf, to a contract. Through the Koppleman/Rubin Associates the White Whale record label signed them up. They recorded an album at Allegro Sound Studios in New York. There were Scully 24-track tape machines making all the recordings state of the art. The only problem was that the studio sat directly on top of the subway system. When a train came by, they would have to shut down temporarily because of the noise and rattle. This was where Tommy James did most of his recording.

Musically the self-titled *Plant and See* album shows the talents of Willie and his guitar with psych tendencies and slight special effects. There was one single pressed *Put Out My Fire b/w Henrietta* that was ready for distribution but the White Whale label was in disarray and did not promote the album at all. Shortly thereafter Plant and See took a break, but the hiatus was short lived. They reformed and renamed themselves as Lumbee after Willie's tribal heritage and added a second guitarist Rick Vannoy. Ron Sieger left and was replaced by Bobby Paul. The band now included Willie Lowrey (lead guitar, vocals) Carol Fitzgerald (vocals), Rick Vannoy (rhythm guitar, vocals), Bobby Paul (bass) and Forris Fulford (drums, vocals).

They traveled to Philadelphia and were signed by the very obscure Radnor record label. Another album was recorded at the newly established Sigma Sound Studios with production help of Ralph Dino and John Sembello. The LP was called *Overdose* and the album package was quite elaborate. At the time, the country was still lamenting over the deaths due to overdose of Jimi Hendrix, Janis Joplin and Jim Morrison and the album title was named as a tribute to their legacy. The packaging included a board game that encouraged marijuana use and the cover picture depicted young children sitting around a table playing the enclosed game. It was very controversial.

Musically you could hear positive progressions from their Plant and See days. Heavy guitar and four-part choir like harmonies akin to the UK bands Design and Arrival. Carol Fitzgerald's voice really bellows out and there's a general funk happening throughout. Although implied, there were no obvious references in the songs to drugs or vices and the Radnor label single from the LP *Streets of Gold b/w Get Ready* went to #1 on the local radio charts in Philadelphia, North & South Carolina and Virginia.

But there was a lack of backing by the label because of the perceived drug connotations and no promotion or distribution occurred for the LP. They did play several venues on the east coast opening for other well-known bands including The Allman Brothers, Canned Heat, Linda Ronstadt, Tower of Power, The Brooklyn Bridge and others. Carol and Willie married but the band fell apart again and it ended permanently.

Forris Fulford retired musically and lived in New York.

Rick Vannoy got into the coffee craze and opened a coffee house and tattoo parlor.

Bobby Paul and Ron Seiger disappeared.

Together Willie and Carol had boys. Proud of their sons, Clint wound up as the guitarist for the heavy metal band Sevendust. He toured and played with other bands like Seether, Dark New Day and Korn before branching out on his own as a solo artist. His brother Corey played bass and guitar for Seether and Dark New Day as well and played with other metal bands. Both boys are quite successful.

Carol and Willie lasted a while but eventually split apart. She settled down and lived her life in Fayetteville.

Willie performed with Clyde McPhatter as leader of his backup band, but he spent most of the time involved promoting the ideals and visions of the Lumbee tribe. He had a studio, promoted other bands, toured all over the country and wrote songs with a long list of production credits. Unfortunately, Willie Lowery had an extended bout with Parkinson's disease and gave in the year of our Lord 2012.

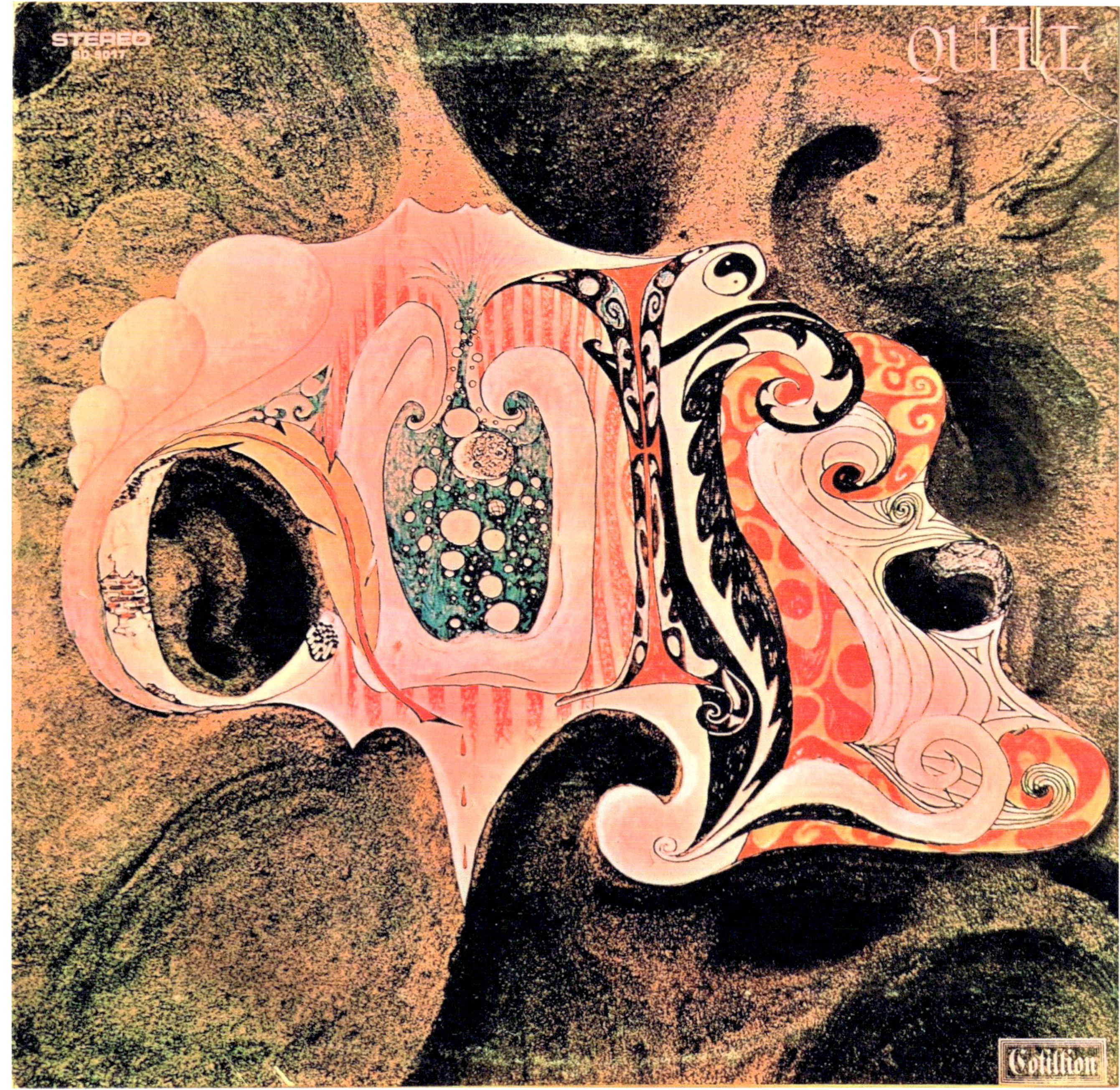
STEREO
SD 9017
QUILL
Cotillion

QUILL 1967-70

Brothers Jon and Dan Cole grew up in Merrimac, Massachusetts. The five kids in the family were all musically inclined. Both Jon and Dan attended Northfield Mount Hermon Prep School, where noted movie theater celebrities Uma Thurman, Laura Linney, beat poet Lawrence Ferlinghetti and singer Natalie Cole were former students. The school encouraged music and taught the procedural aspects of recording with students who played instruments and wrote songs. Each year they would go through the process of making a record album, schedule time at Ace Studio in Boston to rehearse and record the LP and get it distributed. The ever evolving rock band was called The Hermon Knights. As young students Jon and Dan joined the band and were included as players on the 1965 edition of the rock album release called *Knights Off Campus*.

In his junior year Jon went abroad and studied in Germany where his enthusiasm for roots music and blues gained him some celebrity status. He joined a rock band, The Black Beat Brothers, as lead singer. Jon came home for high school graduation, then returned to Europe and rejoined the Black Beat Brothers, which became well known in southern Germany winning a Polydor recording contract for victory in a Battle of the Bands. But he left Europe before the contract was signed. Returning to Cambridge, he attended the School of the Museum of Fine Arts at Tufts University to study painting.

When Dan graduated, he aspired to study art and went to Bard College in New York. But Dan left Bard and came to Boston to study acting. He met up with Jon and they refocused their energy on music. With both brothers having capabilities for writing songs, they met Ray Paret, who was managing several Boston bands at the time, including The Ultimate Spinach and Bead Game, and he liked their songs and singing.

Ray's partner was David Jenks in the startup company Amphion, and Jon and Dan were brought aboard. Dave found players Roger North (drums, percussion) and Phil Thayer (piano, sax, flute, Hammond organ, percussion) from the band Catharsis and Norm Rogers (guitar, vocals, percussion) from the Morning Star Blues Band to join Jon

Cole (bass, vocals, percussion and guitar) and Dan Cole (vocals, trombone, percussion and guitar) to form the full band. Norman Rogers came up with the name Quill.

After honing their skills in the small rehearsal studio behind the offices of Amphion Productions located at 331 Newbury St in Boston, Ray Paret got them into many known Boston clubs as well as gigs in New York and Philadelphia. They also played at many colleges throughout the northeast and clubs as far away as Aspen, Colorado. Gaining popularity, they encouraged their audiences to participate by handing out various percussion items like sticks, bells and blocks of wood building their shows with a euphoric rhythmic frenzy. As hometown favorites, they outperformed such bands as Janis Joplin, The Who, Blue Cheer, The Kinks, Lee Michaels, Rhinoceros, The Velvet Underground and they were highlighted 9 times at The Boston Tea Party. Dave Garroway also featured them on his popular TV show called *Tempo Boston.*

Ray had been working for weeks with Michael Lang, who was then promoting what would become the Woodstock Music Festival. He convinced Michael to come and see Quill at Steve Paul's Scene in New York. They were scheduled to open for Johnny Winter who was appearing there for a showcase in the presence of record company moguls. But Quill also had a short session in Indianapolis that Saturday morning to lip sync to one of their songs for a local WLWI TV (channel 13) broadcast with "*Bandstand Thirteen*" hosted by Jimmy Mack. This show was a local knock-off teen dance show much like Dick Clarks *American Bandstand*. The road crew stayed behind in New York to haul the big equipment and set up the stage at the venue.

There was plenty of time to fly to the state of Indiana, do the show and return, but direct flights back to New York were all suddenly cancelled due to severe weather. It was an all day ordeal but they were able to catch a return flight to Philadelphia and took a taxi back to New York. Fortunately, their equipment was already set up on stage at The Scene and they arrived just in time to plug in and play. All went very well and because of this performance Ahmet Ertegun, who was present, was so impressed with Quill that he signed them to his Atlantic record label. Michael Lang was also dazzled, and they were one of only three bands without a record album release to be asked to play and accepted the deal for Woodstock. The others being Sha-Na-Na and Santana.

Michael Lang was fresh from organizing the May 1968 rendition of the Miami Pop Festival a year earlier. He and his partners initially tried to set up another big event in Woodstock, N.Y. but there was so much resistance from the town locals that they found another nearby township to present their ideas. The town of Wallkill only had a populace of about 10,000 people and they found a thirty-acre industrial park that seemed to be perfect. After signing Creedence Clearwater and other big name rock bands, word got out and they had already sold nearly 50,000 tickets in anticipation of the gathering.

Again, there were rumblings from the Wallkill folks about a hippie takeover but a PR campaign was in place to promote the "low key" concert. There were several goodwill meetings with the town hall and event organizers along with community baseball games. In support, Michael Lang chose Quill to represent the Woodstock event and put on free shows at schools, community centers, prisons and mental hospitals to promote the Festival. Ultimately the rock concert in Wallkill was banned due to the potential for an overused city water and sewer system.

An agreement was finally made with the town of Bethel. Members of Quill along with the construction and set up crews stayed at the El Monaco Motel owned by the parents of Elliot Tiber. Woodstock may not have occurred without this man as he generated the town permit for the event, but that's another story. Opening day for the festival happened on Friday August 15^{th,} 1969, at Max Yasgur's farm featuring mostly folk artists with Richie Havens, Sweetwater, Joan Baez, Tim Hardin and others. Quill was set to be the opening act on day two featuring heavies like The Jefferson Airplane, The Grateful Dead, Country Joe and the Fish, Mountain, The Who, Canned Heat and more. Heavy rains occurred overnight and into the morning. Quill was flown in by helicopter overlooking cows and nearly half a million people. The rain had finally stopped and it cleared up enough for Quill to take the stage.

It was much different than playing in the small venues they were used to. They were very energetic but the stage here was set up about 8 feet high, the front stage crowd was 30 feet back and the speakers were situated to broadcast the sound all the way back to the row of Honeypots at the far reaches of the fields. Tossing out a bucketful of rhythm instruments to the front crowd and trying to get them absorbed into the music always worked before, but with 450,000 people the intimate connection was not there. The largest crowd Quill had played to previously was 7,500 at The Music Hall in Boston when they were the opening act for The Who.

After their 45 minute set Dan and Jon mingled backstage with Grace Slick, Carlos Santana, Keith Moon and others who were waiting their turn on stage. Quill's Woodstock performance was good enough to be included in the film and organizer Michael Lang really liked the band. There was every intention to include them in the documentary but the sequential sound was out of sync and didn't match the video. It's thought that the torrential rainfall affected some of the equipment and there wasn't any way at that time to make corrections. Their portion of the film was scratched and left out. A real shame as Sha-Na-Na and Santana took off because of Woodstock.

Gigs came to Quills door after the event because of how big and newsworthy the festival was. Woodstock certainly gave them the notoriety that they would not have had otherwise. All set to record their first LP, Ray Paret wanted to bring in a producer but the band insisted upon doing it themselves. Jon, who was 22 at the time, blames himself for this youthful misjudgment. The first self-titled *Quill* album was recorded back at Amphion in the small rehearsal studio and later mixed at Aengus Studios in Maynard, Mass. The band listed stage names for each member with Jon as Ju-unk Khol, Dan as Da-ank Khol, Phil as Phil Stan 'D There, Norm as Red Rocket Rogers and Roger as R. Willie North. The curious should know that the album cover picture was hand sketched and colored by Norman Rogers, the guitarist. There's a surrounding grainy look because the drawing was cut out and laid on a sandy beach near Boston with wet sand sculpted around the picture.

After the album was released, Norman left the band for a short time and Jimmy Thompson was brought on as the lead guitarist. But he didn't last long and departed. Jon was interested in doing production work with his partner Bill Reisman at Aengus Studios where Andy Pratt, Richard and the Rabbits, Jonathan Edwards and other local acts were recorded. Norman then returned to the band. They were still relatively unknown and with the documentary footage of Quill at Woodstock on the cutting room floor there was no promotion from the Cotillion Record label that the LP was released on. Most were relegated to the cut out bins. There was also no single released but several songs were played on FM underground radio including the catchy *Thumbnail Screwdriver.*

The album was quite diverse with great guitar licks and feedback, some horns, jazz licks, drums, bells, tabla, wood, sticks and their signature song *They Live The Life* which was the only song performed at Woodstock from the LP. This was in part because up until the day of Quill's performance, Dan was sick with a flu-type illness and it was not sure whether he would be able to perform. The record album didn't come on the market until a year later. By then Jon and Norman had left the band. But Norm was asked to rejoin and he along with Dan Cole, Phil Thayer and Roger North returned to the studio to record another set of songs for a second LP. Jon was not present. Cotillion did not release the second LP and further discouragement caused the band to split apart for good.

Roger North later played with Odetta and The Holy Modal Rounders before developing and patenting a unique design of molded curved drums called North Drums. He moved to Portland, Oregon and was last heard performing with The Freak Mountain Ramblers.

Norm Rogers went to Vermont, where he was from, and continued playing with local bands. He passed away in 2011.

Phil Thayer moved to Florida and still plays music, especially horns and flute and is an accomplished musician.

Dan Cole went on to manage Intermedia Sound Studios in Boston and produced other bands as well. He worked with Sony Professional Products group and then moved to Portland, Oregon as a management consultant.

Jon Cole worked with other bands in the Boston and Cambridge areas as producer/manager. He later moved to Hawaii, began a Solar Energy business and became active in alternative energy systems. He still plays music every week with friends on Hawaii Island.

Phil and Jon reunited to play at Yasgur's Farm for the 50th anniversary of the original Woodstock Festival. The complete Quill original performance was released as part of the enormous CD collection of all the music played at the first Woodstock called *Woodstock - Back to the Garden: The Definitive 50th Anniversary Archive* which includes a staggering 38-discs and a total of 432 tracks. All the music from bands who were known and unknown are here.

Quintessence
In Blissful Company

QUINTESSENCE

Quintessence
Dive Deep

QUINTESSENCE 1967-72

Ron Rothfield was born in Melbourne, Australia. He moved to New York, got a music degree playing flute and studied Jazz with Lennie Tristano. He then met Richard Vaughn and they played the folk and coffee clubs in Greenwich Village for a while. They moved to the UK, found a big house and settled in Ladbroke Grove in Notting Hill, England. At the time, this area was the perfect place for the Hippie counterculture where bands formed. Hawkwind, The Pink Fairies, The Deviants, Steamhammer, Mighty Baby, The Third Ear Band and others got their start here. These bands were all experimenting with otherworldly vibes and once established they were more than just a rock music band; they became an experience as a live act.

The Beatles had all experienced positive vibes in India so many people were looking for that inner peace during the tumultuous times of the later 60's. Ron met Swami Ambikananda and he became a spiritual teacher and advisor. Ron and Richard were living in a house on Blenheim Crescent and wanted to start a band. They advertised in Melody Maker Magazine for players and had about 200 respondents to the add. Auditions occurred at Powys Hall located at 124 Ladbroke Grove.

Weeding their way through the auditions they found Phil Jones who was from Australia and had fronted a band called The Unknown Blues. Phil and his band already had studio recording experience with 4 singles to their credit. Luckily, he had found his way to the UK and lived nearby so he was happy to join in on (vocals). Allan Mostert was only 16 years old and joined as a fabulous (lead guitar) player as well as Dave Codling on (rhythm guitar). Finally, Canadian born Jeremy Milton joined in on (drums). The band was set.

Swami was living at the house along with poet Stanley Barr who wrote many of the lyrics and wound up managing the band. Ron named the band Quintessence which was the essence of all things that permeate earth, wind, fire and water. Swami gave the band members names, reflective of their individual characteristics. Ron Rothfield became (Raja Ram) (flute, percussion), Phil Jones was called (Shiva Shankar), (vocals, keyboards), Allan Mostert stayed as Allan (lead guitar), Dave Codling was renamed (Maha Dev) (rhythm guitar), Richard Vaughn was (Shambhu Babaji) (bass) and Jeremy Milton became (Jake) (drums).

They practiced in a basement underneath a fish and chips restaurant on Portobello Road. The first gig was at the Art Lab located at 182 Drury Lane, London where six gigs occurred over a three-week period. They jammed and mesmerized the crowd with strobes and black lights for their light show and heavy rock guitar with Indian music vibes. Word got around and then they played the All Saints Church, a place where Pink Floyd had practiced and played. 400 people showed up strictly by word of mouth. There was also a show at The Roundhouse in Chalk Farm, London.

The band was showcasing themselves and not charging cover or if they were it was for the benefit of those who had been incarcerated on drug charges. Raja would do interviews for The Melody Maker after each show. This weekly UK magazine is noted for being one of the first publications dedicated to music and founded by Lawrence Wright for dance band musicians in 1926. Quintessence garnered a huge following. When they practiced and honed their talents in that basement the whole block could hear the band rehearsing. They'd been together for only 4 months and the record label reps were clamoring to sign the band.

The Reprise/Warner record label pursued the band for a month trying to sign them, but they wanted artistic freedom for any kind of deal. Island Records owner, Chris Blackwell, came to hear the band with Muff Winwood, older brother of Steve Winwood, doubled the highest offer and signed them on the spot. They gave them an advance of 5000 lbs, full control in the studio, a van and new equipment.

Through the NEMS agency, they were booked back at The Roundhouse and then at Hyde Park for a concert on stage with The Soft Machine, The Deviants, Edgar Broughton Band and others. This concert was filmed. Quintessence recorded all five LPs at Morgan Recording Studios Ltd. in Willesden, London 3 miles north under the guidance of John Barham who studied under Ravi Shankar and worked with George Harrison. No expense was left on the table. Gopala was Dave Codling's brother in law, and he designed the elaborate cover for the first LP, a foldout, with several inner pages, full lyrics and pictures to the cost of 1000 English Lbs. Early pressings of this album included a large color poster of Krishna.

The album *In Blissful Company* swirls with wah-wah guitars, deep penetrating vocals, echoes, chants and they rock. The single *Notting Hill Gate b/w Move Into The Light* was the only single released. During the shows they enchanted their audiences with mantras and long solos of hypnotic psychedelic guitars. Many disciples followed them to every show and there were 100s of concerts at places such as St. Pancras Town Hall in Camden, The Roundhouse in Chalk Farm, London, college gigs, outdoor concerts and festivals. They played the first two Glastonbury Fayres and toured all over Europe selling out the Royal Albert Hall twice.

Between gigs they recorded two other albums for Island Records, the self-titled *Quintessence* and *Dive Deep*. Heavy religious innuendos are present on every record and fans would try to typecast the band as Jesus Freaks. But the band admitted that they were not evangelists, they were just dedicated to a higher universal presence. BBC broadcasts with Euro TV exposure and dozens of features in the major music press assured this band as a huge success, but they were a band lacking a radio hit.

They wanted to go to America and Chris Blackwell worked out a deal with Bell Records, but they were offered a lower advance than expected. There was heavy interest for Quintessence in the US, but only Dev and Jones agreed to the advance. Admittedly, Raja Ram pushed this issue with the band, preferring a better deal and causing a bit of a "tiff" amongst the members. Ultimately Maha Dev (guitars) and Shiva Jones (lead vocals) were sacked, The US deal fell through and Island records released them from further recordings. The band became a quartet.

They signed with RCA records and the fans were puzzled about where the lead singer went. There was no official press report about how, when or why Shiva and Dev left the band. Meanwhile, album four *Indweller* and album five *Self* was recorded and released, but both LPs lacked the energy and verve of the first three. Shiva's vocals were missing and interest was sidelined. They were described as Led Zeppelin without Robert Plant, Free without Paul Rodgers and Jethro Tull without Ian Anderson. The band moved on to other adventures.

By now Dave Coding and Phil Jones stayed together, formed a band with other musicians and recorded a self-titled album, *Kala,* on the small Bradley's Records Ltd. label. Kala never got a break and only a few gigs were played because it was thought that Shiva just up and left Quintessence high and dry. No further LPs were recorded or released, but they continued playing into the 80's before they broke up for good. The band eventually fell apart.

Allan Mostert (Allan) relocated to Spain, continued in music but didn't record very much.

Richard Vaughn (Shambhu Babaji) disappeared.

Jeremy Milton (Jake) helped to form the band Blurt with his brother Ted and played well into the late 1990's. It's noted here that Jake was the first to coin the phrase *The Old Grey Whistle Test* from the famous late-night BBC television music series. Bands that played here were not in the top BBC hit list. If the night desk guard could whistle the tune's he heard during the night sessions to the players when they left in the morning, he passed the test.

Dave Codling (Maha Dev) reactivated Quintessence with Shiva Jones for a 40-year reunion of the band. They played concerts sporadically thereafter. Maha Dev released one solo album. Regrettably, he (as Dave Codling) passed away in July 2019.

Shiva Jones and Raja Ram never settled their differences over their initial separation.

Phil Jones (Shiva Shankar) stays active with music and lives his life on a higher level. He married and rediscovered the (Digeridoo) which he says gives him focus. He lives in the USA and continues playing gigs as Shivas Quintessence.

Ron Rothfield (Raja Ram) still lives in the same house in Ladbroke Grove. He retired from music for 10 years, but then developed a liking for Psychedelic Trance music, formed his own record label and has released several albums of his own. He was a part of another ambient psych trance band called Shpongle and currently fronts the band 1200 Micrograms.

There are many live recordings of Quintessence and these concerts have been marketed on CD on and off for years.

G9003
STEREODISC
The Rainbow Press
mr. g records
The National Newspaper
THERE'S A WAR ON
THE GIRL THAT CANNOT LOVE
NO ONE FOLLOWS THE DAYTIME
Seeks New Effort by Allies, Especially to Bring Their Units to Full Strength
STEP ABOARD
THERE'S A WAR ON
I'VE FOUND SOMEONE
CYCLIC EPIC
BETTER WAY
LIGHTNING STREAK
A SIMPLE WAY
OUR COUNTRY'S STILL O.K.

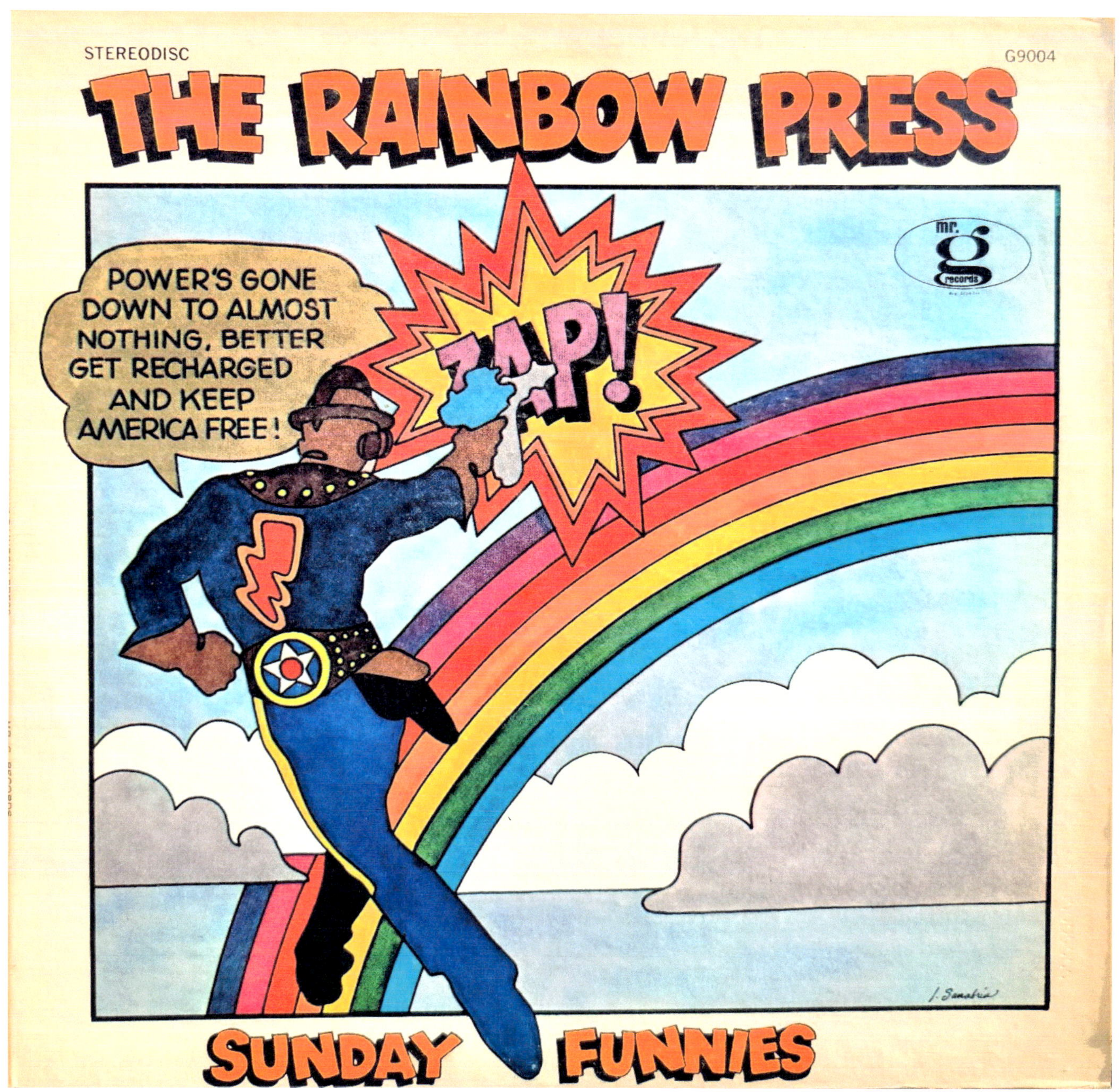
STEREODISC
G9004
THE RAINBOW PRESS
mr. g records
POWER'S GONE DOWN TO ALMOST NOTHING, BETTER GET RECHARGED AND KEEP AMERICA FREE!
ZAP!
SUNDAY FUNNIES

THE RAINBOW PRESS 1968-69

Marc Ellis was from Larchmont, New York and was the son of Ray Ellis who was noted for producing and arranging songs for many well-known singers (Johnny Mathis, Sarah Vaughn, Billie Holiday, Ben E. King, Liza Minnelli, Barbara Streisand and others). Marc played guitar and was in a band at Mamaroneck High School called The Specs. The band included Marc Ellis (guitar, vocals) Tony Bouchard (lead guitar), Mike Lange (bass) and Bill Yergin (drums). They played sock hops and teen dances and had some fun but when graduation was over so was the band.

They all moved onto College. Marc's Dad knew the owner of Audio Fidelity Records, Herman Gimbel, and was asked if he knew anybody who wanted to record an LP. Herman needed a tax write off and wanted to put out a cheap album to take the business loss. So, Ray asked his son Marc if he wanted to record an album. Why not? He and Dave Troup were friends at Ithaca College and had a common interest in music. Dave had also been the bass player in a band at Suffern High School located about 30 miles west of Larchmont. The band name was called The Group and included Larry Milton (keyboards, 12-string guitar, vocals), Charlie Osborne (organ) and Joe Groff (lead vocals). They came aboard at Dave's request and all that was needed was a drummer. Marc asked his former friend from The Specs, Bill Yergin, to join in on (drums).

Larry and Marc spent many weeks writing songs and the band practiced relentlessly at Dave Troup's house. They called themselves Continental Divide. The formal band included Marc Ellis (rhythm guitar, vocals), Joe Groff (vocals, recorder), Dave Troup (bass, vocals), Larry Milton (keyboards, guitar, vocals), Charles Osborne (organ, vocals) and Bill Yergin (drums). Their first gig was at The Suffern High Senior Graduation Prom. They played a couple other minor events, then signed a contract and scheduled studio time. It was at this point that they all decided to make the recording but not to play any more live gigs. The real focus was on college degrees and a stable livelihood.

They headed for Plaza Sound Studios located on the eighth floor of Radio City Music Hall in New York. (No longer active, it should be noted here that this is the same studio where The Ramones recorded their first LP in 1976). Unloading their equipment, they knew they hit the big time when they rode up the elevator with some of The

Rockettes. The time was right in the middle of the Hippie "heydaze" and social unrest due to the Vietnam War. They felt that the band's name should reflect the times. The Hippie scene was vibrant with rainbow colors and there were lots of news headlines about The Vietnam War and the anti-war protests occurring daily. So, they changed their name from The Group to The Rainbow Press.

During the sessions, executive producer Herman Gimbel made one appearance and commented about a peculiar lyric that ended with "that colorful box." He said "colorful box" had sexual connotations and the censors would never allow that song *Cyclic Epic* to air on the radio. There was some protest by the band members, but the lyric was eventually changed to "that colorful top." That was the only time they ever saw Herman. Entitled *There's A War On*, the album was completed and a minor lot of LPs along with the single *Better Way b/w There's A War On* was pressed and sent out to some of the major cities in the US.

An album full of psych tendencies, wild fuzz guitar, special effects, Vogues-like harmonies, echoes, pop sounds and memorable tunes, the music is similar in sound to other psych bands like Orpheus, Ford Theatre, The Racket Squad, The Paisleys and The Mystic Astrologic Crystal Band. The Mr. G Record label (with Mr. G identified as Mr. Gimbel) was a subsidiary to Audio Fidelity Records and made all the right moves promoting and distributing the LP. But that wasn't the intention.

The record was supposed to die on the shelves. However, in the blossoming psych scene in San Francisco, the LP got some real notice and radio airplay. The initial distribution of 500 albums sold out. Several requests for more copies resulted in about 20,000 LPs being sold. This perceived dead duck recording started making a profit. The guys were surprised and ecstatic. But Herman was beside himself. He wasn't losing the money as planned. Ray Ellis suggested another LP recording by the boys, this time with no promotion.

Only a couple months went by and they were back in the studio, this time at A&R Studios - Studio 2 under the guidance of production guru Phil Ramone. Another great LP was recorded. This second LP was called *Sunday Funnies* and had much of the same sound found on the first LP. But this time there was limited quantities pressed, no promotion and no distribution. It became the tax loss Herman Gimbel wanted. The band broke apart shortly after the recording was completed. There were never any thoughts about Rainbow Press making a mark and they never played at any of the local clubs live. All the players moved on.

Joe Groff graduated from Hamilton College and became a Music Major. He taught music in private school but spent most of his life as a data processor for Hartford Insurance Company. He retired & bought a farm in rural New York.

David Troup got his Fine Arts Degree at Ithaca College. He joined the Air Force and was a member of The Singing Sargent's while active. He gave vocal lessons and became a cruise ship entertainer.

Charles Osborne studied at The Jewish Theological Seminary of America and became a Jewish Cantor. He has written, directed and recorded numerous classical choral, full orchestra and small group performances in North America and Europe. Performances have occurred at The Lincoln Center in NY and the Kennedy Center in DC.

Larry Milton spent his years after college in music with several rock bands, some featuring Fran Sheehan (bass) and Sib Hashian (drums) both former players with the band Boston. He currently lives North of Boston and is leader and musical director of Tuxedo Junction, a band that caters to Weddings and other occasions.

Bill Yergin graduated from Case Western Reserve School of Dentistry. He was a retired DDS and lived in Ohio. About 2001 he began playing drums again with bands of all genres, Classic Rock, Blues, Country, Big Band and Jazz but sadly passed away Sept 2021.

Marc Ellis completed his studies at Ithaca College, moved to California and got into the media and music industry. He writes songs for commercials, TV, film scores and theatre musicals. Successful, he has owned and operated Mooncrest Productions for over 30 years.

There was a 50-year reunion of The Rainbow Press celebrating their first album release in late 2018. They all met at Joe Groff's farm outside of New York where they rehearsed and played a one-off show at a nearby church auditorium for an audience of adorning fans. It went very well and prompted a 3rd Rainbow Press album *Only Love Is The Truth* with all the original players. Released in the later months of 2021 you can hear it on YouTube and purchase it through the Bandcamp website. It's as if they never parted.

Columbia
Stereo
RAVEN

RAVEN
live at 'the inferno'
THE RISING SONS ARE RISING

RAVEN 1967-70

Stan Szelest played keyboards with Ronnie Hawkins in Toronto with Robbie Robertson, Rick Danko and Levon Helm who eventually formed the nucleus of The Band. Stan, who was originally from the states, left the Hawks and moved back to Buffalo, New York. He formed Stan & The Ravens with himself on (keyboards, vocals), Chuck McCormick (guitar), Pete Haskell (bass) and Sandy Konikoff (drums). They were loud and Stan was like a Jerry Lee Lewis player kicking his foot out hitting an amp, a bass drum or one of the players during the stage action. Their featured home clubs where they played the most was a corner bar on Delevan Ave called The Hideaway and Lulu Belles Restaurant on Best St. They had a few years together and towards the end the band replaced Pete and Sandy with Tom Calandra on (bass) and Gary Mallaber on (drums).

Tony Galla and The Rising Sons were a band that had included Tony on (vocals, bass), John Weitz (guitars), Jimmy Calire (keyboards, piano) and Fred Mayer (drums). They had a national hit on the airwaves with, *In Love b/w Guys Go for Girls.* Stan Szelest was known to depart his band occasionally to join Ronnie Hawkins and sit in with other bands and it was suggested that Tony Galla and Jimmy Calire fill in when Stan was absent. Stan objected to this, which resulted in Tom Calandra and Gary Mallaber joining Tony and the boys. Tony gave up bass playing duties to Tom and Gary replaced Fred Mayer on drums. So, the official band was Tony Galla (vocals), John Weitz (all guitars), Jimmy Calire (piano, keyboards, vocals), Tommy Calandra (bass) and Gary Mallaber (drums). Simplifying their name to The Rising Sons, they recorded another single *There's Nothing Going for Us b/w I'm Feeling Down* and played gigs back at The Hideaway, The Mug, Gilligan's, Alliotta's and others in Buffalo.

Marty Angelo, a former keyboardist for Shakey's Blues Band, met the band in performance at the Grandview Ballroom in Angola, New York and he eventually became their manager. John Weitz was only 17 and when they played the Glen Park Inferno in Williamsville, he was underage and the owner of the club wouldn't allow him to be on stage with the band. But the gig went on anyway with John outside, sitting in his car with a monitor for him to hear and a 200-foot guitar cord connected to the stage Amp inside. This show was recorded. He turned 18 a month or two later, which was legal drinking age in areas of the east coast and he could finally join the band on stage.

They attended the first Woodstock Sound Festival in 1967. This was before the more famous Woodstock Music and Art Fair that occurred later. Located at Pan Copeland's farm just outside the town, the event drew maybe 500-1000 attendees and included folksters like Tim Hardin, Phil Ochs, Richie Havens, Jackson C. Frank, Bunky and Jake and others. Raven was the only electrified band at the time and because of this they were scheduled as the last to perform. When they started to play, they were booed off stage by all the folk-oriented festival patrons.

By 1968 The Woodstock Sound Festival had evolved and for just $1 you could see such acts as The Soft Machine, Fear Itself, The Blues Magoos, Lothar and the Hand People, Rebecca and the Sunnybrook Farmers, Cat Mother and the All Night Newsboys, Procol Harum and other rock bands. The event had two good years of success and was the inspiration for Michael Lang to choose the Woodstock area for his dream festival in the first place.

Marty was trying to get more notice for the band outside of Buffalo and tried to persuade Steve Paul to book the band at his Scene night club located at 301 West 46th St. in New York. Steve was reluctant at first, but one night Jimi Hendrix happened by there and Marty was able to play him the Inferno club live tape. Jimi loved it and talked Steve into booking the band. It was at this point Marty realized that The Rising Sons name conflicted with another band who was already established, so in respect of their founder, Stan Szelest, they renamed themselves as Raven.

Jimi Hendrix and Eddie Kramer both wanted to get Raven over to Electric Ladyland Studios to do some recording. But Marty had also sent a tape of the live Inferno recording to George Harrison who expressed interest in the band as well. George wanted to bring them to England and record on the newly formed Apple Record label, but that never happened. By 1969 there was much interest in Raven who had high respect from both Steve Paul and Bill Graham, who owned The Fillmore East. Both club owners put Raven, a band without a record deal, on their stage.

After opening for Led Zeppelin at The Boston Tea Party, Jimmy Page revered John Weitz and was quoted as saying he was "one of the best guitar players in the world." After seeing the band live, Janis Joplin tried to hire Jimmy Calire for her newly formed Kosmic Blues Band but was turned down. George Harrison sent Peter Asher over to the states to get the band to sign a record deal but he was turned away. All the English bands that came to the states wanted to tour with Raven and they played several times at The Electric Circus in New York, The Fillmore East, The

Kinetic Playground in Chicago, The Grande Ballroom in Detroit, The Rockpile Club in Toronto, Canada, The Electric Factory in Philadelphia and many other places.

Michael Lang offered a deal for them to play at Woodstock and he wanted them to sign a contract. But after the debacle at the previous Woodstock Sound Festival in 1967 they were reluctant and walked away from a sure deal, a concert that became worldwide history. Who knew? They eventually signed a five-year deal through Marty Angelo at Columbia Records with legal backing and a producer, John Hill, who believed in the band.

The first self-titled album *Raven* was recorded at Columbia Recording Studio A located at 799 7th Avenue, NY. This is an album full of raw rock and blues. There are no special effects, psychedelic mind melts or studio embellishments. But Tony's voice is beyond belief. I guess the best voice comparison would be to that of Steve Walsh from Kansas. Tony doesn't sound like Steve but has a voice that makes you stop what you're doing and take notice. Columbia put out the single *Feelin' Good b/w Green Mountain Dream* and a non-album release *Children At Our Feet b/w Here Come A Truck*. They continued playing concerts and got a spot on Cleveland's *Upbeat* TV Show.

These guys could rock and the testament comes from Janis Joplin, Jimmy Page, Jimi Hendrix, George Harrison and so many other big names in the industry. The fans who saw them live knew exactly what this band was about. They were chosen as one of the first rock bands to perform a live one-hour show broadcast nationally on PBS. The Kinescope recordings of this performance have either been lost or tossed. The album had major distribution all over the country but only had sporadic play on the air waves. The band was disappointed with the studio sound and production and the album didn't have the verve and energy that they exhibited during the live shows.

Because of this it was decided to put the Live at Glen Park Inferno tape to record. Originally recorded in 1967, a limited number of private pressings *Live At The Inferno* were hastily printed up. The cover of the LP shows the band members superimposed over a picture of the burned ruins of the venue which had since burned to the ground in 1968. The album was distributed locally in hopes of enlightening folks to the raw power of Ravens sound, missing on the studio LP. They did a tour of England, playing places like The Lyceum Theatre in London, The Roundhouse in Chalk Farm, The Marquee Club in Chelmsford and others. There were no albums released in the UK, so they took

50 copies of the live album with them to pass out at the shows hoping to generate some interest in the UK, alas it never happened.

It was shortly after they returned to the states that the players started to drift apart. Other songs had been recorded at the initial Columbia sessions and left off the first LP. John Hill had hopes of using these and others to complete a second LP, but the band was faltering and eventually fell apart. Tiring of it all, they decided to separate.

Tommy Calandra stayed in Buffalo and opened up BCMK Recording Studios where he had a long career recording local Buffalo bands. He wrote a theme song for the Buffalo Sabers NHL Stanley Cup quest and several radio jingles. He sadly died in 1998.

John Weitz formed a jazz/fusion band called JR Weitz and moved to San Francisco in 1973 playing clubs for over 10 years. He recorded one self-titled jazz/fusion LP with the help of Billy Cobham and then became an audio engineer and designed and patented digital electronic devices. Unfortunately, he left us in 2012.

Jimmy Calire played with the band America for several years. He relocated to California and produces music for art and major theatre productions. Winning several awards over the years, his career has always been fluent. Jimmy's son Mario Calire was the drummer with Jakob Dylan and The Wallflowers.

Gary Mallaber is still one of most sought-after session drummers in the industry. Working with Bruce Springsteen, Eddie Money, Van Morrison and Bob Segar he had a 20-year stint with The Steve Miller Band and has over seventy gold and platinum records to his credit.

Tony Galla has had a long career with his voice from heaven. After he moved to California he sang for several acts in all genres (blues, rock, gospel) and has constantly toured throughout the years keeping the pipes fresh and clear. He has written songs for Movies and TV and recorded four of his own CDs available on his website.

Of note, Raven did reform for one show in 1993 with all original members at the Tralf Music Hall in Buffalo. Excerpts of this show can be found on YouTube.

STEREO
Repairs
Already
A
Household
Word
R532L
Repairs

repairs
CREELAND AV
CREST
MOWEST
MW121L

KUCKUCK
2375 025 Stereo
REPAIRS
LIVE

REPAIRS 1971-72

Four of the members of Repairs, Peter McCann, Jim Honeycutt, Mike Foley and Larry Treadwell all met up while attending Fairfield University in Fairfield, Connecticut between 1966 and 1970. Peter McCann began performing in his freshman year with the Fairfield University Glee Club. There he met Jim Higgins and George Mathias. They began to perform together as a trio calling themselves Peter, Jimmy and George and performed various folk song covers at local colleges and venues. They broke up after a year or so and Peter began to play and perform as a duo with Jim Honeycutt. Both played guitar and Peter sang.

During their junior year, bassist Mike Foley joined them. Occasionally, Jim's girlfriend, Sukie Propst also joined them on stage to sing with Peter. At the end of their Junior year Larry Treadwell, who was a seasoned electric guitarist, was added. Tim (Ace) Holleran joined playing drums and Sukie, who would marry Jim after graduation, was asked to join the band permanently.

Calling themselves Repairs, they honed their skills playing at colleges and local venues. They were invited to play at the first Earth Day celebration in Westport, Connecticut in the Summer of 1971. While performing, Andrew Loog Oldham, the producer of The Rolling Stones, lived nearby at a house in Wilton. He happened by the show on his way to a movie at a Westport theater and overheard the music playing. He sent his wife to the movie and stayed behind to listen. He was taken by Repairs performance and offered to represent them for a record deal.

Signing with the Motown subsidiary Rare Earth Records, they recorded their first album at Syncron Studios located in Wallingford, Connecticut. The band's first album was entitled *Already A Household Word* and certainly gave you your money's worth as it ran for 58 minutes. It starts a little slow and country like, almost like John Denver or Seals and Crofts, but as each song drills into your head, you realize how unbelievably beautiful this band is. Great fuzz guitar, female vocals, four-part harmonies, special effects, virtual stereo and great infectious songs. The music is very much in the mold of the best of the highly collectable flower pop sunshine bands like Growing Concern,

Pidgeon and Love Exchange. A real shame that it didn't sell better. No singles were released in the US. Local promotion was great, but nationally nobody knew.

However, they did well enough to be invited to record a second album. Simply called *Repairs*, the second LP effort has more of the same infectious songs which complements the first with a refined sound like that of Michaelangelo without the autoharp. You'll also find more than 50 minutes' worth of great songs on this second album. It was released on the other Motown subsidiary Mowest, but unfortunately again had zero promotion and the album sank out of sight.

No singles were released from either LP in the US, however there was an extremely rare EP promo featuring four songs from the second LP. Repairs did get notice in Germany which prompted them to record a last and final album at Syncron Studios in front of a live audience. The album was entitled *Repairs Live* and was only released on the German record label Kuckuck Schallplatten. Two singles from the first album were also released *Songwriter b/w Nowhere* and *O Lonesome Sorrow b/w Circle Won't Take Me Around.* These were only released in Germany.

The show was recorded and filmed with portions of the show now seen on YouTube. What was especially nice about this album was Repairs ability to perform and especially sing live, which really showed how talented this band was. With no vision of national success, the band broke up after a six-week tour of Florida. Jim and Sukie left the band. Peter, Larry, Mike and Ace decided to give it one more shot as a foursome. They did record one more album which was never released. Then they moved to the west coast and California.

Working hard six nights a week didn't pay off either. With notice from nobody, it wore them out and they soon disbanded. Repairs was woefully overlooked as a band and their albums stack up musically to most of the high-priced biggies. Except for the live album, the first two studio LPs appear to be common, are easy to find and relatively inexpensive. No CD reissues yet, but they should be. It's all about the music here.

Jim and Sukie divorced amicably.

Sukie moved to Naples, Florida having success with a different career. There in Florida she opened a restaurant with Tony Ridgway. Her other passion was cooking and wine which she took to great heights. She is a renowned wine expert, has two wine distribution shops and provides a select list of wines for 13 different high-end restaurants in Florida. She is also recognized as a top wine specialist in Wine Spectator magazine.

Jim Honeycutt stayed at home and settled in Westport, Connecticut as a long tenured teacher at Staples High School. He became the media high school teacher and ran the Media Lab teaching students, among other things, on how to record and make records & CD's. It turns out that Jim is an identical look-a-like cousin to Walter Egan who scored a top ten hit (1978) with *Magnet and Steel* and went on to release 10 albums during his career. Strangely both Walter and Jim were born on the same day and in the same hospital.

Mike Foley stayed in Connecticut and continued to write music and play bass guitar, but he never hooked up with any serious recording bands.

Tim (Ace) Holleran joined the band Orchestra Luna back in Connecticut and stayed with them for quite a while, then joined Burton Cummings, Meat Loaf, Linda Ronstadt and Bette Midler on tour and in the studio. For a short while, he wrote comedy for some of the Saturday Night Live skits. He is currently a freelance writer for several publications and a web designer.

Larry Treadwell is still in Los Angeles, California. He joined the band Sumner for a couple of years, then toured the world and played with Thomas Dolby, Cindi Lauper, The Pointer Sisters and others before building a studio. He has been involved with many TV and movie scores and is currently with The Enzymes partnered with Rob Lewin who was the bass player with Illinois Speed Press.

Peter McCann released two albums and finally got fame with the top 5-hit single *Do You Wanna Make Love b/w Right Time Of The Night*. This generated into a lifetime of songwriting for the likes of Whitney Houston, Jennifer Warnes, K.T. Oslin, Crystal Gayle, Karen Carpenter and many others. He currently lives in Nashville, TN.

sage and seer

SAGE AND SEER 1969

David Rea and Don Beckmann met at Thomas Jefferson High School in Denver, Colorado. Don, a year older and David both played guitars. They practiced in the basement where Dave lived and started playing the familiar Beatles tunes heard on the radio. They soon began writing songs and shortly thereafter felt comfortable enough to start playing in public. Looking for a band name, David's Mother suggested that the duo be called Sage and Seer. *(please note that David is not the same David Rea that played with Gordon Lightfoot and Ian and Sylvia)*

Their first gig was in a ward at Fitzsimmons Hospital located in Aurora, Colorado. From the start they played their own songs and compositions. The show was a complete disaster according to David and the two nearly gave it all up. But thinking the better of it they decided to press ahead. There weren't a lot of venues around town for an acoustic duo to play at, but they did find a few, playing high school parties, the Bullfighter Restaurant, the Red Lion Inn, the Denver Athletic Club and the Denver Folklore Center. They played other high school events and emceed a talent show. Their shows featured all their own compositions which was very unusual, but they got a good response.

Enough confidence convinced them to think about recording some of their songs. David remembered a former high school music teacher that had retired. Bob Ashton had started his own local record company called Stylist Records. He and his partner Al Davis, the Stylist records producer, agreed to take a listen to their stuff and asked them to record a demo. They set up at Summit Studios in Denver and recorded a four-song acetate. Bob and Al were impressed enough and were on board to record an official single. A backing band was put together with an unnamed session drummer and bass player along with Bob Ashton on (harpsichord, piano) and David and Don on guitars and vocals. They recorded *Calling b/w I Can't Take You Home*. The song *Calling* got some local radio airplay and some minor interest from Billboard but it never made the official charts.

Undeterred, Stylist Records worked a deal with a producer in Los Angeles at the Warner Brothers label. So, Don, Dave and Al Davis flew to LA to hook up with the big label. They were too young to play any of the known clubs on the Sunset Strip like the Whiskey Au Go-Go or The Rainbow and their accommodations wound up being a cheesy

Sunset Blvd motel. But they were dazzled the next day when they passed through the gates of Warner Bros with dreams of becoming famous. When they met with the WB executives, they were informed that their designated producer had experienced a nervous breakdown and was gone. So, they were sluffed off to another producer that wanted to pair Dave and Don up with studio musicians to become a funk band.

There was no way that was going to happen, so they headed home with much discouragement. Tails between their legs, they somehow found Dan Goodman who was a music major and film editor with connections at the University of Colorado. He came to David's house and listened to the Sage and Seer duo play live and really liked what he heard. Stylist Records hired him to arrange their songs for an album. He realized the challenge and hired Mark Schuster, another music major at Colorado University and keyboardist, to assist with the project. They split arrangement duty for the songs. Mark knew and performed with another student, Jack Olesen, a bass player and invited him to the sessions. Along with Jack, Mark gathered some other musicians and set up additional sessions to practice the arrangements at a big house in the hills near Golden, Colorado.

The recordings for the LP occurred back at Jackson Sound Studios located at 1401 S. Lipon St. in Denver. A 16-track tape machine was used which was new and state of the art for the times. Members of the Denver Symphony were hired and conducted by Ben Kaufman. So, the band was David Rea (Harmony Sovereign guitar, lead vocals), Don Beckmann (Gibson lead guitar, vocals), Mark Schuster (organ, harpsichord, keyboards), Jack Olesen (bass) and an unknown session (drummer). Joe Jackson, the studio owner, engineered the session. When the recording session dragged on too long, there was some friction towards the end of the sessions and during the mixing, but after a week the recording was complete.

The self-titled album *Sage and Seer* has a home-made sound with innocence, soft psych moves, echoes, fuzz guitar, some studio effects and all the good things that make a band special. The best likeness in sound would be to another obscure unknown band called JAIM. The album cover was designed by JVR Inc. in Denver that shows David (standing) and Don (sitting) silhouetted through the lens of a liquid oil and water light show. Two singles from the album were released to the airwaves *Pictures Thru a Sunday Afternoon b/w Clarissa* and *Candle b/w She Died Again*, but things just didn't work out as they had hoped.

David and Don followed the Lennon/McCartney format agreeing to split the royalties for all songs written equally. But nothing ever occurred, the record label didn't have a clue how to market the album or have enough money to promote the band and set up gigs. A limited number of LPs were pressed, some were passed out to the session players and the others relegated to the cut-out bins. David remembers throwing the LPs as frisbees with a friend back in Boulder. Stylist recorded others acts, including the FAB Company, but soon folded and faded away. Don and David never gigged after the sessions and as a band they split apart.

The other studio players (Mark and Jack plus others) stayed together for about a year and played at various venues in and around the area. But no songs from the album were played as they were just a covers band.

Afterwards, Mark Schuster relocated to Los Angeles absorbing himself in the bustling music scene, but his current whereabouts are unknown.

Jack Olesen moved to LA and taught Chemistry at a small college for a while, then went back to Boulder, earned his PhD and worked for DuPont Chemical as a technical sales specialist. Now retired and living in Texas, he's always found casual work as a bass player here and there during his spare time.

Don Beckmann moved to the San Francisco area and went into social work. As he describes it, he's "Living in the Bay Area, retired from public service and doing what he can for the people he loves."

David Rea moved to Boulder playing his songs at local clubs. Then he got a creative writing scholarship to an art college in San Miguel de Allende in Mexico. He lived there for a while. During that time, he sometimes sang with a Mexican rock band called Los Mexicanos at La Econdida, a late-night club. Years later he went into advertising, eventually becoming Executive Creative Director for Re/Max, the world's largest real estate organization.

He wrote and produced dozens of big-budget TV commercials shot around the world. Then in the mid-90's he began writing songs again and released another CD in 2004 recorded at Pacifica Studios in Culver City, California near Santa Monica called *Nation of One*. Now retired, he currently writes novels for his own amusement.

The Sage and Seer album is rare and well worth the asking price if one is ever found. David admits his regrets for tossing the LPs as toys back in the day.

SALVATION
MONO ABC-623
abc RECORDS

ABCS-653 STEREO
abc
RECORDS
SALVATION GYPSY CARNIVAL CARAVAN

SALVATION 1967-68

Joe Tate grew up in St. Louis, Missouri. His Mom and Dad were both involved with The Salvation Army Church. He started playing violin at an early age but got disinterested and wanted to play guitar. His main influence was Ike and Tina Turner. He saw them several times at The New Lindy Ballroom before they received national attention with the single *A Fool in Love b/w The Way You Love Me*. After that, they were gone and playing the big cities all over the US. Joe relied on a friend at Normandy High School, Dennis Linde, to teach him how to play guitar. Dennis is noted for moving to Nashville and writing the song *Burning Love* which Elvis Presley took to #1 on the cashbox charts. It was his last #1 hit. Joe got good enough on guitar and joined a band playing parties but never experienced a serious paying gig.

He got involved with the ICBM Missile program in Lincoln, Nebraska and then attended the University of Missouri and was totally absorbed into social issues and anti-war events. Migrating to California he met Gary Blum. He and Gary joined the band Red Shepard and the Flock. They played clubs in the area and toured out of state but when playing a place in Colorado, found themselves stranded. Red Shepard had picked up all the tour earnings and split. Joe returned to San Francisco and formed a three-piece band called The Creatures, but this band was short-lived.

He was jamming with Al Linde, a singer he had met on the road during his days with Red and the Flock, and they decided to form another group. The band was formalized with players, Joe Tate (guitar), Al Linde (vocals), Art Resnick (US of Arthur) (keyboards), Artie McClean (bass) and Teddy Stewart (drums). In respect for his Father, and a play on words, he decided to name the band The New Salvation Army Banned.

Initially they found a big old 1937 Packard Twelve Limousine that was large enough to carry the band members and all the equipment to get around to the gigs, but later located an old beat up school bus and had a painting party to flower it up all psychedelic like with vibrant colors.

Bryant Cohen became their manager and booking agent and asked the band if they wanted to play a club called The Roaring Twenties. This was a five night per week gig but it was a topless place. They agreed and were not together long before Chet Helms asked them to perform at The Avalon followed by Bill Graham at The Fillmore.

Word got out and the band was getting all kinds of grief and disapproval from the real Salvation Army organization over the use of their name. They didn't like the fact that their name was being associated with a bare breasted club of ill repute and a letter was sent to manager Bryant Cohen asking if the band could change their name.

Joe and the band didn't really see any problem. It was a tribute to his dad as a representative of The Salvation Army organization and the band he performed with playing music on the streets about love, hope and happiness for everybody to hear. The music was different but Joes band was playing and singing about peace, love and turning on. There was no need to make the name change according to Bryant. But the Salvation Army, as it turns out, was a big corporation and they decided to hire a big-time lawyer to invoke a misuse of the name. As stated in the press "This constitutes an unauthorized appropriation of The Salvation Army's property right in that name."

The lawsuit indicated that the band was also wearing uniforms that replicated those that were worn by the official church players as inappropriate and mocked the band members of the real The Salvation Army. The band's so called uniforms were WW1 army jackets purchased at a thrift store. A letter was sent to Bill Varnie, owner of the Roaring Twenties club, detailing their misgivings and he decided to cancel all the shows by the band at his place until something was done. They moved on to other places, were getting a good fan following and favorable reviews in the press, so they continued without heeding the warning.

They were scheduled to play the Central City Street Fair. The Fair was part of an effort to revitalize a depressed area in San Francisco and the original Salvation Army Band was also going to participate but they backed out when they found that The New Salvation Army Banned was also going to perform. They made an official statement, "We can't appear with them." Other bands on the bill were The Freedom Highway, Mount Rushmore and The Freudian Slips, all of whom could conceivably have been in violation of name misrepresentation.

Then a threat was sent to Bryant by Charles Thurber, Vice President of The Better Business Bureau, that stated the use of that name was not authorized and did not represent what was implied. Suddenly, venue announcements of upcoming shows excluded the New Salvation Army Banned, the press wouldn't mention them for ads or review their performances and the Musicians Union was giving them problems. Basically, they were blackballed. Deciding to give in rather than fight, they changed their name to simply Salvation.

ABC records came to them, gave them a $10,000 advance and signed them up to a contract. Their first album was recorded at Universal/Western Studios in Hollywood, California. The sessions included Tom Scott (sax) and Bill Plummer (sitar). Produced by Bob Thiele, everything was done in about 3 days. Fuzz guitar, echoes and slight special studio effects were all part of the mix. Similar bands that come to mind are Country Joe and The Fish, Notes from the Underground and Dr. Wests Medicine Show. Two singles were put out, *Think Twice b/w Love Comes in Funny Packages* and *Cinderella b/w The Village Shuck* but the song G*I Joe* on the LP was the one that got heavy airplay on the FM underground stations up in the Seattle area. As a result, they were extremely popular up in the Northwest and traveled north to play at the first Sky River Rock Festival in front of 60,000 fans.

There was little promotion for the first self-titled LP entitled *Salvation*, but they were brought back in to record a second record album. Drugs were the highlight for experimentation, the band and sound engineers partook in various substances and it shows on the second LP effort entitled *Gypsy Carnival Caravan*. Much more weirdness and studio effects permeate this disc with echoes, screams, phase shifting guitars and harpsichord making for a perfect FM radio underground sound. There were no singles and no promotion, however they were scheduled to play at The Fillmore East and traveled back to New York in their freaky looking Land Yacht.

As soon as they arrived, some of their equipment was stolen right out of the bus. They were set up at the famous Chelsea Hotel, where Bob Dylan wrote the songs for the album *Blonde on Blonde* and were also featured at some clubs in Greenwich Village. During this time, they met with the ABC executives and had a discussion about general happenings but Al Linde spoke his mind and was so embittered over ABC's handling of the band and unseen royalties that he got up on the table in anger and reprimanded those in control. The Fillmore show went off as planned but any national tour on the horizon was immediately canceled.

To make matters worse, their tour manager, Mike Silverberg, was handling the advance money to pay for trip expenses. He reluctantly didn't pay the Hotel bill for the band members and skipped out of town. Mike was nowhere to be found and Joe, Teddy and Al were arrested for failure to compensate for their stay. Artie McClean and US of Arthur were elsewhere when this occurred.

The road manager, Carlos, took over duties to get them back to San Francisco and once there the band stayed at his house in The Presidio. They played at many of the clubs, venues and festivals on the west coast promoting the albums where they could but then US of Arthur was arrested for possession and spent time in jail. The rest of the band just sort of burned out and fell apart.

Unfortunately, Al Linde succumbed to cancer.

Teddy Stewart worked for the US Post Office and played drums locally in the East Bay area of San Francisco with other bands.

Artie McClean had always lived on a big old boat in Southern California where he still resides.

Arthur Resnick lives in St Paul, Minnesota fronting his jazz band The Art Resnick Trio.

Joe Tate took a hiatus for a while and was living on his houseboat in Sausalito. This location is where many artists and musicians lived. He formed The Redlegs basically with former musicians and neighbors. Big things could have happened as they had a contract offer but after reading the fine print it was clear that it didn't benefit the band. They were together on and off for over 40 years. Joe fronted The Blue Monday Band and The Hippie Voices for weekly gigs in Sausalito. But gave up performing and retired at the ripe young age of 82. Joe was always highly intelligent. In his spare time, he invented the Ambient Power Module which converts radio frequencies to usable electrical power. Albeit only as Millivolts, it is sufficient to operate clocks, smoke alarms, Ni-Cd battery chargers and Seismic Warning Systems for Earthquakes which curiously emit radio signals when they happen.

SPACE
"MUSIC TO THE PEOPLE"

SPACE 1969

The Merchant Marines were noted for bringing rock 'n' roll to San Juan, Puerto Rico. Many of the ships that came to port had their own musicians and would set up to play in clubs located in town. People would come to dance and the music influenced those who aspired to play in a rock band. Carli Muñoz was quite young but he was a pianist that also played bass guitar. His first experience with rock 'n' roll occurred at a place called The Quiet Village where he joined a band called Hot Papa Jr. The band included Hot Papa (drums), Pepito Maldonado (guitars), Carli (keyboards) and Tito Allen (bass). He eventually started his own band called Los Colegiales and they were able to play social dances and make money. Players came and went, and when The Beatles were seen on Ed Sullivan, he formed a three piece band called The Red Fever with Carli on (bass), Vinnie Urrutia on (guitar) and Jorge Marién (drums).

Carli was also fortunate to start playing with well-respected jazz musicians. He showed a real knack for playing keyboards at an early age accompanying local greats like Charlie Robles, Julio Angel, Chucho Avellanet, Lissette, Celinés and others. He also became a bass player as part of the featured band on *La Nueva Ola* (The New Wave) which was a TV show featuring local rock talent as well as rock bands from other countries.

He was barely 15 and was already a seasoned keyboard and bass player. One night he filled in on (double bass) for Freddie Thomas in the house jazz band at The Holiday Inn that included Sabu Martinez, Monchito Muñoz, Freddie Thomas and Juancito Torres. Carli became a permanent player on keyboards. They backed several performers and were backing a well-known jazz singer, Mirna Rodriquez, and her escort of dancers called The Paper Dolls.

Carli took a liking to one notable dancer, Diana Costello. She was older (at 24) and was from New York. A former singer (as Diana Lee) she toured with The Royal Teens that had a big hit single *Who Wears Short Shorts b/w Planet Rock* back in 1957. There is a live video of her singing with the band, on YouTube, on the very first episode (Feb. 15th, 1958) of *Dick Clark's Saturday Night Beechnut Show*. This show was broadcast for three years from Manhattan's Little Theatre in New York and was before he hosted the more famous *American Bandstand*.

The Voltures were a rock band that included Jorge Calderón (guitar), Amaury López (drums) and Osvaldo Torres (bass). They had just broken up. Jorge happened to see Carli at the Holiday Inn and approached him to see if he would like to form a rock band. Carli agreed to join if he could bring Diana along. Diana was a proven singer and they practiced at Carli's house. Calling themselves The Living End, they gigged at places like The Miramer Charthouse and The Elk Club in Candado. They became the hottest rock band in Puerto Rico and won every Battle of the Bands contest that happened. Things got thick between Carli and Diana. There were plans to get married, but then Carli decided against it and backed out. Diana left the band and went back to New York.

Continuing without female vocals for a short period of time, Jorge took over singing duties. Roberto Puras (Casals) was a fan of the band and became their equipment manager, helping to set up gigs. Osvaldo taught him how to play bass guitar. Roberto then left the band to play with others including Los We, The Undertakers and The We Know You group. One evening The Living End were playing at a club called The Scene Au Go-Go and did an instrumental version of a huge current hit *The Girl from Ipanema*. During the song they heard this wonderful female voice singing the lyrics over the PA System from the DJ booth across the room. Her name was Tessy Coen and she was stunning. The looks and the voice were what the band needed, so they hired her on the spot.

They were together for over a year, then Osvaldo Torres decided he wanted to leave the band and go back to College. So, they brought back Roberto Puras, who by now had become a proven (bass) player. They also hired Billy Soto, who had been with a band called The Sonset that recorded an album and had some success with an AM radio hit. He was added as (lead guitar). Members officially became Jorge Calderón (guitar, vocals), Carli Muñoz (keyboards), Billy Soto (lead guitar), Tessy Coen (vocals, congas), Roberto Puras (bass) and Amaury López (drums). The band traveled to St Thomas to open a new club at Duffy's Hotel and played there for a while.

Members began experimenting with LSD and the music expanded and got exciting. But they were getting some "heat" from the local authorities. So, to avoid any problems they decided to travel to New York which turned out to be a medicine cabinet where the drugs were plentiful. Within a week of their arrival, they were able to audition for Scott Muni's Rolling Stone and became the house band there. Jack Rieley was their manager and depending on the venue or evening gig, they began to rename themselves as Space. They were paired with The Elephants Memory at The Wagon Wheel, run by mafia mobster Johnny Biello. Located at 128 West 45th St., this place was formerly The Peppermint Lounge. There was also a long-running summer gig at The Castaway's on Long Island.

Their fan base was growing and record labels came calling. Capitol records signed them to a record deal. Although they were highly creative, they were very green in the recording studio set up at Ultra Sonic Studios located on Long Island, New York. Being thrown into the sessions with no direction they were given an assigned producer, George Francis "Shadow" Morton, so nicknamed because he could never be found. He had formerly been with The Markeys and is credited with writing the songs *Remember, Walking in the Sand* and *Leader of the Pack* putting The Shangri-Las at the top of the heap.

True to his name Shadow Morton was usually so intoxicated for the studio sessions that he never showed up, so The Living End was left on their own without any technical knowledge of how to put an album together. Fortunately, John Linde stepped in with quality engineers Bill Stahl and John Bradley to help with the project. But the sessions took quite a while. Musically, they have an infectious psychy sound with some wild guitar riffs. The (congas), played by Tessy, gave them a unique sound and the female vocals, vibes, guitars, echoes and special effects show a band with a lot of talent. Tessy has a voice that is similar to Laura Nyro especially on the song *Baby*.

By 1968 Space was falling apart. Capitol Records had granted them their own offshoot record label called Hand Records for release and distribution. The album, which was officially released in September 1969 and simply called *Space,* sat on the shelves for over a year. When the LP finally came out on the market there was no promotion and no singles were released. The cover of the LP is bright red, picturing the band from left to right Amaury López, Jorge Calderón, Tessy Coen, Carli Muñoz, Roberto Puras and Billy Soto. By the time the album was put on the market, the drugs and band relationships had taken their toll. Carli was living with his manager, Jack, in New York and was invited to accompany him out to California for a weekend trip. A decision that molded him and secured his livelihood in performance and music for the rest of his life.

Carli was gone, he stayed in California and the band all went their separate ways.

Amaury López moved on and was not involved in music. His whereabouts is unknown. The rumor is that Amaury López (Jackson) was the same musician but he was a keyboard player. He did join Roberto Puras in the band Raices and later fronted the band Apocolips but this Amaury López was never a drummer and was not the same person.

Roberto Puras moved back to San Juan and joined a band called Raices that released one self-titled LP. It's reported that he survived a drive by shooting while exiting a club in San Juan. He worked in management in the healthcare industry providing supplies, through different corporations, to Pharmacies and Pharmacy chains for most of his life and retired to Florida.

Billy Soto was part of a band called Tribe that released one of five funk and soul LPs with him called *Dedication.* He disappeared into normal life hereafter.

Jorge Calderón had released one highly rated LP in 1975 called *City Music* that included a virtual who's who in the music industry, Waddy Watchel (guitar), Willie Weeks (bass), William Smith (keyboards), Jim Kelter (drums) and many others. He had a great career working with Ry Cooder, Jackson Browne, David Lindley and many others with tours, writing and recording. But he was mostly involved with Warren Zevon and credited on all of his albums (post 1976) for production, arranging and songwriting. He won a Grammy for Warren's last album release called *Wind.*

Tessie Coen is listed as Tessie Calderon with vocals and percussion on other recordings with Jorge Calderón, David Clayton Thomas, Claudia Lennear and Carol King. It's not confirmed but she may have married Jorge at some point.

Carli Muñoz spent 16 years in California and was remarkably successful with The Beach Boys when he replaced Daryl Dragon on keyboards recording and touring all over the world. He produced Dennis Wilson's *Pacific Ocean Blue/Bambu* album rerelease. Carli had written songs for *Bambu* as an initial follow up to his *Pacific Ocean Blue* LP. *Bambu* was never completed and the sessions weren't released until 2008. Carli has also played with George Benson, Wilson Pickett, Charles Lloyd, Chico Hamilton, Al Jarreau and many others. He then opened his own jazz club which was still active as of this writing called Carli's Fine Bistro and Piano located in Old San Juan, Puerto Rico. He is the featured musician here and has had an illustrious career releasing several solo LPs and CDs.

A VERY
STRANGE
BREW
ABCS-672 STEREO
abc
RECORDS

STRANGE BREW 1969

Strange Brew formed in East LA and included former members of local R&B cover bands playing various venues and private parties. Ron Reyes (guitar, vocals) had been with The Impalas and had already recorded a couple of noteworthy singles backing John and George Ochoa as The Slauson Brothers, *Power Glide b/w Rosalie* and *Baby Come Home b/w 2 O'clock Blues*. Art Sanchez (bass, vocals) and Mark Mora (drums) had both been with The Unusuals and The Runabouts and John Mekenian had played (keyboards) with Mark Mora in a band called The New Edition. By now they had all departed their respective bands and were looking to move in a new direction.

Ron was responsible for pulling the players together to form a new band. Tommy Lozano was also from this Los Angeles area and had been a backing vocalist for Cannibal & the Headhunters touring the East coast. He had just returned to LA and came aboard for (lead vocals). They all met in The City of Commerce and practiced in the garage at the house where Ron's mother lived. The group picked the name *Strange Brew* from the song made famous by Cream but it was intended to represent the various ethnic backgrounds of the band members – Italian, Armenian, and Chicano. As seasoned musicians they put together an assortment of current hit cover songs. John Ochoa took over management duties and booked venues like The Alhambra High School Auditorium, The Montebello Armory, places in Orange County and Gazzarri's on the Sunset Strip.

Art's friend, Steve Lawrence, played saxophone and Hammond organ with The Ever-Green Blues band. Strange Brew was scheduled to play an outdoor event and share the stage with this band at a park in Lynwood, Ca. The Ever-Green Blues had already recorded one LP and were represented by Jimmy King (aka Lou T. Josie). He was a singer songwriter who wrote the song, *Midnight Confessions,* originally performed by this band, and released as a single from their first album. Subsequently this song charted to a top 10 national hit on the radio airwaves by The Grass Roots.

Art asked Steve if Jimmy might want to come to the show and preview Strange Brew. He did show up and liked what he heard from the band but when he asked if they had any original songs, they did not. Still, he saw potential in the band and the boys went back to the garage where they rehearsed at The City of Commerce and holed up for a few days writing new material. Two songs were written *If You Want Me* and *Crossroads of Life*.

Jimmy arranged to have recording sessions take place at American Recording Studios in Studio City where bands like Iron Butterfly, Three Dog Night, Steppenwolf and The Grateful Dead recorded their early albums.

He had written two additional songs *Three's A Crowd* and *Yesterdays Coming* and brought them to Strange Brew. They went ahead and recorded demos of the four songs and based on these, Jimmy King replaced John Ochoa to oversee the band and secured a deal with ABC Records for a full album.

But John was not completely excluded as he co-wrote two songs that the band subsequently included on their LP. Sessions occurred after hours, to accommodate the regular day job schedules and the fact that Art was still in high school. Horns were added to the song *Always On My Mind* courtesy of Steve Lawrence, Kenny Walther and Tom Bray, all members of The Ever-Green Blues. This was not the same song written in 1972, made famous by Willie Nelson. The Ever-Green Blues released two albums and then they became the band Elijah for two more LPs.

One weird thing occurred during the recording of another song. The sound of a cricket was heard through the speakers during the playback and it was overwhelming. Things had to stop while they all looked around the studio trying to find the little creature. They wound up rerecording the song once the orthopteran was deposed of. Overall, the album is full of harpsichord, organ, screaming fuzz guitar, wah-wah, three-part harmonies, special effects including Jimmy King's bubbling aquarium on the album's intro, infectious tunes and a nice AM Radio pop atmosphere with an edge prevalent for the times. Similar in sound to The Soul Survivors, The Buckingham's and Louie and the Lovers but with much more guitar.

A photo op occurred for the album cover that shows a distorted view of the band members with a lens shot through a glass bottle. There were empty clear glass wine bottles superimposed over the band picture for a double exposure. This was to promote a weird psychedelic effect used to market the LP. The players pictured from left to right are Mark Mora, Tommy Lozano, Ron Reyes, Art Sanchez and John Mekenian in that order.

The back cover lists the band as The Brew which may have been a typo or a quick decision by the label that led to some confusion. There has always been a misunderstanding about this amongst record collectors, but the band always billed themselves as Strange Brew wherever they played. Adding to the muddle was the thought that this band may have been related somehow to another band known as Impala Syndrome. This was probably due to Ronnie's former band The Impalas and the fact that Impala Syndrome was clearly displayed in the wild cover painting on the last LP released by this other band from Venezuela. They were known as Los Impalas or (The Impalas) but there was no connection at all between the two bands.

To Strange Brews knowledge there was no specific promotion for their formal LP called *A Very Strange Brew* put out by ABC Records however one single was put on the market *Union Man b/w I Can Hardly Wait To Live*. No special tour or showcase occurred for the band. After the release they continued playing many of the same venues as before.

Jimmy King helped to promote the album by assisting Strange Brew in booking performances at various venues like Thee Experience, a club owned by Marshall Brevetz that was hip to featuring local new bands with a newly released LP. Other venues on The Strip including The Troubadour and The Whiskey A-Go-Go also featured Strange Brew. They were the opening act for the band Seatrain for a show in Lancaster and appeared on stage opening for The Standells at the legendary El Monte Legend Stadium. This was a huge auditorium outside the city limits of Los Angeles that could hold more than 3000 people. Art Laboe was a local DJ who broadcast his show live here and was responsible for organizing all the rock 'n' roll events at the stadium for over 10 years.

Strange Brew lasted about two years and fell apart. They didn't know if there was any marketing of their band by the record company and there was little if any revenue from sales. A great band that was lost in the constant shuffle who put out a noteworthy album that they should be proud of.

Tommy Lozano married and later worked in security for a major hotel/casino in Las Vegas.

John Mekenian is also married and currently owns and operates a successful tire sales and vehicle service center.

Mark Mora continued in music and studied extensively with Joe Porcaro, a great session drummer who worked with Stan Getz, Madonna, Pink Floyd, Frank Sinatra and the legendary Don Ellis. His sons Jeff and Steve Porcaro formed the well-known supergroup Toto in the 80's with brother Mike Porcaro joining later. Mark Mora has toured with various groups and continues to work in the studio.

Art Sanchez and Ron Reyes were invited to rejoin George Ochoa and a new project called Olde Tyme Religion. This band recorded two singles *Itchy Feeling b/w The Swimmer* and *Glori b/w 47 Cents* on the Warner Brothers label. Olde Tyme Religion evolved into *Yaqui* and recorded one self-titled LP on the Playboy Record label. This was a Santana flavored band with heavy guitars and is highly recommended. It was recorded at Bolic Studios, owned by Ike and Tina Turner in Inglewood, Ca. and at Capitol Studios in Hollywood. They frequented The Starwood club in West Hollywood opening for such bands as Love, Cheap Trick and Funkadelic.

Together and individually Art Sanchez and Ron Reyes have recorded, performed and toured with several regional and national acts too many to mention and are still active to this day.

CREATION OF SUNLIGHT

SUNLIGHT 1970

At an early age Jerry Griffin had learned to play piano. He lived in Long Beach, California and remembered his parents buying him a Baldwin Organ called a Howard Combo. His immediate thoughts were to start looking for a band. There was an ad in the Press-Telegram, the local Long Beach newspaper, for a band looking for an organ player. Jerry answered the call and found a band that had moved to the area from Oklahoma called The Torques. This was not the band from Lexington, Kentucky with all the hits. They practiced together and Jerry honed his chops, but before they played a gig, most of the band moved back to Oklahoma leaving their singer, Gary Young, behind along with Jerry.

Determined to make a real go of playing in a band, Jerry recruited friends at Millikan High School. Don Sain (rhythm guitar), Steve Montague (bass), Ron Clark (flute, sax, percussion) and Bob Morgan (drums) to form the new band. They were all seniors and had all been playing in bands for a couple of years, so they already had the experience. Teamed up with Jerry Griffin (keyboards, vocals) and Gary Young (vocals) they also hired Carl Estrella (lead guitar) who was Don Sain's guitar teacher. Carl was from another school. They called themselves The Sunlights Seven.

As a covers band they would play USC and UCLA frat parties, teen clubs and any of the five high schools in the area on a Friday night. The high schools had big auditoriums and people just wanted to dance to familiar tunes. Jerry remembers playing at a USC Sigma Chi Fraternity party attended by many football players. Mike Holmgren, the backup quarterback for USC was there. Of course, he became a big-time football coach later winning the Superbowl in 1997 with the Green Bay Packers.

Jerry and Gary were writing original songs and would throw one or two in during a set. They entered a Battle of the Bands at the Hollywood Bowl and came in second place. That summer the band also played the Hollywood Palladium for a teen fair. As a band they were busy. Gary Young was the older guy and he met up with Bobby Engemann who had formed The Lettermen in the early 60's. This band had several top 40 hits. By 1967 Bobby had left the band to get into the business side of music. He had just built a studio called Independent Recorders Inc., located in Studio City at 4028 Colfax Ave. only a few miles from the Hollywood Hills. The Sunlights Seven had no signed deals with any record label at the time, but they did record a few songs at this top studio. There was a small local shop called DCT Recorders that had a disc cutting lathe. This was a place where anybody could come in and record something (voice, sound or music) and press their own record. So, Gary and Jerry took a tape of the first three songs that they recorded at Bobs studio and had DCT cut about five acetates. These first acetates with three recorded songs were given a handwritten title as *Heaviness*. These acetates were supposed to be for reference only to give to any of the band members who wanted them and to interest any record labels as demos.

Two more studio recordings happened, so they went back to DCT and had them cut 10 more acetates with 5 songs each. This disc was called *Sunstroke*. There might be only 10-12 copies of the acetates in existence. It was decided that the song *David b/w Judy In Disguise* should be released as a single. They still didn't have a record deal yet and rather than going through all the trouble of trying find one, Bobby Engemann and Gary Young created the Entra record label to release the single. The hope was to get radio airplay for the songs and get interest in the band.

The deal was that Bobby was putting up all the studio costs for the band. His brother was Karl Engemann, who at the time was vice president of Capitol records. When an album was recorded and complete, Bob figured he would recover his costs by putting the record out on the Capitol Records label. Gary Young, Jerry Griffin and Howard Gayle produced and engineered all the recordings at Independent Recorders and the album got finished. By this time, they felt that bands with names like The Four Seasons, The Dave Clark Five and themselves as The Sunlights Seven were too old school and early 60's sounding, so they shortened their name to Sunlight.

The sessions and master tapes were complete and they were ready to sign with Capitol but were passed over for Neil Merryweather's band who had recorded at the same Independent Recorders Studio and made a self-titled album called *Merryweather*. For some reason Capitol Records executives thought there might be a conflict of interest between Bobby and Karl and signing Sunlight was inadvisable.

However, the album was ready to be released. So, Bobby Engemann got some other investors to form another new record label he called Windi Records. A single by the band Sunlight was pressed and ready for radio airplay *Sometimes A Woman b/w Color of Love*. The full album was complete and was entitled *Creation of Sunlight*. They never played anywhere as Creation of Sunlight; this was simply the album title. They pressed up 500 copies. The cover design was a picture of the band taken by a friend through a fish-eye lens.

Musically, this is a top of the heap flower pop band with transcendental guitar jams and infectious beats. Some say the band comes across like Strawberry Alarm Clock. Because of the harder edged guitars and Hammond B3 Organ with spinning Leslie Speakers, the album is near perfect pop-sike with great harmonies, running bass riffs, echoes, sound effects and great psych guitar.

Reluctantly, Bobby Engemann just sort of walked away taking a loss on the band. Sunlight did no gigs promoting the record album. They never played any of the big clubs backing any already known bands and continued to simply play as a cover band throwing in a few of their own compositions. The single that was released *Sometimes A Woman b/w Colors Of Love* was credited to Sunlight but there was no other reference on the album cover that the band was called Sunlight. To make matters more confusing, another single was released *David b/w The Fun Machine* credited to the band Creation of Sunlight.

It had been about two years, recording songs and trying to make their mark. During the summer after high school, Jerry decided to move on to heavier Rock & Roll bands. Bobby didn't have any way to distribute the album and with no interest and no radio airplay, the band broke apart. Windi Records lasted 5 years but other than a few single releases, had only one other noteworthy rock record album on their label from the band Merkin in 1973.

The band was done but the single had some interest and airplay in Florida and other parts of the Midwest. Gary Young decided to re-establish the band and put together some players. Steve Montague and David Sain couldn't join and Jerry Griffin was already gone. So, Gary grabbed Roger Dines (guitar), Kerry Greene (keyboards) and Vince Pescatore (bass) to join him, Ron Clark, Carl Estrella and Bob Morgan. They drove to Oklahoma to do a small tour and when they arrived in Oklahoma City, they heard their song *David* being played on WKY radio 930. It hit number one on their local charts due to so many requests. Sunshine was featured live on WKY TV channel 4. This was a local low frequency VHF station that broadcast their performance at the Armory. There was no recording of this event. They also played at The Cheyenne Social Club and The Gaslight Dinner Theatre which were both big events back there. However, only about 8 to 10 venues in total were played. Afterwards, they fell apart and all moved on to separate colleges to take advantage of the military draft deferment to stay out of the Vietnam war.

Gary Young returned to California. He stayed on with Bobby Engemann to produce all the Windi album and single releases but disappeared afterwards. His current whereabouts is unknown.

David Sain worked with Fender guitars in Los Angeles for years. Now retired, he currently is a member the American Kountry Band out of Peoria, Arizona.

Ron Clark relocated to Vermont and was last heard from working with the State Services there.

Bob Morgan moved to Colorado and got into real estate investment, flipping houses.

Carl Estrella is a professor of Biology and Anatomy at Merced College in California.

Jerry Griffin played in a few bands for a while, but eventually opened his own successful business as Griffin Productions based in Arizona. He sadly passed recently in 2019.

Steve Montague moved to Portland, Oregon and worked in manufacturing and inventory control for CompUSA. He has since retired and does live action videos and filming for local bands in the area.

STEREO
DS 51004
COLISEUM
LONDON

TOUCH 1968

Don Gallucci played (organ and keyboards) for the Kingsmen at gigs locally in Portland, Oregon. The single *Louie, Louie b/w Haunted Castle* made the top ten nationally and stayed there for 16 weeks. Don Gallucci and Jack Ely (guitar, vocals) penned the B-side to the revered single. The Kingsmen became famous, *Louie, Louie* became a rock standard and is credited as having a key influence on the music of rock n roll as we all know it. Because of this, the band would have to journey on the road for a national tour.

Don was only 15 years old and couldn't travel, so he stayed behind and formed Don & the Goodtimes with Don McKinney (lead vocals, sax), Pierre Ouelette (guitar), Dave Child (bass) and Bobby Holden (drums). They were immediately signed to Jerden Records, a single was released *Turn On b/w Make It* and they played clubs in the Northwest area promoting the song. Dressed in white suits and top hats, they were influenced by Paul Revere and the Raiders and dressed the part. A couple more singles were recorded that got them notoriety nationally. They played the teen shows in Los Angeles at the Hollywood A Go-Go and were hired as the weekly featured band on TV with Dick Clark's *Where the Action Is*. Members came and went during this time.

The band evolved to include Don Gallucci (vocals, keyboards), Joey Newman (guitar), Ron "Buzz" Overman (bass), Jeff Hawks (lead vocals) and Bobby Holden (drums). By 1967 they settled in LA and began working on an album. Recorded at Columbia Studio A at 6121 W Sunset Blvd, the album was produced by Jack Nitzsche and included session musician's Ry Cooder, Glen Campbell and Hal Blaine. The album was released on EPIC records and nearly reached Billboards top 100 at #102. The single from the album *I Could Be So Good To You b/w And It's So Good* reached the No.15 spot in the LA area. But music was transforming into psychedelia.

FM underground radio was making noise with 10-minute songs, special studio effects and full album sides being played. By years end Ron Overman and Bobby Holden had left. The psychedelic music scene was blossoming. With times and music changing, Don wanted to get away from the "Teeny-bop" image. Altered states substances came into play and the band went through a metamorphosis. He reclused himself and wrote a mind-blowing song called

Seventy-Five. This set the pace for a new band with members Don Gallucci (vocals, keyboards), Jeff Hawks (lead vocals), Joey Newman (guitar), Bruce Hauser (bass, vocals) and John Bordonaro (drums, vocals).The band called Touch was set.

They needed money at times, so they did play gigs. Mostly featured at Rose Deitch's Club Galaxy in West Hollywood, they played gigs as Don & the Goodtimes with all the familiar songs, but the set also included some of the new creative material. Some of these songs were extraordinarily complex and psychedelic. The fans weren't sure what to make of the strange sounds.

They also helped *Elyse Weinberg* on her self-titled debut LP as her backing band calling themselves The Band of Thieves. But the music here, although quite good, is nothing like what it was about to become. They finally hired a manager and their gigs, though few, had more Touch songs than Don & the Goodtimes songs. The buzz was on about the band.

Howard Greer, a famous fashion designer, owned a huge mansion known as The Castle up in the Hollywood Hills. The place was vacant and would be the area where they would live and rehearse. Record labels were scrambling to sign this band. They invited label executives to their "Castle" in Southern California, got them stoned, positioned them in certain hot spots and played a private concert. A bidding war occurred between the record companies to sign these guys before they recorded a note. Finally, Coliseum/London Records advanced them $25,000 which was a huge sum in those days.

Things were set up at Sunset Sound Recorders founded by Tutti Camarata, a well-known sound producer for Disney. The production for the album would be something never done before. Producer Gene Schiveley conceived the 20-20 sound so that the listener could hear each player and instrument separately like witnessing a live performance. The only unusual instrument was a Tone Generator which artificially created sound frequencies. There were no synthesizers or mellotrons being used in the studios yet. Gene would do experiments with sound until he found the right amount of magic. The songs were great, but the sound was in true stereo with everything up front. Something that you could only find previously on a MONO recorded LP. There were many studio embellishments for the recording.

It was not long before word got out about the mind-blowing music going on at Sunset Sound. The curious started showing up like Mick Jagger, Grace Slick, Jimi Hendrix and others. Hendrix paid for extra studio time just to hear the playbacks. They all agreed to a center fold-out for the album cover with the band name, Touch, spelled out with a mirrored image in the shape of a brain. Some albums included a poster of a playboy centerfold.

When the self-titled *Touch* album was released, it created a buzz, tabbing Touch as "Gods of the new rock". This was spring 1969 and Touch is noted as a direct influence of the bands Yes, Genesis, Kansas, King Crimson and Renaissance. It's said that they were the first art rock progressive era band. The complexities of each tune, the four-part harmonies, psych guitar, wah-wah, echoes, studio effects and the keyboards really set them above all other bands at the time. Don got all these strange sounds out of his organ. Amazingly he was only 19 years old. The catchy single with both album songs *Miss Teach b/w We Feel Fine* was the only 45 released to radio stations.

Kerry Livgren, from the band Kansas, recalls when he first heard the album being played on the airwaves. He was driving home after a gig with his band The Gimlets at about 2 o'clock in the morning listening to an FM radio station. They were playing the aforementioned song, *Seventy-Five*. It was about 12 minutes long and he was so blown away he had to pull over and close his eyes just to "see" the sounds spewing from the radio speakers. On the vinyl disc this final song on side two never ended because it played all through the trail off groove emitting a continuous high-pitched noise to end the song. But it never faded out. If the tone arm didn't automatically retract from the record the high pitch was there until the arm was manually lifted by hand.

The radio stations were behind the record album and the label wanted them to go out on the road to promote it. But Don said the record couldn't be duplicated on stage live. True or not, the band was drained, they began having internal problems and just wanted to be done with the project. Promotion stopped, sales slowed down and Touch was finished. Diminished visions of what could have been. Way ahead of their time, the industry didn't have the equipment to reproduce the sound for a live performance.

John Bordonaro retired from the music business, became a realtor in California, bred Arabian Horses and got into Equestrian Horse sales.

Joey Newman showed up in a band called Blue Buffalo, formerly The New Buffalo Springfield, which evolved into *Blue Mountain Eagle* and released one self-titled album. He reunited with Jeff Hawks and Bruce Hauser to become the band *Stepson* in 1974 for an album release and formed *Bandit* releasing an album on ABC Records in 1975.

John Hauser got out of music and went to work in Florida.

Jeff Hawks became a Hairdresser.

Don Gallucci became a producer for Iggy and the Stooges and their second album *Fun House*. He produced Tom Waits and others and then changed his name to Don Caverhill to remove any notoriety while pursuing another career. He helped on soundtracks for a couple of B movies and got into the financial aspects of the Real Estate Industry where he has done well in Southern California.

Stereo
CS 9614
COLUMBIA
THE UNITED STATES OF AMERICA
GORDON MARRON
DOROTHY MOSKOWITZ
CRAIG WOODSON
RAND FORBES
JOSEPH BYRD
THE UNITED STATES OF AMERICA

Columbia
Stereo
MS 7317
MASTERWORKS
THE AMERICAN METAPHYSICAL CIRCUS
The Sub-Sylvian Litanies
American Bedmusic I
The Southwestern Geriatrics Arts and Crafts Festival
Gospel Music for A. R. Byrd III
JOE BYRD AND THE FIELD HIPPIES

THE UNITED STATES OF AMERICA/JOE BYRD AND THE FIELDS HIPPIES 1969-70

Joe Byrd was raised in Arizona and played accordion and vibraphone in a few pop and country bands. He formed his own jazz quartet and studied music composition under Bernie Childs while he was a student at Arizona University, completed his graduate studies at Stanford University and then traveled to New York to learn Avant Garde music with composers Morton Feldman and John Cage. Joe became a member of the Proto-Fluxus experiments in art and music along with Yoko Ono, Charlette Moorman and others and experimented with electronics creating odd sounds with his musical compositions. This was early 1960-61.

John Cage was creating strange beats and sounds for dance and utilized what was then called "Happenings". Joe was absorbed and influenced greatly. He was very curious about the sequence of sounds and chords and focused his compositions on that. Working as an assistant to Virgil Thompson he got some notice for his works integrating voice and instrumentation. The New York Times recognized him and gave him credits for a Carnegie Hall concert that he performed in 1962. Virgil recommended him to Time-Life Records to record music for a project they had about the Civil War. Then he met Dorothy Moskowitz.

He and Dorothy traveled to California where Joe began studies in music at UCLA. He became a teaching assistant and studied acoustics, psychology and Indian music. After a while, Dorothy grew tired of LA and went back to New York. Meanwhile Joe started his own "Happenings" events in LA. Happenings were initially started in New York by Allan Kaprow, a pioneer in establishing the concepts of performance art. They combined elements of dance, theater, music, poetry, and visual art. Joe put together a blues band with his friend Linda Ronstadt as vocalist and he realized that his experimental sounds, integrated with rock music, could reach a much larger audience.

The times were changing and rock music was heavy into experimentation. He and Dorothy were still in contact and she came back to LA to help him with his new project. He quit school to go full time into music as a living. Joe asked for backing from Art Kunkin who was just starting up the LA Free Press at the time. Heavy into electronics Tom Oberheim, a fellow UCLA student, built a Ring Modulator for the band which was an early form of a synthesizer with electronic oscillators. Joe focused on a political, avant-garde group of musicians and hired folks that he had played with back in New York. With himself Joe Byrd on (harpsichord, organ, calliope), Dorothy Moskowitz (vocals), Ed Bogas (keyboards), Gordon Marron (ring modulator, electric violin), Rand Forbes (bass, guitar) and Craig Woodson (drums) they recorded a very unusual LP at Columbia Studio D that was either loved or hated.

The self-titled *United States Of America* album packaging was odd as the jacket came in a brown paper bag and although it had heavy distribution in the marketplace, it wasn't promoted at all by Columbia records. The critics loved it, but it didn't sell. The music was truly diverse and mesmerizing at times with lots of weird special effects, echoes, dreamy airy vocals and a variance of electronic sounds. One single came from the album that was only released in Europe, *The Garden Of Earthly Delights b/w Love Song For The Dead Che.*

The first gigs were played at the Ash Grove in LA. They opened for Country Joe and the Fish and Moby Grape at the Shrine Exposition Hall in LA. Traveling to the east coast, they stayed a week and opened for The Velvet Underground at the Boston Tea Party, Richie Havens and The Troggs at The Fillmore East and were the headliner at the Café Au Go Go in Greenwich Village. The stage show was dreamlike with some of the first fog machines used, there was low lighting with the band seen only in the shadows except for Dorothy who was in the spotlight. The show along with the music was an experiment in art form.

Joe was difficult to deal with during the studio sessions, wanting full control of how the music sounded. On the road, there were fist-a-cuffs between Joe and the band over musical differences. Joe was a control freak and he later admits that he concentrated on the music and performance and didn't think about the personalities of the band members. Every rehearsal and performance became group therapy. They fell apart very quickly.

After the breakup of USA Joe was back in the studio with more of the same musical ideas. But instead of an actual band, there was a plethora of studio musicians. Horns and woodwinds, several vocalists with choral like harmonies, psychedelic guitar, synthesizer, heavy special effects, backwards sounds, echoes and plenty of studio magic continued. As Joe Byrd and the Field Hippies this album called *The American Metaphysical Circus* was never played live. Critics and fans were drawn to the album for years. Both albums pretty much represent what psychedelic music is all about, experimentation mixed with chilling vocals and harmonies.

In the aftermath of the band, Dorothy Moskowitz toured with Country Joe and the Fish for a while then became a local San Francisco voice over artist. She continued to write songs for children and did session work throughout the 80's and 90's and wound up teaching vocal techniques in the Piedmont, California school district. She worked with Todd Clark singing two songs on his recent LP *Whirlwind Of The Whispering Worlds.*

Craig Woodson completed his studies at UCLA and has a PhD. He started Ethnomusic Inc. which is a developmental music education agency that promotes instrument making, educational workshops, concerts and teaches groups about world music. He played with The Kronos Quartet for a while.

Gordon Marron became a session artist recording with Barbara Streisand, Madonna, Natalie Cole, Joni Mitchell and others before he moved to Hawaii and formed The Kauai Musical Arts Agency.

Ed Bogas wound up doing studio work as back up musician on records and for Movies and Television. He took over for Vince Guaraldi on piano behind all the *Peanuts* and *Garfield* TV specials after Vince passed away in 1976. He currently fronts Bogas Productions in San Francisco.

Rand Forbes left music and became a software engineer eventually owning a development company and was an Oracle database Administrator.

Joe Byrd was/is truly a musical innovator. For 10 years from the 70's through the 80's he released synthesized Christmas music and Patriotic songs on the Tacoma record label with *Christmas Yet To Come* and *Yankee Transcendoodle* and two additional synth LPs to follow. As a result of these, he became a music historian and began production work for Ry Cooder and others along with writing musical scripts for Movies and TV. He moved to Northern California and was a food columnist for the local Humboldt newspaper and then formed a group called Catskills Revival where they researched and performed forgotten songs from stage shows and films. He also taught music history and theory classes occasionally at The College of the Redwoods.

Vision of Sunshine
AVCO EMBASSY
STEREO AVE 33007

VISION OF SUNSHINE 1970

This band was formed by Gerald Hauser who grew up in Hollywood. His Dad was Dwight Hauser who was a Hollywood screenwriter, actor and producer of films in the movie theatres and on TV. Gerald was a high school football star but blew out his knee during a game. As a wing-back he was known as Wings Hauser, a name he still uses today. After the injury he knew his athletic career was over, so he focused on the arts and music. In 1967 he had a bit part in one of his Dad's films *First to Fight* that starred Gene Hackman, Chad Everett, Claude Akins and Dean Jagger all of whom went on to greater stardom later in life.

Dwight Hauser died two years later leaving Gerald at liberty to take on the 60's scene. He played guitar and piano and was inclined to form a band. His girlfriend at the time, Jane Boltinhouse, had this angelic voice, so she and Gerald put together some songs. Gerald was still living in his Dad's house which was located directly behind Bob Denver's home on Lake Sherwood near Thousand Oaks, Ca. Bob was a star in Hollywood having played Maynard on the TV show, *Dobie Gillis*, and then was Gilligan on the long running weekly TV show *Gilligan's Island*.

Bob was also good friends with Mike DeTemple who was a prominent banjo player that had won many times at the annual Topanga Canyon Banjo-Fiddle Contest. Mike was invited to be the featured player at an upcoming Young Peoples Concert, sponsored by Leonard Bernstein, designed to bring orchestra music to young people. He performed a piece called *The Winterfest Concerto for 5-String Banjo* written by Earl Robinson, a celebrated song writer who was an activist and friends with Pete Seegar and The Weavers. As a screenwriter in Hollywood, Earl wound up being blacklisted with several others who were tabbed as Communists.

Bob Denver had just purchased another home and was living there. When he moved into his new place, he offered Mike an opportunity to house-sit his old place. This would give Mike privacy and he spent about a year and a half trying to learn this difficult project for Banjo. The concert was held at the Dorothy Chandler Pavilion located in Los Angeles, a venue that held over 3000 people. Conducted by Lawrence Foster, director of the London Symphony

Orchestra, Mike was proud to have pulled it off in front of a sold-out show with full orchestral support of The Los Angeles Philharmonic.

Back at Bob's house, Mike was always entertaining musician friends and would have jam sessions in the large living room. Wings Hauser would come over and hang out and eventually he asked Mike if he could rehearse there with his newly formed band. At the time the band consisted of Wings (guitar, celeste, vocals), Jane Boltinhouse (vocals) and Sean Nelson (harpsichord, organ).

The practice sessions for a proposed album occurred in the house rec-room that overlooked the pool and Lake Sherwood. Mike DeTemple (guitar, banjo, bass), Andy Douglas (drums) and Rabbit MacKay (guitar) were there at the house to embellish the rehearsals. Mike had a pet Doberman on the premises named "Pecker" that gave some of the players fits during practice. Once Wings and the players were comfortable with the songs they wrote and because of his Hollywood connections, he was able to land a one album deal with AVCO Embassy records.

Wings asked Mike, Andy and Rabbit if they could assist with the recording at the studio. The musical compositions were recorded at Sunset Sound Recorders in Hollywood. Howie Kane, formerly of Jay and the Americans, produced the band. The full recording session with players included Wings Hauser (vocals, acoustic guitar, celeste, calliope), Jane Boltinhouse (vocals), Mike DeTemple (bass, guitars, banjo), Sean Nelson (harpsichord, organ) and Andy Douglas (drums). There were some in-house studio musicians and they were asked to help as well, Mary Till (flute, vocals), Terri Osiecki (flute, vocals), Joyce Miller (cello) and Jessie Eurlich (cello). The sound engineer was Bill Lazarus and he is heard playing (congas) on one of the songs.

The band was named on a whim and the self-titled *Vision Of Sunshine* album was released with *Stranger Here b/w Bizarrek Kind* as the album single. The child's voice heard on one of the songs is Sean Nelson's 10-year-old brother. There were no heavy psychedelics here, but the songs have that mysterious sound that draws one in. Perfect for the underground FM radio airwaves, the album is full of echoes, harpsichord, dual cellos, tandem flutes and some screaming guitar. Jane has a haunting dream-like voice. There are great vocals from Wings as well. The music and harmonies take you to another level when your eyes are closed. There are religious overtones, but it relates more towards flower power and positive self-images.

The critics made mention of the recording because of the unusual instruments used by a rock band (celeste, recorder, dual flutes, cellos, calliope, guitars) and Jane's voice shined. Musically, the album hints of the band Sweetwater and approaches an uncanny resemblance to Tom Rapp and Pearls Before Swine feel on the song *You Get What You Pray For*. They promoted the album at The Troubadour, The Greek Theatre and other clubs around Ventura, Ca. The tour band was only Wings Hauser, Jane Boltinhouse and Sean Nelson along with Terri and Mary on flute and harmonies.

Wings and Jane were married by then and had a daughter, but things soon began to fall apart. She knew of Charles Manson and had already begun taking an interest in religious cults and the practices thereof. She was conflicted about playing in a band or following her obsession, so she decided to pick up and leave everything behind, the band, Wings and her daughter. This spelled doom for any big aspirations Vision Of Sunshine had and they broke apart. Wings had to raise his daughter, Bright Hauser, as a single parent.

Sean Nelson never played with any other known musicians and settled in Ventura, Ca. with his wife.

Andy Douglas joined the Navy shortly after the album was released and worked for the Government for years before playing drums again with the DC-4 band in Washington DC. He now lives in New Mexico and works with "The Freedom in Music Project" playing with The High Desert Blues Band, a charity that helps at-risk kids through music.

Mike DeTemple did a few film scores including the backtrack banjo during scenes in the Oscar winning movie *Bonnie And Clyde*. He played with Dave Mason on the album *Alone Together* and did session work in LA with Eric Clapton and Paul Butterfield. He also toured with Rick Danko during his on and off status with The Band, worked with Theodore Bikel in New York and played in South Africa with Albert Hammond. By age 50 he settled down and began to build high-end guitars. He "tap-tunes" the wood he uses and makes the pick-ups, bridges, frets and other hardware for the guitars out of Titanium. The DeTemple guitars are highly sought after for their quality.

Jane Boltinhouse hooked up with Brooks Poston who was originally with the Charles Manson family but was converted to normalcy by Paul Crockett on the Barker Farm and Ranch he was helping to maintain for money. Brooks was aware of what was going on but left the family just before the famous Tate/LaBianca murders. He was key in the court proceedings and conviction of Charles Mason that landed him in jail. Brooks Poston, a great guitar player, along with Paul Watkins, another Manson family member, formed a folk duo called Desert Sun. Jane joined them and they played around Burbank, Venice and other southern California areas. They would quote Manson in-between songs during the shows and would hand out tapes of songs they recorded. Many songs were written by Charles Manson which Brooks vehemently denied. Paul Watkins never really left the family cult, eventually he took off and Desert Sun disbursed.

Jane and Brooks relocated to the Seattle area playing clubs as The Northern Lights in the 80's. Brooks passed away in 2015 but Jane Boltinhouse, as last heard from, still resides in Washington state.

Wings Hauser, also known as DJ Hauser, had an acting ambition take over. He became a steady movie and TV character actor appearing in many TV series including *The A Team, Magnum PI, Beverly Hills 90210, Roseanne* and several films over the years. A familiar face on TV and movies, he is father to Cole Hauser who is also now a big-time character actor. Notable for movies *Good Will Hunting, Hart's War* and playing opposite Kevin Costner as Rip Wheeler on the popular TV series *Yellowstone*.

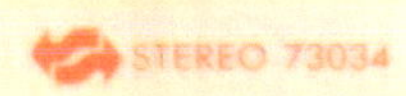

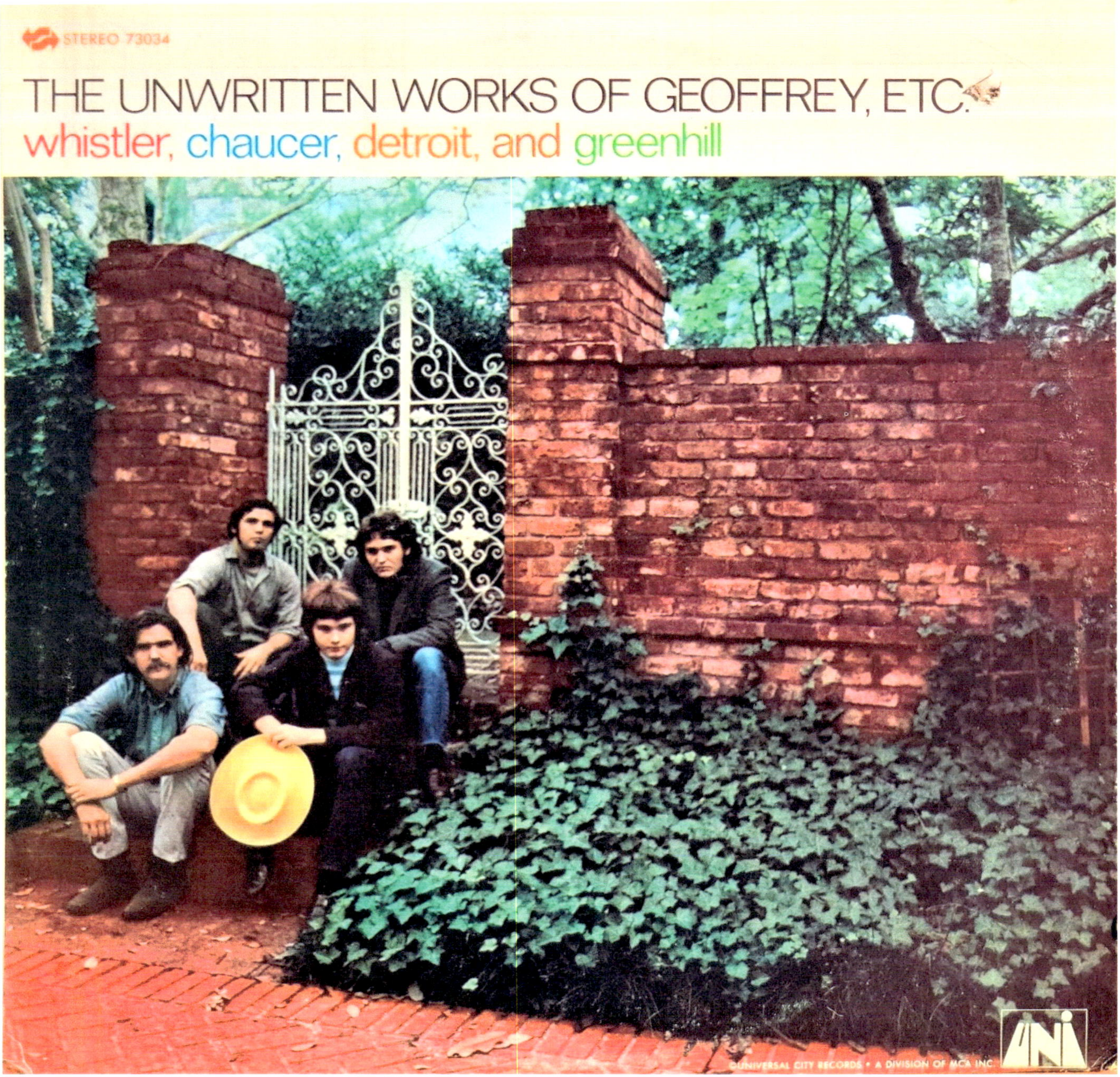
STEREO 73034
THE UNWRITTEN WORKS OF GEOFFREY, ETC.
whistler, chaucer, detroit, and greenhill
UNI
©UNIVERSAL CITY RECORDS • A DIVISION OF MCA INC.

WHISTLER, CHAUCER, DETROIT AND GREENHILL 1968

This band had its roots in Fort Worth, Texas and started with a collaboration of players from bands playing at private parties, high school dances, teen clubs and talent show competitions. All said and done the initial band was called The Mods and included players Scott Fraser (drums, vocals), Edd Lively (lead guitar, vocals), Danny Hawkins (guitar, vocals), Rick Finley (bass, vocals) and Don MacGilvry (vocals). They formed at RL Paschal High School where they all attended.

The Mods had an admirer who was a friend. Caswell Edwards III had inherited a fortune through his Grandfathers Texas land deals. He fronted the money to set the band up to record at Sound City Recording Studios located in Fort Worth, Tx. Major Bill Smith owned the studio. A character who was credited with producing three #1 chart hits. *Hey! Baby,* by Bruce Channel, *Hey Paula,* by Paul and Paula and *Last Kiss* by J. Frank Wilson & The Cavaliers. The Mods first and last single was *Days Mind The Time b/w It's for You*. The sound engineers were Frank Henderson and Phil York who trained a young T-Bone Burnett who at the time was calling himself Jon T. Bone.

Cass Edwards, as he was called, became their manager and had the funding to back the band. The B side to the 45 *It's For You* was a song written by the Beatles but was never recorded by them. Nobody could believe that a sixteen year old Cass could get permission from them to record the song, but he did. *Days Mind The Time* had significant airplay and traveled up the charts to number one locally. They all sang and the 4-part harmonies rivaled The Beatles. The Mods had a huge fan club and got a weekly gig playing Teen-A-Go-Go hosted by KFJZ's top radio DJ, Mark (Mark E. Baby) Stevens. Other local teen dance shows popped up including Action-A-Go-Go and Peppermint-A-Go-Go. The Mods were featured every Saturday night on Panther-A-Go-Go that was held at Panther Hall and televised through Channel 11, KTVT.

They were only in High School and the constant gigging and weekly TV started taking its toll. Don MacGilvry and Danny Hawkins both left along with Rick Finley. Scott and Edd wanted to keep a band together and through T-Bone found Phil White and David Bullock who each sang and played guitar and bass. They rehearsed at the studio and T-

Bone had an idea to give each band member a pseudonym. This is where Scott became "Benjamin Whistler", Edd became "Geoffrey Chaucer", Dave was known as "Nathan Detroit" and Phil was "Philip Greenhill". David really had no plans to join as a band member. He had a voice from heaven but thought his friend, John Carrick, was better vocally. So, he suggested that Scott, Edd and Phil go down to Houston and look up John Carrick, who along with his Mother, ran a folk club called The Sand Mountain Coffee House.

This club had frequent players like Jerry Jeff Walker, Townes Van Zant, Janis Joplin, Johnny Winter and others. John himself had previously been heavy into the folk scene with a band called The Balladeers and previously had played as a trio that included David Bullock on stage there. It was summer break so Phil, Scott and Edd just showed up one evening and talked John into playing for him after hours. He was reluctant at first but agreed to give a listen. Their equipment was in the car, so they unloaded, set everything up and played some tunes.

John couldn't believe his ears. These zit-faced high schoolers played way beyond their years. They wanted him to come back to Fort Worth and help be the lead vocalist for their band. They said a recording contract was all set up through T-Bone Burnett. John agreed to join and they practiced and rehearsed to hone their sound there at the club during the day.

Eventually they moved to a house they called The Castle. John played some tapes of songs the boys recorded for Dave Bullock, who had since returned to Houston, and told him their voices together would be something special. So, Dave had a change of heart and they all headed back to Fort Worth spending most of their time recording at Sound City Studios located at 1705 W 7th Street. A demo was recorded *Rock and Roll Woman b/w There Goes Another Day* with songs written by John Carrick, Jon T. Bone and credited to the band Whistler, Chaucer, Detroit, Greenhill. But it never got beyond the acetate stage.

T-bone, Scott and Edd were avid readers and wrote all the songs with Edd Lively having inspiration from characters in history and Scott, whose Mother was a music teacher, also collected literature classics. They also did studio sessions as a back-up band with whomever T-Bone had recording in the studio. The sessions for an album took about 8 months to complete. Studio musicians helped with the sessions. The band really wasn't official yet and it was T-Bone who just wanted to put things together with what and who he had.

After a while, things began to sour and Edd felt he was a weak link. No band lives in perfect harmony and he left. It was a bitter split. John Carrick was disappointed and was apparently just a guest artist as a harmony singer in the sessions but was asked to replace Edd's vocals for the recording. So, the studio band as recorded was John Carrick (lead vocals), Scott Fraser (guitars, drums), David Bullock (guitar, vocals) Phil White (bass, vocals), T Bone Burnett (accordion, keyboards), an unnamed session drummer and they added in the tapes of Edd Lively on (guitars, flute). Officially the album was a "concept LP" called *The Unwritten Works of Geoffrey, etc.* by the band Whistler, Chaucer, Detroit and Greenhill.

Major Bill Smith was a slick hustler who helped T-Bone get a negotiation with UNI records. With the album finished T-Bone got an offer from the UNI record label but thinking he could get more dollars, turned it down and counteroffered for a higher package deal. UNI reneged on his offer and gave the same deal to Fever Tree who took the money no questions asked. UNI did sign them, but it wasn't the lucrative contract they were originally offered. The album went directly to the cut-out bins.

The LP cover pictures Scott Fraser (Whistler) upper right, David Bullock (Detroit) lower right and Phil White (Greenhill) upper left. Guy Clark is with them sitting on the lower left. Guy was an upcoming musician and an artist who later recorded over 20 LPs. He won a Grammy award in 2016 and is remembered for his songwriting. But at the time, he was an unknown and was asked to do the album cover artwork because he had a fancy camera. When Edd left, the band had only three official members, and with Edd gone and four guys needed for a picture, Guy included himself in the photo. The cover pictures were taken without John Carrick's knowledge.

The exclusion of John in the photo and being only credited as a footnote to the project really hurt, as the guys drove all the way to Houston specifically to include him for their new band. He was the lead vocalist on record for most of the songs. The album has some haunting moments with jangling guitars, fiddle, accordion, echoes, backwards guitar, flute and three-part harmonies. Country tinged folk and psych, like Hearts and Flowers, Plain

Jane and West. The songs *Ready to Move* and *Tribute to Sundance* really showed how things would sound later but the LP just tanked and there was no promotion, so they all took a break.

John Carrick migrated back to Houston and started an "electric" band with John Tuttle, former drummer with Fever Tree. Calling themselves The Texas Rangers, several clubs were played including the famous Vulcan Gas Company. They also backed Creedence Clearwater for a tour of Texas and John Fogerty asked if the boys wanted to make a record. But it occurred to Mr. Carrick that he might still be under contract to UNI, so it never happened. The rock life took its toll. He was heavy into heroin for a couple of decades but got through it and brokered guitars for musicians and collectors for a living.

Edd Lively moved on and played with his band Edd Lively and the Movers in and around Fort Worth, Texas. There were no recordings made.

Scott, David and Phil continued to write songs and they finally hired a (drummer), Tony Lee, with (keyboards) by John Harris and billed themselves as The Unwritten Works for one concert only at the W. E. Scott Theatre in Fort Worth.

Scott Fraser, David Bullock and Phil White then formed Space Opera and recorded some magical music.

KE 32117
Epic
SPACE OPERA

SPACE OPERA 1973

After the demise of Whistler, Chaucer, Detroit and Greenhill, Scott Fraser (guitar, vocals), David Bullock (guitar, vocals) and Phil White (bass guitar, vocals) hired an official band manager Michael Mann who gave them stability as a band and brought them some success. He was the one who set up the only concert for the previous band at the W E Scott Theatre in Fort Worth where they were billed as The Unwritten Works. He set up gigs for them to play at clubs around the area but there was always a fill-in drummer to fill the void. They needed someone who would commit full time.

Brett Owen Wilson was someone who played drums and was somebody Scott knew back at Paschal High School. He played around town in various jazz combos, so they set up an audition. Brett was going to college, had no plans and felt that joining the group was the thing to do. They all decided to name the new band as Space Opera because of their love for Science Fiction and because of the space program and the Moon landings that were happening.

Meanwhile Cass Edwards, who had bankrolled the band as The Mods in their high school days returned from Cornell College and became the band's audio sound engineer. The first official gig as Space Opera was at the End of Cole club in Dallas in June of 1969. They were constantly playing gigs at Zeke's, The House of Pizza and others to sharpen their sound. Playing the Texas International Pop Festival was noteworthy, but they weren't known enough to perform on the main stage where the headliners Led Zeppelin, Ten Years After, Santana, The Rotary Connection and others played. Instead, they played in the free stage area. Behind this stage was where the big groups set up for the main stage. Wavy Gravy and The Merry Pranksters were parked directly behind and guys like Johnny Winter & B B King would show up and join in with whomever was playing the free stage.

At one-point, Grand Funk Railroad had to cancel their last performance for the event, a Monday show on the main stage. Space Opera was asked to play in their place. Gaining a reputation, it was time to start recording again so they went back to Sound City and laid down one song. T-Bone Burnett was involved with Whistler Chaucer in the studio previously but was unavailable this time. It was suggested that they go up to Nashville and record at

Columbia Studios there. They hooked up with Bob Johnston and Elkin 'Bubba' Fowler. A few more songs were recorded and they were introduced to Jim Meeker, who was an oilman in the music business.

He took over all the financing and paid the bills for the band. Michael Mann continued to be the go between, for the band and Meeker. Then they flew to New York to audition for Warner Bros records. An audience of 50 people were present including Clive Davis, Columbia records guru, along with Kris Kristofferson and Eric Andersen, both high on the vine at Columbia Records. The session there was recorded and was to be remixed at Columbia Studios. But they played on rented equipment and it didn't go well. Clive didn't hear a hit song during the audition and became disinterested. The interest also waned as the Warner Bros. executives were focusing more on their fortunes through The Allman Brothers Band.

Tails between their legs they flew back to Texas with the audition tapes and rerecorded some songs. Presenting them to KFDA-FM radio, they got some local radio airplay. Space Opera had a real cult status following and that grew into opening for the likes of Quicksilver, Jefferson Airplane, Jethro Tull and others at the big arenas. The Exit 4 Studio was located just off Interstate 30 on Fitzhugh Ave in East Dallas. This is where the main songs were recorded for an LP by the band that included Scott Fraser on (piano, guitar, vocals), David Bullock (all guitars, flute, vocals), Phil White (upright bass guitar, vocals) and Brett Wilson (drums, vibraphone).

The album was completed and they sent the tapes to Roger Bland who apparently had connections to The Four Seasons. Nothing happened as a result. But there was an agent in Canada who had heard the band perform in Fort Worth and wanted them to play clubs in Canada near Toronto. Mike Mann got them a place in Williamsville, New York where they could cross the border without hassle and play the clubs up there. They stayed in a house on acreage that had room enough for all the band members and crew.

An in-house studio was built for rehearsals and recording. Wonderful! They gigged at clubs near Toronto, at the State Universities of New York and in Ohio, Virginia and nearby states in the US. They courted record company executives at the house hoping to get the best record deal through a big label company. The band turned down a lot of record labels because of control issues. Space Opera wanted full control of the band name, self-production arrangements, cover artwork and artistic control, unheard of and deal breakers in the record industry. There was a lot of overhead with big staff, A&R guys, engineers, studio costs and the list doesn't end.

Manta Sound Studios had just been built in Toronto and Space Opera was asked to try out the sound and all the new innovative equipment there. Recording a live version of their song *Guitar Suite* they loved the studio. Based on what they heard, Columbia Records of Canada offered the band full artistic control which was the stumbling block for all the other interested labels. They signed a lucrative contract and moved to Southampton, NY, 500 miles away, to write other songs and refine old ones for a major label LP.

When ready they relocated to Toronto and set up camp at The Waldorf Astoria Hotel. The first obstacle was that the label wanted their own producer. It wasn't what they wanted and the band felt that having a stranger with his own opinions would change the overall sound. They previously produced all the songs themselves, but did agree to have some guys come in. A big-name producer could help sales. But no one fit the mold, so they wound up producing themselves anyway. Cass Edwards and Lee DiCarlo engineered the sessions. Manta Sound Studio A had a 16-track board and two 16-track recorders and they spent 16-18 hours per day in sessions. Re-recording songs over and over until things were flawless, they wanted the project to be perfect.

But the monetary cost was extreme. After three months the tapes were sent to Crystal Sound in Hollywood for mixing and the mastering was to be done in New York. They were happy with the results but to duplicate the studio sound, tour equipment and high-tech amps along with foot switches had to be specially made in Chicago and the speakers were being hand built. They were reluctant to hit the stage before they had any new equipment. Scott was adamant about waiting until everything was set in place.

This was a major momentum killer. Capitol of Canada wanted them on the road and the band wasn't ready. They went back to Fort Worth and just waited for the equipment to show. It was a six month wait and $50,000 in cost. The stuff showed up, but when they were ready to go, the record label had lost interest and moved on. The album finally hit the stores, on the Epic label in the US, 2 months before the equipment arrived. There was no album promotion or tour support.

It was nearly a year without serious practice or stage exposure and then they finally played The San Pedro Playhouse in San Antonio. Epic Records sent a PR man to view the show and get a feel about a possible second LP, but the band had no new material and they were very rusty from not practicing the album songs completed in the studio up north. The Epic representatives tried to come backstage to converse with the band but the security guy guarding the door didn't know who they really were and slighted them off.

Their second chance came at the W E Scott Theatre in Fort Worth. A sold-out show in their hometown with a great audience reception. They hit all the notes on the new equipment and they were pleased but the Epic representative was not impressed and flew back to New York the next morning. Only three other shows were played, two of them performed at a club called Gertie's in Dallas.

Full control and perfection came at a cost. The artistry was there, the album was great, but they had no thoughts about the aftermath, about how to promote the LP or how to generate distribution. Record Companies were usually a thorn in the side of every band but in this instance, they should have listened to the Columbia label folks that gave them what they wanted, believed in them from the very start and supported them throughout.

The buzz about the band was hot when the *Space Opera* album was finished but the wait for perfection on the stage cost them everything. Before dissolving they played their last show on January 2nd, 1976, at the House of Pizza where it all started. About 80 people, friends and family witnessed 3 hours of magic. Afterwards they all went their separate ways.

David Bullock left for New York followed shortly by Scott Fraser. The two of them studied music theory and played at clubs in Greenwich Village as a duo. Eventually they formed a chamber orchestra with some friends from Juilliard including Cello, Violin, Oboe, etc. As the Bullock Fraser Chamber Orchestra there was some interest, but things never panned out.

Twenty years later, the digital age caught up with Space Opera. There was a resurgence. Fans remembered the band and the guys never stopped talking. David had moved back to Texas and by 1995 the boys were back rehearsing together. They scheduled a concert at the Caravan of Dreams club in the area and wanted everyone to know that they were back and not going away. They all had personal lives and other jobs but found the time to play clubs in the area and by the new millennium (2000) had formed a website on the computer to interact with fans.

Plans were made to record a second LP. Eagle Audio Recording was the studio used in Fort Worth. It didn't take long at all and *Space Opera II* was available on CD through their website in 2002. Music that they had written between '96 and '99. It was sporadic but they gigged around town promoting this album locally. Collectors Choice reissued the original first album on CD in 2004 and things were going well. But nothing lasts forever.

Brett Wilson worked at a fancy restaurant keeping the books. This led him to becoming an accountant. He never stopped looking towards a possible formal reformation of Space Opera but unfortunately passed away in 2005.

Scott Fraser moved back to Fort Worth from New York, bought a Synclavier, a digital Synthesizer, and recorded an EP called *SS-433* of Philip Glass type material. He taught music at colleges and schools. Sadly, he passed away in 2006 due to Melanoma.

Phil White went back to playing for local jazz bands then wound up in Los Angeles playing here and there and producing bands. He was always a recluse and always seemed to be on the road. He never married and being a free soul took its toll. Having problems breathing, he was dragged into the doctor's office. The news was not good and he died in 2008.

David Bullock got into film and video production. He kept a journal with all the notes and had all the dates about who, what, when and where, involving the band. Without his input Space Opera would have become just another lost obscurity. He kept the website going for a while and put together a third album. This involved the unreleased LP recorded at the Exit 4 Studios back in 1970-71 plus other recordings from 1975-78. Called *Safe at Home* the music here is dreamlike, like Big Star and Year One but with wonderful dual guitars, phase shifting, echoes and stereo panning. This album should have been released back then. It is just drop-jaw magical and brings real tears of joy upon each listen. The rare CD was available through the website which has now disappeared. The members are gone but the beauty of their music left the legacy of a band that will live forever.

ABOUT THE AUTHOR

As a kid I grew up in Garden City, Michigan. My Dad had a few records that he would put on the Hi-Fi for cocktail parties when Mom and Dad had the neighbors over. When Dad was at work, I remember listening to various records on the HiFi playing *Ira Ironstrings Plays Music For People With $3.98 (Plus Tax, If Any),* the original Samuel Goldwyn soundtrack album *Porgy and Bess,* Leonard Bernstein's *Copeland - Billy The Kid/Rodeo* and any of the weekly series of LP records that my parents bought at the supermarket. Then I saw a weird looking record with a wild cover by Dave Brubeck called *Time Out*. When I listened to the songs from the album like *Blue Rondo A La*

Turk, Strange Meadow Lark and *Take Five*, I just melted. I was just a young kid but this was the most awe-inspiring music I had ever heard. I'd listen to this record repeatedly and stare at the wild colorful cover painting by Neil Fujita. I couldn't get enough of the oddball time signatures and Paul Desmond on Saxophone. WOW!!!

But this record just didn't fit in with the other stuff that Dad and Mom had like Percy Faith, Mitch Miller, Folk Songs of The World and so many others. Later in life I asked Dad about that Dave Brubeck record and he said somebody gave it to him at work. He never listened to it.

My first memory of rock music was watching the Beatles on *Ed Sullivan*. This was everyone's favorite Sunday night TV show. I talked my dad into a transistor radio, so I could listen to some more Beatles music. I was 13 years old and soon heard other bands and remember riding my bike up to K-Mart to buy *Gloria b/w Here Comes The Night* by Them (my first record). I listened to WKNR out of Detroit and CKLW out of Windsor, Ontario, Canada from across the Detroit River. These were the two big radio stations for garage bands and one hit wonders from my listening area back then.

Dad got a job with Boeing in Seattle, so the summer of 1966 was my last in Michigan. I had purchased very few records by then (maybe 10 single 45's or so, but the last record I bought before we left, was the single *I'm Gonna Miss You b/w Tried To Hide* by the 13th Floor Elevators. On the way to Seattle, we stopped in Missouri to visit relatives and I remember hearing another weird tune called *Good Vibrations*. Not knowing the term at the time, songs like this were my introductions to Psychedelic music.

When we got to Seattle I settled into school and had a regular radio set up next to my bed where I found a couple of cool AM radio stations KOL and KJR. They played many of the same songs and bands I heard back in Detroit like The Beatles, The Animals, Them, but others were different like The Collectors, The Wailers, The Springfield Rifle, The Surprise Package and others. I happened to be out shopping once with Mom and saw an album of radio record hits. It was called *KRLA-Solid Rock Hits*. This record had *Dirty Water* by The Standells, *Psychotic Reaction* by The Count Five, *Little Girl* by The Syndicate of Sound, *Hey Joe* by The Leaves, *Hang on Sloopy* by The McCoys and 19 other Garage Band radio hits. All these songs I heard on the radio, all of them were on one record and I could listen to them over and over. I was very content.

Sometime in 1967 (probably my birthday) I acquired a stereo radio with separate speakers. I promptly replaced my little AM radio with this. I set the speakers on either side of the bed so I could hear the songs in stereo panning through my head from one ear to the other. I immediately discovered another radio station, KRAB, which had a couple hours on a Friday or Saturday night when they would play some very strange rock music. Of course, the DJ never said who the band was that was playing on the radio. So, I would try and envision what this band would look like. KOL FM and KISW FM were the local Underground radio stations and they would play full sided LPs and the songs were long. Live songs like *Spoonful* by Cream and *Whipping Post* by The Allman Brothers seemed to go on forever. *Wind* by Circus Maximus was also a favorite and then there was 17 minutes of *In-A-Gadda-Da-Vita*. I also found Captain Midnight, a real freaky DJ, on CKLG that would broadcast out of Vancouver, B.C. in Canada. That station came in clear as a bell from 115 miles away.

By this time, I had a mutual friend, Richard, who was into music as well. We would find our way to some choice used record stores near the University of Washington and explore through the record bins. I was looking at all the covers and trying to figure out who the band was that I had heard on KRAB. Or I would see a wild colorful album cover and buy it for the artwork alone. There were listening stations, where you could listen to the record before you bought it, but there was always a waiting line, so I would just take a chance. When I got home and put the record on the player, I discovered a different band with another strange sound and another weird album cover.

In the late 60's there were two popular used record stores in the area, Puss 'N' Books & Cellophane Square, near the University of Washington campus. These were the establishments that I frequented most on the weekends with my best friend Richard. I found albums by bands like The Freeborne, The Chocolate Watchband, Appletree Theatre, Kak and many others during my high school years here. But K-Mart had cut-out bins where new records were found cheap. A dollar or two could get you an album by many of the unknown psychedelic bands that had been consigned to the cut out bins. An affordable and worthy chance at some unknown band purchased on the cover art alone. It was obvious I was into the strange and beautiful musical sounds and weird cover artwork found. The odder the sound, the better it was to my ears. *Trout Mask Replica* by Captain Beefheart and the Magic Band was (to me) the ultimate record. The music was just so weird and the cover was so bizarre.

Every Friday after the latest football game we had a dance back in the high school commons area and would gather for the local band talent like The Gates Of Trapezoid, Sun, Gray Stone, The Beard of Joseph Palmer, Porcelain Yogi and others. These were bands that never went anywhere, but they had that psychedelic live sound and us kids were hopping and spinning around to the strobe lights and wild music. This was truly a magical time in my life.

I was hooked on the music and continued to buy records for years. My wife Elaine, who I met in high school, tolerated my hobby (she still calls it a sickness). We went to the skating rinks and saw bands like Crabby Appleton, Buffalo Springfield and Sugarloaf. Over the years, I evolved with the music. Elaine and I took disco lessons and we did the disco thing for a while. Then into the mid 70's and 80's where we danced at the clubs and saw other bands like Bighorn, Shyanne, Huge Spacebird and other AOR one hit wonders. New Wave and Techno came along, then the 90's. I bought records that made my foot tap and put a chill down my spine. Then I got into CD's (but that's another story).

I have around 30-40 thousand records in various categories stored within my house (three floors worth). Although I have many different genres of music, Swing, Country, Lounge, Jazz, Celtic, Soul, Pop, AOR, Orchestra, Comedy, Folk, Bluegrass, HipHop and even some Rap, my passion has always been with Psychedelic music from the 60's.

Check out the record website - Ina-Gadda-Da-Records at www.inagadda.com

All the album covers pictured with only three exceptions are from my personal collection.

Special thanks to Dwight Payne, Keith D'Arcy, Debbie Parke and Joe LaChew for allowing me to borrow one album from their personal collection for photography purposes only. I just didn't have it all and they were gracious enough to oblige my request.

Thanks to Irwin Chusid for the use of the Book Cover Artwork by Jane Sinnickson - title unknown.

Courtesy www.JimFlora.com and the Heirs of Jane Sinnickson

Circa 1940-50's - the painting is lost in the archives and has never been found.

And a very special thank you to my son Cameron Handyside who helped put this all together.

Hear his music at www.youtube.com/c/apologuemusic or visit his website at www.apologuemusic.com

I wish to thank all those who helped to provide the information and allowed me to walk down memory lane with them.

I was honored to speak with all of you.

Acknowledgements

Various issues of magazines dedicated to the bands in question were an invaluable reference:

Goldmine Magazine, Trouser Press, Ptolemaic Terrascope, Ugly Things, Flashback Magazine, Fuzz, Acid and Flowers, Tapestry of Delights, Guitar Player Magazine, Dreams Fantasies and Nightmares, The Archivist

The various books and articles written by the players about their times:

Space Traveler by James Vincent, It Came From Memphis by Robert Gordon, Walk Don't Run by Steve Jae Johnson, Lost in Space by Frank Gutch Jr., The Miami Pop Festival (A Photographic Experience) by Ken Davidoff

Newspaper and magazine articles dedicated to the band:

The Omnibus Press, The Independent Star News – Pasadena, Life Magazine, The New Haven Register

Special thanks to those I personally spoke with by phone, through email or via text messaging. Through your invaluable help this book would not have happened.

THE ABSTRACTS thanks to Henry Dandini Jr., THE AFFECTION COLLECTION thanks to Mike Doggett, AGGREGATION thanks to Bayard Gregory, AFTERGLOW thanks to Larry Alexander, Ron George, Gene Resler & Roger Swanson, AIR thanks to Tom Coppola, ALEXANDERS TIMELESS BLOOZBAND thanks to Charles Lamont, THE AMERICAN DREAM thanks to Don Lee Van Winkle, AORTA notes from "Space Traveler" by James Vincent, THE APPLETREE THEATRE thanks to Terence Boylan, ARS NOVA thanks to Wyatt Day, ARZACHEL tales from the Egg Archives, BEAD GAME thanks to Robert Gass, BEAR thanks to Happy Traum and Eric Kaz, BEAST from the Bob Yeasel website, BIG LOST RAINBOW thanks to Ridley Pearson & Otis Read, BIRMINGHAM SUNDAY thanks to Debbie Parke & Joe LaChew, THE BLACKWOOD APOLOGY thanks to Joe Piazza & Dale Menten, BLOODROCK thanks to John Nitzinger, BLUES IMAGE thanks to Skip Konte, BO GRUMPUS thanks to Jim Colegrove, JOLLIVER ARKANSAW thanks to Jim Colegrove, BOLD thanks to Steve Walker, BOW STREET RUNNERS thanks to George Graham & Steve Struthers, BROTHER FOX AND THE TAR BABY, From Alan Lorber's interview in Goldmine Magazine, THE BUBBLE GUM MACHINE thanks to Vicki Spenser & Independent Star News July 7, 1968, THE CAKE notes from interview with the band, CHAD AND JEREMY from bio at the Chad Stewart and Jeremy Clyde website, CHARISMA thanks to Richard Tortorigi & Bernie Kornowicz, CHIRCO basic notes from Roger Maglio, THE CHURLS thanks to Bob O'Neill & Sam Hurrie, THE COLLAGE thanks to Jerry Careaga, COLOURS thanks to Jack and Wally Dalton, CONDELLO thanks to Dennis Kenmore, COTTONWOOD thanks to Dave Weyer, CROWBAR thanks to Sonnie Bernardi, John Gibbard and Roly Greenway, CROWFOOT thanks to Russell DaShiell, THE DEEP / THE FREAK SCENE thanks to David Bromberg, David Rubinson and the archived Rusty Evans website, DESIGN basic notes from Barry Johnson, THE DEVIL'S ANVIL from WRUL radio interview with Eliezer Adoram, EARTH OPERA thanks to Peter Rowan, EAST thanks to the Aman Ryusuke Seto website, EASTFIELD MEADOWS thanks to Dwight Payne & Wayne Grajeda, EDEN'S CHILDREN thanks to Richard Lee, ETERNITY'S CHILDREN thanks to Bruce Blackman, EUPHORIA thanks to Bill Lincoln

THE FABULOUS FARQUAHR from New Haven Register dated 10-25-2004, THE FALLEN ANGELS thanks to Jack Bryant, FANTASY (US) thanks to Greg Kimple, FARGO thanks to Dean Willden, FAT WATER thanks to Lance Massey, Bill Schneider & GE Stinson, FEATHER thanks to Johnny Townsend, FEDERAL DUCK / OGANOOKIE thanks to Bob Stern, Jack Bowers and George Stavis, FELT thanks to Mychael John Thomas, FEVER TREE thanks to the Michael Knust memories and Rob Landes, FIRE (US) thanks to Paul Gene, FLAT EARTH SOCIETY thanks to interviews with Jack Kerivan, Paul Carter & Phil Dubuque in Ptolemaic Terrascope, THE FLOATING OPERA thanks to John Nemerovski & Artie Alinikoff, FORD THEATRE based on notes from R. Stevie Moore, James Altieri & Harry Palmer, FORT MUDGE MEMORIAL DUMP thanks to Rich Clerici, THE FREEBORNE thanks to Nick Carstoiu and Bob Margolin, THE FREE DESIGN from the Chris Dedrick website, FUSE thanks to the Chip Greenman website, GAME from Chuck Kirkpatrick commentary, GANDALF thanks to Peter Sando, GENTLE SOUL thanks Pamela Pollard, GIANT CRAB thanks to Ernie and Brian Orosco, THE GLASS FAMILY thanks to Jim Callon & Dave Capilouto, GLASS HARP from the Glass Harp website, GLASS PRISM thanks to Tom Varano, THE GLITTERHOUSE thanks to Hank Aberle, THE GODZ based upon "This Is the Godz Truth" by Ray Brazen, GOLIATH thanks to Butch Barbella, THE GORDIAN KNOT thanks to Jim Weatherly, GRAFFITI thanks to Jorge Strunz, HAMILTON STREETCAR thanks to Tom Fannon, HEART from the Dave Butterfield memoirs, THE HOBBITS thanks to the Jimmy Curtiss interview with Michael Shelley for WFMU Radio, H.P. LOVECRAFT from the Ptolemaic Terrascope interview with Ethan Kenning, ILL WIND from Ken Frankel and the Ill Wind website, INDELIBLE INC. thanks to Dave Dister and Mark Miceli, THE INSECT TRUST based upon notes from Perfect Sound Forever & “It Came From Memphis” by Robert Gordon, JAIM thanks to Fal Oliver and Mike Bono, J.K.& CO. thanks to the Jay Kaye website, THE LAST RITUAL thanks to Michael Beskin, CHELSEA BEIGE thanks to Billy Cross & Stafford James, MICHAELANGELO based upon Tiffany Anders interview with Angel Peterson, THE MOON from Matthew Moore’s memoirs of the band, THE NEW YORK ROCK & ROLL ENSEMBLE from Dorian Rudnytsky’s memoirs of the band, THE OTHER HALF thanks to the Geoff Westen website, PACIFIC OCEAN notes from “Walk Don’t Run” by Steve Jae Johnson, THE PAISLEYS thanks to Bob Belknap, PLANT AND SEE / LUMBEE from the Joel Rose band biography, QUILL thanks to Jon Cole and Ray Paret, QUINTESSENCE thanks to Ron Rothfield and the Raja Ram Anthology, THE RAINBOW PRESS thanks to Bill Yergin, Larry Milton & Charles Osborne, RAVEN thanks to Tony Galla, REPAIRS thanks to Jim Honeycutt, SAGE AND SEER thanks to David Rea and Jack Olesen, SALVATION thanks to Joe Tate and Art Resnick, SPACE thanks to Carli Muñoz , STRANGE BREW thanks to Arthur Sanchez, SUNLIGHT thanks to Jerry Griffin & Steve Montague, TOUCH thanks to Don Caverhill, UNITED STATES OF AMERICA / JOE BYRD AND THE FIELDS HIPPIES from Dorothy Moskowitz interview in Ptolemaic Terrascope, VISION OF SUNSHINE thanks to Mike DeTemple and Andy Douglas, WHISTLER, CHAUCER, DETROIT AND GREENHILL notes from "Lost in Space" by Frank Gutch Jr., SPACE OPERA notes from "Lost in Space" by Frank Gutch Jr.

Made in United States
Troutdale, OR
06/03/2024

20300874R00345